Led Zeppelin
FAQ

Series Editor: Robert Rodriguez

Led Zeppelin FAQ

All That's Left to Know About the Greatest Hard Rock Band of All Time

George Case

Backbeat
Books

An Imprint of Hal Leonard Corporation

Published in 2011 by Backbeat Books
An Imprint of Hal Leonard Corporation
7777 West Bluemound Road
Milwaukee, WI 53213

Trade Book Division Editorial Offices
33 Plymouth St., Montclair, NJ 07042

The FAQ series was conceived by Robert Rodriguez and developed with Stuart Shea.

Book design by Snow Creative Services

Printed in the United States

Library of Congress Cataloging-in-Publication Data

Case, George, 1967–
    Led Zeppelin FAQ : all that's left to know about the greatest hard rock band of
all time / George Case.
        p. cm.
    Includes bibliographical references and index.
    ISBN 978-1-61713-025-0 (alk. paper)
1. Led Zeppelin (Musical group)–Miscellanea. I. Title. II. Title: Led Zeppelin
frequently asked questions.
    ML421.L4C37 2011
    782.42166092'2—dc23

                                                                2011033450

www.backbeatbooks.com

Contents

Foreword

Light and Shade

In the summer of 2011, as I began to write this foreward to George Case's informative and passionate book, I could not help but reflect on why Led Zeppelin remained so alive in the minds of fans more than thirty years after they announced in December 1980 that they "could not continue as we were," in the wake of John Bonham's death. Judging by the number of T-shirts one sees on the skinny frames of kids who were not alive when the band was together, there is clearly something about their music and their essence that has also translated to younger generations, which is certainly not the case for all '70s arena bands. Try getting a glimmer of recognition from a teenager about Jethro Tull or Emerson, Lake and Palmer.

I worked for Led Zeppelin for three years, starting in April 1973, primarily as their American publicist, and even then my fascination with the music and the epic scene around them was matched with an appreciation for the powerful impact I could nightly see on the faces of their fans.

I asked Andrew Loog Oldham, the legendary former producer and manager of the Rolling Stones, for his thoughts and he suggested that one of the keys to Zeppelin's mystique was the exact timing of their ascent, which uniquely bridged the '60s and the '70s. Oldham used the young Jimmy Page as a session guitarist on Marianne Faithfull's "As Tears Go By" and later employed Page to do A&R at Immediate Records. "He was very, very quiet but keenly aware of the business. We had a blues series that included John Mayall and Eric Clapton, and Jimmy's method of producing was to have people jam and have a Grundig tape recorder in the bathroom."

When Page created Led Zeppelin in the wake of the breakup of the Yardbirds, he had a fully developed vision about what aspects of British '60s rock culture to emulate and which to jettison to make the new band uniquely powerful.

Page picked the absolute best musicians and left no weak spots. John Bonham's talent towered above that of Cream's Ginger Baker or the Jeff Beck Group's Cozy Powell. Robert Plant had a personal artistic vision that dwarfed that of the Who's Roger Daltrey or Cream's Jack Bruce. It is no accident that Robert has been able to have a vibrant solo career while the other lead singers from guitar hero bands have not. (Rod Stewart emerged from the Jeff Beck Group but, lacking Plant's rock gravitas, he quickly became pop.) And of course John Paul Jones, who had also cut his teeth playing on many of Oldham's sessions, was the premier arranger and bass player of his generation.

Page emphasized graphics rooted in a mythical band image instead of the tired convention of ensemble band photos. He was highly attuned to the rapidly developing language of the underground and the concepts of credibility that rock audiences were establishing. FM rock radio in the United States and John Peel in the UK had made it unnecessary for bands to contort their music into three-minute pop singles in order to reach a mass audience. "Jimmy had seen the perils of the wrong kinds of singles with the Yardbirds," Oldham reflects. "You couldn't have a single like 'For Your Love' and then profess to be a blues band that played Mose Allison and be taken seriously." Led Zeppelin was the first unapologetic "album" group to reach the apex of commercial success. No pandering to the pop culture, no singles, no television (Jimmy hated the tinny sound of TV speakers). From the beginning, Zeppelin invested in the best equipment for concerts and recognized that their real bond with their audience was created in person.

Zeppelin liked making money and they were justly proud that their manager (and my boss), Peter Grant, changed the economic terms of the business in their favor, and they liked sex and drugs. However, when I worked for them, amidst the record-breaking grosses, the dark glamour, and the wild consumption, I was always impressed with how seriously the band took its art. John Bonham got to every arena earlier than the others to do his own sound check. Jimmy and Robert agonized over the smallest mistakes, whether made by their crew or by themselves.

Zeppelin retained just enough hippie idealism to cast a wider psychological net than the "heavy metal" they inspired. (Page complained to me when critics lumped Zeppelin in with other heavy bands. "Don't they hear the light and shade?") Even bands whose first albums came out just a few years later, such as Aerosmith and Kiss, were oblivious to the '60s idea of "credibility." It is impossible to imagine Steven Tyler or Gene Simmons doing an album with Allison Krauss or a documentary about guitars and equally implausible to think of Robert Plant or Jimmy Page hosting *American Idol* or a reality show.

My friend Peter Newman, now a New York real estate executive, is a typical Zeppelin freak who was in tenth grade when Bonham died. "The first album I owned was *Led Zeppelin IV*, which I got when I was nine. Later, when I saw *The Song Remains the Same*, I couldn't believe what I was watching. I was a drummer and I couldn't figure out how to replicate what Bonham played. I must have listened to that live album a thousand times." Now in his forties,

Newman still brims with emotion when he talks about the band "Nothing else has stayed with me they way they do."

Ultimately, I think there is some alchemy between the members of the band that made them distinct from anything they did in other configurations—and the intensity of the fans. I remember standing with Peter Grant in Tampa Stadium, which held 56,800 fans who helped Zeppelin break the Beatles' record for attendance at a single-artist show. Pointing to cars zooming by on an adjacent highway he said, "In here people are having this great time, and out there they don't have any idea." A secret held by millions of people. Lucky us.

Danny Goldberg

Acknowledgments

I n the over two years it has taken to research, write, edit, and revise *Led Zeppelin FAQ*, I have made contact with a range of people who have helped me check facts, track down images, offer opinions or insights, confirm (or refute) rumors, and generally assist in digging into the ever-challenging mysteries of Led Zeppelin. Specific responses from some individuals are referred to in the main text, others took questions and fulfilled requests, the answers to which are scattered throughout the book, and still more at least had the time to reply with civility when queried. My gratitude goes out to:

Roger Berlin, Richard Cole, Thea Dunn, Roger Farbey, Danny Goldberg, Ross Halfin, Roy Harper, Steve A. Jones for his Zeppelin scholarship, Trevor Lee, Clare Morris, Ron Nevison, Joe Petagno for his recollections of creating the Swan Song logo, Sam Rapallo, Marcus Reeves for thoughts on African Americans' interest in Led Zep, Duane Roy for donating bootlegs and artwork, Evan Schechter for generous info on everything from Aleister to ZoSo, John Shap for reflections on classic rock radio, Len Ward for memorabilia and memories, John Watson, Beth Wilks for remembering the SCTV "Stairway" parody, and John Wright.

A whole lotta love goes out to Bernadette Malavarca, Rob Rodriguez, Polly Watson, and the Backbeat Books team, for getting me there.

And to my captive audience of hardcore Zep-heads Tonya, Genevieve, and Olivia, for everything: "If the sun refuse to shine, I would still be loving you."

Introduction

I Never Did Quite Understand

t would be both easy and, on the surface, accurate to begin by stating that no artists in rock music have been the subject of as much hearsay, rumor, and conjecture as Led Zeppelin. Most modern public references to the foursome make seemingly obligatory allusions to their larger-than-life history of legendary albums, legendary concerts, legendary offstage proclivities, and the legendary swirl of exaggeration, suspicion, and superstition that trailed in their wake. A critical, oft-repeated tale from their annals tells of guitarist Jimmy Page demanding that publicity photographs of Led Zeppelin convey a sense of "power, mystery, and the hammer of the gods." This description has been the convenient cue for a majority of Led Zeppelin's journalistic and popular citations ever since.

Yet any researcher today can sift through this mystery to avail him- or herself of dozens of Led Zeppelin books, numerous official and unofficial sound and video recordings of Led Zeppelin, and thousands of Led Zeppelin newspaper and magazine articles, in addition to the very contemporary resources of Wikipedia, YouTube, and other online indices. Indeed, a growing body of latter-day collectors, archivists, and authors have done scrupulous jobs of investigating relevant primary sources (interviews, press releases, concert bills, musicological analyses, et cetera) to lay bare anecdotes or technical secrets that would have been revelations (not always welcome) during the group's prime. Really, a more honest introduction must ask, What riddles about Led Zeppelin *haven't* been solved? Is there anything we *don't* know about one of the most successful, celebrated, and documented rock 'n' roll bands of all time?

Yes, in fact. The problem is that Led Zeppelin's career as a permanent legend has lasted over twice as long as the act's career as a regularly performing and recording ensemble. Over this posthumous time—from 1981 to the present—many of the outfit's achievements have become enshrined as pop music's equivalent of the Battle of Britain, the conquest of America, or the discovery of fire: events so self-evidently momentous, memorable, or influential that their original circumstances have been left unexamined. What Led Zeppelin did in the studio, on the stage, or in private has been covered so thoroughly, and covered and re-covered again, that critics, fans, and curious listeners have been denied a more realistic perspective on what specifically happened and why audiences responded as they did. The better topic to address, then, might not be Frequently but Infrequently Asked Questions, the musical, personal, and cultural issues around the quartet that are rarely raised, rarely resolved, or which are rarely considered at all.

Such is the mythology spun around the biggest rock names of the 1960s and 1970s—hagiographic accounts of fateful beginnings under the spell of Chuck Berry or Elvis Presley, of historic tallies of Top Tens or number ones, of tragic dissolutions under the weight of fame, self-indulgence, and personal acrimony—that the confused, coincidental, and very hurried narratives of their professional lives are often forgotten. Led Zeppelin's story is among many where image and reality have only occasionally overlapped. Thirty, forty, or fifty years on, the epic sagas of uniquely compatible players brought together by destiny to create a timeless series of million-selling records or play an epochal run of concerts seem etched in stone, but the day-to-day truths underlying these sagas were far more prosaic. In 1969 or 1975, rock stars like the members of Led Zeppelin were people scarcely past school age, rarely with formal musical training, struggling to survive in a fickle commercial medium where hard work and raw talent alone could not guarantee artistic or economic viability. They were in constant competition with older and newer acts of widely varying styles, were often overlooked by the day's arbiters of cool, and were affected as much by the routine demands of their industry as by any musical inspiration or spiritual epiphany. Hindsight might portray their fame as foreordained, but more probing study will unearth a different and in many ways more illuminating trajectory.

Led Zeppelin FAQ is not an attempt to debunk or disparage the band. It does sort out the basic information on Led Zeppelin any novice follower will want to know, highlight the most important aspects of the band members' lives and work, and catalogue as many confirmed details and bits of trivia and arcana as are possible to track down. However, I have also tried to bring in fresh insights and ideas to familiar controversies, shake up a few fallacies, and to remind readers of the fundamental roles celebrity and commerce have played in creating—and sometimes distorting—the standard Led Zeppelin biography. Asserting from the outset that Led Zeppelin were a great rock group who more than earned their acclaim, I believe both the reputation of the act and the sentiments of its fans are secure enough to withstand the scrutiny to which they will be subject herein: frequently asked questions, infrequently asked questions, and questions never dared until now.

The Mystery of the Quotient

Led Zeppelin Quick FAQ

Led Zeppelin's total record sales: At least 250 million and possibly up to 300 million copies in all formats worldwide.

Backward messages on "Stairway to Heaven": There aren't any. If persuaded of such beforehand, listeners might pick out intelligible language when the music is played in reverse, but nothing the band ever deliberately put on the recording.

Jimmy Page, Satanist: Page was not. He was interested in alternative religions that were sometimes categorized under "the occult," but he did not practice anything that meets the usual criteria of devil worship.

Led Zeppelin's music and mystique have entranced listeners for more than forty years. *Courtesy of Robert Rodriguez*

John Paul Jones was allegedly a member of Herman's Hermits: As a session musician in the mid-1960s, Jones played on and arranged some recordings by the lightweight British Invasion act, and accompanied them at a handful of 1967 performances in Germany, but he was never officially a member of the band.

The meaning behind the four symbols on *Led Zeppelin IV*: The icons are less significant than many assume. John Bonham's and John Paul Jones's (the interlocking circles and arcs, respectively) were taken from a preexisting book of designs; Robert Plant's (the feather in the circle) was from a nineteenth-century text that purported to describe the heraldry and culture of a lost civilization; Jimmy Page's ("ZoSo") was a representation of an astrological sign for Saturn, adapted from a sixteenth-century manuscript.

The Shark Incident: On tour in the US in 1969, Led Zeppelin's tour manager used a freshly caught fish to stimulate an acquiescent nude groupie at a drunken hotel party.

Led Zeppelin's reputation for stealing other people's songs: In a few cases, legal decisions have awarded other composers a share of royalties from some Zeppelin tunes whose lyrics had been casually or inadvertently appropriated. In others, snatches of various older pieces were still identifiable when combined into new Zeppelin music. Had Led Zeppelin not been so successful and so influential, most of the "plagiarisms" would have gone unnoticed.

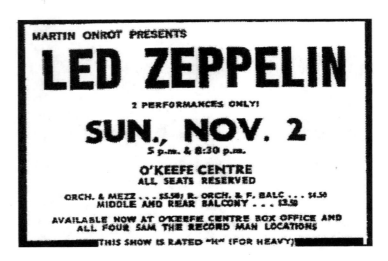

This book is also rated H (for "heavy"). · *Author's Collection*

Why Jimmy Page played a guitar with two necks:
One neck had the conventional six strings, the
other a more resonant twelve. By alternating
between the two in a single performance, he
could replicate the multiple overdubs of such
studio epics as "Stairway to Heaven" on stage.

**Led Zeppelin's reputation for smashing up
hotel rooms and abusing women:** In the 1970s
world of traveling rock bands, the musicians and
their entourages were granted wide latitudes of
sexual enjoyment and offstage pranks, but the
four members of Led Zeppelin were no more or
less destructive or self-indulgent than most other
acts of the period.

**John Bonham is widely believed to have choked
to death on his own vomit:** A coroner's inquest
concluded the drummer had died of "accidental
suicide" brought on by a pulmonary edema, the
swelling of blood vessels in the lungs. He had
passed out too drunk to properly regurgitate the
forty ounces of alcohol in his system.

Author's Collection

Robert Plant's feelings about "Stairway to Heaven": Though Plant is
reputed to hate the song, he does not. At several times since 1980 the vocalist has said he is not as impressed with the song as many Zeppelin fans. He
has never performed it as a solo artist and rarely agrees to sing it in company
with the surviving members of the group, but he has also said he is very
proud to have had a hand in its creation.

Jimmy Page is said to have lived in Aleister Crowley's house: From 1970
to the early 1990s, Page owned the Scottish Boleskine House, which had
been registered to the occultist in the early twentieth century. Page rarely
resided there for any length of time.

All Will Be Revealed

The Led Zeppelin Basics

We're Gonna Groove: Personnel

Led Zeppelin were a British-based rock group that recorded and played from 1968 to 1980. They are widely considered to be one of the greatest acts of the rock 'n' roll era. The four members were:

James Patrick "Jimmy" Page (January 9, 1944–) Electric guitars, acoustic guitars, pedal steel guitar, mandolin, banjo, backing vocals, theremin, tape effects.

Robert Anthony Plant (August 20, 1948–) Lead vocals, backing vocals, harmonica, conga, tambourine, occasional guitar.

John Paul Jones (née John Baldwin) (January 3, 1946–) Electric bass guitar, electric upright bass, piano, electric organ, mellotron, synthesizer, mandolin, conga, acoustic guitar, lap steel guitar, recorder, backing vocals.

John Henry Bonham (May 31, 1948–September 25, 1980) Drums, conga, gong, tympani, tambourine, backing vocals.

It's Been a Long Time: Life Span

The group's first rehearsals took place in August 1968; the band first performed under the name Led Zeppelin on October 25, 1968, and their debut album was released (in the US) in January 1969. John Bonham was found dead on September 25, 1980, and a formal press release announcing Led Zeppelin's disbandment was issued on December 4, 1980. Thus, the band was officially extant for twelve years, give or take a few weeks.

This measurement is qualified by the actual amount of time Led Zeppelin were performing and recording. A sterner look might conclude that the act's most fruitful years were from 1969 to 1973, when they were touring constantly and when their most popular records were made. After that, they made one complete tour of the US and did the Earl's Court gigs in 1975, performed an American tour in 1977 that was prematurely canceled, made a total of four appearances in 1979, and ran a short European jaunt in 1980. Led Zeppelin's first four albums, generally regarded as their best, were produced between October 1968 and mid-1971 (*Led Zeppelin IV* was in stores in November, but the tracks had been completed in the spring of that year), a span of about thirty months. *Physical Graffiti*, their last really well-received album, came out in February 1975, using material that had been put down in 1974 or even as far back as 1970. The low-key, only partially successful last studio album, *In Through the Out Door*, was recorded in late 1978 and on sale in the late summer of 1979. Like many, perhaps most, of the great rock 'n' rollers, Led Zeppelin rose and fell in a far shorter duration than a mere chronology will reveal. The various reasons for this decline are addressed elsewhere, but, for a band whose fame has extended over four decades, Led Zeppelin had no more than five or six years of peak productivity.

Measuring a Summer's Day: Sales Figures

The question of the band's absolute record shipments is a more complicated one than a simple statement of numbers will answer. Though Led Zeppelin are routinely described as one of the highest-selling acts ever, arriving at a definite statistic to corroborate this is not easy. In the first place, record companies, even in their heyday before the advent of home cassette recordings and, later, Internet "piracy," have often been reluctant to disclose hard figures. Releasing accurate data on record sales is (or was) for the labels a double-edged sword: Hit records could be talked up to promote further purchases, but talking up hit records also invited the attentions of artists or managers who would then demand a bigger share of the revenue generated, and eventually government tax collectors, with their sharp eyes and long arms, would take an interest in any corporation making too loud or too specific boasts of product shipped. Press-friendly phrases like "broke all records," "went double platinum," or "all-time best seller" are usually hyperbole that have no real application in the accounting department.

Another factor is the price and durability of the items being counted. Vinyl records, eight-track tapes, audio cassettes, CDs, and DVDs are, like books, relatively inexpensive and can last indefinitely; many a Led Zeppelin collector owns original LPs as well as remastered compact discs of the same material. Whatever the medium, an album in good condition can change hands several times over its life where only the single original purchase (by retailer from manufacturer) will ever be counted. A measure of Led Zeppelin's record sales will also leave out the even murkier subject of bootleg discs (called "audience recordings" in polite company), and some Zeppelin examples of these, such as *The Destroyer* or *Listen to This Eddie*, have acquired almost as much a following as the authorized studio releases. And there is simply no telling how much Led Zeppelin music was copied to tape at home and passed around from friend to friend, all of it of course without the sanction of the authors, their manager, or their corporate partner. Even today, copyright matters are vexing ones at all levels of the entertainment industry, not only in view of lost income but lost accuracy.

Third, statistics of absolute record sales are often confused with chart positions of sales measured against competing discs. Trade publications such as *Billboard*, *Goldmine*, *Cashbox*, and *Variety* track weekly movement of units in the familiar hierarchies of Top Tens, Top 40s, Hot 100s, or number ones, without acknowledging that what constitutes a Top Ten or a number one will necessarily vary from one interval to the next. Paralleling best sellers' lists and television ratings, the actual count of records bought in stores has declined over the last twenty-odd years, reflecting changes in demographics, economic conditions, and technology, but there must by definition always be a "most popular" title whatever the total transactions or viewers. In 1971, Led Zeppelin's untitled fourth album failed to register as the biggest-selling LP in America when Santana's *III*, Sly and the Family Stone's *There's a Riot Goin' On*, and Carole King's *Tapestry* were all shifting more copies, but over time *Led Zeppelin IV* has proven the bigger seller. Conversely, most of Led Zeppelin's albums made number one in Britain shortly after their respective releases, but the band have sold altogether fewer records there than many other British acts of their own and later eras, including Queen, Oasis, Dire Straits, and the Spice Girls.

For a medium so dependent on another—broadcast radio—for advertising, records' popularity on the airwaves does not automatically translate into popularity at the cash register. Though Led Zeppelin albums were heavily rotated on North American FM stations in the 1970s (and the band are fixtures of "classic rock" radio today), they were well removed from the playlists of more hit-oriented networks, and because Led Zeppelin put out relatively few singles as an operating band and never catered to the formats of AM stations (much less TV spots), they were often beat out by briefly more successful songs that reached more listeners in a shorter space of time. Thus

1973 was not the year of "Over the Hills and Far Away" but the year of "Tie a Yellow Ribbon Round the Ole Oak Tree" by Dawn, featuring Tony Orlando, and 1979's most requested track was not "Fool in the Rain" but the Village People's "YMCA." This has also clouded the issue of which artists have won the greater success: Is it the multimedia superstar sensations whose flurry of catchy 45s and glitzy television appearances were inescapable for a few weeks or months, or the secretive, anonymous cult act generations of fans have actually forked over hard cash to seek out and hear?

Here again is a complication, namely the expanding and fragmenting market for recorded music. The most popular works, as indicated by total sales, are frequently skewed toward more recent issues, as growing populations are more likely to buy records by newer artists. Because young people are generally the most consistent spenders of entertainment money, modern releases will gradually surpass earlier ones in terms of copies bought—as aging audiences devote their disposable income to products other than popular songs, the overall stature of their own favorites will be eclipsed by those of their children and grandchildren. Globally, too, emerging economies like those of Brazil, India, and China have already begun to develop their own domestic followings for homegrown talent, and the conventional first-world rankings of hits and blockbusters will be obsolete; the "universal" appeal of Bing Crosby's "White Christmas" or Pink Floyd's *Dark Side of the Moon* can no longer be assumed in coming decades.

Considering all this, the long-disbanded and British-based rock 'n' roll group Led Zeppelin have proven a remarkably resilient and worldwide musical attraction. If they cannot be proven as the most popular musical act of all time (can anyone be, in the final analysis?), they have certainly enjoyed a commercial fortune very few performers from any genre have known. Not only is their catalogue relatively small—a mere eight studio albums issued between 1969 and 1979, in addition to the live *The Song Remains the Same* and the funeral *Coda*—but it has been anthologized in only a few collections. The box sets of 1990 and 1993; the *BBC Sessions* of 1997; the *Early Days* and *Latter Days* best-of packages from 1999 and 2001, respectively; the triple-disc live *How the West Was Won* in 2003; and the remastered *Mothership* from 2007 have boosted the ultimate figures, but not in the way other acts have reconfigured their songs into literally dozens of Greatest Hits, Not Sold In Stores, All-Time Classics, or Christmas assemblies.

According to the Recording Industry Association of America (RIAA), Led Zeppelin sold 111.5 million records in the United States through 2009. This number puts them behind the Beatles, Garth Brooks, and Elvis Presley but ahead of the Eagles, Billy Joel, Pink Floyd, and Barbara Streisand. With the US still the biggest market for sound recordings, Led Zeppelin's sales

"Hey Hey, What Can I Do," the B side of 1970's "Immigrant Song," was the sole Led Zeppelin song released only in the 45-rpm format.   *Author's Collection*

in that country can be extrapolated to an estimate of between 250 million and 300 million records purchased around the planet.

You'll Be My Only: Led Zeppelin's "No Singles" Policy

Between 1969 and 1979 ten 45-rpm Led Zeppelin records were available in North America; there were others released in overseas markets like Japan and elsewhere. "Whole Lotta Love," "Immigrant Song," "Black Dog," "D'yer Mak'er," "Trampled Underfoot" and "Fool in the Rain" were all Top 40 hits in the United States. No singles, other than a promotional issue of "Trampled Underfoot," were made available in Britain.

Perhaps difficult to fathom for generations grown up on videos and the Internet, the "no singles" policy identified with Led Zeppelin refers to their practice of not putting out new music *only* as a single. In both the US and the UK, the music industry had up until the mid-1960s been dominated by the single, which served the demands of broadcasters and teenage listeners adequately, but which also tended to produce a high rate of turnover for the artists, all vying for more airplay and hook-based material than most could ever have. Before the Beatles and Bob Dylan, pop records' low cost and typical reliance on two-minute gimmickry made most of them critically and economically disposable.

In contrast, all Zeppelin's 45s were "teaser" rather than "stand-alone" releases that were taken from—and promoted—a recent album. By the time of the band's inception in 1968, the size and affluence of the baby-boomer audience, especially in America, had made the sale of cohesive and original pop LPs (i.e., not anthologies) increasingly viable: the Beatles' *Sgt. Pepper's Lonely Hearts Club Band*, Bob Dylan's *Blonde on Blonde*, Jimi Hendrix's *Are You Experienced*, and Cream's *Disraeli Gears* were highly successful records unto themselves rather than just platforms for one or two radio hits. Jimmy Page and Peter Grant, Zeppelin's manager, saw the commercial opportunities in this trend—albums were more profitable than singles, of course—on top of the artistic respectability. "We didn't have to create songs for a pop singles market," Page told *Guitar World* magazine in 2003. "That would have been the kiss of death for us. . . . By not releasing a traditional single, we forced people to buy albums, which is what we wanted. We wanted them to see the band's complete vision."

The "no singles" stance of Led Zeppelin was, on one hand, a calculated approach to capitalize on a lucrative market by offering only premium product; on the other, it was a conscientious gesture of principle in making whole, self-contained albums the band's prime medium. A dearth of singles has meant that Zeppelin's total record sales are artificially lower than those of other acts who put out many more of their songs in a cheaper and more palatable format, but it has also made the group's music appear more serious in being communicated in a more substantial way.

Maybe More than Enough: Led Zeppelin's Biggest Hit

The group's most popular record is *Led Zeppelin IV*. The RIAA credits this disc with 23 million copies sold in the US since 1971, below the numbers for the Eagles' *Greatest Hits, 1971–1975* and Michael Jackson's *Thriller* and above Pink Floyd's *The Wall*, AC/DC's *Back in Black*, Garth Brooks's *Double Live*, and Shania Twain's *Come On Over*. This list is only of albums, not discs of any format, but considering the scarcity of Led Zeppelin singles and their commitment to the medium of long-playing albums, it is certain that this record is their single most popular releases. That it has reached this level of sales almost forty years after its first appearance, and long since the demand for most of its contemporaries has tapered off, is in the world of pop music a striking achievement. Judging again by its American popularity, it is probable that between 30 million and 40 million copies of *Led Zeppelin IV* have been bought internationally.

Overlords: The Strengths and Weaknesses Each Member Brought to the Group

Another of the clichés according to which classic rock groups are characterized is their alchemical balance of personalities and abilities, as if their resultant music was a magical creation only the musicians in question could have made, or wanted to make. In fact, although compatibility is of course a crucial component to a functioning ensemble, many of the best-loved bands came to their sounds through a combination of rehearsal, accident, compromise, and convenience, with each individual member attempting to pull the songs in his preferred way and forced to accept the others' opposite influences. "The only heavy band I really dig is the Zeppelin," Robert Plant once said, while John Paul Jones has pointed out that "none of us had remotely the same record collection." More than that of most of their peers, the music of Led Zeppelin was a product of widely varied leanings and techniques that blended in an unforeseen and volatile mixture.

John Paul Jones

Jones was the band's most formally disciplined and versatile player, raised in a musical family and having served an apprenticeship in the London studio scene since the early 1960s. A multi-instrumentalist with solid chops on bass, piano, organ, guitar, mandolin, and reeds, and fluent in music theory and the crafts of arranging and orchestration, he was the consummate professional in Led Zeppelin. Despite his low-key demeanor on- and offstage, Jones was the prime mover behind some of Zeppelin's standout tracks: "Good Times Bad Times," "Your Time Is Gonna Come," "Heartbreaker" (probably), "Celebration Day," "Since I've Been Loving You," "Black Dog," "No Quarter," "Trampled Underfoot," "Ten Years Gone," and "All My Love." Without his skills, Led Zeppelin might have been just another bunch of English bluesmen endlessly jamming around three chords, pedestrian riffs, and wandering solos. A jazz and soul fan whose heroes included Ray Charles and Charles Mingus, he told scholar Susan Fast, "[B]ands often form from people who all listen to the same (one) type of music and therefore lack the variety of listening that I think is necessary for a well-rounded and interesting musical group." Likewise, Jones's post-1980 involvement with alternative darlings like Sonic Youth, the Butthole Surfers, Diamanda Galás, Uncle Earl, and the Mission lent Led Zeppelin a retroactive credibility their snootier critics of the 1970s had always denied them. With his eclectic tastes, Jones embellished Zeppelin's music just as he had done for numerous performers' music as a session hand: made it tighter, trickier, more sophisticated, and often more exciting.

Like all the famous "quiet ones"—cf. George Harrison, Bill Wyman, John Entwistle, et al—Jones received less credit for his group's success than he might have claimed, both for specific pieces like "Stairway to Heaven" and "Kashmir," and for a general elevation of its all-round sonic identity. He was no lyricist, however, and it may be significant that the album where his stamp is most audible, *In Through the Out Door*, is also Zeppelin's least powerful. Though his role as a unobtrusive, behind-the-scenes fixer was an asset during the first years of the quartet, his detachment and willingness to avoid the spotlight may have put undue pressure on the already stressed Jimmy Page, Robert Plant, and John Bonham from 1975 onward (although he did agree to try singing Sandy Denny's parts on "The Battle of Evermore" during the 1977 tour). Some of his concert solo turns on keyboard, where he would drop in snatches of Miles Davis, Sergey Rachmaninoff, and Tchaikovsky's *The Nutcracker*, embodied the self-indulgent, virtuosity-for-its-own-sake pretensions punk rockers sought to puncture, and his droll, family-man persona (however authentic) made him the squarest personality among some otherwise notoriously colorful characters. Though known to enjoy a joint and to be an occasionally remote or difficult interview subject, he carried little of Page's enigma or Bonham's danger and less of Plant's charisma. Still, John Paul Jones's preference for the challenges of high-quality rock music over the rewards of high-living rock stardom was his singular, inimitable value in Led Zeppelin.

Robert Plant

Plant, along with Jimmy Page, was the public face of the band, and as chief wordsmith the man who gave Led Zeppelin a large share of their mystical, countercultural dimension. With his encyclopedic knowledge of obscure lines and phrasings it was R&B buff Plant who first placed the group in its class as a high-powered blues meltdown, and it was the literate and sensitive Plant who eventually took them beyond the language of Chicago or the Mississippi Delta to the visionary ranges of "Ramble On," "Immigrant Song," "That's the Way," "The Rover," "Kashmir," "Achilles Last Stand," and above all "Stairway to Heaven." A sincere proponent of the transformative potential of music, Robert Plant also lifted Zeppelin up from merely a faithful, dilettante's exhibition of amplified folk idioms to achieve something like mass catharsis—in their Houses of the Holy, Plant was what their biographer Stephen Davis called a "high priest of rock communion and a true believer." His leonine hair, bare chest, tall frame, and confident stage moves—so confident he could even pose as a radiant feminine other to Page's dark wizard—secured his stature as the act's prime sex symbol, a conquering hippie Viking whose image thousands of female fans still find irresistible.

But Robert Plant's most tangible ability was as a vocalist, and this is where his influence may be widest. Jimmy Page, John Paul Jones, and John Bonham were all heroes on their instruments, but no more than Plant was with his voice. His devastating work on *Led Zeppelin* and its three sequels was an unprecedented display of range, control, and projection, melding the blues affectations of Joe Cocker or (especially) Janis Joplin with the technical effects of Enrico Caruso. By the climactic bars of "Good Times Bad Times," "Dazed and Confused," "Whole Lotta Love," "Heartbreaker," "Since I've Been Loving You," "Stairway to Heaven," and "When the Levee Breaks" he is hitting and sustaining notes few pop singers before him dared to aim for. Although certainly untutored, Plant's quasi-operatic moans were taken up by many front men in other hard rock bands of later years: Journey's Steve Perry, Judas Priest's Rob Halford, Foghat's Dave Peverett, Boston's Brad Delp, Vince Neil of Mötley Crüe, Klaus Meine of the Scorpions, Paul Stanley of Kiss, Ronnie James Dio, Sammy Hagar, Iron Maiden's Bruce Dickinson, and the blatant David Coverdale. Not until the grunge reactions of Nirvana and Pearl Jam did the standard male rock vocalist's repertoire drop from Plant's exuberant octaves to the mumbled, mangled phrasings of today.

Precisely because Plant had no formal training as a singer, however, his high wails were gradually grounded over the course of Led Zeppelin's flight, and neither did he do his instrument any favors as a regular smoker of tobacco and cannabis. His bouts of tonsillitis and other throat woes forced cancellation of some Led Zeppelin concerts and subdued performances in others, and he was quietly sidelined with throat surgery around 1973 or 1974, after which some contend he never sounded the same. By Zeppelin's later tours he was relying on an electronic harmonizer effect to cover some of his strained melismata, and at the band's 2007 reunion several songs were played in lower keys than the original to preserve Plant's pipes, although this may have been an inevitable nod to his fifty-nine years. Moreover, the singer's surreal experiences as a twenty-one-year-old rock star and his tragic misfortunes as an individual have left him with a conspicuously embarrassed perspective on his Led Zeppelin career. While acknowledging his pride in having been a part of the band, and crediting Zeppelin as the basis for his four decades as a prominent and highly respected artist, Plant has always

With worldwide sales of almost 40 million units, *Led Zeppelin IV* is the band's most successful record.   *Courtesy of Robert Rodriguez*

tended to downplay the more extravagant aspects of Zeppelin's music and mythos (refusing to sing "Stairway to Heaven," for example), citing them as the exaggerated or juvenile follies of someone too young to be forever held accountable to them. To many fans, Plant's maturity and humility have allowed Led Zeppelin to maintain their dignity, in contrast to the graceless aging of Rolling Stone Sir Mick Jagger, but others complain he has been a holdout in blocking a reunion of the surviving members and in unduly dismissing the group's greatest work. For all his efforts to outgrow it, and for better or worse, Robert Plant will be always be tied to the majestically romantic role he played and sang so well as part of Led Zeppelin.

John Bonham

Bonham was the true source of Led Zeppelin's heavy sound and the member who truly lived and died the rock 'n' roll excess with which the band has always been linked. His drumming has been imitated by countless other percussionists in rock and other fields, and his recorded work has been frequently sampled for use in later artists' digital creations. Many of Zeppelin's classic tunes are virtually defined by his beat: the bass triplets on "Good Times Bad Times" (which prompted no less a listener than Jimi Hendrix to compare the dexterity of Bonham's pedal action to a castanet player's), the explosive snare on "Whole Lotta Love," the eruptive hi-hats on "Rock and Roll," the cascading entry in "Stairway to Heaven," the cavernous meter of "When the Levee Breaks," the relentless groove of "Kashmir"—it is a list that can encompass most of the songs in the band's canon. But for his combination of Motown taste and industrial-strength authority, Led

Zeppelin would have had lost much of its audio hallmark and been more like a watery Jimmy Page Group or Robert Plant Blues Explosion. Bonham remains one of the symbols of pop music performance at its most overwhelming and pop music lifestyle at its most decadent. (He and the Who's Keith Moon were the likely archetypes for the feral drummer Animal on *The Muppet Show*, a staple of US television in the late '70s.) Arguably the Zeppelin member with the best command of his instrument and by many accounts the most consistent of the four musicians in concert, he is the only man from the group to be remembered in not one but two biographies. John Bonham is an inspiration, a titan, a legend, and finally a tragedy.

Some of this reputation has only come posthumously. In 1984's *The Book of Rock Lists* his name is nowhere to be found on "The 25 Greatest Rock and Roll Drummers," although he is included in "Rock and Roll Hell: A List of Probable Inductees." During the 1970s his playing was, along with Led Zeppelin's generally, relegated to a category of mere "heavy metal," meaning loud, hard, and simple, and it is also the case that other rock drummers of the era—Stewart Copeland of the Police, Carl Palmer of Emerson, Lake and Palmer, Bill Bruford of Yes and King Crimson, Alan White of Yes, Neil Peart of Rush—were playing with more subtlety and finesse than Bonham usually displayed. Bonham's drums were recorded by Jimmy Page in a way that would have magnified anyone's talents, adding to his larger-than-life sound: The Herculean intro to "When the Levee Breaks," for instance, was recorded in a naturally echoing stairwell and slowed down in the final mix for a deeper, more plodding cadence. His heavyweight physical stature was an advantage when generating the driving meters of "Dazed and Confused," "Immigrant Song," "The Wanton Song," "Achilles Last Stand," or his solo "Moby Dick," but in other numbers it gives a leadenness to material that might better be timed to a lighter touch, like the ballads "Your Time Is Gonna Come," "Tangerine," or the attempted reggae of "D'yer Mak'er." Just thirty-two when he died, he might have started to suffer long-term manual or carpal damage had he grown older, owing to his hard-hitting overhand "match grip" percussion (never mind his solo spots where he played with his hands alone). Bonham's recorded legacy is well considered by Chris Welch and Geoff Nicholls in *John Bonham, A Thunder of Drums: The Powerhouse Behind Led Zeppelin and the Godfather of Heavy Rock Drumming*, whose title implies that, for all his immortal licks, rolls, and fills, his influence is still mostly felt as an especially aggressive musician more than an especially imaginative one.

John Bonham's fatal deficiency, really, lay not in any limitations as a percussionist (though the unassuming "Bonzo" was always the first to admit that he had them), but in his penchant for violence and self-destruction.

Had he never joined Led Zeppelin, the likeable and homey lad from the Midlands might have lived out a happier life as a husband and father, perhaps jamming with some mates in local bands and hitting his favorite pub every Saturday night, closing down a busy work week as a building contractor or lorry driver. Instead, swept up into one of the most popular rock acts in the world at the age of twenty-one and sent to the far corners of the earth to perform, he lost much of his inherent modesty and grounding—the provincial, working-class drummer of truncated education was turned loose in the fleshpots of America, Europe, and Asia and afforded the opportunity to behave far more recklessly than he ever would in his English hometown. Stories of Bonham vandalizing hotels and dressing rooms, and bullying or assaulting bystanders and hangers-on, have become fixtures of Led Zeppelin lore, scarcely alleviated by survivors' apologies that he was a nice guy when sober, that he was a down-to-earth chap who just missed his family, that deep down he meant no harm. If all the men of Led Zeppelin were to varying extents caught up in the chaotic licentiousness around them, John Bonham was the one least able to deal with it. Coming before an era when interventions and rehabilitation clinics were regular retreats, and before anger management and chemical dependency were known concepts, Bonham's Zeppelin stardom was well deserved but still came too soon. It is to the band's credit that they deemed him irreplaceable after he died, but it is to the band's shame that his sad and sordid death had to happen at all.

Jimmy Page

Page is one of the most famous rock musicians ever, both for his enduring music and his still-shadowy private predilections. He was the founder and producer of Led Zeppelin; the main or collaborative composer of almost all the quartet's songs; the man who selected the other three players for membership; the final authority on Zeppelin's official recorded output, tour schedules, and set lists; a guitar hero; a star concert attraction (considering he took no lead vocals and rarely spoke to the attendees); the curator of the band's post-breakup archives; and the key figure in Zeppelin's occult legendry. His skills on electric and acoustic guitar led many other professional and amateur players to emulate (or further) his techniques, and his ingenuity and improvisations in the studio are some of the most crucial developments in the science of recorded pop music. Photographs of Page as the long-haired, open-shirted instrumentalist with his Les Paul slung to his thighs; as the backstage emperor guzzling Jack Daniel's whiskey; as the spotlit soloist triumphantly hoisting his double-neck; or as the black-, white-, or SS-uniformed rock 'n' roller taking adulatory center stage are some of the most iconic visions in popular culture. To sum up the artistic and intellectual ideal of "rock star," it would be hard to find a better illustration than Led Zeppelin's Jimmy Page.

It is ironic, then, that Page was perhaps the least proficient musician of the group and the remaining member with the least adventurous track record after 1980. Though obviously a talented guitarist and a dynamic live performer, his actual playing from cut to cut and from concert to concert was erratic; though he instigated many of Led Zeppelin's most indelible songs, they were immeasurably improved by the others, in some examples far beyond Page's initial ideas. For a shrewd and sensitive industry professional, he, too, like the naïve Brum John Bonham, suffered badly from overindulgence in drugs and alcohol through the Zeppelin years, and the group's final records and shows reflect the depths of his personal decline. His offstage pursuits of esoteric religions and sexual kinks, though verified well enough, have been repeated and exaggerated to the point where they have taken on a mystique disproportionate to Page's substantive involvement with either. Strip away the fable and urban legend, and Jimmy Page emerges as a good but seldom brilliant artist smart and lucky enough to have placed himself in the middle of phenomena that have added to his renown more by passive association than deliberate action.

As an electric guitarist, Page had a knack for creating memorable sounds that was superior to his actual agility at playing, and many of his signature riffs—"Communication Breakdown," "Whole Lotta Love," "Immigrant Song," "The Ocean," "The Wanton Song," "In the Evening"—are marked more by their infectious hooks than by any fingerboard complexity (beginning players can get the hang of them with little difficulty). He was in fact

Popular releases of bootleg Led Zeppelin music, such as *Physically Present*, are difficult to factor in to the band's official sales figures.   *Courtesy of Duane Roy*

a more advanced acoustic player, inventing a range of unusual tunings and demonstrating some quite delicate finger-style work on "Black Mountain Side," "Bron-y-Aur Stomp," "Stairway to Heaven," "The Rain Song," "Over the Hills and Far Away," and "Bron-yr-Aur." This diversity of ability, moving from idiosyncratic acoustic strumming on "Black Mountain Side" to solid electric boogie on "Communication Breakdown," or from distorted guitar on "Rock and Roll" to pretty mandolin on "The Battle of Evermore," helped Page sound more accomplished than he would have had he confined himself to any single genre—the songs and the styles change before his shortcomings become apparent. More than anything, Page's strength was in isolating and perfecting (abetted by Jones and Bonham) the progressions or rhythmic figures he hit upon by chance, with his training as a session player instilling in him the ear and control required to go over tryout performances and shape them into something more striking or monolithic. Contemporaries such as Jimi Hendrix, Eric Clapton, and Jeff Beck; later hard rock heroes including Deep Purple's Ritchie Blackmore, Black Sabbath's Tony Iommi, and AC/DC's Angus Young; and virtuosi such as Eddie Van Halen, Al Di Meola, and Leo Kottke were better than Page at executing their own parts than he was at his, but Page was the master of recognizing effective notes when he heard them and then maximizing their impact.

Many critics today assert that Page was more influential as a producer than a guitar player. In interviews, to be sure, he has spoken volubly about his use of Altair tube limiters, EMT plate reverbs, UREI compressors, the art of microphone placement, and other studio trickery, while only vaguely recalling his choice of guitars or guitar lines: "I really don't like showing people how I play things. . . . It's a little embarrassing because it always looks so simple to me." His careful orchestrations of guitar, bass, drums, and voice; finely tuned monitoring of volume levels, stereo spacing, and ambient sound; canny choices of album packaging and design; and inspired song-by-song album sequencing have proven to have the longest and broadest reverberation in pop music from his own time; his songwriting and playing are uniquely his but therefore harder to replicate. Typecast as the bow-wielding Sorcerer or the laser-bathed Hermit of stadium gigs, Page enjoyed his finest moments at the mixing desk with a mere handful of accomplices. Though he is now a wealthy and justly lauded musician whose achievements in his field are unsurpassed, his intriguing but unspectacular early career and fitful latter-day record have shown that his highest capacities were expended during the few years he was in command of Led Zeppelin.

Any appraisal of the Led Zeppelin musicians' respective attributes must note that they, like their contemporaries in other famous rock groups, were working in a very exclusive field. They were not just craftsmen but entertainers, demonstrating their skills nightly to thousands of people who had come to see and hear them—their popular titles of Best Rock Guitarist or Greatest Rock Drummer should come with the addendum, "who was widely known." Becoming Led Zeppelin, international pop music sensation, required a crucial flamboyance and showmanship (even on the part of the usually retiring John Paul Jones) beyond mere facility, and there were almost certainly other players of the band's time who were more technically capable or creatively inventive who, for whatever reasons, never connected with a large audience. Led Zeppelin's millions of records and tickets sold were not flukes but the consequence of determined effort and deliberate self-promotion.

All the Zeppelin members have spoken of how their live gigs were more fulfilling—and in some ways more important—to them than the laborious recording process; even though the shows were ephemeral and the albums are forever, it was on the boards where Page, Plant, Jones, and Bonham felt they really earned their pay. "In the first two years of any band, you just work solidly," Page has said. "If you're going to make an impact, that's what you have to do. . . . In fact, we probably worked for three years straight." "Live shows were what Led Zeppelin was all about for me," Jones echoed. "The records were kind of starting points for the live shows." "We figured the best thing to do was shut the fuck up and play, you know?" Plant shrugged of Led Zeppelin's response to bad press. Meeting his rock star subjects following their 1970s concerts, *Rolling Stone* reporter Cameron Crowe recounted what he saw as the performers' real motivations: "These guys, most of them, seemed to be in it for the feeling they got on stage, and hopefully girls and acclaim *after* that." Part of the foursome's status, then, must rest on their work not as brilliant composers or genius instrumentalists but as energetic touring performers happy to show off for public consumption and hardy enough to keep doing it until their fan base was secure.

Father of the Four Winds: What Peter Grant Did for Led Zeppelin

Manager Peter Grant was the undisputed "fifth member" of the band, and without his fierce loyalty and imposing management strategies Zeppelin could well have wound up as no more than another Jethro Tull, Ten Years After, Savoy Brown, or the Strawbs—a psychedelic, progressive blues or folk act of the late 1960s that could only score occasional success before fragmenting in a welter of shoddy deals, cheap shots, bad scenes, and blown chances. Like a salesman convinced of his own pitch, Grant stuck by Led

Zeppelin as his prime client, turning the group from promising newcomers beset by hostile reviews into a very early example of entertainment industry "branding." It was Grant and Page who designed Led Zeppelin together, as much a corporate enterprise as an artistic one, with Page having only general notions of what the music would be; the important thing they had both learned from years in the industry was that acts had to have control of their own material. Credited as "executive producer" on Led Zeppelin's ten original albums (the term was taken from film production and has no relevance in the music industry, other than to acknowledge his business oversight), Grant ensured the group stayed a steady and lucrative draw over its working life and beyond. With his heavy hand on the balance sheets, Zeppelin benefited from a consistency that eluded many of their rivals: between 1968 and 1980, the same four members had the same manager; same producer; same record label; same links to the same network of promoters, lawyers, booking agents, and road support; and the same security in knowing that their money and creative endeavors were safely guarded at the front office.

Serious rock management, at the beginning of Led Zeppelin's career, was still in its early stages. Many artists were guided by people who were hardly more than eager fans with a few inside contacts, like the Beatles' Brian Epstein or the Rolling Stones' Andrew Loog Oldham. They were devoted to their charges and sincere in their admiration of the music, but they were blindsided by savvier operators smooth-talking their way into the royalty statements and bank accounts. Other men, like Don Arden or onetime Yardbirds producer Mickie Most, were mostly in the game for themselves, holding on to acts only as long as they were generating hit songs or sold-out venues—once the commissions stopped coming, bands could be dropped in favor of some other, hipper prospect. These were the smarmy types satirized by Pink Floyd (and Zeppelin's friend Roy Harper) in their "Have a Cigar" from 1975's *Wish You Were Here*: *"The band is just fantastic, that is really what I think. . . ."* The advent of "name" groups with identifiable personnel and styles ran ahead of managerial culture's traditional tendency to see performing bands as generic, interchangeable, or disposable providers of dance accompaniments and two-minute singles.

Peter Grant was, along with disparate actors like Allen Klein or David Geffen, one of the first in the profession to realize just how huge the market was for rock music, how much single clients could be potentially worth over time, how little audiences (then) needed persuasion via advertisement, and how even small percentages of the take could represent major sums of cash. For this reason Grant had no patience with traditional showbiz payoffs, cut corners, or side deals. All of them, to him, were ruses put out as a means to scoop proceeds from long-haired kids too innocent or stagestruck to know when they were being ripped off. Jimmy Page and John Paul Jones, seasoned in the London studio scene, were aware of these pitfalls, but Robert Plant and John Bonham were not, and no one was more aware of crooked bargains and cooked books than Peter Grant. In the long run his instinctive nose for every last legal and financial concession the band was rightfully due made them superstars, but in the short term Zeppelin drew complaints of thuggery and exploitation.

During the 1970s, Grant's brutal demands for record-breaking advances, cash up front, and nine-tenths of ticket sales per concert alienated some of those he negotiated with. A huge physical presence who on several occasions used the threat of force to get his way, he sometimes seemed to win Led Zeppelin's earnings out of intimidation more than good faith, and *The Book of Rock Lists* scoffed at Zeppelin's claims to be "the Greatest Rock and Roll Band in the World": "They just got more money than anyone else." Certainly the band was filling arenas and hitting the top of the charts well after their music entitled them to, and a less insistent or single-minded backer than Grant might not have been able to justify their fees to record executives or average punters after 1975. Like John Bonham and Jimmy Page, Grant too became a drug addict, severely curtailing his health and professional aptitude while continuing to feed the very crudity and belligerence middlemen so resented. He still managed Page for a couple of years following Bonham's death, but had to sit out most of the 1980s while getting clean and never was very active in the industry subsequently (he died of a heart attack in 1995). Current disputes over exorbitant ticket surcharges or monopolized concert promotion are at least partly due to precedents set by him forty years ago. While Peter Grant can take credit for transforming the music business in its most remunerative years—guaranteeing artists the money that had hitherto been frittered away on peripheral players—his tactics and his lifestyle came with decided downsides.

Walking Side by Side: Led Zeppelin's "Sixth Members"

During the quartet's life its circle of associates was quite small and few were ever allowed ongoing access to their inner workings. The following individuals are the most likely candidates for honorary membership.

Richard Cole

The band's original and most notorious road manager, Cole has been a major fount of information on Led Zeppelin's private life. His reminiscences loom large in Stephen Davis's *Hammer of the Gods*; an unauthorized documentary, *A to Zeppelin*; and he also cowrote a salacious autobiography, *Stairway to Heaven: Led Zeppelin Uncensored*. Cole definitely was in on the group's infamous touring debaucheries, and even his critics admit he was, for most of his stint, a reliable employee who handled the logistics of travel, accommodation, security, and equipment competently. In view of the band's hectic schedules of 1968–73, this is no small accomplishment. On the other hand, Cole was rarely party to any of the members' efforts in songwriting and record production, and his relationships with Robert Plant, Jimmy Page, and John Paul Jones were not overly close; indeed, the surviving members have all but disowned him for his public revelations.

Roy Harper

A quirky English poet and musician who was taken up by Page and Plant following their introduction to him at the Bath Festival in 1970, Harper is actually named in a Zeppelin title, "Hats Off to (Roy) Harper," although the song itself makes no mention of him. Jimmy Page played on some of Harper's 1970s records, including *Stormcock* and *Lifemask*, and the two made an entire album together in 1985, *Whatever Happened to Jugula?* Part of the group's entourage in their high-flying heyday, Harper even opened the odd Zeppelin show, offering typically eccentric numbers about cricket and other English in-jokes to baffled American hard rock fans. Admired by some in and out of the group for the perverse anticommercialism of his art but heard by others as a full-fledged nutcase, Harper was nothing if not an original. His involvement with other big names such as Pink Floyd and Kate Bush has made him a curious footnote in the history of British rock music.

B. P. Fallon and Danny Goldberg

Publicists for the group in the 1970s, and both welcomed into the group's inside circles, the Irish Fallon and the American Goldberg were faced with the challenge of making Led Zeppelin a mainstream act like the Rolling Stones—or, failing that, T. Rex. Goldberg seems to have made further inroads in this than Fallon, although it is also true that Zeppelin's rise to the rock aristocracy was most accelerated after 1980. Both have granted interviews discussing their connections to the band, and Goldberg, who has since served as a high-level executive for Warner Music, has authored his own memoir, *Bumping Into Geniuses: My Life Inside the Rock and Roll Business*.

Eddie Kramer, Glyn Johns, Andy Johns, George Chkiantz, Keith Harwood

The engineers regularly hired by Page as his studio assistants between 1968 and 1975, these technicians participated in the recording of Led Zeppelin's most important cuts. Page has said that he deliberately changed engineers with every album—"I didn't want people to think they were responsible for our sound"—but collectively Page's old Surrey chum Glyn Johns (*Led Zeppelin*), Johns's younger brother Andy (*Led Zeppelin II, III, IV*), George Chkiantz (*Led Zeppelin II, Houses of the Holy, Physical Graffiti*), expatriate South African and Hendrix alumnus Eddie Kramer (*Led Zeppelin II, Houses of the Holy, Physical Graffiti, The Song Remains the Same*), and young Englishman Keith Harwood (*Houses of the Holy, Physical Graffiti, Presence*) had no little part in realizing Page's audio conceptualizations. Kramer's operation of the console while mixing the abstract interlude in "Whole Lotta Love" alone entitles him to special mention in the Zeppelin discography, as do Andy Johns's experiments in miking Bonham's drums to send "When the Levee Breaks" off the Richter scale.

Cameron Crowe

Now a Hollywood writer-director, Crowe began as a teenage reporter for *Rolling Stone*, where his youth and enthusiasm (or fawning, it's been said) won him appreciative access to such stars as David Bowie, Elton John, and Led Zeppelin. Crowe filed some of the more illuminating interviews with Page and Plant during the 1970s, wrote the liner notes for *The Song Remains the Same*, and contributed an essay to the booklet accompanying the 1990 Zeppelin box set. His 2000 film *Almost Famous* was an autobiographical look back at his early career, with the fictional band Stillwater based partly on Zeppelin. Out of his ongoing ties to Page and Plant he has been able to secure use of their music for his cinematic projects, including *Almost Famous* and *Fast Times at Ridgemont High*, for which he wrote the screenplay. Crowe was also married to Nancy Wilson of the group Heart, longtime Led Zeppelin admirers.

Steve Weiss, Jerry Weintraub, Frank Barsalona

Zeppelin's legal and business enablers, these three American heavies were, behind Peter Grant, the key players in constructing the quartet's financial organization. Weiss was the US entertainment attorney charged with sorting out the fine print of Led Zeppelin's various deals, including the establishment of Swan Song records. Known to be a very tough negotiator, he is seen silently backing Grant in *The Song Remains the Same* while the manager lights into a Madison Square Garden employee for selling contraband Zeppelin souvenirs. As head of Premier Talent, booking agent Barsalona is credited with single-handedly reinventing the American rock concert industry, taking a hitherto haphazard and exploitive model driven by local figures and turning it into a nationwide system that treated acts as artists and not commodities; along with his value to Led Zeppelin in the band's conquest of the American market in their touring heyday of 1969–72, Barsalona also nurtured the careers of such legendary live performers as Bruce Springsteen, U2, and Van Halen. Promoter Jerry Weintraub, who also served for big names including Elvis Presley, Bob Dylan, and Eric Clapton, ensured Zeppelin's huge concert grosses of '73, '75, and '77. Weintraub took promotion out of the hands of regional middlemen and into those of his own Concerts West firm, allowing his superstar rosters to retain even more of the gate from their sold-out gigs.

Ahmet Ertegun

The head of Atlantic Records who first signed ex-Yardbird Jimmy Page's untried new group, Ertegun was known in the music industry as a gracious and farsighted executive, with a previous roster that included Ray Charles,

Jimmy Page and John Bonham lived the decadent rock star life to the fullest—and paid the price.   *Courtesy of Duane Roy*

Aretha Franklin, and other R&B legends, all of which reflected well on Led Zeppelin. "I made it very clear to them that I wanted to be on Atlantic rather than their rock label, Atco, which had bands like Sonny and Cher and Cream," Jimmy Page recalled in a *Guitar World* interview. "I didn't want to be lumped in with those people—I wanted to be associated with something more classic." Ertegun and his partner Jerry Wexler's sincere support of Led Zeppelin from 1969 to 1980 was deeply gratifying to Peter Grant and the four musicians, and he attended many Zeppelin concerts, accompanied them on their touring jets, and made it through the premier screening of *The Song Remains the Same* ("Who was the guy on the horse?" he asked Peter Grant). The 2007 Led Zeppelin reunion show at London's O2 arena was held to raise funds for the Ahmet Ertegun Education Fund, a charity established after the record man's death the previous year.

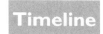

Cross the Sea of Years

Led Zeppelin's Timeline

Many accounts of the band's working life describe the four musicians exist-
ing in a social or cultural vacuum, as if the only thing going on when Led
Zeppelin was making music was Zeppelin itself. In fact, while the group was
of course popular and busy from 1968 to 1980, they were rarely the biggest
story, or even the biggest show business story, of the day. "We all lived in the
real world as much as you can," John Paul Jones looked back in an *Uncut*
interview from 2008. "I mean, it is a bit of a bubble that you travel around
in, but we were all pretty well informed." The timeline running throughout
this book, juxtaposing the key events and achievements of Led Zeppelin's
career with the most influential events and achievements in current affairs
and the arts, should put things into a wider perspective.

1968

June 5: Robert F. Kennedy assassinated, Los Angeles.
June 5: Jimmy Page retains rights to Yardbirds' name as the group dissolves.
July: Jimmy Page scouts recruits for the New Yardbirds.
August 19: First New Yardbirds rehearsal of Page, John Paul Jones, Robert
　　Plant, John Bonham.
August 22: Soviet military forces suppress the "Prague Spring" pro-
　　democracy movement in Czechoslovakia.
August 29: Youth protesters and police clash at the Democratic National
　　Convention, Chicago
September 7: First New Yardbirds performance, Gladsaxe, Denmark.
October: Mexico City Olympics; black athletes Tommie Smith and John
　　Carlos give "Black Power" salute from the podium.
October: Recording *Led Zeppelin*.
November 6: Richard Nixon defeats Hubert Humphrey in a close US election.
December 26: Led Zeppelin begin first tour of the US.
Movies: *2001: A Space Odyssey*; *Romeo and Juliet*; *Rosemary's Baby*; *Yellow
　　Submarine*; *I Am Curious (Yellow)*.
Music: Jimi Hendrix, *Electric Ladyland*; the Beatles, *The Beatles*; the Rolling
　　Stones, *Beggar's Banquet*; Bob Dylan, *John Wesley Harding*; Big Brother
　　and the Holding Company, *Cheap Thrills*; Steppenwolf, "Born to Be
　　Wild"; the Beatles, "Hey Jude"; Marvin Gaye, "I Heard It Through the
　　Grapevine"; Cream, "Sunshine of Your Love."

3

To You I Give This Tune

Led Zeppelin's Ten Best, Worst, and Most Overlooked Songs

L
ists such as the following are of course subjective and usually highly contentious, but given the finite duration of the Zeppelin catalogue (eighty-one studio songs issued between 1969 and 1982, taking up less than ten hours of music), over forty years a pretty secure fan and critical consensus has arisen around the band's highest, lowest, and least recognized attainments.

The Best

For desert island castaways, condemned prisoners, or others with limited time and space, these ten Zep tracks are the absolute, bare-bones, indispensable crème de la crème. For everyone else, these are a good start.

"Stairway to Heaven"

There is no escaping it, as the song allegedly claims when played backward. Leave aside its reputation as a secret bearer of Satanic messages, as an overplayed FM radio anthem, or as a "we're not worthy" 1970s cliché, and "Stairway" endures as Led Zeppelin's crowning marriage of acoustic and electric, light and shade, heavy and soft, power and mystery, hammer and god: their "A Day in the Life," "Like a Rolling Stone," "Layla," "Hotel California," "The Star-Spangled Banner," "Won't Get Fooled Again," and "Gimme Shelter" rolled into one. A mandatory component in the group's concerts from 1971 to 1980, a showcase for all four group members at their most polished, and the most popular track on the group's most popular album, the opus has since found a place atop Led Zeppelin's oeuvre and near the summit of all rock 'n' roll artistry. There is room for debate in sorting out many of the band's most valuable pieces, but the status of "Stairway to Heaven" is off-limits.

"Whole Lotta Love"

Only one Led Zeppelin song rivals "Stairway to Heaven" in fame and influence, and it's this one. Boasting a minimal riff sustained, amplified, and echoed to titanic scale, its opening twenty-five seconds are among the most suspenseful and dramatic fanfares in pop music, with its orgasmic fadeout marking perhaps Robert Plant's finest moments as a vocalist. Combine these with a middle section that is quite likely the most recognizable snippet of abstract composition in the world—over and above anything by Philip Glass, Karlheinz Stockhausen, or John Cage—and it is both the crucial template for a thousand other imitative hard rock cuts and a singular, pioneering experiment in sonic architecture.

"Kashmir"

Rarely does any popular musician manage to create one magnum showstopper, let alone a second one that compares well with the first. This prime cut from *Physical Graffiti* has actually held up better than "Stairway to Heaven" in its richness of sound and meaning—Led Zeppelin's most ambitious, ornate, and ominous number. A fully realized and fully successful divergence from their bluesy roots, "Kashmir" is also the piece that best belies the Zeppelin stereotype as dealers of one-dimensional heavy metal, and can quite possibly claim responsibility for opening the ears of millions of listeners to exotic non-Western tonalities. Its elephantine meter and chromatic ascension have been widely copied and sampled (including by Jimmy Page in tandem with rapper Puff Daddy), but the song remains in a class by itself.

"When the Levee Breaks"

The grand finale of *Led Zeppelin IV* is the quartet's mightiest rearrangement of a blues song, yet it is in its way the most faithful to the blues spirit—Plant's singing and harmonica, Page's open-tuned guitars, and of course Bonham's catastrophic drums give Memphis Minnie's Mississippi Delta original the scope and melodrama of Richard Wagner. Like "Whole Lotta Love," "Levee" is a landmark recording of no less than a landmark performance.

"Dazed and Confused"

Still synonymous with the druggy pleasures of headphone-wearing, couch-sprawled lethargy, "Dazed" was Led Zeppelin's original calling card, the mainstay of their early sets and their choicest holdover from the Yardbirds. This was what Jimmy Page intended in 1968 when he was devising an improvisatory, psychedelic blues act that could begin where Cream and Iron Butterfly left off: built around his bowed Telecaster concert platforms, his roiling solo in the Yardbirds' "Think About It," and the basic structure of Jake Holmes's freak-folk model. Acid rock doesn't come any more acidic than this.

"Rock and Roll"

Employed as both a volcanic show opener and a celebratory encore, this elemental fanfare is the link between the heavy metal volume and attack of Zeppelin's followers and the primeval boogie-woogie of their antecedents. Along with the song's I-IV-V chord progression and rollicking lyric, its title alone makes it a perfect illustration of what it calls itself. Timeless.

"Thank You"

Led Zeppelin's balladry always came as a departure, their gentler moments serving to emphasize the band's trademark electric riffs, but this warm and moving love song is the one which perhaps best stands on its own. Page's glistening twelve-string and Plant's palpable devotion raise this from being a mere change of pace to an early indication of artistic range; taken up years later as a fan favorite of the reunited Page and Plant outings, it proved to be one of the pair's most listenable and most positive collaborations.

"Achilles Last Stand"

Long, loud, and intentionally self-mythologizing, "Achilles" represents a late high point in Led Zeppelin's epic constructions. The interplay between Page, Jones, and Bonham is particularly effective, and the introductory and concluding guitar figures are haunting brackets to an otherwise unstoppable rhythmic thrust. A devastator.

"Black Dog"

Led Zeppelin never wrote a more intricate or more memorable hook than they did for "Black Dog" (one of their few tracks put out as a single), which features just about the densest, darkest, and funkiest guitar run in rock music traded off with a virtual dictionary of blues phraseology. The cliff-hanger punctuation of Plant's a cappella verses with the serpentine cohesion of Page, Jones, and Bonham is a compelling device from an ensemble who knew how to wring every last drop of tension and release from their work.

"Immigrant Song"

Composed of yet another technically simple yet irreducible chord fragment from Page, coupled with Plant's battle-horn howls and Norse god lyric atop Bonham and Jones's maelstrom underlay, the heaviest Zeppelin song can still hold its own against the detuned nu-metalers of today. "Immigrant Song" has been widely copied for its breakneck speed, intense audio weight, and thematic invention (see Iron Maiden, Judas Priest, Deep Purple, et al), but rarely duplicated.

The Worst

Few would wish to accuse Led Zeppelin of having made substandard music, but these are the most likely to get all but the least critical punters reaching for a guilty lift of the needle or touch of the fast-forward button. None are absolutely terrible songs, just rare faux pas from a usually very classy outfit.

"Carouselambra"

A lengthy and tedious swirl of synthesizer and guitar, "Carouselambra" wants to be big but just comes across as a muddle. Zeppelin at their most gaseous.

"The Crunge"

For a white rock act that could do very credible takes on soul and R&B modes, "The Crunge" is a real embarrassment, starting off with some nice drum work but soon deteriorating into an all-too-Caucasian hunt for a groove and the bridge. This is an outtake that never was but should have been.

"Hot Dog"

Another genre pastiche, this time of country music, "Hot Dog" is fine as a comic jam session, but the flop sweat starts to show after a few spins. The band whose serious moments were practically biblical in depth never seemed to do tongue-in-cheek humor well, and this is an obvious example.

"Hots On for Nowhere"

Murky vocals and a very fussy arrangement make this penultimate *Presence* number that album's closest to a throwaway. The song is admirable for its swing-style bounce but too elaborate to enjoy much.

"Hats Off to (Roy) Harper"

Despite its titular salute to their folk singer friend, Page and Plant are just covering bluesman Bukka White's "Shake 'Em On Down" here—complete with 78-rpm scratches and authentic slurring of vocals and acoustic guitars. A very accurate re-creation of country blues, sure, but accurate re-creations of country blues aren't what we want from Led Zeppelin.

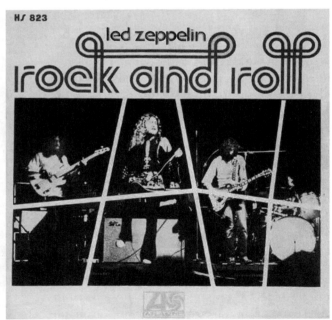

"Rock and Roll": Zeppelin's timeless tribute to their genre.
Courtesy of Robert Rodriguez

"Four Sticks"

There's no doubt the musicians were masters of unusual timings and extra beats, but sometimes, as in this black sheep from *Led Zeppelin IV*, the audience can't find the same rhythm. Although "Four Sticks" is well placed in Page and Plant's 1994 *No Quarter* experiments, it's significant that this is the one of eight tracks from its album that didn't make it on to the 1990 box set.

"Living Loving Maid (She's Just a Woman)"

The lightweight on an album bristling with heavy riffs, "Living Loving Maid" is one of the group's poppier tracks, down to its smiley backing harmonies and cute little guitar solo. Think of "Heartbreaker" or "Sick Again" remade for a G rating.

"Black Country Woman"

A leisurely afternoon outdoors with acoustic instruments, a half-written parody song, and an airplane buzzing overhead, but spoiled by the distracting presence of a tape recorder. "Black Country Woman" is Led Zeppelin's lazy filler equivalent of the Beach Boys' "Barbara Ann" or the Beatles' "You Know My Name (Look Up the Number)."

"Darlene"

Taken from the strained *In Through the Out Door* sessions and finally inserted on *Coda*, this is an expert approximation of piano-heavy good-time rockabilly—*too* expert. Here's another case of talented players vamping away at an older style without adding anything different or fresh.

"Dazed and Confused" (*The Song Remains the Same*)

Although this song could be a major mind-blower in Led Zeppelin's concerts, the thirty-minute live version presented here is just far too long and wandering—an entire vinyl album side—when bereft of the visuals that accompanied the film. Snatches of Scott McKenzie's "San Francisco (Be Sure to Wear Some Flowers In Your Hair")" and other departures uplift the track, but only temporarily. Even Jimmy Page was lukewarm on the shows from which this was taped, and he was the guy in charge.

The Most Overlooked

It's difficult to imagine any Zeppelin tracks that haven't been heard a million times, especially as the band has been sanctified on North American FM radio for more than thirty years, but somehow—for reasons of duration, genre, or the popularity of adjacent cuts—these have never got the attention they deserve. Though these songs have been long known and loved by hard-core Led-heads, latecomers would do well to check these out along with the more familiar classics.

"The Rover"

An anthem for an imagined utopia and Robert Plant's most idealistic vision, "The Rover" features grinding guitar passages and thudding drums that show Zeppelin at their swaggering supreme. Started as an acoustic song some years before its release on *Physical Graffiti* and seldom performed in its entirety in concert, only the long shadows of "Stairway to Heaven" and "Achilles Last Stand" keep this from being the group's greatest epic.

"Tea for One"

The saddest piece in Zeppelin's repertoire and a rock 'n' roll torch song, "Tea for One" utilizes the chords of the well-liked "Since I've Been Loving You" slowed and stretched to an inconsolable tempo and pierced with one of Page's most emotional solos. The party's over, the bar's closed, the lover's gone—this is what that sounds like.

"I'm Gonna Crawl"

A third minor-key blues piece to stand beside "Tea for One" and "Since I've Been Loving You," "I'm Gonna Crawl" reveals Led Zeppelin's underrated feel for expressive slow soul. John Paul Jones's synthesized string intro is a lush opening that almost portends a Frank Sinatra monologue, and Page again hits home with one of his most fluid solos.

"Poor Tom"

If there's such a thing as heavy mellow or folk metal, this is it. Bonham's dancing stomps drive the bittersweet outlaw ballad beneath Page's droning acoustic guitar and Plant's vivid storytelling: "Poor Tom" is outdoorsy country blues redone with real flair and a hard rock kick.

"Wearing and Tearing"

Made for but inexplicably left off of *In Through the Out Door*, this song is a blisteringly sped-up variation on "Train Kept A-Rollin'," usually heard as Led Zeppelin's affected stab at the raw motifs of punk rock. Except the four musicians chugging through this could have eaten the Sex Pistols for breakfast.

"Out On the Tiles"

Crowd-pleasing, mindless heavy rock à la Grand Funk Railroad, but with the incomparable Zeppelin instrumental chops. Listen for the raucous fade-out where Page throws Bonham's extemporaneous drumming all over the stereo spectrum. This is the band having fun and hitting hard.

"Going to California"

Perhaps the loveliest of all the band's acoustic songs and their most convincing take on the singer-songwriter genre, "Going to California" wafts on mandolin and open-tuned guitar to blissfully evoke the Laurel Canyon Eden Page and Plant had always dreamed of. It sounds even more ethereal when followed by "When the Levee Breaks."

"Candy Store Rock"

A sparse, no-nonsense jukebox workout anchored by Jones and Bonham's merciless lockstep, light in mood but dark in performance, "Candy Store Rock" is quintessential Zeppelin in its blend of 1950s R&B simplicity and 1970s stadium power.

"Bron-yr-Aur"

This unaccompanied pastoral is more melodic and more original than Jimmy Page's other acoustic turns of "Black Mountain Side" and "White Summer," yet rarely gets credit as such. Officially a Led Zeppelin song but actually a Page solo, it highlights the guitarist's knack for alternate tunings, introverted fingerpicking, and bucolic mood-setters: the solitary, sunlit Welsh countryside rendered in sound.

"The Wanton Song"

Utilizing the same octave-jumping chord shape as "Immigrant Song" but in a tauter time, and featuring a nakedly hedonistic Plant, "The Wanton Song" describes Zeppelin's nightly routs of the local groupie populations. The stop-start pace is augmented by Page's inserts of vertiginous backward echo, and Bonham's surprise fill in the last verse is heart-stopping.

4

Back to Schoolin'

The Roots of Led Zeppelin

The Days of My Youth: Zeppelin's Prime Influences

The varied personal and professional histories of Jimmy Page, Robert Plant, John Paul Jones, and John Bonham meant that the four had unusually diverse listening habits, which translated into the diversity of styles evident in Zeppelin's music. "I've always said that Zeppelin was the space between the four individual musicians, and it was bigger than the sum of its parts," Jones told *Bass Player* magazine in 2007. Though they were collectively happy with the work they made together, individually they each preferred sounds quite different from the others' tastes; considering that they passed most of their twenties and early thirties in collaboration, their private choices had been set before then, and they all continued to evolve in different musical directions while pooling their talents in one of rock 'n' roll's most distinctive quartets. Make a sound collage from snatches of the following musicians' output and you just might get something that sounds a little like Led Zeppelin.

Jimmy Page

Page had first been inspired by Elvis Presley's original sideman Scotty Moore, as well as Cliff Gallup and Johnny Meeks, who provided similar services for Gene Vincent, and James Burton, who backed up teen idol Ricky Nelson. All were masters of rockabilly, a hybrid style that paired the chords and licks of blues music with the biting attack and galloping rhythms of country or bluegrass. Other of Page's boyhood heroes were skiffle strummer Lonnie Donegan, twang experts Link Wray and Lonnie Mack, and the jazz-pop icon Les Paul, with his futuristic innovations. Discovering the real blues a little later, the young guitarist had his ears further opened by the authentic grit of Elmore James, B. B. King, Freddie King, Chuck Berry,

Memphis Slim accompanist Matt Murphy and Howlin' Wolf's partner Hubert Sumlin.

Together with electric pioneers, Page has often cited as influences such jazz and classical players as Andrés Segovia, Django Reinhardt, Tal Farlow, and Manitas de Plata. He was also indebted—more directly than he might care to admit—to the great British folk guitarists of his own era: John Renbourn, Davey Graham, and especially Bert Jansch. During Led Zeppelin's prime he also reported an admiration for unsung American rockers Amos Garrett (who played on Maria Muldaur's "Midnight at the Oasis") and Steely Dan's Elliott Randall, no less than the obligatory Jimi Hendrix. Further out, he told of enjoying classical composers Gustav Mahler and Krzysztof Penderecki, and he was also struck by the unique tunings and structures favored by singer-songwriter Joni Mitchell.

Robert Plant

Plant began as a blues buff and remained Led Zeppelin's in-house scholar of the genre. Like every young English singer, he couldn't avoid coming under the spell of Elvis Presley, but he soon moved on to the giants of original country blues and city R&B, like Muddy Waters, Howlin' Wolf, John Lee Hooker, Sonny Boy Williamson, Snooks Eaglin, Bukka White, Peetie Wheatstraw, Sleepy John Estes, Tommy McClennan, Big Bill Broonzy, Charley Patton, Son House, and the magisterial Robert Johnson. Plant gradually expanded beyond hard blues to the West Coast psychedelia of the 1960s, naming such acts as Love, Kaleidoscope, Buffalo Springfield, Moby Grape, and the Jefferson Airplane as favorites; still later he took to the exotic tones of Arabic singer Om Khalthoum.

John Paul Jones

Possessing the most thorough and disciplined musical education of the four, Jones naturally had the widest spectrum of musical interests—and the most highbrow. Among his first fixations he has named composers Sergey Rachmaninoff and Claude Debussy; jazz geniuses Charles Mingus, John Coltrane, and Miles Davis; boogie giant Fats Waller; bluesman Big Bill Broonzy; rock 'n' roller Jerry Lee Lewis; and the legendary soul singer and pianist Ray Charles. On his specialty of the bass, Jones was affected by earlier talents Phil Upchurch, Willie Weeks, Motown great James Jamerson, Stax Records anchor Donald "Duck" Dunn, and jazz notable Scott LaFaro. "I wasn't really involved in the white group side," he admitted of his

Scottish guitarist Bert Jansch was a major influence on Jimmy Page's acoustic
guitar style.   *Redferns/Getty Images*

allegiances as a behind-the-scenes session player in Swinging London, in
Andrew Loog Oldham's autobiography, *Stoned*. "We were into Otis Redding
and the Mar-Keys, they were all into Chuck Berry and the Chess people. . . .
As a musical scene they just didn't rate, really—the Yardbirds, it was like 'Oh

dear,' it was more punk than R&B." Jones has also spoken of his fondness for soul godfather James Brown.

John Bonham

Like many other drummers of his generation, Bonham was motivated by the stardom of swing heavyweights Gene Krupa and Buddy Rich, then found inspiration closer to home with the visibility (and audibility) of English rock 'n' rollers Keith Moon and the singular Ginger Baker. Sandy Nelson, the American session ace of the early 1960s known for "Let There Be Drums" and "Teen Beat," was another likely influence. Young Bonham had also attended to the subtleties of Dave Brubeck's timekeeper Joe Morello, the irresistible grooves laid down by James Brown, Motown's Benny Benjamin and Uriel Jones, and New Orleans legend Earl Palmer, and in time checked out the radical fusion drumming of Larry Coryell percussionist Alphonse Mouzon.

Devil He Told Me to Roll: Jimmy Page's Pre-Zeppelin Gigs

The bright and sensitive youngster who became Led Zeppelin's enigmatic sorcerer started off his musical career in the manner of thousands of other British lads of the 1950s: discovering first the homey busking of skiffle music, then the darker strains of the blues, and eventually immersing himself in the first wave of the new American fad of rock 'n' roll. Before slotting into his pivotal job as a London session guitarist, Page had already paid dues in many amateur and professional engagements around Britain.

c. 1955 Sings in choir at St. Barnabas Church in the London suburb of Epsom
1958–60 Sits in and performs with various school chums, including Malcolm Austin and the Whirlwinds
1958 Appears with neighborhood friends in the J. C. Skiffle Group playing "Cotton Fields" and "Mama Don't Allow No Skiffle Around Here" on the *All Your Own* children's talent television show
1960–61 Plays guitar in Epsom dance hall house bands; plays guitar with Red E. Lewis and the Red Caps
1961–62 Plays guitar with Red E. Lewis and the Red Caps, and with Neil Christian and the Crusaders; accompanies poet Royston Ellis at spoken-word performances
1962 Performs occasional gigs with the Cyril Davies R&B All-Stars
1962–63 Occasionally sits in with the Marquee Club house band

1962–66 Gigs as session musician
1963–64 Holds nominal membership in Carter-Lewis and the Southerners, Mike Hurst and the Method, Screaming Lord Sutch and the Savages, and Mickey Finn and the Blue Men; accompanies Sonny Boy Williamson on English recording sessions
1965 Releases a solo single, "She Just Satisfies" b/w "Keep Movin'"
1966–68 Plays with the Yardbirds
1968 Gigs as a session musician, forms the New Yardbirds

You've Been Learnin': John Paul Jones's Pre-Zeppelin Gigs

In contrast to his future bandmates, young John Baldwin entered the music business as a practical family trade rather than in a vague quest for fame and fortune. Quickly learning the basics of sight-reading and the discipline of playing in a range of styles, he also became proficient on not one but two instruments, his versatility ultimately adding greatly to Led Zeppelin's work. As a bass player he was enlisted in several ephemeral acts that disbanded as soon as they were formed, giving him valuable experience without requiring a commitment to any one lineup or set list. Instrumentalists of Jones's caliber were more common in a time when live entertainment—house bands, dance orchestras, nightclub journeymen—had yet to be replaced by the DJs and piped-in music that have transformed the entire music industry. Wherever his vocation took him, it seems Jones, perhaps alone of the foursome, would have maintained a lifelong career as a performer, accompanist, arranger, or instructor, whether or not he became a rock star.

1960 Serves as organist and choirmaster in his local church; accompanies Joe Baldwin on bass at a summertime residency
1961–62 Performs in various groups with schoolmates; plays bass with the Deltas; performs shows with several pro acts at US military bases in the UK
1962–63 Serves as bass player with Jet Harris and the Jet Blacks; occasionally sits in for gigs, e.g., playing keyboards for saxophonist Mick Eves, bass for the Ronnie Jones and the Night-Timers, and playing in the backing band for Herbie Goins
1962–68 Works as a session musician
1964 Releases a solo single, "Baja" b/w "A Foggy Day in Vietnam"
1967 Reportedly accompanies Herman's Hermits at a few German gigs
1968 Plays in the New Yardbirds

Stars to Fill My Dreams: Robert Plant's Pre-Zeppelin Gigs

Unlike his future compatriots Jimmy Page and John Paul Jones, Plant remained on the edges of the English pop music scene throughout the 1960s. Though never lacking in enthusiasm, dedication, or fundamental talent, the vocalist lived too far from the metropolis of London and had no formal credentials as a singer, and as a result he was for several years only one of thousands of hopefuls struggling to find the right combination of musicians to front and a steady schedule of gigs to earn a living. Though he is today a wealthy and honored performer whose position in rock 'n' roll history is secure, the fact is that, but for the chance opportunity of meeting ex-Yardbird Jimmy Page, the twenty-year-old Robert Plant might very well have abandoned his dreams of musical success and resigned himself to a life revolving around humdrum office jobs, a private collection of rare country blues records, the complete works of J. R. R. Tolkien, and a discreet marijuana habit.

Plant was no amateur, however. He had sung in professional or semi-professional acts since his teens, gaining valuable stage experience at local shows and regional tours, and he had learned by heart an extensive number of obscure blues, folk, soul, psychedelic, and R&B tunes—perhaps learned them a little too well for Led Zeppelin's initial critics. Since Plant became famous, a retrospective of his promising but unfulfilled work before autumn 1968 has gradually been pieced together, including short- and long-term employment in several bands around mid-1960s Birmingham and even an abortive recording contract. Despite being the creator of an immortal rock god persona, it was to this modest background he would eventually return following the Zeppelin's deflation.

1962–63 Sings with Andy Long & the Original Jurymen
1963 Sings with the New Memphis Bluesbreakers, the Brum Beats, and the Sounds of Blue
1964 Sings with the Delta Blues Band and Black Snake Moan
1964–65 Performs with the Banned
1965 Sings with the Crawling King Snakes
1966 Performs with the Tennessee Teens, and Listen; records one single with Listen for CBS: "You'd Better Run" b/w "Everybody's Gonna Say"
1967 Performs with the Band of Joy / Robert Plant and His Band of Joy; records two singles as a solo performer on the CBS label: "Our Song" b/w "Laughin', Cryin', Laughin'," and "Long Time Coming" b/w "I've Got a Secret"

1968 Records demos of "For What It's Worth," "Hey Joe," and "Adriatic Sea View" with the Band of Joy (none of which is released for many years); performs with Alexis Korner's band; records "Operator" and "Steal Away" with Alexis Korner (the tracks remain unreleased until 1971 and 1996, respectively); sings with Obs-Tweedle; performs with the New Yardbirds

Over the Top: John Bonham's Pre-Zeppelin Gigs

Along with Robert Plant, the teenage Bonham was one of many young people hoping for a big showbiz break that had yet to materialize. In his case, however, "Bonzo" had the advantage of all rock 'n' roll drummers over singers and guitarists: rarity. The size and investment represented by a decent drum kit was enough to dissuade all but the most committed, and thus Bonham was quickly taken up into several working acts around Birmingham from his earliest forays into the pop music scene.

Because of his loud and hard-hitting style, however, Bonham was sometimes ejected from groups who found his playing to be a liability in scoring club dates. He was unapologetic about this and, until 1968, rarely strove to toe anyone's line. More than most percussionists, Bonham moved from band to band, sitting in with whoever needed him at the moment while keeping his ear open for better opportunities with others. This ultimately worked in his favor in Led Zeppelin, where he at last found the right combination of musicians to keep time for, but in the mid-1960s, the struggling Midlands stickman's long-term future looked uncertain.

Though Bonham was obviously a natural drummer for whom even marriage and fatherhood weren't cause enough to steer into steadier work (he wed Pat Phillips in 1966 and Jason Bonham was born the same year), his professionalism was raw and he was not the type to plot a diligent climb up the career ladder. Before he joined Zeppelin his last gig was with Tim Rose, best known for the moderate hits "Hey Joe" and "Morning Dew," but how long the association might have lasted is dubious, and Bonham might have continued bouncing from prospect to prospect—impressing with his talent and his technique but always just a little too noisy for the bands who hired him. Fortunately for the music world, but perhaps unfortunately for Bonham himself, his connection to Robert Plant landed him the biggest gig of his life and the last one he would ever know.

1963 Gigs with the Blue Star Trio
1963–64 Plays with Gerry Levene and the Avengers

1964 Plays with Steve Brett and the Mavericks, Terry Webb and the Spiders, and the Senators; records "She's a Mod" with the Senators, which is released on a local compilation, *Brum Beat*
1964–65 Performs with Locomotive
1965 Gigs with the Nicky James Movement; performs with A Way of Life
1965–66 Plays with the Crawling King Snakes; rejoins A Way of Life
1967–68 Plays with the Band of Joy
1968 Gigs with Tim Rose's band and with the New Yardbirds

Now I've Reached That Age: Jimmy Page as a Session Musician

An indelible part of his legendary stature, Page's employment as a versatile and in-demand studio guitarist in London from 1962 to 1966, and briefly again in 1968, is invariably mentioned when tracing his artistic and professional growth. That some of the songs to which he contributed became worldwide hits predating his successes with Led Zeppelin only adds to the legend.

The story is complicated, however, by Page's own downplaying of his session years as an apprenticeship that he eventually sought to leave behind. Sometimes he has credited his studio career as a valuable training he would later recall when producing, playing, and orchestrating the Zeppelin canon. "I learned an incredible amount of discipline. . . . [H]aving to vamp behind people like Tubby Hayes, who was a big jazz saxophonist in England, or play on several of Burt Bacharach's pop sessions, gave me a fantastic vision and insight into chords." In other instances, he has dismissed most of the material he backed up—"I've got a lot of skeletons in my closet"—and openly admitted to not remembering a large percentage of the songs in whose recording he was hired to assist. "I learned things even on my worst sessions," he has compromised. "And believe me, I played on some horrendous things."

Some of the divide between myth and reality here is due to the nature of studio work in the 1960s. Jimmy Page's job at most of these dates was not to produce, arrange, or otherwise supervise the music being made, but only to chip in a suitably polished guitar part—sometimes only a guitar solo—on songs that had already been laid out by the artist, the manager, or the studio overseer. In this capacity, he would have had no say in where his performance figured in the eventual mix or which take was finally put to disc; he was paid for being on hand, ready to play, regardless of what the finished record sounded like or its ultimate commercial fate. Some of his work went no further than preliminary or demo tracks before later musicians would copy his ideas, and at other times he would just fake his way through the session (with amplifier turned down or unplugged altogether), then collect his fee and walk away when the rest of the personnel were satisfied with the day's productivity.

A few of Page's sessions were controversial jobs where he and other professionals secretly substituted for less experienced players whose names and faces were shown on the resulting product, but more often the guitarist was a welcome backup to performers with no permanent band of their own. Indeed, some acts he played for were "studio-only" outfits whose sole income came from record sales rather than live concerts. Despite the growing draw of such self-contained groups as the Beatles, the Rolling Stones, the Kinks, and the Who (and, in time, Led Zeppelin), the music industry of the 1960s was still based around an elaborate hierarchy of songwriters, instrumentalists, technicians, A&R (Artist and Repertoire) officials, and other contributors, all of whom might claim a part in putting together a hit song or hit record. Page's role on the studio floors was therefore a limited one that any young and ambitious musician would find increasingly frustrating.

How did his session stint affect Jimmy Page's subsequent career? Certainly the practice of repeatedly putting down take after take of similar passages prepared him for the music he made with Led Zeppelin, where he would layer two, three, four, or more tracks of his own guitars on top of each other: the massed "guitar armies" of "Black Dog" or "Achilles Last Stand" depended on his ability to carefully replicate given riffs or progressions, bulking up their sound without letting them deteriorate into a mess of overdubs. While there are some brilliant spontaneous single takes in his oeuvre, much of Led Zeppelin's acoustic identity comes from his experience going over songs until they were just the way he wanted them, a skill which would have been foreign to rawer musicians more accustomed to the randomness of stage performance than the formal routine of the studio. As a session man Page also saw and heard a range of recording techniques—some effective, some not—he would recall when producing all of Led Zeppelin's albums, and he has often noted how his innovations in microphone placement and stereo imaging were learned from observing and then listening to the indifferent, by-the-book regimens of journeymen like Shel Talmy or Mickie Most. "When I was playing sessions," he remembered, "I noticed that the engineers would always place the bass drum mic right next to the head. The drummers would then play like crazy, but it would always sound like they were playing on cardboard boxes." Usually Page kept his head down and did as he was told in such circumstances, but when he elected himself Led Zeppelin's producer, he had already spent several years absorbing the dos and don'ts of recording pop music.

The most important legacy of Page's session period was to confirm his position as an industry professional. Not only did he make a name for himself as a reliable and more than competent guitar player, but he had also made connections with numerous other newcomers, budding stars, and confirmed heavies he would befriend and work with in the decades to come: producers Joe Meek and Andrew Loog Oldham, songwriters Burt Bacharach and Jackie DeShannon, record executives Ahmet Ertegun and Jerry Wexler, engineers Glyn Johns and Eddie Kramer, and performers as diverse as Chris Farlowe, David Bowie, the Rolling Stones, and Donovan. All these links gave him entrée to business and creative circles traditionally cool toward the starry-eyed amateurs, teenage hopefuls, and Next Big Things whose publicity shots and audition tapes were cluttering their in-boxes. In 1968 Jimmy Page asked one studio colleague, a soft-spoken, formally trained young arranger and player named John Paul Jones, if he'd be interested in joining his new band. The rest was history.

A complete discography of the pre-Zeppelin Page is probably impossible to assemble. Some estimates have him playing on over three-quarters of the pop and rock 'n' roll music recorded in Britain between 1963 and 1966, although such a percentage can never ascertained and—in view of the thousands of songs commercially released during these peak years of the British Invasion—is physically implausible to associate with single musician. Page has reported, "At one point I was playing at least three sessions a day, six days a week," but this schedule does not necessarily translate into eighteen completed songs available on album or single. Nor was Jimmy Page the only guitarist employed in the London recording rooms of the mid-1960s, as regulars such as Vic Flick and Big Jim Sullivan were heard on memorable tracks like John Barry's inimitable *James Bond* theme (Flick) and P. J. Proby's "Hold Me" (Sullivan), and later "name" guitarists like Deep Purple's Ritchie Blackmore and rockabilly ace Albert Lee were also honing their chops in the same studios as Page. At different times any of these players, or other anonymous guitarists, could join up or trade places with Page for session jobs while they, like Page, were also scoring occasional work in performing bands (Page even wangled his friend Jeff Beck a few studio bookings). The following list is drawn from various accounts from the musicians involved, compilation records anthologized to appeal to Zeppelin completists, and credible if not infallible documentation that ties Page to particular artists or producers. Though some songs provide tantalizing tastes of his later work with Led Zeppelin, more are ordinary mid-'60s pop where guitar heroism is scarcely in evidence. For Jimmy Page, the best was yet to come.

- Chris Andrews: "Yesterday Man"
- The Authentics: "Without You," "Climbing Through"

- Burt Bacharach: *Hit Maker*
- Long John Baldry: *Looking at Long John*
- John Barry/Shirley Bassey: "Goldfinger"
- Paul Bedford: "Will You Follow Me," "Head Death"
- Dave Berry: "The Crying Game," "My Baby Left Me," "Baby, It's You," "One Heart Between Two," "Little Things," "This Strange Effect"
- The Blue Rondos: "Baby I Go for You," "Little Baby"
- Brook Brothers: "Trouble Is My Middle Name," "Let the Good Times Roll," "Once in a While"
- Sean Buckley and the Breadcrumbs: "It Hurts Me When I Cry," "Everybody Knows"
- Carter-Lewis and the Southerners: "Your Momma's Out of Town," "Somebody Told My Girl," "Skinnie Minnie," "Who Told You," "Sweet and Tender Romance," "Mama"
- Neil Christian and the Crusaders: "The Road to Love," "Honey Hush," "I Like It," "A Little Bit of Somethin' Else," "Get a Load of This"
- Petula Clark: "Downtown"
- Joe Cocker: "With a Little Help from My Friends," "Bye Bye Blackbird," "Marjorine," "Just Like a Woman," "Sandpaper Cadillac"
- Louise Cordet: "Two Lovers"
- Jackie DeShannon: "Don't Turn Your Back on Me"
- Charles Dickens: "So Much in Love," "Our Soul Brother"
- Donovan: "Sunshine Superman"
- Val Doonican: "Walk Tall"
- The Everly Brothers: *Two Yanks in England*
- The Factotums: "Can't Go Home Anymore My Love"
- Marianne Faithfull: "Come and Stay with Me," "This Little Bird," "Summer Nights"
- Chris Farlowe: "Moanin'," "Out of Time," "Think," "Don't Just Look at Me"
- Fifth Avenue: "Just Like Anyone Would Do," "The Bells of Rhymney"
- Mickey Finn and the Blue Men: "This Sporting Life," "Night Comes Down"
- The First Gear: "Gotta Make Their Future Bright," "The In Crowd," "A Certain Girl," "Leave My Kitten Alone"

- Les Fleur de Lys: "Circles," "So Come On," "Moondreams," "Wait for Me"
- Wayne Fontana and the Mindbenders: "Hello Josephine," "Roadrunner"
- Billy Fury: "I'm Lost Without You," "Nothin' Shakin' but the Leaves on the Trees"
- Wayne Gibson and the Dynamic Sounds: "See You Later, Alligator," "Kelly"
- Bobby Graham: "Zoom, Widge & Wag"
- Johnny Hallyday: "Psychedelic," "A Tout Casser"
- Jet Harris and Tony Meehan: "Diamonds," "Hully Gully"
- Herman's Hermits: "Silhouettes," "Wonderful World," "Just a Little Bit Better," "No Milk Today"
- Brian Howard and the Silhouettes: "The Worryin' Kind," "Bald-Headed Woman," "Come to Me"
- Engelbert Humperdinck: "The Last Waltz"
- Brian Jones: *A Degree of Murder* (soundtrack)
- Davy Jones and the Lower Third: "You've Got a Habit of Leaving," "Baby Loves That Way"
- Tom Jones: "It's Not Unusual"
- The Kinks: "You Really Got Me," "Bald-Headed Woman," "Revenge," "Long Tall Sally"
- Kathy Kirby: "Dance On," "Playboy," "Secret Love," "You Have to Want to Touch Him," "Let Me Go Lover," "The Sweetest Sounds"
- The Lancastrians: "She Was Tall," "We'll Sing in the Sunshine," "The World Keeps Going Round," "Not the Same Anymore"
- Brenda Lee: "Is It True," "What I'd Say"
- Leapy Lee: "Little Arrows"
- Lulu: "I'll Come Running Over," "Shout," "Surprise, Surprise," "Leave a Little Love," "He Don't Want Your Love Anymore"
- The Manish Boys: "I Pity the Fool," "Take My Tip"
- The Marauders: "That's What I Want," "Hey, What'd You Say"
- George Martin: "This Boy (Ringo's Theme)" (*A Hard Day's Night* soundtrack)
- The Masterminds: "She Belongs to Me," "Taken My Love"
- The Scotty McKay Quintet: "Train Kept A-Rollin'"
- The McKinleys: "Sweet and Tender Romance"

- Mickie Most: "The Feminine Look," "Money Honey," "That's Alright," "Mr. Porter," "Yes Indeed I Do," "Sea Cruise," "It's a Little Bit Hot"
- The Nashville Teens: "Tobacco Road," "I Like It Like That"
- Nico: "I'm Not Sayin'," "The Last Mile"
- The Andrew Loog Oldham Orchestra: *16 Hip Hits*
- The Orchids: "Love Hit Me," "Don't Make Me Sad"
- Gregory Phillips: "The Last Mile," "Please Believe Me," "Angie"
- The Pickwicks: "Little by Little"
- Brian Poole and the Tremeloes: "Candy Man," "Three Bells," "I Want Candy"
- The Primitives: "You Said," "How Do You Feel," "Help Me," "Let Them Tell"
- P. J. Proby: "Hold Me," "Together"
- Chris Ravel and the Ravers: "I Do," "Don't You Dig This Kinda Beat"
- The Redcaps: "Talkin' 'bout You," "Come On Girl"
- Cliff Richard: "Time Drags By"
- Chris Sandford: "Not Too Little, Not Too Much," "I'm Lookin'"
- The Sneekers: "I Just Can't Go to Sleep," "Bald-Headed Woman"
- Al Stewart: "Turn into Earth," *Love Chronicles*
- Crispian St. Peters: "You Were on My Mind," "Pied Piper"
- The Talismen: "Castin' My Spell," "Masters of War"
- Jimmy Tarbuck: "Someday," "Wastin' Time"
- Them: "Baby Please Don't Go," "Gloria," "Here Comes the Night," "Mystic Eyes"
- Twice as Much: "Sittin' on a Fence," "Step Out of Line," "Baby I Want You"
- Twinkle: "Tommy"
- The Untamed: "I'll Go Crazy"
- Pat Wayne with the Beachcombers: "Roll Over Beethoven"
- Houston Wells and the Marksmen: "Blowin' Wild," "Crazy Dreams"
- The Who: "I Can't Explain," "Bald-Headed Woman"
- John Williams: "Dream Cloudburst," "Early Bird of Morning"
- The Zephyrs: "I Can Tell"

From Seven to Eleven: John Paul Jones as a Session Musician

Like Jimmy Page, the future Led Zeppelin bassist and keyboardist was highly sought in the London studios of the mid-1960s; as it is for Page, a select catalogue of his contributions is difficult to determine. This not only reflects how busy he was over this time (about 1962 to the formation of Zeppelin in 1968), but his range of musical skills. Besides supplying bass lines, Jones was also called to arrange and orchestrate sessions where his actual playing was nowhere to be heard but where his involvement was nonetheless audible. "Arranging and general studio direction were much better than just sitting there being told what to do," he looked back. "I always thought the bass player's life was much more interesting in those days, because nobody knew how to write for bass. They used to say, 'We'll give you the chord sheet,' and get on with it. So even on the worst sessions, you could have little runaround." The sprawling diversity of artists whose paths he crossed as a session man—everyone from Herman's Hermits and Lulu to Paul Anka and Tom Jones—indicates something of the transitional, cross-generational state of the pop music business before it became dominated in the next decade by youth-oriented rock and its offshoots. The cornier credits also reveal him slipping into a hackdom only membership in Led Zeppelin could redeem. "After a few years of nonstop sessions it got too much," he told Zeppelin archivist Dave Lewis. "I was making a fortune but I wasn't enjoying it anymore." Again, as they had done for Page's, the combination of overwork and boredom threatened to stale Jones's talents in the last months before joined the band that would make him famous.

Since Jones did not have the wider stage experience gained by Jimmy Page in the Yardbirds—or for that matter by Robert Plant and John Bonham in various Midlands acts—his concert performances cast him as the quintessential sideman, where he was dependable and well rehearsed but usually inconspicuous. The versatility and reliability Jones acquired from his studio stint were what Page sought when inviting him to join the group, not any flamboyant showmanship. He memorably recalled Plant's expectations of him being "some old bloke with a pipe" at the first New Yardbirds jam session, which, though he was scarcely two years older than the young singer, was not far off the mark as an assessment of his professional temperament.

Jones's low-key role in Led Zeppelin has meant that less research has been made into his early credits, but his presence on some material has been confirmed by him (on his own website) and by others. Because he was employed full-time in studios for several years, many of the gigs have long since slipped his mind, whether he had performed or served as musical director or both, and few of the dates in which he participated resulted in timeless hits. "So many sessions were run-of-the-mill, banal, mundane, very boring, you couldn't wait to get out of them," he has confessed. Much of his job entailed conducting other session hands' own playing, or advising producers on what instruments and instrumentalists to use on particular parts, qualifying him as an all-around (probably not very interested) consultant rather than merely an occasional hired hand. The following names and titles are the best-known fraction of the hundreds or thousands of performers and records John Paul Jones is known to have worked with or worked on.

- Paul Anka
- Burt Bacharach
- Pearl Bailey
- Lionel Bart: "Maggie May"
- Jeff Beck: "Beck's Bolero," "You Shook Me," "Hi Ho Silver Lining," "Love Is Blue"
- Madeline Bell
- Dave Berry
- Marc Bolan
- The Cherokees: "Land of 1,000 Dances"
- Petula Clark: "Downtown"
- Sammy Davis Jr.
- Donovan: "Mellow Yellow," "Hurdy Gurdy Man," "Sunshine Superman"
- The Downliners Sect: "Rocks in My Bed," "Waiting in Heaven"
- Marianne Faithfull
- Julie Felix: *Changes*
- Wayne Fontana and the Mindbenders: "A Groovy Kind of Love"
- Freddy and the Dreamers
- Graham Gouldman
- Françoise Hardy
- Herman's Hermits: "A Kind of Hush," "No Milk Today" (Accounts differ as to the degree of his involvement with the Hermits. Singer Peter Noone has claimed Jones played bass on most of their repertoire, including hits like "I'm Into Something Good," while other members have angrily disputed this.)
- Engelbert Humperdinck: *Release Me*
- Davy Jones and the Lower Third: "You've Got a Habit of Leaving," "Can't Help Thinking About Me"

- Kathy Kirby
- Jay and the Americans
- Tom Jones: "Delilah," "The Green Green Grass of Home"
- Lulu: "To Sir with Love," "The Boat That I Row"
- The Magic Lanterns
- The Mighty Avengers: "Blue Turns to Grey"
- Mickie Most
- Billy Nicholls
- Nico
- Des O'Connor
- The Andrew Loog Oldham Orchestra: *16 Hip Hits*
- Carl Perkins
- Peter & Gordon
- P. J. Proby
- Cliff Richard: "Shoom Lamma Boom Boom"
- The Rolling Stones: "She's a Rainbow"
- Harry Secombe
- Del Shannon
- Dusty Springfield: *Dusty . . . Definitely*
- Cat Stevens
- Rod Stewart: "Good Morning Little Schoolgirl" b/w "I'm Gonna Move to the Outskirts of Town"
- Robert Stigwood
- Barry St. John: "Everything I Touch Turns to Tears"
- The Walker Brothers
- Dinah Washington
- Ian Whitcomb: "You Turn Me On"
- The Yardbirds: "Ten Little Indians," "Little Games," "Ha Ha Said the Clown"

1969

January–February: Led Zeppelin tour the US and Canada.

January 12: *Led Zeppelin* released.

January 20: Richard Nixon sworn in as US president.

March 2: First flight of Concorde supersonic airliner.

April: Major anti-Vietnam-war demonstrations in US.

May: Led Zeppelin touring North America; recording *Led Zeppelin II*.

June 22: Judy Garland dies, age 47, London.

July 3: Rolling Stone Brian Jones found dead, age 26.

July–August: Led Zeppelin tour North America.

July 20: Moon landing.

July 30: Edward Kennedy's companion Mary Jo Kopechne drowns, Chappaquiddick Island, Massachusetts.

August 9: Savage murders of Sharon Tate household, Los Angeles.

August 15–17: Woodstock music festival.

October–November: Led Zeppelin tour North America.

October 21: Paul McCartney denies rumors of his death.

October 22: *Led Zeppelin II* released.

November: Anti-war demonstrations in Washington, DC.

December 6: Rolling Stones Altamont concert ends in murder of a fan by Hells Angels.

Movies: *Easy Rider*; *Midnight Cowboy*; *Butch Cassidy & the Sundance Kid*; *The Wild Bunch*.

Music: The Beatles, *Abbey Road*; the Rolling Stones, *Let It Bleed*; the Who, *Tommy*; Sly and the Family Stone, *Stand!*; the Grateful Dead, *Live Dead*; Dusty Springfield, *Dusty in Memphis*; Elvis Presley, "Suspicious Minds"; the Supremes, "Someday We'll Be Together"; B. B. King, "The Thrill Is Gone"; the Archies, "Sugar Sugar."

5

I'm Gonna Join the Band

The Formation of Led Zeppelin

For Your Love: Led Zeppelin and the Yardbirds

Though there is no denying that the foursome eventually known as Led Zeppelin played their first concerts as "the New Yardbirds," or "the Yardbirds featuring Jimmy Page," the original Yardbirds' biggest successes preceded Jimmy Page's entry into the group. As a quintet, with Eric Clapton on lead guitar, they had made the smash single "For Your Love" in March 1965, and, following Clapton's replacement by Jeff Beck, they made the hits "Heart Full of Soul," "Shapes of Things," and "You're a Better Man than I," but the overworked and underpaid band were deteriorating and bassist Paul Samwell-Smith quit in June 1966. Jimmy Page was initially recruited first to take over Samwell-Smith's bass spot, then to complement Beck on lead guitar while rhythm player Chris Dreja switched to bass; the erratic Beck himself quit for good (just before he would have been fired) after an exhausting American tour in late 1966. From 1967 to the spring of 1968 the four-piece Yardbirds were highlighted by Page's guitar spots—and they continued to play the hit songs Page never had a hand in making—but Dreja, vocalist Keith Relf, and drummer Jim McCarty had long since tired of the treadmill and consented to Page taking over the rights to the act's name after their final shows in July 1968. Page had recorded a smattering of new cuts with the Yardbirds (both with and without Jeff Beck), but management woes and public apathy kept "Happenings Ten Years Time Ago," "Little Games," and "Ten Little Indians" from rising beyond the middle levels of the charts. Aside from Page's presence on lead guitar (though not, significantly, in the studio control booth), the connection between Led Zeppelin and the Yardbirds is only a contractual one.

It is true that Jimmy Page's later work with the Yardbirds explored some of the sonic territory he would eventually chart with Led Zeppelin. Several

Yardbirds numbers ended up as part of the Zeppelin oeuvre, including "I'm Confused" and "Think About It" (merged to become "Dazed and Confused"), "Train Kept A-Rollin'" (played live and adapted into "Stroll On" for the Yardbirds' appearance in the mod 1966 film *Blow-Up*), Page's instrumental showpiece "White Summer," and the abandoned "Knowing That I'm Losing You," which evolved into "Tangerine." For that matter, the very first New Yardbirds performances also sounded covers of the older band's favorites "For Your Love" and "I'm a Man." By the Yardbirds' concluding tour of North America Page was stroking his Fender Telecaster with a violin bow and taking longer and more psychedelic solo breaks, clearly headed in the direction he would travel with Led Zeppelin, though perhaps leaving his Yardbird bandmates behind. In 1967–68 it was the Yardbirds themselves who had already become a different band than they had been during the tenures of Eric Clapton and Jeff Beck.

The last incarnation of the Yardbirds had been managed by Peter Grant, who continued as Page's representative while the guitarist sought to assemble a fresh act. The Yardbirds had been booked for a series of Scandinavian shows in September '68, so Page was obligated to have some semblance of a set ready to satisfy promoters in Denmark and Sweden. Page and Grant's intentions following the Yardbirds' dissolution were to complete that group's outstanding commitments, then to use them as a springboard for more forays into the North American concert and record market, where opportunities for other electric, improvisational blues performers (like Cream, Jimi Hendrix, and Iron Butterfly) appeared to be good. The two then went about scouting signed and unsigned talent in the few weeks they had. Hearing audition tapes and catching a live performance by singer Robert Plant, Page first invited Plant to join, who in turn recommended his Midlands friend and occasional bandmate, drummer John Bonham; then Page's own studio colleague John Paul Jones (whose work was already known and respected by the guitarist and Peter Grant) volunteered to step in. During this short stretch vocalists Terry Reid, Chris Farlowe, and Steve Marriott; drummers Aynsley Dunbar, Clem Cattini, Bobby Graham, and Paul Francis; and erstwhile Yardbirds bassist Chris Dreja and the Move's Ace Kefford were all under consideration for membership. Page also was impressed with Cream bassman Jack Bruce and Jimi Hendrix's drummer Mitch Mitchell, though neither were likely hires, and Ron Wood, then playing bass with the Jeff Beck Group, claims he was asked by Peter Grant to come aboard the New Yardbirds as either a guitarist or bass player, though this claim remains uncorroborated.

Two points are obvious from this—admittedly rather jumbled—time line. One is how quickly Keith Relf, Jim McCarty, and Chris Dreja were replaced by other players, suggesting Page had no great desire to duplicate any of their stylistic contributions. The other is how soon Robert Plant, John Bonham, and John Paul Jones jelled together: There was no long audition period, and no other combination of musicians ever rehearsed together with prospects of becoming the group now known as Led Zeppelin. Through a

Yardbirds, 1966.   *Courtesy of Robert Rodriguez*

mixture of necessity and luck, the one singer, bassist, and drummer available and willing to join Page in carrying on the Yardbirds turned out to be the best men for the jobs. A counterfactual New Yardbirds, consisting of Jimmy Page backed up by Terry Reid, Clem Cattini, and Chris Dreja, might have been put together with similar designs in the summer of 1968, but it's unlikely that combination would have gained the response of the fateful four.

Sunshine Superman: Led Zeppelin and Donovan

Donovan Leitch, the English minstrel responsible for the 1968 hit "Sunshine Superman" as well as flower-power classics "Jennifer Juniper," "Wear Your Love Like Heaven," and "Mellow Yellow," has often claimed that Led Zeppelin was a direct by-product of his own studio dates. Most recently he has put forward the story in a 2005 autobiography, *The Hurdy Gurdy Man*, suggesting that all the future members of Led Zeppelin but Robert Plant provided the backing tracks for "Hurdy Gurdy Man." This seems to be another case of intentional amnesia: Busy pros Jimmy Page and John Paul Jones had worked for Donovan on "Sunshine Superman" and other material, and it may well have been at a session for the eventual *album* titled *Hurdy Gurdy Man* that Page and Jones first mentioned working together in a full-time band (though it would not have been the occasion of their first meeting), but John Bonham was not a studio drummer and did not work with either Page or Jones prior to the formation of Led Zeppelin. Moreover, the guitarist on the "Hurdy Gurdy Man" cut has been variously identified as Alan Parker, Allan Holdsworth, or an Ollie Halsall, not Jimmy Page. In the 1960s the popular Donovan was close to other luminaries like the Beatles and Bob Dylan, but his recollections of being the catalyst for Zeppelin are either deliberately exaggerated or chemically confused. It's possible, too, that Page and Jones had earlier talked of future plans while in the studio for Keith De Groot's *No Introduction Necessary*, released in 1968. Page, Jones, Bonham and Plant did provide backing together in sessions for P. J. Proby's *Three Week Hero* just before their initial Scandinavian shows as the New Yardbirds.

Ain't Disclosin' No Names: The Origins and Significance of "Led Zeppelin"

Given that stages are usually elevated from the floor of any theater, show people of all varieties have always sought to "go over" with their audiences, meaning to hold the attention of the people sitting out from and below them; for a play, song, or joke to "fall flat" is to have the performance receive no enthusiasm from whoever has come to watch, metaphorically tumbling down from the musician or actor on the boards to some humiliating space in front of the first row. In an idiom that seems to have originated somewhere in the early twentieth century, any presentation or speech that receives a welcome reception has "gone over." From this, a mocking opposite arose: something floated in hopes of applause or approval but which gets none has "gone over like a lead balloon."

In 1966, Jimmy Page, then one of London's most in-demand session guitarists, participated in a recording date with his friend Jeff Beck, guitarist for the Yardbirds, along with session bassist John Paul Jones, Keith Moon, drummer for the up-and-coming Who, and keyboardist Nicky Hopkins. Though the lineup was only an ad hoc one that produced the lone instrumental "Beck's Bolero" (eventually included on Beck's 1968 album *Truth*), the musicians enjoyed working together. Page and Beck especially liked collaborating with the frenetic Moon and knew he and his partner in the Who's rhythm section, thunderous bass player John Entwistle, were each dissatisfied with their roles in that quartet. Excited by expectations of making "super hooligan music" together, Beck, Page, Moon, and Entwistle casually discussed forming a permanent band. Nothing came of it, especially as their preferred singer, Steve Marriott of the Small Faces, was managed by a hard-nosed and very protective Don Arden ("How would you like a group with no fingers, boys?" he threatened), but Moon and Entwistle were each said to have remarked ironically that their union would "go down like a lead zeppelin." "Keith and I decided we'd go off and form a band with Richard Cole, who used to be our chauffeur," Entwistle was to remember in Geoffrey Giuliano's Pete Townshend biography, *Behind Blue Eyes* (Cole, of course, became Led Zeppelin's road manager). "A big band making much more money than the Who could ever make . . . I'd designed a cover of an R-101 zeppelin going down in flames. I was gonna do it in black and white, very subtle." Two years later, Page resurrected the quip and the picture when naming his new group.

It says much about Led Zeppelin's influence that the word *zeppelin* today is probably more likely to summon images of long-haired rock stars than of German dirigibles, but in the late 1960s the original zeppelins were still a fearsome living memory in Britain and, to a lesser extent, the United States. Devised and championed by an aristocrat of Kaiser Wilhelm's Germany, Count Ferdinand von Zeppelin, the vast lighter-than-air craft were in the early twentieth century the state of the art in aeronautics, first deployed as passenger carriers and then recruited into the military for reconnaissance and, later, bombing (each of the count's airships were numbered by the designation *Luftschiff Zeppelin*, hence *LZ 1*, *LZ 2*, and so on). During World War I more than five hundred Britons were killed in zeppelin air raids, and more than a thousand injured. German bombs and rockets caused even more British fatalities in World War II, leaving a grudging, vengeful respect for Teutonic militarism that was still current in 1968. Of course, the airships were borne aloft by very flammable hydrogen gas, making them spectacularly vulnerable to accidents or British gunfire, and the giants were finally outmoded by the late 1930s when airplanes proved speedier and safer. The Nazi zeppelin *Hindenburg* exploded and burned in Lakehurst, New Jersey, on May 6, 1937, following a transatlantic flight; photographs and newsreels of the disaster captured its awesome horror for posterity. "Going down like

Led Zeppelin shortly after their ascension in the fall of 1968.

Courtesy of Robert Rodriguez

a lead zeppelin," then, invoked not merely an embarrassing flop but a kind of holocaust, a cataclysm that destroyed performer and spectator alike.

Jimmy Page and his manager Peter Grant had already rejected "Mad Dogs" and "Whoopee Cushion" as names for Page's nascent band, although Page later claimed he would have christened it as casually as "the Vegetables" or "the Potatoes," such was his preoccupation with the group's sound. But in 1968 there was already a trend for rock groups (most

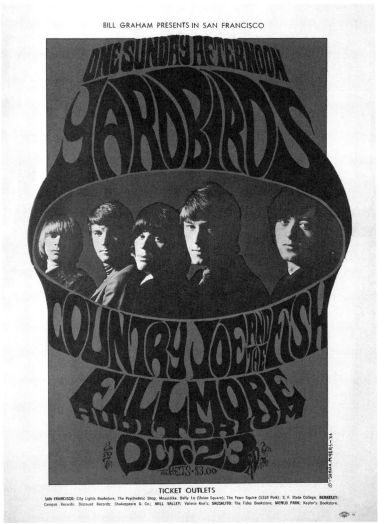

The Beck-Page incarnation of the Yardbirds lasted only a few months in late 1966.
Courtesy of Robert Rodriguez

of them American) billed with incongruous, oxymoronic juxtapositions: Moby Grape, the Strawberry Alarm Clock, Soft Machine, the Electric Prunes, Pink Floyd, the Jefferson Airplane, and notably Iron Butterfly, whose droning "In-a-Gadda-da-Vida" had been a huge underground hit. As well, the literal senselessness of all these terms would have carried a druggy resonance for their target audiences of the late 1960s. The final touch was to modify the adjective, subtracting the *a* from *Lead* to avoid mispronunciation. "I played around with the letters," remembered Peter Grant, "doodling in the office and realized that 'Led' looked a lot simpler." Though most readers would have got the pun soon enough, the intentional misspelling was a blunt, brutal sneer at phonetic niceties, which had a huge impact on pop linguistics in years to come, culminating in the likes of Def Leppard, Megadeth, Ratt, Mötley Crüe, the Geto Boys, Ludacris, Boyz II Men, and their unlettered brethren. For an offhand aside meant to be self-deprecating, "Led Zeppelin" has proven one of the most memorable and effective show business titles of all time.

6

When the Guitars Play

Led Zeppelin's Key Musical Instruments

How Much There Is to Know: Guitars, Basses, Drums, Keyboards, and Other Gear

A band that made musical virtuosity so much a part of its spectacle—epic guitar solos, superhuman drum marathons, tasty keyboard excursions—was bound to have its equipment heavily scrutinized by listeners and aspiring players, wondering just what made performers like Jimmy Page, John Bonham, and John Paul Jones so good. The visual appeal of Page's double-neck guitar or Bonham's see-through drums is as much a part of the Led Zeppelin attraction as any song, album cover, or personal reputation; no self-respecting Zeppelin tribute band would today take the stage without at least a Les Paul, a Fender Jazz bass, or a Ludwig kit.

It's often forgotten, however, that the Led Zeppelin band members considered themselves a working act with little time to fuss over what tools they did their jobs with. Jimmy Page's summary of purchasing his 1959 Gibson Les Paul from Joe Walsh in 1969 has been a simple "It just seemed like a good touring guitar," and he has characterized his early lineup of instruments and accessories as "basically whatever we could afford at that time." He has also said his main consideration in picking Marshall amplifiers was their "state-of-the-art reliability. They were really good for going out on the road." Likewise, John Paul Jones told *Guitar Player* magazine in 2003 that John Bonham would "sit down on horrible kits that hardly sounded better than the cases they came in, and he still sounded like John Bonham." *Led Zeppelin III* engineer Terry Manning has confirmed, "As nostalgic, vintage, or mythological as it may seem to people now to have worked in these supposedly golden days with all that vintage gear, it just wasn't thought of in that way at that time. We just used what we had and did the best we could."

Notwithstanding the claims of advertisers and the scholarship of curators, all the great instrumentalists in pop music considered their axes to be mere vehicles for their art; logging the make and model of each implement could be left to someone else. The research and debate expended over the provenance of Led Zeppelin's guitars, basses, keyboards, amplifiers, effects, and drums have far outstripped whatever research and debate went into selecting them in the first place. Referring only occasionally to the hazy memories of their owners and custodians, collectors and archivists have arrived at a complete inventory of the instruments played by the group from 1968 to 1980. From a musical standpoint, here are Led Zeppelin's most valuable pieces of equipment.

Jimmy Page

Page began Led Zeppelin's onslaught with a 1959 Fender Telecaster, acquired around 1965 as a gift from Jeff Beck. He'd used this guitar in the Yardbirds, then on the *Led Zeppelin* LP and for the band's live sets up to the spring of 1969. This Tele began its life white but was given an op-art paint job by Page while a Yardbird, then scraped down sometime in 1967 and decorated with a psychedelic dragon. It was also the source of the soaring "Stairway to Heaven" guitar solo. The Telecaster was retired after a friend of Page's repainted it yet again, affecting its wiring, although Page managed to save the neck and attach it to another Fender, a brown 1953 Telecaster. That guitar was equipped with a B-bender device, a push-button effect that allowed the player to get pedal-style tremolo effects with the B string alone; Page took it out for Led Zeppelin's appearances in '77, '79, and '80. Another Tele, this one a cream-colored '66, was taken on the 1980 European tour.

In April of '69 Page bought a 1959 Gibson Les Paul for $500 from Joe Walsh. Until the late 1960s, Gibson solid-body electrics, with their humbucking pickups that produced a lower, thicker sound than those of the bright Fender line, were something of a second choice among rock 'n' roll guitarists. It was ex-Yardbird Eric Clapton who revived the Gibson brand as a member of John Mayall's Bluesbreakers (Les Pauls were discontinued by the company between 1961 and 1969), demonstrating the effectiveness of a Les Paul when plugged into an overdriven amplifier: suddenly the round tones made by the pickups became the sustained, stinging notes that virtually defined hard rock and its descendants from then on. Page first told Walsh, "I'm quite happy with my Telecaster," but after trying it out he was converted—"[T]he Les Paul was so gorgeous and easy to play." Guitar hero Page won even more public attention for Les Pauls in the following decade. The Walsh instrument went through much wear and tear during

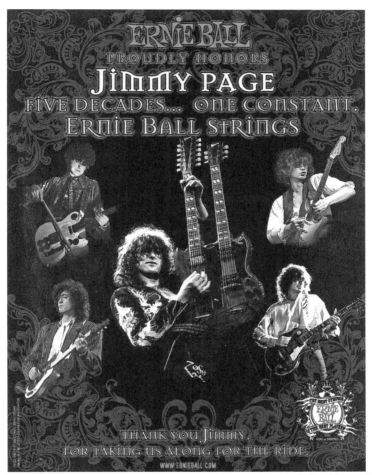

Jimmy Page's various instruments, such as his Gibson EDS-1275 double-neck, have become stars in their own right.   *Author's Collection*

the next few years but remained Page's "Number One" electric guitar over his Zeppelin career and beyond. The guitar was customized with a neck shave to ease playability while Walsh owned it (which erased its serial number); Page himself fitted the Number One with Grover tuning heads shortly after taking it on, and commissioned electronic modifications on it well after 1980. Because it lacks an accurate registration stamp some buffs debate whether Number One is a 1959 or '58 issue, but most Gibson experts cite it as a '59.

A second Les Paul, this one a definite 1959, was purchased by Page in 1973 and used onstage for Zeppelin's '75 tour. "Number Two," serial number

91703, was nearly identical to Walsh's sunburst Les Paul and is sometimes assumed to have been interchangeable with it, but the Number One has seen considerably more stage time. A 1969 or '70 Gibson Les Paul, painted crimson, was also employed during Page's Zeppelin tenure, and a 1950s Les Paul, also made over in red, was brought out on the '77 tour. A *fifth* Les Paul owned by Page was in fact his first, a three-pickup Custom "Black Beauty" that he used on his studio work in the 1960s, and at Led Zeppelin's 1970 Royal Albert Hall show, but the guitar was stolen in transit between the US and Canada later that year. It hasn't been seen since. Given that all Page's electrics were maintained and given spot repairs by him, members of the road crew, or local servicemen, the confusion around which exact axe he was wielding at any one time is understandable. In retrospect it's obvious that the guitarist's main concern was having at least one functioning guitar on hand for every show or studio date, regardless of which one it was or to what cosmetic work it might be subject. Photographs from the Zeppelin years show him playing his quintet of Les Pauls for different performances in different settings (Number Two was tuned to DADGAD for "Kashmir" in 1975), although the Walsh Gibson was his most favored. Number One and Number Two are still in his possession.

The guitar most casual fans would associate with Jimmy Page is his custom-made Gibson EDS 1275 double-neck, serial number 911117, acquired in early 1971. Gibson had made a number of double-neck models in different configurations, but their weight and price made them little more than novelties; Page requested the company specially build him a twelve- and six-string instrument on which he could play "Stairway to Heaven" (the original recording of which utilized *four* guitars) in concert. It also carried an undeniable aesthetic quality, especially as it was associated by spectators mostly with "Stairway" and other anthems such as "The Rain Song" and "The Song Remains the Same." This guitar too is still owned by Page, and its value has been appraised at £50,000.

For songs played with a slide or in open tunings, Page used a low-cost Danelectro 3021 electric—or rather, selected components of two married together. This odd and distinctly homely guitar was seen onstage while he performed "White Summer / Black Mountain Side," "In My Time of Dying," and, in 1977 and after, "Kashmir." A 1964 Lake Placid Blue Fender Stratocaster, bought by Page in 1975, was played at Zeppelin's Earl's Court, Knebworth, and 1980 European concerts, and on songs from *Presence* ("For Your Life") and *In Through the Out Door* ("In the Evening"). A Fender XII twelve-string electric chimed through studio renditions of "Stairway to Heaven," "When the Levee Breaks," "The Song Remains the Same," and possibly "Thank You."

Page's acoustic arsenal was smaller but still eclectic. Most Led Zeppelin sit-down sets were played on a Martin D-28, although he also owned and used a Harmony Sovereign (this was also likely used for the intro to "Stairway"), a lute-shaped Giannini Craviola, and borrowed from session colleague Jim Sullivan a Gibson J-200 for "Babe I'm Gonna Leave You," "Your Time Is Gonna Come," and "Black Mountain Side" on the group's first record. Gibson A-2 and A-4 mandolins were on hand for recording and live performances of "The Battle of Evermore." A Vega banjo was plunked through "Gallows Pole," while a Fender 800 pedal steel can be heard warbling in "Your Time Is Gonna Come" and "Tangerine."

Though he tried several varieties of guitar amplifiers during Led Zeppelin's busy working nights of 1968 and 1969, including Rickenbackers, Voxes, Hiwatts, and Oranges, Jimmy Page seemed to settle on Marshall units for stage shows from about 1972 to this day. All of Page's amps were modified and customized by the manufacturers or outside electricians—Page himself was no techie—with the guitarist's key issue being the consistency of their gain (distortion) and the endurance of their tubes over many nights of being trucked to and from venues and played at high volume. Page again brought a number of amp models to the studios, including Marshalls, although a smallish Supro Coronado supplied the killer crunch of *Led Zeppelin*, where its twelve-inch speaker projected a bigger sound onto tape than a larger amp's set to a lower volume.

Page was among the first rock 'n' roll guitarists to base his sound around outboard effects such as fuzz, echo, and wah-wah. As a session man in the 1960s he'd asked electronics whiz Roger Mayer to alter or scratch-build some devices for him, but once in Zeppelin he stuck with a Sola Sound Tonebender distortion footswitch pedal, a range of Vox wah pedals (including the popular Cry Baby), a Maestro Echoplex, and later an MXR Phase box. Of these, the Tonebender probably had the biggest impact on Led Zeppelin's sound. Compared to the highly specialized delay and distortion gadgets and entire digital rigs available to musicians today, all of these were primitive tools that Page was plainly trying out and choosing in a hit-or-miss fashion (especially given the unpredictable acoustics of concert sites). "All I had to really work with was an overdrive pedal, a wah-wah, an Echoplex, and what was on my guitar," he admitted in a 2007 *Guitar World* interview. "It wasn't a lot, and I had to create the entire range of sounds found on the first five Zeppelin albums." Though Page has long had a relationship with the Gibson guitar firm and licensed several "signature" replicas of his most famous guitars, he has never endorsed or been tied to any single effects product. The one non-guitar accessory specifically identified with Page was his Sonic Wave theremin, an updated, compact version of the futuristic

1920s antenna instrument that produced musical notes and interplanetary sounds by the player manipulating his hands around it; Page's theremin was run through an Orange amp and the Echoplex in concert, where it made the freaky timbres of "Dazed and Confused," "Whole Lotta Love," and "No Quarter." Page has also said that he took old violin bows to use on his guitar for live settings, where a single rendition of "Dazed and Confused" was enough to leave a bow useless. "[N]ew violin bows are expensive, so what we would do is buy a bunch of warped ones and take them on the road."

John Paul Jones

Unlike Jimmy Page, the versatile "Jonesy" is not linked in the public mind with any one or two famous basses or keyboards. "I have a vast collection of instruments, but I'm not a collector," he told Dave Lewis in 2002. "Instruments are for playing." As much as the other performers in Led Zeppelin, Jones had many gigs to make and parts to play—how and with what were secondary to him. His most recognized axe was a 1961 Fender Jazz bass, serial number 74242, that he played in the studio and live throughout his stint in Led Zeppelin (it's alternately said to date from 1962). He was also seen with a lovely 1951 Fender Precision bass (sometimes called a "Telecaster bass" for the resemblance of its head and hardware to the guitar's), a 1970 Fender fretless Precision (brought out again at Zeppelin's 2007 reunion show), and, in 1973, a five-string 1967 Fender Bass V. In the later Zeppelin years he took out two very advanced Alembic instruments, one a four- and the other an eight-string, the latter of which delivered a heavy punch to cuts such as "Achilles Last Stand." "The one good thing about that period [recording *Presence*] was that I'd started using the Alembic eight-string, which I felt really added to our sound," he recalled.

Tapped to play other string instruments for the quartet's acoustic interludes—"Oh, Jonesy will do it," was the reasoning—Jones picked up Martin, Harmony, and Fender mandolins, an Ovation twelve-string guitar, an Arco upright bass, and, not to be outdone by Page with his double-neck, a spectacular *triple*-neck acoustic that incorporated mandolin, twelve- and six-string guitars, handcrafted by Englishman Andy Manson. That's Jones tickling the mandolin on "Gallows Pole" and "Going to California," and guitar onstage for "The Battle of Evermore." As keyboardist with the group, Jones was pragmatic in his choice of implements: Hohner, Hammond, and Farfisa organs or electric pianos, a Fender Rhodes piano, a Hohner clavinet for the relentless funk of "Trampled Underfoot," and Steinway and Yamaha grand pianos. The Mellotron M400, an early step toward what would become the synthesizer, was played onstage for

'so good I use
12 at a time'

john paul jones · led zeppelin
(instrument player)

Toll free: 1 800 675 2501
www.rotosound.com

John Paul Jones has played a range of unique instruments over the course of his career.   *Author's Collection*

"Stairway to Heaven," "The Rain Song," and "Kashmir." "I used to use a mellotron, which was the only way you could get a string or flute sound in those days," he told *Bass Player* magazine in 2007. "But you'd never know when it was going to be in tune." His most significant keyboard acquisition, in terms of its effects on Led Zeppelin's music, was a Yamaha GX-1 synthesizer in 1978, which was prominent on such *In Through the Out Door* cuts as "In the Evening," "All My Love," and "I'm Gonna Crawl." In concert and in studios Jones sometimes stepped on Fender or Moog bass pedals to play simplified foundations of songs he was already doing on another instrument, e.g., "Since I've Been Loving You," "That's the Way," or "Ten Years Gone." Some quintessential 1970s electronic music was generated by his EMS VCS3 (an acronym for Voltage Controlled Studio with 3 oscillators) unit for "No Quarter," "Four Sticks," and "In the Light"—this prog rock fixture is better known for its deployment by Pink Floyd, and the Who on "Won't Get Fooled Again." Like Page, Jones tried and rejected many amplification setups with Led Zeppelin: Vox, Rickenbacker ("In a matter of seconds I blew it up"), and Gallien-Krueger, but decided his Acoustic 360 preamps and speaker cabinets worked best and so used them for most of the group's stage sets.

John Bonham

Perhaps the most remarkable aspect of the drum kits John Bonham played with Led Zeppelin is their simplicity: In the years where the flashiest percussionists were burying themselves behind virtual fortresses of pedals, heads, cymbals, and hardware, Bonham stuck with a more modest set of components. The difference was that his drums, though fewer in number than Ginger Baker's or Keith Moon's, were all the largest dimensions available (even his Premier, Ludwig, and Promuco drumsticks were oversize). Though he did seek to add a second bass drum to his kit for some of Zeppelin's first rehearsals and gigs, the ensuing calamity was just too much for Page and Jones to keep up with: "They freaked everyone out," remembered roadie Clive Coulson. Black Sabbath drummer Bill Ward, a friend of Bonham's from his Birmingham days, also spoke of the Zeppelin drummer complaining to him, "Them bastards won't let me use two bass drums." No matter. For his historic drum work he mainly relied on the basic configuration of a single bass drum, a fourteen-inch Ludwig Supraphonic snare, a rack-mounted tom-tom, one or two toms on the floor, and a hi-hat, plus two or three crash and ride cymbals.

John Bonham used several kits during his employment with Zeppelin, starting with a Slingerland assembly in 1968 but moving to—and staying with—Ludwigs thereafter. He hit Ludwig Black Diamond Pearls in 1969, with a twenty-four-inch bass drum and a single sixteen-inch floor tom. A Ludwig Natural Maple kit was played from 1969 to 1970, now with a twenty-six-inch bass, a Ludwig Speed King bass pedal (his preferred pedal from then on), two floor toms, and a Paiste thirty-eight-inch symphonic gong. From 1970 to 1973 Bonham sat at Ludwig Sparkle Green drums, now with two Ludwig twenty-nine-inch tympani to his left, and the gong behind him.

Led Zeppelin's record-breaking 1973 North American tour immortalized Bonham's Ludwig Amber Vistalite drums, clear instruments (bass and toms) tinted off-yellow with his *Led Zeppelin IV* symbol imprinted on the bass head; he took them out again in '75. Now he had four cymbals besides the hi-hat, the sixteen- and eighteen-inch floor toms, two tympani, and a gong with which to blow fans away. Some drummers say the acrylic material of the Vistalites doesn't sound as nice as the usual wood, but for eye-catching allure they're supreme. This unforgettable kit was later auctioned off for charity for more than £100,000. In 1977, '79, and '80 Bonham was seen and heard with a stainless steel Ludwig collection, although the number of drums and cymbals remained constant. His live renditions of "Kashmir" and "Moby Dick" in latter-day gigs were given electronic phase effects. For Zeppelin's quieter moments he handled a tambourine or congas, spoons, and castanets for the jug band fun of "Bron-y-Aur Stomp," and a tambourine-like Ralph Kester Ching Ring atop his hi-hat for soloing. Timbales were played on "Bonzo's Montreux." Occasionally a cowbell was seen attached to his bass drum, audible on the studio version of "Moby Dick," "Houses of the Holy," "We're Gonna Groove," and the electrifying opening to "Good Times Bad Times."

Robert Plant

As Led Zeppelin's vocalist, Plant of course had no guitar, keyboard, or drum to play, but he could be as plugged-in as his mates for concerts and studio work. As with Page, Jones, and Bonham, his pick of equipment was as practical as it was considered, and although in his post-Zeppelin days he has endorsed guitar models he probably had no great preference for any particular piece of the band's inventory. He did appear in ads for Shure microphones in the 1970s—not that he held a Shure at every single Zeppelin show—and he is known to have used the common Hohner harps and harmonicas in various keys for such bluesy Zeppelin cuts as "You Shook Me," "Bring It On Home," "When the Levee Breaks," "Poor Tom," and "Nobody's Fault but Mine." Plant was also photographed at congas when recording, and banged a tambourine during live performances of "Stairway to Heaven" and other songs. Learning the instrument in the early 1970s, he is believed to have borrowed the others' guitars to strum simple backings for "Boogie with Stu," "Night Flight," and "Down by the Seaside." Possibly the most important device the singer took up was an Eventide Harmonizer, a signal-altering unit (also used by Jimmy Page for some concert guitar solos, and on Bonham's "Bonzo's Montreux") that enabled him to double his vocals (hence the name) when his natural projection failed him, as it began to over Led Zeppelin's many long and loud performances. This was first employed by Plant on the 1977 US tour, then again at Knebworth in '79. Though the Harmonizer could make for some spacey sound effects when sung through, some listeners, including bandmate Jones, felt Plant relied on it overmuch.

1970

January: First reports of 1968 My Lai massacre by US troops in Vietnam.

January–March: Led Zeppelin tour Britain and Europe.

March–April: Led Zeppelin tour the US and Canada.

April 10: Paul McCartney announces he is leaving the Beatles.

May: Page and Plant at Bron-yr-Aur cottage.

May 18: Student protests at Kent State University leave four dead.

June 6: Led Zeppelin plays the Bath Festival, England.

June–July: Recording *Led Zeppelin III* at Headley Grange and Island and Olympic Studios.

August–September: Led Zeppelin tour the US and Canada; conduct more recording work in Memphis.

September 14: Arab militants hijack five airliners, blow up three.

September 18: Jimi Hendrix dies, London.

October 4: Janis Joplin dies, Los Angeles.

October 5: *Led Zeppelin III* released.

October 18: Canada invokes War Measures Act against militant Quebecois separatists.

November 12: Charles de Gaulle dies, Paris.

December: Preliminary work on *Led Zeppelin IV*.

Movies: *Five Easy Pieces*; *M*A*S*H*; *Love Story*; *Patton*,

Music: Van Morrison, *Moondance*; Neil Young, *After the Gold Rush*; Miles Davis, *Bitches Brew*; Black Sabbath, *Black Sabbath, Paranoid*; Derek and the Dominos, *Layla and Other Assorted Love Songs*; Simon & Garfunkel, "Bridge Over Troubled Water"; the Kinks, "Lola"; Edwin Starr, "War"; John Lennon, "Instant Karma."

7

Wonders What It's All About

Led Zeppelin Songs That Reference Real People, Places, or Events

I Was Told What It Means: The Stories Behind the Songs

Obviously, the lyrical sources for any song can come from the writer's imagination, from his or her personal experience, or a combination thereof, and Zeppelin tunes are no exception. Some of the foursome's best-known verses and choruses were derived from the blues, and others came out of simple experimentation with rhythms and rhymes, but a surprising number of them arose out of day-to-day feelings or circumstances that have been uncovered since. This list is of Led Zeppelin tunes that are known to have origins in the authors' own reality.

"How Many More Times"

Robert Plant is borrowing from several other songs in his improvisations here, but his mention that he had a child on the way was accurate insofar as the birth of his daughter, Carmen, was imminent when the song was recorded in October 1968.

"What Is and What Should Never Be"

According to Richard Cole in *Hammer of the Gods*, the mysterious damsel Plant is singing to was an actual clandestine liaison of his in 1969.

"Thank You"

On one of his very first attempts to sit down and compose a song, Plant is here in faithful husband mode, writing for his wife, Maureen, in gratitude for her support of him and his rock 'n' roll career.

"Living Loving Maid (She's Just a Woman)"

Though it's never been confirmed, the subject of this scornful rocker was probably one of the aggressive but unwanted groupies who pestered the band in America during 1969, or a composite of several.

"Immigrant Song"

The lyrics of Zeppelin's Viking battering ram were inspired by the band's visit to Reykjavík, Iceland, in June 1970, settled by seaborne Scandinavian conquerors centuries before. If not a historically coherent depiction of Norse invasions, "Immigrant Song" did rise out of *the land of the ice and snow, from the midnight sun where the hot springs flow.*

"Tangerine"

Jimmy Page's rewrite of a 1968 Yardbirds demo is conceivably a ballad that recalls his girlfriend of the mid-1960s, singer Jackie DeShannon.

"Bron-y-Aur Stomp"

Named for the Welsh cottage where it was written, the song is obliquely about Plant's canine companion Strider.

"Hats Off to (Roy) Harper"

Though nothing about the actual Roy Harper is heard in this blues pastiche, his inclusion in the title was a compliment from Plant and Jimmy Page, who'd recently met the folksinger and admired him for his scruffy independence.

"Black Dog"

Named for, if not about, a stray Labrador that wandered in and around the Headley Grange house where the blistering blues track was first recorded.

"There was an old black dog around the Grange that went off to do what dogs did and came back and slept," noted John Paul Jones.

"The Battle of Evermore"

The pastoral, archaic vibe of this duet with Sandy Denny was partly based on Robert Plant's recent study of the Anglo-Scottish border wars between the thirteenth and seventeenth centuries, when English kings and Scot chieftains warred across the Roman marker of Hadrian's Wall. "You can live in a fairy land if you read enough books and if you're interested in as much history as I am," he told an interviewer in 1972. "The Dark Ages and all that."

"Misty Mountain Hop"

This song is connected to Plant's enjoyment of marijuana and escapades with law enforcement cracking down on same.

"Four Sticks"

John Bonham played the song with two drumsticks in each hand.

"Going to California"

The *"Queen without a king"* who *"plays guitar and cries and sings"* is Joni Mitchell, much admired by Page and Plant, and a resident of the Californian hippie haven of Laurel Canyon in Los Angeles.

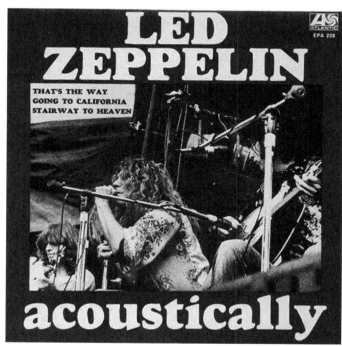

"Going to California" was inspired by the gentle folk of singer-songwriter Joni Mitchell. *Courtesy of Robert Rodriguez*

"When the Levee Breaks"

A cover of Memphis Minnie's original, which described the catastrophic Mississippi River floods of 1927 and the subsequent migration to Chicago and other northern urban centers by the region's African-American populace. The song became newly relevant after the 2005 Hurricane Katrina disaster that befell New Orleans, where levees were once again breached.

"The Song Remains the Same"

The travelogue of sites named in this *Houses of the Holy* opener—California, Honolulu, Calcutta—reflects the band's globe-trotting tour schedule of the previous three years. Though Led Zeppelin as a group never performed in India, Page and Plant had visited there and enjoyed their jams with local players.

"The Rain Song"

Musically if not lyrically spurred by John Bonham's conversation with George Harrison, during which the ex-Beatle chided him and his group: "The problem with you guys is you never do ballads." "I said, 'I'll give him a ballad,'" Jimmy Page recollected, "and I wrote 'The Rain Song'. . . . In fact, you'll notice I even quote 'Something' in the song's first two chords."

"The Ocean"

Robert Plant would introduce the song in concert by telling fans, "This is about you," meaning the undulating waves of longhairs filling the stadiums where Zeppelin gave their concerts. The three-year-old girl who has won the singer's heart is once again his daughter, Carmen.

"Houses of the Holy"

Related to "The Ocean," the piece refers to the communal feeling inside the halls and arenas of the quartet's live appearances. Plant was deeply affected by performing to such numbers as came to see Led Zeppelin. "I love my work, which is communication on a vast level," he once said. To another reporter he was more secular: "Some nights I just look out there and want to fuck the whole first row."

"Kashmir"

Quick to qualify that no member of the group had traveled to the India-Pakistan border region, Plant has explained that the exploratory, questing lyrics for the *Physical Graffiti* masterpiece came from his journeys in the comparably exotic Morocco, driving down "a single-track road which cut neatly through the desert . . . [T]here was seemingly no end to it."

"Bron-yr-Aur"

Like the earlier (misspelled) "Bron-y-Aur Stomp," the warm acoustic guitar interlude is titled for the Welsh cottage where it was initially strummed into being.

"Ten Years Gone"

Plant revealed that this epic ballad described a first love, presumably from about 1964, with whom he'd broken over his pursuit of show business success.

"Black Country Woman"

Another disguised admission from Plant of infidelity with his wife's sister, who likewise hailed from the English Midlands, or Black Country.

"Boogie with Stu"

What it is: a *boogie with* friend and auxiliary Rolling Stone Ian *"Stu"* Stewart.

"Sick Again"

One of Led Zeppelin's most explicitly carnal songs, both celebrating and regretting the bevies of teenage beauties (*"the circus of the LA queens"*) who latched onto them during their West Coast American visits.

"For Your Life"

A murky note of warning creeps into this firsthand *Presence* tale of Angeleno late nights and white lines, *"paying through the nose . . . in the City of the Damned."* "Addiction to powders was the worst way to see yourself, a waste of your time and everybody's time," Plant later avowed. "You make excuses for yourself why things aren't right or about what's happening to your potential. You lie to yourself and rub your nose later."

"Royal Orleans"

Different interpretations have been made of the cryptic verses here. Led Zeppelin stayed at the Royal Orleans hotel in Louisiana in 1973, where John Paul Jones partied with a local drag queen and ended up unconscious with his room on fire; this song refers to the misadventure. Jones, however, has denied that he was *"kissing whiskers left and right"* or that he learned *"if you take your pick, be careful how you choose it."* "The transvestites were actually friends of Richard [Cole]," he told *Mojo* magazine in 2007. "That I mistook a transvestite for a girl is rubbish—that happened in another country to somebody else." Well, it did happen.

"Hots On for Nowhere"

The almost indecipherable line *"I've got friends who would give me fuck-all"* could be Plant's complaint against Page and Peter Grant, forging ahead with Zeppelin's next album while he was apart from his family and recovering from a serious injury.

"Tea for One"

Plant's lyrics on the heartrending rewrite of "Since I've Been Loving You" lament his separation from his wife due to his tax exile and their near-fatal Greek car accident of 1975. "I was just sitting in that wheelchair and getting morose," the singer remembered. "We had just finished a tour, we were away from home, and Robert was in a cast, so I think everybody was a little homesick," Page was quoted in *Guitar World*. "Our attitude was summed up in the lyrics for 'Tea for One.'"

"Hot Dog"

The electric honky-tonk breakdown, where Plant sings that he'll *"never go to Texas anymore,"* is supposedly about his Lone Star groupie Audrey Hamilton. The lines *"I took her love at seventeen / A little late these days, it seems"* are best left without comment.

"Carouselambra"

Many of the lyrics on *In Through the Out Door* were Plant's response to the tragic death of his young son and his reevaluation of rock stardom. *"Powerless the fabled sat, too smug to lift a hand . . . Where was your helping, where was your bow?"* could be a dig at Jimmy Page's incapacitation by drugs.

"All My Love"

In the vocal's emotion as well as in its words, the record's highlight is quite likely a tribute to Plant's child and an affirmation of family loyalty.

8

Sounds Caressed My Ear

Led Zeppelin Music Trivia I

To Trip Is Just to Fall: Audible Technical Mistakes in Led Zeppelin Songs

Aside from Page's much-discussed "sloppy" guitar solos, where his choked or faltering lines have a personality that more fluid players' do not, there are several Zeppelin songs where one or more of the band noticeably fumbles his part. None of these errors were serious enough to warrant discarding the entire take, and most add a measure of authenticity to the numbers, showing that they were performed by real people in real time. To the extent that they are musical flubs, only the individual listener can decide just how much they detract from the piece they're in—if at all.

"Your Time Is Gonna Come"

Jimmy Page's pedal steel guitar is not quite in tune with the rest of the song, as even he admitted to *Guitar Player* magazine in 1977. "I had never played a pedal steel before, but I just picked it up. . . . It's more out of tune on the first album because I hadn't got a kit to put it together."

"I Can't Quit You Baby"

"There are mistakes in it, but it doesn't make any difference," Page said in the same '77 interview. "[T]here are some wrong notes." He's right about the lazily executed soloing: Listen for some clams at 1:30, 2:07, and 3:20, at least.

"Heartbreaker"

Of his solo, Page told *Guitar World*, "That whole section was recorded in a different studio and was sort of slotted in the middle. If you notice, the whole sound of the guitar is different." In fact, the solo guitar is tuned a little higher than that for the rest of the song.

"Moby Dick"

There are some awkward edits during Bonham's drum solo, clearly spliced from several takes.

"Immigrant Song"

At about 1:40, Plant hesitates on the line *"So now you better stop. . . ."*

"Since I've Been Loving You"

Discovered with the cleaned-up CD releases of 1990, Bonham's bass drum pedal is squeaking throughout the song. "It sounds louder every time I hear it," Page has noted. Other songs where this is audible—barely—include "The Rain Song," "Over the Hills and Far Away," and "The Crunge."

"Stairway to Heaven"

Not exactly a mistake, but the overdubbed twelve-string-guitar fanfare before the solo, at about 5:31, is slightly out of sync. There's also an open G string sounded during Page's electric solo, near 6:00, that isn't a bum note but probably wasn't intentional.

"Misty Mountain Hop"

The band briefly seem to fall out of time around 2:11, at the line *"There you sit. . . ."*

"The Rover"

Page misplays an E chord at 2:57.

That Confounded Bridge: Studio Noises or Talk in Zeppelin Songs

It was a fashion in the post-Beatles, post-Dylan era of rock 'n' roll to include snatches of nonmusical dialogue or sounds on album tracks, to impart a realism to the work that distinguished it from the carefully groomed productions of an earlier generation of artists. The device was, in a way, a parallel of the 1960s' cinematic trends for handheld cameras and improvised scenes that replaced the Hollywood models of technical perfection. Led Zeppelin didn't intentionally leave studio chatter in very often—other performers of the time were much more casual that way—but several of their cuts contain deliberate or inadvertent sounds besides instruments and singing that can be picked out by careful ears. Here are among the most distinct.

"Babe I'm Gonna Leave You"

The first Led Zeppelin albums were recorded hastily, either in a concentrated couple of weeks or in scattered sessions at a variety of studios, and thus many taping accidents were left in the final mixes: guide takes left audible under masters, vocals "bleeding" into instrumental tracks, and so on. An example of the former comes at 1:45 in this number, where Robert Plant's ghostly *"I can hear it callin' me"* is heard very low. This would have not gone unnoticed by Jimmy Page or engineer Glyn Johns, but it had a cool resonance and so was kept in.

"You Shook Me"

This is another case of one recorded take incompletely erased by a subsequent overdub, with Plant's off-mic laughter at 1:45 and his faraway moaning around 5:50.

"Whole Lotta Love"

Once more, Plant's voice came through under another track at around 4:00 but was given a dollop of echo to add another sonic dimension to the recording. The acoustical depth suggested by this kind of production is just not possible with the digitized layering of most current pop music.

"Friends"

The very faint dialogue in the song's first few seconds is said to be Page mumbling "fuck" as he hesitates on his guitar part.

"Out On the Tiles"

Someone seems to say "stop" at 1:22—possibly to coordinate the tune's tricky rhythmic breaks.

"Tangerine"

This beautiful ballad enters with a plainly deliberate count-in after Page noodles around some A-minor guitar chords. "That's commonly known as a false start," he said in 1970. "It was a tempo guide, and it seemed like a good idea to leave it in. . . . I was trying to keep the tempo down a bit. I'm not so sure now if it was a good idea."

"The Crunge"

The song begins with Page's studio direction to engineer George Chkiantz ("One more straight away, George") and ends with Plant's obvious "Where's that confounded bridge?"

"The Ocean"

This track starts off with John Bonham's count-in (which he would repeat in concert performances of the song) and, at about 1:38, some listeners insist a ringing phone can be heard.

"In My Time of Dying"

As this lengthy blues jam winds down, some pleased comments from the musicians are left in after Plant mimics Bonham's coughs and Page picks some celebratory notes: "That's gonna be the one, then!" (probably Bonham), "Come have a listen, then" (possibly engineer Andy Johns), and "Oh yes, thank you" (probably Bonham again).

"Boogie with Stu" / "Black Country Woman"

The tail end of the first song hears Plant's laughter, which leads into the intro to the next, recorded outdoors, where engineer Eddie Kramer asks, "Shall we roll it, Jimmy?" The sound of a passing plane is pointed out by Kramer, but the easygoing Plant says, "Nah, leave it." These and the "In My Time of Dying" close are the two most au naturel bits of Led Zeppelin's shoptalk to have made it onto their official records.

"The Wanton Song"

Led Zeppelin was really cooking on this knockout rocker, and Page's enthusiastic "Go!" in the background urges the band on around 3:18. Play loud to hear.

"For Your Life"

Another very attentive listen identifies the sound of snorting through a straw, relevant to the song's subject, after Plant sings *"paying through the nose,"* at about 5:30.

Way Down Inside: The Sounds in the Abstract Section of "Whole Lotta Love"

Between 1:23 and 3:00, Zeppelin's juggernaut went off on the most extreme example of *musique concrète* ever heard in a Top Ten hit. *Hammer of the Gods* author Stephen Davis described it as "clamoring trains, women in orgasm, a napalm attack on the Mekong Delta, a steel mill just as the plant shut down," but the tracks employed for the passage are more prosaic. The main elements were Page's theremin, Plant's voice, and Bonham's snare, hi-hats, and conga—there are no "sound effects" in the sense of prerecorded samples of ordinary noises, and certainly no clips of sex or air raids. "We already had a lot of the sounds on tape, including a theremin and slide with backward echo," recalled Jimmy Page. It was engineer and Jimi Hendrix collaborator Eddie Kramer who helped the producer realize the potential of the instruments he had on hand. "[H]is knowledge of low-frequency oscillation helped complete the effect. If he hadn't known how to do that, I would have had to try for something else." Page also said of the interlude that "all that other stuff, sonic wave sound and all that—I built it up in the studio and put effects on it and things; treatments." Page's Sonic Wave theremin produced some pretty weird sounds on its own, but with Page and Kramer's work at the mixing console they became even weirder: distorted, echoed, reverse echoed, and panned back and forth across the stereo field. Perhaps the final component of the "Whole Lotta Love" surrealism is the studio equipment itself. Page and Kramer mixed the song at an eight-track deck in New York's A&R Studios, "playing" the faders and pots while the tapes rolled. The methodology seems primitive in today's programmed, sixty-four-track, digital environment, but in 1969 such an approach—to physically tinker with the technology as it was operating—was sheer ingenuity. Like the song "Whole Lotta Love" itself, Page and Kramer's performance represented a finite amount of musical input built up into a monster.

Her Face Is Cracked: The Sound at the Beginning of "Celebration Day"

"I was very good at salvaging things that went wrong," Page said in his revelatory *Guitar World* interview of 1991. "For example, the rhythm track at the beginning of 'Celebration Day' was completely wiped by an engineer. . . . The engineer had accidentally recorded over Bonzo! And that is why you have that synthesizer drone from the end of 'Friends' going into 'Celebration Day,' until the rhythm track catches up. We put that on to compensate for the missing drum track." It's been said that engineer Andy Johns ran out in terror after the glitch, though he's never recounted the story, and at the time of the album's release Page claimed, "The tape got crinkled in the studio and wouldn't go through the heads." The implement used to make the electronic hum was likely John Paul Jones's VCS3, an early machine whose artificial tones were high-tech sci-fi in 1970.

Didn't Take Too Long: The Sound at the Beginning of "Black Dog"

There are three of Page's guitars overdubbed in the *Led Zeppelin IV* blastoff, a favorite technique of his when building up the sonic weight of his riffs. The distortion is jacked to the maximum through use of direct injection and compression—the amplifier is bypassed and the instrument is instead plugged straight into the recording deck, where its tones are scrunched into the thickest possible frequency. "Each riff was triple tracked," Page explained in 1993. "One left, one right, and one right up the middle." The hissy tape noise of practice strums and string scratching that precedes Robert Plant's entry is what Page called "the massing of the guitar armies," as the separate tracks were rolled and synchronized before the master take was put down. Though the warming-up sounds could easily have been edited out, it makes for an ominous few seconds of calm, like a stray rifle shot before the massive artillery barrage begins.

The Disregard of Timekeeping: The Meter of "Black Dog"

"Black Dog" is the best of many examples of Led Zeppelin's mastery of time signatures that would have stymied less expert musicians. Not a few of its millions of listeners have thought the main guitar riff is fumbled when it is repeated a fourth lower after the three identical opening salvos, yet somehow Page, Jones, and Bonham stay together without the whole thing turning into a train wreck. Very few well-known songs in Western pop music are timed to irregular numbers—Pink Floyd's "Money" is in 7/8, and jazzman Dave Brubeck's classic *Time Out* album is full of fives and sevens, but most rock 'n' roll is built on a steady two, four, or eight beats per bar. The trick to "Black Dog" is in the sympathetic ears of the three instrumentalists, who play an idiosyncratic line that really has no formal rhythmic structure with just the right amount of metrical give and take. Page later spoke of his enthusiasm for "shifting the goalposts," inspired by the quirky stop-start cadences of such blues artists as Howlin' Wolf and Skip James, and "Black Dog" is similarly basic but with a very funky sense of syncopation.

"When I wrote ["Black Dog"]," John Paul Jones told Susan Fast, "the 'B' section of the riff was actually phrased as three 9/8 bars and one 5/8 bars over the straight 4/4 but nobody else could play it!" The bassist has also counted this original conception as 3/16 time, "but no one could keep up with that," and he clarified to Cameron Crowe. "We struggled with the turnaround, until Bonham figured out that you just count four-time as if there's *no* turnaround. That was the secret." Some transcribers of "Black Dog" time the riff as three bars of 4/4, followed by a single bar of 5/4 and then another 4/4, but anyone trying to do their own version of the song should play it as Led Zeppelin did in 1971: by feel.

Cryin' Won't Help You: How the Echo in "When the Levee Breaks" Was Created

John Bonham's intro to the *Led Zeppelin IV* Memphis Minnie cover might be the heaviest instrumental performance in the group's record, and it is certainly one of the classic moments in rock 'n' roll audio production. Though the song was first attempted in a conventional studio, the trials were unsatisfactory and it was set aside until the band went to the Headley Grange home to lay down tracks with the Rolling Stones' mobile setup. What the listener hears on the completed take is the combination of three elements. First, Bonham's spare drum kit happened to have been set up in the three-story entrance hallway, known as the Minstrel's Gallery, of Headley Grange. "Bonzo went out to test the kit and the sound was huge because the area was so cavernous," Jimmy Page recalled. "The acoustics of the stairwell happened to be so balanced that we didn't even need to mic the kick drum." Upon listening to Bonham's first tryouts of the drums in the spacious area, Page decided to record the rhythm track of "When the Levee Breaks" on the spot. Secondly, the natural reverberation of the Minstrel's Gallery was augmented with compression, echo, and compressed echo by engineer Andy Johns, who ran the signal through a Binson echo chamber, a kind of analog reverb unit that used a steel drum rather than electronics for its effect. This process gave the already palpable attack of the drums an even more physical presence. Finally, the instrumental section of the song (drums, guitar, and bass) was *slowed down* by Page when mixed, making for an even fuller, more plodding beat. "If you slow things down, it makes everything sound so much thicker," said Page. "The only problem is you have to be very tight with your playing, because it magnifies any inconsistencies." That is, an irregular tempo played back at normal speed will sound even more irregular when spaced out more widely by deceleration. Fortunately, Bonham, Page, and Jones were locked in well, securing the vast echo of "When the Levee Breaks" and a milestone recording.

Many Times I've Listened: The Sound at the End of "Over the Hills and Far Away"

The haunting fadeout of this number, from about 4:09 on, has puzzled many listeners. A wispy figure that seems to repeat with a harp or keyboard the main acoustic guitar run of the song, it has been explained by Jimmy Page as a recording of pure echo from an electric guitar: "There's no send on there, just the return," he told *Guitar World*, adding that the final notes were achieved with John Paul Jones's synthesizer. As producer, Page would know what elements are heard in the final mix as well as what instruments were present at the basic take. Elsewhere the sounds are said to come from a harpsichord of Jones's, although the liner notes credit him with only bass on the track. The consensus seems to be that "Over the Hills and Far Away" ends with the reverberations from Page's guitar combined a swell from one of Jones's keyboards, perhaps his mellotron or VCS3 .

In Through the Out Door: The Sound at the Beginning of "In the Evening"

Another portentous album opener, "In the Evening" is introduced with John Paul Jones's Yamaha GX-1 synthesizer underneath Page's bowing a heavily distorted Fender Stratocaster and clanging a mechanical device called a Gizmotron across its strings. "It's like a hurdy-gurdy type of thing, an electronic wheel," said Page. "You'd hold it near the bridge [of the guitar] and depress whichever strings you wanted. It kind of rolled the strings." The abstract tones of this passage were similar to the ones Page had created for his abortive *Lucifer Rising* soundtrack.

1971

January: Led Zeppelin continues work on *Led Zeppelin IV*, Headley Grange.

January 25: Charles Manson, three others, found guilty in Tate-LaBianca slayings.

February 1: Reports say one-third of US college students have tried marijuana.

February 10: Los Angeles earthquake does substantial damage; aftershocks coincide with Jimmy Page and Andy John's mixing work at LA's Sunset Sound.

March: Led Zeppelin's "Return to the Clubs" tour in the UK.

June 30: "Pentagon Papers," charting US involvement in Vietnam, published in the *New York Times*.

July 3: Jim Morrison dies in Paris at 27.

July 6: Louis Armstrong dies, age 71.

August 1: Concert for Bangladesh, New York, featuring George Harrison, Eric Clapton, Ravi Shankar, Bob Dylan.

August–September: Led Zeppelin tour the US and Canada.

September: Led Zeppelin play Japan.

September 13: Attica prison riots leave several dead.

November 8: *Led Zeppelin IV* released.

Movies: *A Clockwork Orange*; *The French Connection*.

Music: The Who, *Who's Next*; the Rolling Stones, *Sticky Fingers*; Marvin Gaye, *What's Going On*; Sly and the Family Stone, *There's a Riot Goin' On*; Carole King, *Tapestry*; Joni Mitchell, *Blue*; Jethro Tull, *Aqualung*; John Lennon, *Imagine*; Don McLean, "American Pie," Isaac Hayes, "Theme from *Shaft*"; Alice Cooper, "Eighteen"; Three Dog Night, "Joy to the World."

9

Sitting Round Singing Songs

Led Zeppelin Music Trivia II

Sing My Song: Zeppelin Songs with "Song" in the Title

- "The Lemon Song" (*Led Zeppelin II*)
- "Immigrant Song" (*Led Zeppelin III*)
- "The Song Remains the Same" (*Houses of the Holy*)
- "The Rain Song" (*Houses of the Holy*)
- "The Wanton Song" (*Physical Graffiti*)

Walter's Walk: Led Zeppelin Songs That Could Refer to Dancing

Though seldom heard in Broadway musicals, several of the group's tunes have titles that imply the listener should kick up his or her heels.

- "Bron-y-Aur Stomp" (*Led Zeppelin III*)
- "Misty Mountain Hop" (*Led Zeppelin IV*)
- "Rock and Roll" (*Led Zeppelin IV*)
- "Dancing Days" (*Houses of the Holy*)
- "Boogie With Stu" (*Physical Graffiti*)
- "Candy Store Rock" (*Presence*)

Only Drive You Mad: Why "Houses of the Holy" Was Left Off the Album of That Title

Unlike the Rolling Stones' *Let It Bleed*, the Beatles' *Sgt. Pepper's Lonely Hearts Club Band*, Jimi Hendrix's *Are You Experienced*, Sly and the Family Stone's *Stand!*, or Van Morrison's *Moondance*, there are no Led Zeppelin albums with the same name as one of their songs. Possibly such a move would have been too "poppy" for the band, who downplayed the importance of hit singles and who always insisted their albums were meant to be appreciated as organic entities—highlighting any one piece by calling a whole collection after it might relegate the rest of the material to filler in the mind of the audience. The general view is that the song "Houses of the Holy," recorded in 1972, was heard to be incompatible with other tracks on the record *Houses of the Holy*, released in 1973. It was not until the next Zeppelin disc, 1975's *Physical Graffiti*, that the cut made it on an LP.

Style Is New, Her Face Is the Same: Back-to-Back Zeppelin Songs with the Same Lyrics

Both "Heartbreaker" and the following "Living Loving Maid (She's Just a Woman)" feature lines that end with the words *lay their* or *lay your money down*.

Communication Breakdown: Led Zeppelin's Instrumentals

A total of four studio tracks have no vocal accompaniment: "Black Mountain Side" (*Led Zeppelin*), "Moby Dick" (*Led Zeppelin II*), "Bron-yr-Aur" (*Physical Graffiti*), "Bonzo's Montreux" (*Coda*). Onstage, the band stretched out many songs to hand solo spots to Jimmy Page ("Heartbreaker," "Dazed and Confused," the unreleased "White Summer" merged with "Black Mountain Side," and a stand-alone guitar showcase on the '77 US tour), John Bonham (the drum solos "Pat's Delight" or "Over the Top," which later evolved into "Moby Dick"), and John Paul Jones on keyboards ("Your Time Is Gonna Come," "No Quarter"). "I had to learn how to snap my fingers, because that looked quite jazzy," conceded Robert Plant, left out of such displays. "And sometimes, when I was at a loss, I used to sit cross-legged on the piano looking like an interested gnome."

10

To Build a Dream

Other Musicians Featured in Led Zeppelin's Music

M ost of Led Zeppelin's four- or five-piece contemporaries freely brought in outside performers to augment their songs, often retaining them as regular hires to join them in the studio or in concert. But Jimmy Page, Robert Plant, John Paul Jones, and John Bonham were a more self-contained unit that very seldom required anyone else to step in (particularly with the multitalented Jones in the lineup), and when they did it was by choice rather than necessity. Thus there are only a handful of people besides Led Zeppelin who can be heard playing Led Zeppelin.

Four Already, Now We're Steady: Recorded Music

Viram Jasani plays tabla on "Black Mountain Side." (Now a promoter with the UK-based Asian Music Circuit, Jasani declined to be interviewed for this book.)

Sandy Denny sings a duet with Robert Plant on "The Battle of Evermore."

Ian "Stu" Stewart plays piano on "Rock and Roll" and "Boogie With Stu."

Mick Bonham (John Bonham's younger brother) blows the whistle, beginning at 2:30, in "Fool in the Rain."

Unidentified string players play backup on "Friends."

Unidentified string players provide orchestration on "Kashmir." Peter Grant recounted a tale of road manager Richard Cole being sent to London's Southall district to find "a Pakistani orchestra" for the song, although John Paul Jones has said of the track that "we did the strings with an English orchestra in Olympic Studios."

It Was Really, Really Good: Live Performances

In concert, Led Zeppelin occasionally brought extra players onstage with them, more for spontaneous get-togethers than as any indispensable accompanists. Jimmy Page admitted that he was sometimes stretching to incorporate all of a given song's overdubbed guitars into a single live performance but, as he noted, "There are times when I'd just love to get another guitarist on [stage], but it just wouldn't look right to the audience."

Jack Lancaster and Mike Evans, saxophonists for Blodwyn Pig and the Liverpool Scene, respectively, came on to jam "Long Tall Sally" with Led Zeppelin following the Pop Proms show at the Royal Albert Hall on June 29, 1969.

An unidentified female bassist subbed for John Paul Jones, called back to England to see his ailing father, for the medley finale of a Cleveland show on August 26, 1970.

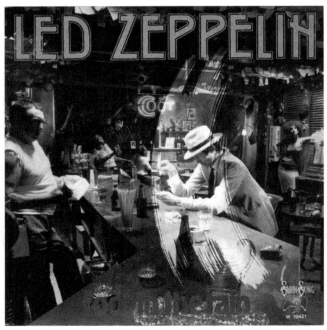

"Fool in the Rain" featured a brief contribution from John Bonham's brother, Mick.
Courtesy of Robert Rodriguez

Richard Cole, Zeppelin's road manager, occasionally got to sit in on congas during the "Whole Lotta Love" finale of some English and European dates.

Chris Welch, an English rock journalist, played congas on "Whole Lotta Love" in Frankfurt, Germany, on July 18, 1970.

Phil Carson, an Atlantic Records official, friend of the group, and later manager of Jimmy Page, was invited to share the stage with Led Zeppelin on a few occasions. He played bass on "C'mon Everybody" at a Dublin gig on March 6, 1971, and again on the same song at Osaka, Japan, on September 28 of the same year. In Frankfurt, Germany, on June 30, 1980, he participated in a reprise jam on "Money."

Clive Coulson, a Led Zeppelin roadie, hammed it up on "C'mon Everybody" at the aforementioned '71 Osaka show.

Ron Wood, future Rolling Stone and ex-Face, came onstage for an encore of "Communication Breakdown" at Nassau Coliseum on February 13, 1975.

Mick Ralphs, guitarist for Swan Song act Bad Company, played an encore of Jerry Lee Lewis's "It'll Be Me" on May 22, 1977, in the Convention Center at Fort Worth, Texas.

Keith Moon, the uncontrollable Who drummer, partying hard while exiled to Los Angeles, joined the band for Bonham's "Moby Dick" and an encore of "Whole Lotta Love," at the LA Forum on June 23, 1977.

Simon Kirke, the drummer for Bad Company, played along with "Whole Lotta Love" at Munich's Olympiahalle on July 5, 1980.

1972

January–June: Led Zeppelin record *Houses of the Holy.*

February 28: President Richard Nixon makes historic visit to Communist China.

February: Led Zeppelin tour Australia and New Zealand.

March 24: British prime minister Edward Heath imposes parliamentary rule on Northern Ireland following increased violence.

May 16: Alabama Governor George Wallace critically injured by gunfire.

June 17: Five burglars arrested for break-in at the Watergate hotel, Washington, DC.

June: Led Zeppelin tour North America.

August: Heavy US B-52 raids on North Vietnam.

September 5: Eleven Israeli Olympic athletes are killed by Black September terrorists, Munich.

October: Led Zeppelin play Japan.

November 8: Richard Nixon wins US presidential election in a landslide.

December 26: Chilean athletes admit to cannibalism after an Andes plane crash.

Movies: *The Godfather*; *Deliverance*; *Deep Throat.*

Music: The Rolling Stones, *Exile on Main Street*; Stevie Wonder, *Talking Book*; Deep Purple, *Machine Head*; David Bowie, *The Rise and Fall of Ziggy Stardust and the Spiders from Mars*; T. Rex, *The Slider*; Neil Young, *Harvest*; the Temptations, "Papa Was a Rollin' Stone"; Mott the Hoople, "All the Young Dudes"; Johnny Nash, "I Can See Clearly Now."

Are We Rolling?

Led Zeppelin in the Studio

Gauge Is on the Red: Where Zeppelin Recorded

lthough the band maintained the same record label and producer-guitarist over their twelve-year span, they never confined themselves to a single studio to make their music. Already experienced in a range of studios in England and the US when Zeppelin was formed, Jimmy Page always kept his ears open for the most advanced, most convenient, and most comfortable places to record, and at different times different sites met his criteria. Sometimes the spot was determined by the group's peripatetic touring circuit, others by their technical sophistication, and others by their relaxed ambience. A few of these were used no more than once or twice for overdubs or demo takes, while others were where entire albums were rehearsed, taped, and mastered. This list comprises all the recording rooms, jam scenes, and mixing booths where Led Zeppelin's albums are known to have been prepared and finalized.

A&M Studios, 1416 North LaBrea Avenue, Los Angeles

This was one of many North American settings where preliminary takes for *Led Zeppelin II* were laid down in the spring and summer of 1969.

A&R Studios, 112 West Forty-Eighth Street / 322 West Forty-Eighth Street / 799 Seventh Avenue, New York

Led Zeppelin II was given its final mix by Jimmy Page and Eddie Kramer over two days in these New York locations (the studio business occupied several buildings, all of which are listed here). Some takes were also originally recorded in A&R.

Ardent Studios, 1457 National Street, Memphis, Tennessee

Parts of *Led Zeppelin III* were recorded at Ardent in 1970 with engineer Terry Manning. The album's final mix, and the inscription of Aleister Crowley's "Do What Thou Wilt" on the master runoff groove, were also completed here.

Atlantic Studios, New York

Atlantic has been cited as another *Led Zeppelin II* recording site.

Electric Lady Studios, 52 West Eighth Street, New York

Several songs from *Houses of the Holy* received their final mixes at this legendary studio, designed by Jimi Hendrix.

Groove Studios, New York

Parts of *Led Zeppelin II* were recorded here.

Headley Grange, Liphook Road, Village of Headley, Hampshire, UK

Much rock 'n' roll history was made in the country home, originally built in 1795, that became Led Zeppelin's unofficial recording residence. Initial or final tracks for *Led Zeppelin III*, *IV*, and *Physical Graffiti* were put down within its spooky confines (Jimmy Page said he saw a ghost on the premises), most famously the echoing drums of "When the Levee Breaks." Along with the Band's Big Pink, the Rolling Stones' Nellcôte villa, and Sly Stone's 783 Bel Air Drive, Headley Grange is one of the most important improvised recording rooms in popular music.

Island Studios, 8–10 Basing Street, Notting Hill, London

Songs from *Led Zeppelin III* and *IV* were completed at this popular and well-appointed studio, including "Stairway to Heaven."

Juggy Sound Studio, New York

Material for *Led Zeppelin II* was taped at this Big Apple obscurity.

Mayfair Studios, New York

Ditto.

Mirror Sound, Los Angeles

Ditto, only in LA.

Morgan Studios, London

Ditto, only back in the UK. "Thank You" is said to have been recorded here.

Mountain Studios, Montreux, Switzerland

During Zeppelin's tax exile, which began in 1975, the Swiss resort town was a desirable haven. The pulverizing *Coda* drum solo "Bonzo's Montreux" was taped here in December 1976.

Musicland Studios, Arabellastrasse 5, Munich

All of *Presence* was recorded and mixed during a three-week period in November and December 1975 at this in-demand site in the basement of the large Arabella Hotel in West Germany. Robert Plant noted of the hotel that "there was a whorehouse on the fourth floor," but this may be incidental.

Mystic Sound Studios, Los Angeles

Again, parts of *Led Zeppelin II* were recorded here.

Olympic Studios, 117 Church Road, Barnes, London

Olympic was the closest thing to Led Zeppelin's home base in their early years; preliminary or finishing work on *Led Zeppelin, Led Zeppelin II, Led Zeppelin III, Led Zeppelin IV, Houses of the Holy* and *Physical Graffiti* was done here, including all of the classic debut record and the epic "Kashmir." Olympic was one of Britain's premier studios through the 1960s, '70s, and '80s, where music by the Rolling Stones, the Who, the Jimi Hendrix Experience, Pink Floyd, Procol Harum, the Eagles, Queen, and the Beatles ("All You Need Is Love"), among many others, was made. Acquired by

Richard Branson's Virgin company in 1987 and taken over by EMI in 1992, the fabled Olympic was shut down in 2009.

Polar Studios, 58 Sankt Eriksgatan, Stockholm

In Through the Out Door was made at these new Swedish studios, the roost of pop superstars Abba, in late 1978.

Quantum Studios, Los Angeles

Quantum was yet another studio at which portions of *Led Zeppelin II* were recorded.

The Rolling Stones' Mobile Studio

Symbolic of the creative and economic clout enjoyed by rock acts of the epoch, the Stones' £65,000 trailer permitted them and the artists who rented the platform from them to make professional-quality recordings outside the sterile confines of urban office buildings. The "back to the land" ethic infused the resultant music, where the more casual atmosphere and homier acoustics inspired the players to some of their most intimate performances. Sessions for *Led Zeppelin III* and *IV*, *Houses of the Holy*, and *Physical Graffiti* were facilitated by the Stones' studio.

Ronnie Lane's Mobile Studio

Similar in technology to the Rolling Stones' rig but cheaper to use, this portable booth was on hand for various *Physical Graffiti* tracks. Jimmy Page played benefit shows for ex-Face Ronnie Lane's ARMS (Action Research into Multiple Sclerosis) charity in 1983. The well-liked Lane died from MS in 1997.

The Sol Studio, Cookham, Berkshire, UK

All the basic tracks for *Coda* were mixed at this studio, once owned by Elton John producer Gus Dudgeon and acquired by Page in the early 1980s.

Stargroves, Tothill Road, Newbury, Berkshire, UK

A lush country home belonging to Mick Jagger, Stargroves was the site of numerous sessions (using the mobile units) for *Houses of the Holy*, *Physical Graffiti*, and eventually *Coda*.

Sunset Sound Recorders, 6650 Sunset Boulevard, Los Angeles

The basic takes of "Whole Lotta Love" were first recorded here in May 1969. Some of *Led Zeppelin IV* was given a first mix on the premises in 1971, although a technical glitch meant most of them had to be redone at Island Studios.

Unknown Studios, Vancouver, British Columbia

Most accounts of the small Canadian studio where isolated tracks for *Led Zeppelin II* were taped describe it only as a poorly equipped "shed" or "a hut." Today Vancouver is home to many top-level recording buildings, but whatever was used by Zeppelin in 1969 is probably no longer extant.

It Isn't Hard to Recognize: Led Zeppelin's Unreleased Songs

Although hardcore fans have long dreamed of hearing "new" music from Led Zeppelin, there are no remaining pieces in the band's vault that are in as completed a state as the rest of their catalogue. "We weren't the sort of group to hoard tracks," John Paul Jones said to Dave Lewis. "[T]here isn't much studio stuff to work with because we tended to finish only what we were totally satisfied with." Live shows presented many spontaneous covers of other people's work; studio and concert bootlegs have hinted at works in progress that were considerably different than anything that made it to finished albums, and demo or alternate takes suggesting material unlike any other Zeppelin numbers were at least begun, but there is no lost "Stairway to Heaven" or "Whole Lotta Love." The post-1980 issues of *Coda*, the two box sets of 1990 and 1993, and 1997's *BBC Sessions* presented the last hitherto undiscovered Led Zeppelin songs likely to be of interest to a general audience. The following have been the most significant of the quartet's unreleased songs.

"Sugar Mama"

Bouncy boogie with a touch of funk, "Sugar Mama" was recorded in late 1969. With a cleanup it could have been put onto *Coda*, although it's pretty light for Led Zeppelin.

"Traveling Riverside Blues"

An update of the Robert Johnson blues performed on BBC Radio in 1969, the song was known only to bootleggers until its official inclusion in the four-disc 1990 anthology.

"Baby Come On Home"

With a working title of "Tribute to Bert Burns," this soulful outtake from the 1969 *Led Zeppelin* album finally hit the airwaves in 1993.

"I Wanna Be Her Man"

This very raw duet between Page and Plant, demoed on a home tape recorder at Bron-yr-Aur, sounds like Neil Young at his most stoned.

"Hey Hey What Can I Do"

The B side of the 1970 "Immigrant Song" single was, unusually for Led Zeppelin, never fit into an album and seldom heard except by collectors of 45s. It was ultimately put into the 1990 box set.

"Sunshine Woman"

Part of Led Zeppelin's early sets and recorded for the BBC in 1969, this loose blues number resembled both "Traveling Riverside Blues" and another Beeb performance, "The Girl I Love She Got Long Black Wavy Hair," in both lyrics and arrangement. Highlighted by John Paul Jones's piano work, concert takes of this groovy tune have surfaced, but the BBC version seems to have been lost forever.

"Jennings Farm Blues"

Named after Robert Plant's new country home in the English Midlands, this was the working title of an electric track that evolved into the bluegrass "Bron-y-Aur Stomp," from *Led Zeppelin III*.

"The Girl I Love She Got Long Black Wavy Hair"

A hard-hitting riff played on a BBC gig in June 1969, with the band trying a line that grew into the "Moby Dick" intro and Robert Plant freely borrowing Sleepy John Estes's lyrics for the eponymous song, the cut was circulated among bootleggers for many years before starring as the gem from the official *BBC Sessions*.

"In the Morning"

This song is actually early rehearsals of "In the Light," distinct from the ultimate *Physical Graffiti* version.

"Take Me Home"

This is another studio practice bootleg from the *Physical Graffiti* period, where the band gets down to some sizzling funk; parts of it resemble the finished "Custard Pie," although a completed take would have been worthwhile.

"Autumn Lake"

For one scene in *The Song Remains the Same,* Jimmy Page is seen playing a hurdy-gurdy by a moat at his home of Plumpton Place in Sussex. The movie's credits name this spectral short piece as part of the soundtrack, but it has never been issued on any other medium.

"Swan Song"

Perhaps the most legendary of Led Zeppelin's unreleased cuts, this forceful instrumental, consisting of acoustic guitar, bass, and drums, was first sketched around the time of the *Physical Graffiti* sessions in 1974 but never made it past the demo stage. It was resurrected as "Midnight Moonlight" for Page's band the Firm in 1985; the title was adapted into the name of Led Zeppelin's private record label.

"Minnie the Moocher"

Plant sings the lyrics to the old Cab Calloway hit over the chords of what became "Tea for One," in a practice tape from about 1975.

"Fire"

In 1978 Led Zeppelin reconvened at England's Clearwell Castle for some jams and songwriting attempts as Plant recovered from his family trauma of the previous year. An amateur recording of the sessions later emerged, including this fast rocker, which is like an even more savage "Achilles Last Stand."

12

Secrets of the Sorcerer

Jimmy Page's Guitar Heroism

Drop Down: Jimmy Page's Guitar Tunings

Anyone who has studied the evolution of the six-string has recognized that the standard tuning of the instrument—E–A–D–G–B–E, from low to high—is probably the last configuration to lend itself to the player's convenience. In fact, a wide range of guitar tunings have been invented that are more "musical," in terms of producing listenable melodies from an untutored performer. Though guitarist Jimmy Page first became skilled with the conventional E–A–D–G–B–E setup, his horizons expanded as a studio musician when he discovered the great British folk artists Davey Graham, John Renbourn, and Bert Jansch. Less graceful in his electric blues soloing than other guitar heroes Jimi Hendrix or Eric Clapton, Page boasted an arsenal of alternate tunings, which were the ace up his sleeve, and he used many throughout his career—before, during, and after membership in Led Zeppelin.

Page has always referred to the folk standby of D–A–D–G–A–D as his "CIA tuning," for its suggestive Celtic, Indian, and Arabic drones. But as his confidence increased, Page began to make up his own string arrangements beyond those he heard others employ. "I just moved the stings around until it sounded right," he said of his inventions. Of all the star guitarists of his time, only singer-songwriter Joni Mitchell had that kind of audacity. Consequently some Zeppelin songs present great challenges to would-be imitators trying to copy exactly what Page was playing. It is possible, of course, to approximate his chords with other tunings, but note-for-note recreations can be elusive. Some songs were tuned differently between studio and live versions, or were artificially slowed down in the mix to play at a lower pitch (e.g., "When the Levee Breaks"), or are still disputed by subjective guitarists who have arrived at separate tunings to play the same lines. In at least one instance of an overdubbed recording—the unaccompanied "Heartbreaker" solo—slight variations in the tuning of one take's instrument may be discerned from that used on another. Careful listening and Page's own eventual explications, however, have mostly cleared up these mysteries.

- C–A–C–G–C–E: "Friends," "Bron-yr-Aur," "Poor Tom"
- C–F–C–F–A–F: "Bron-y-Aur Stomp"
- C–G–C–G–C–E: "Hats Off to (Roy) Harper"
- D♭–G♭–D♭–G♭–B♭–D♭: "That's the Way"
- D–A–D–G–A–D: "White Summer," "Black Mountain Side," "Kashmir"
- D–A–D–G–B–D: "Going to California"
- D–A–D–G–B–E ("drop D"): "Moby Dick," "Ten Years Gone"
- D–G–D–G–B–D: "When the Levee Breaks," "Black Country Woman"
- D–G–C–G–C–D: "The Rain Song" (studio version)
- E–A–D–A–D–E: "The Rain Song" (live version)
- E–A–E–A–C♯–E: "In My Time of Dying," "Celebration Day" (slide guitar track)
- E–A–D–G–B–D: "Traveling Riverside Blues," "Dancing Days"

The Hand That Sews Time: How Jimmy Page Learned to Bow His Guitar

Perhaps his most memorable performance platform and a technique he used on several Led Zeppelin recordings, Jimmy Page first tried running a violin or viola bow over the strings of an electric guitar while employed as a session player circa 1965. According to Page, he was in a studio with some string players and during a break one of his colleagues asked if he'd ever tried it; both men were curious. The violinist was the London Philharmonic Orchestra's David McCallum Sr. (for some reason, rock superstar Page has always noted the connection to McCallum's actor son, at the time famous for his role in *The Man from U.N.C.L.E.* TV series). "I said I didn't think it would work because the bridge of the guitar isn't arched like it is on a violin or a cello," recalled the guitarist in 2005, "but he insisted I give it a try. . . . Whatever squeaks I made sort of intrigued me. I didn't really start developing the technique for [sic] quite some time later, but he was the guy who turned me on to the idea." When he joined the Yardbirds, Page tried

From the author's collection, circa 1987 and still worn occasionally.

bowing his instrument both in concert and on the numbers "Tinker, Tailor, Soldier, Sailor" and "Glimpses." Later his bow solo was a staple of Zeppelin's "Dazed and Confused" threnodies, and "How Many More Times," "In the Light," and "In the Evening" were also recorded with the accessory.

Some have disputed Page's account, pointing out that guitarist Eddie Phillips of the 1960s English band the Creation was using a bow around the same time, as was Californian psychedelic act Kaleidoscope. As a busy music professional it's likely Page would have at least known of both bands, but in this case his claim to have come across the idea independently, through the friendly prompting of McCallum, seems just as plausible.

As We Go Sliding Through: Led Zeppelin Songs with Slide Guitar

Though Zeppelin is widely thought of as one of the great blues-rock bands, Jimmy Page never developed a reputation as a compelling slide player in the manner of Duane Allman, Ry Cooder, ZZ Top's Billy Gibbons, or Lowell George of Little Feat. Nonetheless, he displayed some impressive slide skills on several Led Zeppelin cuts or parts thereof: "You Shook Me," "Whole

Lotta Love" (the descending slur in the chorus, recorded with backward echo), "What Is and What Should Never Be," "Bron-y-Aur Stomp," "Hats Off to (Roy) Harper," "Traveling Riverside Blues," "Stairway to Heaven" (the fills in the guitar solo at 6:24, 6:28, 6:33, and 6:38), "When the Levee Breaks," "Dancing Days", and "In My Time of Dying." The sliding "Celebration Day" line is actually played by John Paul Jones on a lap steel guitar.

1973

January 21: *Roe vs. Wade* decision legalizes abortion in the US.

January 27: US–North Vietnamese cease-fire.

March 8: 234 injured in IRA bomb attack, London.

March 28: *Houses of the Holy* released.

April 30: Four aides to Richard Nixon resign over Watergate scandal.

May–July: Led Zeppelin's record-breaking tour of North America.

September 21: Chilean armed forces stage coup d'etat.

October 22: Yom Kippur War pits Egypt and Syria against Israel.

December: Arab oil embargo leads to gas rationing in the US.

Movies: *The Exorcist*; *The Sting*; *American Graffiti*.

Music: Pink Floyd, *Dark Side of the Moon*; the Who, *Quadrophenia*; Paul McCartney and Wings, *Band on the Run*; David Bowie, *Aladdin Sane*; Lou Reed "Walk on the Wild Side"; Roberta Flack, "Killing Me Softly with His Song"; Carly Simon, "You're So Vain."

13

They Carry News That Must Get Through

Led Zeppelin Live

Got a Date, I Can't Be Late: Led Zeppelin's Concerts

As with the measurement of the band's total record sales, an accurate accounting of Led Zeppelin's performances is more difficult to come by than it sounds. From 1973 on, their gigs were huge events that drew thousands of people and widespread media coverage, but before then Led Zeppelin tours and shows were less publicized and tended to be organized on the fly. The music itself was exhilarating, venues were often full, and fans came away satisfied; on the other hand, the itineraries were only made up as promoters could commit to a date, a place, and a price. For this reason there are still some Zeppelin appearances that are disputed. Among those least likely to remember the group's full schedule are Jimmy Page, Robert Plant, and John Paul Jones, as well as road manager Richard Cole and members of his crew. They were all too occupied with getting to, setting up, and playing the concerts to confirm when and where they happened.

Some gigs were advertised but never came through, others were played but never advertised, several were canceled—all muddying the final record. As recently as 2009, a "reunion" of fans gathered at the Wheaton Youth Center, in a Maryland suburb of Washington, DC, to celebrate a 1969 Led Zeppelin performance there that local records and Zeppelin historians conclude never happened. In some of their very first shows, too, the act actually played two or more sets in the same location on the same night, while other spots either ran long or were cut short, making an exact number of concerts subject to interpretation. What constitutes a complete show, anyway? A forty-minute club engagement? A festival billing shared with twenty other artists? A three-hour stadium blast?

With these qualifiers in mind, it's certain that Led Zeppelin performed more than five hundred concerts—defined as prepared recitals for a paying audience in a public setting—between 1968 and 1980, with a figure of 533 single appearances the most probable total.

All My Love: Zeppelin's Live Audience

Assuming that many fans saw Zeppelin more than once and that most but not all of their appearances were sold out, the total capacity of every venue the band played comes to some four million, give or take a few thousand. Thus at least two or three million people throughout the world attended one or more Led Zeppelin shows.

Seen Seven Wonders: Countries Visited by Led Zeppelin

The United Kingdom (including England, Scotland, Wales, and Northern Ireland), Ireland, the United States (including Hawaii but not Alaska), Canada, Australia, New Zealand, Sweden, Denmark, West Germany, Switzerland, Belgium, Austria, Finland, Italy, the Netherlands, Japan, and Iceland.

So Glad I Took a Look: Zeppelin's Biggest Audience

The largest crowd Led Zeppelin ever played in front of was at the Atlanta Pop Festival on July 5, 1969, where between 125,000 and 140,000 spectators were present. The festival's artists also included Janis Joplin, Joe Cocker, Canned Heat, Creedence Clearwater Revival, and many others. The largest crowd gathered specifically to hear Led Zeppelin was at the Silverdome in Pontiac, Michigan (outside Detroit) on April 30, 1977, filled to capacity at 76,229 people. Other vast audiences for Led Zeppelin—and Led Zeppelin only—were at Seattle's Kingdome Arena on July 17, 1977 (62,000); Tampa Stadium on May 5, 1973 (56,800); and two final dates at Oakland, California's Oakland-Alameda County Coliseum on July 23 and 24, 1977 (about 55,000 each).

Open Your Arms: Led Zeppelin's Best- and Worst-Ever Shows

All entertainers have good nights and bad nights. Led Zeppelin had more good than bad, and their best have secured their status as one of rock 'n' roll's most effective live artists. Though everyone who saw and

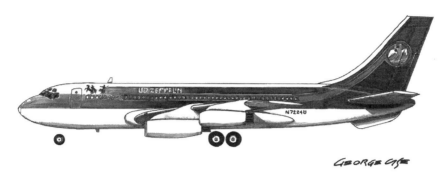

The Boeing 720B *Caesar's Chariot* carried the band around the US on their 1977 tour.   *Author's Collection*

heard Zeppelin has private memories of their shows—as does everyone *in* Zeppelin—in the subsequent decades some key dates have come to the forefront as the band's high- and lowlights, based on published reviews, audience and official tapings, and anecdotal accounts.

Best

Fillmore West, San Francisco, January 9–12, 1969
Led Zeppelin began their conversion of the American rock faithful during a four-night run of two sets each at the famous psychedelic ballroom. "It felt like a vacuum and we'd arrived to fill it," Jimmy Page told Cameron Crowe later. "First this row, then that row—it was like a tornado and it went rolling across the country." San Francisco was a crucial market for emerging acts, and Zeppelin made a lasting impression on the Fillmore punters, with the withering boogie of early numbers such as "Train Kept A-Rollin'," "Communication Breakdown," John Bonham's jaw-dropping drum solo, and "Dazed and Confused." "A Zeppelin show was designed to hit hard from the start," John Paul Jones explained to Dave Lewis. "You know, the first three numbers nonstop—blam!" The bassist also told scholar Susan Fast, "[T]he audiences of 1969–70 simply didn't know what hit them!" At the Fillmore in January 1969, the audiences took a hit they'd never forget.

Boston Tea Party, Boston, January 23–26, 1969
These gigs on the US East Coast have also gone down as Led Zeppelin's breakthrough with the hip youth underground of the late 1960s. With a capacity of no more than a thousand people, the band tore the Tea Party down with crushing volume and spellbinding dynamics, going over the same electric blues riffs that won San Franciscans over: "Train Kept

A-Rollin'," "I Can't Quit You Baby," "You Shook Me," and the metallurgic "How Many More Times," which generated some of the first known head-banging among the fans gathered at 53 Berkeley Street. One performance is said to have run four hours long, including several encores and unrehearsed improvisations on Yardbirds, Chuck Berry, and Beatles songs; the duration is probably exaggerated but the response of the audience is no myth. "The impression, to say the least, is staggering!" wrote Ben Blummenberg of the local counterculture paper the *Boston Phoenix*. He prophesied, "I expect the Led Zeppelin to be flying high for some time. . . . Their raw power is compelling and hypnotic while their complexity makes repeated exposure a pleasure."

Long Beach Arena, Long Beach, California, June 27, 1972
Bootlegged by some of the thirteen thousand spectators present at the time and preserved for posterity on the *How the West Was Won* live CD, this summertime show is considered to be Led Zeppelin at the peak of their musical and theatrical powers. The songs played drew on their first four great albums—"Immigrant Song," "Heartbreaker," "Dazed and Confused," "Stairway to Heaven," and the annihilating finale of "Rock and Roll"—and included acoustic gems like "Tangerine" and "Going to California" as well. There were more fine gigs to come, but the combined vocal and instrumental strengths of Page, Plant, Jones, and Bonham were never again as high as they were here.

Earl's Court Arena, London, May 17–18, May 23–25, 1975
Five brilliant nights of Led Zeppelin's best music and best stagecraft were achieved at these historic events, their last run of wholly successful appearances in their native country. Playing to an estimated 17,000 fans per sold-out show, the foursome had *Led Zeppelin, II, III,* and *IV, Houses of the Holy,* and *Physical Graffiti* from which to select numbers, a true embarrassment of riches. They were also delivering to British fans the mind-blowing visual presentation hitherto reserved for North America, with laser effects, Page's magical dragon suit, Bonham's Vistalite drums, blinding backdrop lights that spelled out the band's name, and, for the first time, big-screen Eidophor TV monitors for the benefit of the back rows. Some of the most reproduced photos of Zeppelin in all their glory are taken from the Earl's Court concerts, and the choicest moments of the video coverage (like the dreamy acoustic interlude) were edited down for inclusion on the *Led Zeppelin* DVD of 2003. "In its field," ran a contemporary report in London's *Daily Mail*, "this is one of the most astonishing examples of pure theater I've seen anywhere," while even the sober *Financial Times* admitted that Zeppelin

"are no longer judged in mere musical terms but as an entertainment industry phenomenon."

Los Angeles Forum, June 21, 1977
From a tour that was often troubled by weak performances and which ended in violence and tragedy, this opening night of a six-date LA engagement had the group rising to a final triumph just weeks before their painful American denouement. Led Zeppelin's set ran over three hours on the summer solstice, taking in long solos ("No Quarter" ran almost a half hour; Page's theremin and bow spot went on over fifteen minutes), but the full house of 18,000 was up for it. Journalist Robert Hilburn of the *Los Angeles Times* wrote that Zeppelin began the gig "with a tenacious, well-paced 45-minute segment that left little doubt about the quartet's continued ability to deliver on stage. . . . After the trauma-edged, two-year layoff, it seemed glad to be back on the road," although he added that "if the show were edited to two hours, the gap between critics' often cold view of Zeppelin and the fans' adoration would be lessened considerably." The Forum shows are how a generation of US Zep-heads would prefer to remember their favorite band.

Worst

Activity Center, Arizona State University, Tempe, July 20, 1977
Led Zeppelin's third-to-last appearance in North America is widely thought to be the nadir of their entire performing career. Much of the blame is placed on Jimmy Page's drug problems, which were all too apparent to his fellow musicians and to many in the audience. "Yeah, I remember that," John Paul Jones conceded in a 1994 Phoenix newspaper interview. "It was a horrible night. Jimmy wasn't . . . well." Missed cues, desultory solos, and Page's wasted condition were all in evidence on the '77 tour, but this evening they combined for a real bummer of a gig that started late, saw flash pots go off at the wrong time and nearly blast Page and Robert Plant off their feet, and ended without an encore. Fans who were there were glad to see Led Zeppelin in any state, but connoisseurs of the foursome's live work rate the tired Tempe recital very low.

Coliseum, Greensboro, North Carolina, January 29, 1975
The 1975 North American tour got off to a shaky start with Jimmy Page injuring the pinkie finger of his left (chording) hand in England and Robert Plant being struck with a bad cold in the depths of the US winter. Some early shows were canceled or postponed. When Led Zeppelin hit Greensboro, Page had been running on Jack Daniel's whiskey and heroin in Los Angeles while the singer recuperated in Chicago, resulting in a

A typically San Franciscan psychedelic ad for a 1969 Zeppelin show.

Courtesy of Robert Rodriguez

disappointing gig where both Plant's voice and Page's guitar were well below par.

Tampa Stadium, Florida, June 3, 1977
When this outdoor concert was canceled two songs in because of an imminent thunderstorm, a riot among almost 70,000 fans and assembled police broke out. Injuries and arrests were plentiful. Though the band's performance was not the issue, punters who expected to see Zeppelin play "Rain or Shine," according to the tickets, were disappointed and a makeup show was canceled in light of the unrest.

Knebworth Festival, Stevenage, UK, August 11, 1979
The back-to-back weekend Knebworth spectacles were intended as Led Zeppelin's English comeback after the prematurely halted 1977 American circuit, but by the second show it was clear that the group had not weathered either the years or new developments in rock music well. Attendance at the open-air event had dropped from as many as 200,000 on August 4 to only around 40,000 on the eleventh, prefiguring the band's equally small-scale and sometimes uneven appearances throughout Europe the following year. Rust, nerves, and technical problems affected both Knebworth shows, and scribes from the New Wave–touting English music press eagerly wrote off Zeppelin as a foundering dinosaur. Quality moments from Knebworth are distilled into a portion of the 2003 DVD, but many of those in attendance left less than impressed.

Gonna Be a Star: Artists Who Shared Bills with Led Zeppelin

By the early 1970s the group was successful enough to be the sole act at most of their events, to the satisfaction of punters and with the bonus of making backstage arrangements and contracts easier for the act and its promoters alike. Interviewed in *Hammer of the Gods*, Richard Cole told Stephen Davis, "If you go to a concert, you don't want to see the Shmuck Sisters singing for thirty minutes. . . . It stopped all that fucking aggravation, the arguments between groups about equipment and all that shit." John Paul Jones told Susan Fast: "Opening acts were more trouble than they were worth. You couldn't get them on [on] time, then you couldn't get them off! Most people only wanted to see the headline band anyway, especially if it did a three-hour set."

Before then, however, Led Zeppelin appeared with a wide variety of musicians, especially at rock festivals. The band played big outdoor shows in Atlanta; New York; Dallas; Milwaukee; Newport, Rhode Island; and Bath, England, in 1969 and 1970, where fans also got to see and hear everyone from the Moody Blues, Santana, the Jefferson Airplane, and Sly and the Family Stone to B. B. King, Chicago Transit Authority, and Buffy Sainte-Marie. During this time Zeppelin also shared stages with Spirit, Zephyr, Alice Cooper, Julie Driscoll, Brian Auger and the Trinity, the Doors, the Who, the Guess Who, and Chuck Berry.

Headliners Vanilla Fudge and Iron Butterfly were both reluctant to go on after Zeppelin in 1969, and Grand Funk Railroad's Don Brewer recalled a backstage clash between their manager Terry Knight and Peter Grant over cutting Grand Funk's set short. "Terry went onstage and made some sort of announcement after they got the PA back on that Led Zeppelin didn't want Grand Funk back on—which just infuriated [audience members] more." Led Zeppelin teased their occasional 1969 opening act Jethro Tull as "Jethro Dull," and suggested Tull's prospective live album be titled *Bore 'Em at the Forum*. Many small-time local players were also booked together with Zeppelin or the New Yardbirds in 1968–69, among them Last Thursday (Schenectady, New York), the Eyes (Brøndby, Denmark), the Spokesmen (Kansas City), and the Trials of Jayson Hoover (Vancouver). Rick Derringer and Judas Priest, both of whom came to enjoy substantial followings, preceded Zeppelin at the Oakland gigs of '77, and at the Knebworth Festival the day's lineup featured Fairport Convention, Todd Rundgren and Utopia, and the Rolling Stones offshoot the New Barbarians, with Keith Richards, Ron Wood, and bassist Stanley Clarke.

Spent My Money: Led Zeppelin's Usual Ticket Prices

The cost to see Led Zeppelin rose as the group went from underground sensation to reigning superstars, but even adjusted for inflation a seat at a live performance between 1968 and 1980 was a bargain compared to what it would cost today. In 1969 tickets for Led Zeppelin's appearance at Chicago's Kinetic Playground went for $5.00, at Toronto's Rock Pile for $2.50, and at Pasadena's Rose Palace for $4.00 at the door. By 1970 a good spot at the Baltimore Civic Center was $7.00. In 1971 attending a club show in Southampton, UK, cost 60 pence, at Wembley's Empire Pool 75 pence; the price went up to £1 (about $5.00 at the time) in 1972–73. Tickets were hitting $10.00 by 1975 (inflation was rampant), and £2.50 would get you on the floor of Earl's Court. Fees topped the $10.00 mark in '77, and getting in to the Knebworth Festival (where other artists were on the bill) was £7.50. Seats for the fall 1980 North American tour had already been sold at $15.00 apiece, but were of course refunded after John Bonham's death.

By contrast, tickets to Led Zeppelin's reunion show at London's O2 arena in 2007 were retailed by an online lottery that was swamped by millions of applicants around the world. The minimum cost to get in was £125, about $250 US.

My Old Blue Dungarees: Led Zeppelin's Stage Costumes

"Page and I were from the school of, 'It's a show so wear something different,'" John Paul Jones explained to Susan Fast in 2000. For many though not all of their live appearances the various members of the group were clad in special attire that was clearly chosen for its visual qualities; while their early gigs saw them dressed pretty casually in T-shirts, jeans, sweater vests, and other fashions of the day, by the early 1970s at least one or two of the musicians were wearing nothing that could be considered street clothes.

Jimmy Page

Page came dressed in a black florally embroidered shirt, left unbuttoned to expose a bare chest, for some shows of Zeppelin's 1972 North American tour; before then he'd worn a sweater with his "ZoSo" sigil woven across the chest for English concerts in '71. Though he never sang and rarely spoke to the audience, his wizardly clothes identified him as Zeppelin's star performer as much as his guitar playing. For 1975's American gigs his shirt and pants were stitched with stars and other glittery insignia, until he debuted his spectacular dragon suit at Earl's Court, a black shirt and pants decorated with matching Chinese-style dragon designs as well as horoscope symbols and a small "ZoSo" patch. By the 1977 US tour he was alternating this outfit with a contrasting white one, embroidered with a winding poppy motif over the pants and top. For one Chicago show on April 10 of that year he made a dubious statement with breeches, jackboots, sunglasses and an SS officer's cap, an ensemble he never tried again but which was widely documented and secured Zeppelin's image as blitzkrieg rock 'n' rollers. At Knebworth in '79 he was back to a vaguely New Wave dress shirt, and for Europe in '80 he was trying a punk look, with the sleeves of his T-shirt rolled up to expose his scrawny biceps.

Robert Plant

Plant never donned anything as outrageous as Page's stage wear, but open shirts or blazers, hippie necklaces, bracelets and belt buckles, and tight, low-cut bell-bottomed jeans were his trademark look from 1971 on. Many fans, indeed, would probably cite Plant's bare chest as one of Led Zeppelin's most valuable recurring spectacles. At New York's Madison Square Garden and San Francisco's Kezar Stadium in 1973 his blouse—more of a vest with puffy sleeves—looks several sizes too small. In 1975 he donned a sort of waist-length kimono with cherry designs. By the 1980 European shows he too was trying to keep up with a return to T-shirts and jeans.

John Paul Jones

The low-key Jones seldom stood out sartorially on stage, the one exception being an outfit seen at some Earl's Court dates in 1975, a truly strange jacket hung with heart-shaped ornaments and other doodads.

John Bonham

Bonham usually came dressed for hard physical work at his drum stool—T-shirts or tank tops, and sometimes a headband to keep his hair out of his face—but in America in '75 his costume rivaled Page's in its distinctiveness: a derby hat and a white jumper and pants, taken from the surreal droog styles of Stanley Kubrick's 1971 film *A Clockwork Orange*. This was appropriate, since Bonham was known to have a taste for ultra-violence when far from home.

The Led Zeppelin gear came from a variety of sources. Some of the articles were likely altered, or sewn from scratch, by friends or wives of the band members. "We came across some people that made these fantastic clothes," John Paul Jones told biographer Mick Wall. "They were very enthusiastic and we bought all this stuff." Fans and groupies may have donated individual pieces in hopes of seeing them worn in concert. Others have speculated the outfits came from the hip London boutique called Granny Takes a Trip, a Chelsea outlet that designed and sold freaky footwear and velvet suits to rock stars like Keith Richards, Rod Stewart, and Mick Jagger. (According to Victor Bockris's biography of Richards, Granny Takes a Trip was also the scene of a drug connection for high-profile musicians, including Jimmy Page.) Page himself has said his dragon suit was made by a Los Angeles seamstress named Coco, possibly a reference to his friend David Bowie's longtime personal assistant, Corinne "Coco" Schwab.

Despite All Your Losing: Led Zeppelin and Hostile or Indifferent Audiences

Considering that any contemporary performances by Led Zeppelin or its remaining members are received with respect more appropriate to a

Led Zeppelin encountered some unfriendly audiences in the US South during the fraught era of the late 1960s. *Courtesy of Robert Rodriguez*

presidential address or the Second Coming of Christ, during their active life the band was not always given the same response. Before they made their reputation they had to work hard to win over skeptical or suspicious crowds, and they sometimes dealt with the common hassles of booing, thrown objects, and general disruption among the attendees. "It was around the time of student unrest in America and obviously the police didn't help," John Paul Jones said to Dave Lewis. "It became a bit of a two-way fight. . . . Robert was always making gestures for calm."

Robert Plant himself has recalled that the first times "Stairway to Heaven" was played, "you could often see people settling down to have forty winks," and the lengthy drum, guitar, and keyboard solos of the '75 and '77 tours saw good business at the concession stands; even late in their career concertgoers could be crass or inattentive to their music. At their best Led Zeppelin were powerful enough to shut down any hecklers, and most of their gigs ended with encores and ovations, but still, there were numerous occasions when the group was in jeopardy of going over like, well, a lead zeppelin.

Bristol Boxing Club, Bristol, England, October 26, 1968

A surly crowd of rural types was in no mood for long-haired electric blues this night, tossing beer glasses and other artillery at opening act the Deviants and continuing the onslaught when the band formerly known as the New Yardbirds came on. A similar response was said to have greeted the band in Exeter, England, a few weeks later.

HemisFair Arena, San Antonio, Texas, August 15, 1969

Led Zeppelin's first ventures into the US's South and Southwest landed them in the thick of a nation rent by social unrest and generational division. Page, Plant, Jones, and Bonham all had *very* long hair at the time, longer than most of the kids in their audiences', making them big targets for local yahoos. Both onstage and off in San Antonio, the group was jeered at by resentful Texan onlookers. Jimmy Page has spoken of other dates in Memphis and Nashville where he and the other players were openly threatened by police and other officials. "It was seriously redneck back then," he said in a *Guitar World* interview. "I mean, what are you gonna do? You aren't going to go against an armed police force that wants to bust your ass."

Konserthuset, Göteborg, Sweden, February 25, 1970

Page reportedly spat on an audience member who tried to accompany his "White Summer / Black Mountain Side" solo with a harmonica outburst.

Olympia Stadium, Detroit, August 28, 1970

On this tour Led Zeppelin tried to perform their acoustic material from the upcoming *Led Zeppelin III* album, but the public address and amplification systems of the era were simply not up to the job, particularly in large halls like Olympia. Fans grew bored and impatient for the hard rock they expected here, shouting "Louder," until Page got up and walked off. "[A]fter two songs' worth of squirming fans and frustrated musicians," ran a Detroit review, "Zep had to plug back in to rescue the evening, which they did with a vengeance."

Vigorelli Velodrome, Milan, July 5, 1971

Led Zeppelin's lone show in Italy ended in a full-fledged riot between fans and police and military units. The melee was impending anyway and wasn't the band's fault, but they did have to escape the venue after only twenty minutes while tear gas and clashing bodies filled the stadium. Zeppelin vowed never to play the country again, and never did.

Stadthalle, Vienna, June 26, 1980

The senseless lobbing of firecrackers and other small incendiaries from the floor has been the bane of rock 'n' roll performers for years, and Led Zeppelin were on the receiving end of their share. "Whoever threw that firecracker deserves to be jerked off by an elephant," Robert Plant scolded San Diego attendees in 1973, and explained Jimmy Page's withdrawal from a Chicago stage in '77, "Jimmy has a bout of gastroenteritis which isn't helped by the firecrackers, so we're gonna take a five-minute break." (The band never came back on and the cancellation was probably due more to Page's drug issues.) "We're used to rowdy crowds," Plant said in a '77 interview, "but this is crazy. . . . We've all been hit by [Frisbees] onstage, but the crackers are much worse; scares the hell out of us." In Vienna, on the band's final tour, a firecracker struck Page while he was playing "White Summer" and he again walked off; crowds were often out of hand for these European shows. Zeppelin only resumed playing Vienna after an announcement chastised the anonymous idiot.

It Might Get Loud: Led Zeppelin's Concert Sound

Though the band never made it to the *Guinness Book of Records* like the Who, nearly all reports of Zeppelin's audio impact when performing attest to their high volume. Many of their first witnesses were put off by the noise and said so. *New Musical Express* writer Keith Altham told manager Peter Grant the group "were far too loud" for the English club where he saw them in 1968, as did the manager of London's Marquee, John Gee: "I thought they were overpoweringly loud for the size of the Marquee." "When Led Zeppelin came on and played at a good ten times the volume of everyone else, the audience nearly freaked completely," was *Disc* magazine's report from the Pop Proms concert of 1969. North American critics could be just as deafened. According to reporter Carl Bernstein (later of Watergate fame) in 1969, Led Zeppelin "rarely came in below the maximum decibel level, resulting in a sound that—no matter how good the fingerwork—became boring." Other unsuspecting listeners were left covering their ears.

Many acts from around the same period—the Jimi Hendrix Experience, Cream, Creedence Clearwater Revival, the MC5, and the notoriously ear-splitting Blue Cheer—had found that sheer decibels could become part of the concert experience for young fans who wanted an all-out bodily assault. Before, British Invaders like the Beatles and the Rolling Stones were dismayed by the thousands of "screamagers" who drowned out the equipment that had served them in small theaters and clubs but which couldn't cut through ten or fifteen thousand pairs of healthy lungs. The next generation of rockers was determined not to be subject to the same indignity: When you came to see *them*, you'd better listen. No excitable high school student could outperform Eric Clapton's Marshall stacks or Keith Moon at maximum overdrive.

Led Zeppelin came armed with John Bonham's God-given might and the high wattage of their speakers, and in some smaller indoor venues they might have had more amplification than the space required. Today many experienced concertgoers cite bands other than Zeppelin as the loudest they've ever heard—AC/DC, Motörhead, Kiss, Metallica—but a typical Led Zeppelin show in a 20,000-seat arena probably came in at a good 100 db. By comparison, the Who's record-setting volume was 126 db. A jet aircraft at close range will register at about 130 db, a level likely to cause hearing damage to the unprotected ear. To this date, no surviving members of Led Zeppelin have complained of auditory injury and, as of 2010, Robert Plant and John Paul Jones are still appearing live and loud.

Sometimes I'd Roll It: Led Zeppelin as Jam Band

The members of Led Zeppelin have often talked of their spontaneity in live settings. "Nothing was ever static," Jimmy Page told *Guitar World* in 2005. "Other bands at the time weren't able to do that; they didn't have

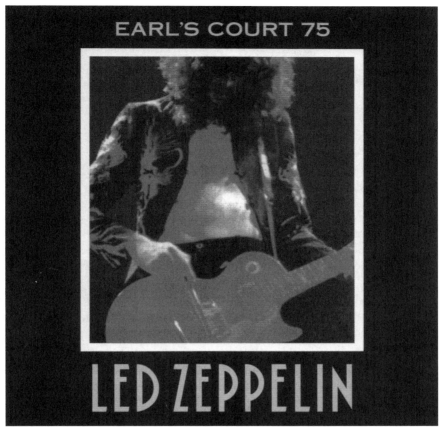

Page's mystical dragon suit was one of his most striking stage costumes.

Courtesy of Duane Roy

the musical freedom and the freedom of collective spirit." "Anybody could take anything anywhere, and we'd all follow," agreed John Paul Jones in *Bass Player.* Many audience recordings from the Zeppelin years capture bits and pieces from dozens of unlikely songs in their sets: Buffalo Springfield's "For What It's Worth," John Lee Hooker's "Boogie Chillun," the Kingsmen's "Louie Louie," Roy Orbison's "Only the Lonely," plus lyrical or musical quotations from Johann Sebastian Bach, Francis Scott Key, James Brown, Bob Marley, Isaac Hayes, and the Woody Woodpecker theme. Medleys of Elvis Presley hits dropped into the middle of "Whole Lotta Love" were standard.

That said, Led Zeppelin were not really doing the same thing as the Grateful Dead or later groups like Phish. The Dead and their followers took improvisation to far-flung realms of drug-inspired possibility, while Zeppelin usually stuck to a regular complement of their own songs that were *occasionally* embellished with unexpected departures but which then returned to the original rendition. Jam bands are also known for their cross-country caravans of listeners who accompany them to each performance, where they are free to make their own recordings of the night's set and trade them with other aficionados. Led Zeppelin and its management often heavily suppressed any unauthorized taping from the stands, and rather than playing outdoor fairs and tribal gatherings mostly stayed inside halls, arenas, and stadiums. Zeppelin did some outstanding jams, but they were not a jam band as the term is today understood.

Walking Side by Side: Led Zeppelin's Road Crew

Immortalized in rock songs from Jackson Browne's "Running on Empty" to Motörhead's pummeling "We Are the Road Crew," the gangs of chauffeurs, stagehands, bodyguards, and other assistants who did the heavy lifting of concert productions are nearly as legendary as the artists who employed them. They lived the rock 'n' roll life without the rock 'n' roll money and the rock 'n' roll fame—seeing the world, partying hard, wrecking hotels, and hearing hundreds of gigs from close range. As the shows got bigger in the mid-1970s, the number of people required to set up and take down equipment and basically ensure the smooth running of touring operations grew. Led Zeppelin's road crew began as just a single manager and his helper, but by the end of the band's life had expanded to a complex hierarchy of technical and personal support. Some were friends and confidantes of the musicians, themselves with performing experience, while others were strictly lighting and sound staffers who had little contact with the stars (like those from the Dallas-based Showco team). Most worked for a variety of other acts, working year-round and internationally while their different bosses took time off. A full roster of the Led Zeppelin's road crew would name the following.

- Richard Cole: Road manager, 1969–79
- Jerry Ritz: Road manager, Scandinavia, 1968
- Phil Carlo: Road manager, 1980
- Billy Francis: Assistant road manager, 1980
- Kenny Pickett: Road crew, 1968–69
- Clive Coulson: Road crew
- Henry "The Horse" Smith: Road crew
- Sandy MacGregor: Road crew

- Patsy Collins: Road crew
- John "Magnet" Ward: Road crew
- Joe "Jammer" Wright: Road crew (guitar tech)
- Ray Thomas: Road crew (guitar tech)
- Tim Marten: Road crew (guitar tech, 1977–80)
- Brian Condliffe: Road crew (bass and keyboards tech, 1975–79)
- Andy Ledbetter: Road crew (bass and keyboards tech, 1980)
- Mick Hinton: Road crew (drum tech, 1971–75)
- Benji LeFevre: Road crew (vocal technician)
- Jeff Ocheltree: Road crew (drum tech, 1977)
- Ian "Iggy" Knight: Road crew (lighting director, 1975–77)
- Dennis Sheehan: Robert Plant's personal assistant / driver
- Rick Hobbs: Jimmy Page's personal assistant / driver
- Dave Northover: John Paul Jones's personal assistant / driver
- Rex King: John Bonham's personal assistant / driver
- B. J. Schiller: Road crew (sound mixing, 1977)
- Brian Gallivan: Tour assistant (1977)
- Mitchell Fox: Tour assistant (1977)
- John "Biffo" Bindon: Tour assistant (1977)
- Dr. Larry Badgely: Tour doctor (1977)
- Dave Moulder: Tour assistant (1980)
- Steve Jander: Laser technician (1977–79)
- Donnie Kretzschmar: Showco engineer (1972–79)
- Rusty Brutsche: Showco engineer (1972–79)
- Kirby Wyatt: Showco engineer (1972–79)
- Gary Carnes: Showco engineer (1977)
- Allen Branton: Showco engineer (1972–79)
- Joe Crowley: Showco engineer (1972–79)
- Tom Littrell: Showco engineer (1979)
- Larry Sizemore: Showco engineer (1979)
- Martin Bushnell: Eidophor projectionist (1979)
- Alan Hogarth: Eidophor projectionist (1979)

Took My Chances on a Big Jet Plane: The *Starship* and *Caesar's Chariot*

In 1973, 1975, and 1977, Led Zeppelin traveled to their concert dates around America by private airliner. These lavishly appointed aircraft—the *Starship* for '73 and '75, and *Caesar's Chariot* in '77—were leased by the band for speed, comfort, and privacy. "Yes, it was extravagant, pretentious, and snobbish," admitted Richard Cole, who'd clinched the $30,000 deal to get the aircraft in 1973, in *Stairway to Heaven*. "But the band felt they had earned it."

Led Zeppelin had gone to and from gigs by van and commercial flight in their initial runs, and by their 1972 North American tour they used a small Dassault Falcon eight-seat corporate jet. This was deemed unsatisfactory, so next year they became the first customers of a rental owned by teen star Bobby Sherman and manager Ward Sylvester, formerly a producer of the *Monkees* TV show. For $600,000, Sherman and Sylvester had acquired a Boeing 720B four-engine jet (serial N7201U), first flown in 1960 as part of the United Airlines fleet, and refinished its interior to suit the lifestyles of high-flying celebrity clientele: shag carpeting, armchairs for up to forty, a bar, an organ, a fake fireplace, a back bedroom with a shower stall, and a video library with the Marx Brothers and *Deep Throat* on hand to entertain. "It was the Bolivian diamond flake of airplanes," Zeppelin photographer Neal Preston was quoted. Though the master chamber was supposedly off-limits at key moments of the flight, Jimmy Page repaired there with female company when he chose. "I did like the idea of a horizontal takeoff," he later said.

In time, other *Starship* riders included a Who's Who of music industry figures from the decade: Peter Frampton, the Rolling Stones, Alice Cooper, Elton John, Olivia Newton-John, and Deep Purple ("The *Starship* was a great place to join the mile-high club," reported Purple drummer Ian Paice). Flown by qualified pilots and staffed by professional hostesses named Suzee Carnel and "Bianca," the *Starship* represented the ultimate in comfort and convenience for its famous occupants. It eased transport between concerts, as the players and their entourage could bypass the hassle of waiting rooms and baggage checks; kept intrusive fans, unwanted bystanders, and nosy police out of range; and permitted the artists to commute back and forth from hub bases rather than move to new hotels every night. In April 1977, when the *Starship* was unavailable, a similar Boeing 720-022 named *Caesar's Chariot* (N7224U) was subleased by Led Zeppelin from a Las Vegas firm named Desert Palace, and operated by Sinclair Air Services. The two

Boeing designs were essentially customized updates of the basic Boeing 707 airframe, a machine first flown in 1954.

Symbolic of the rock lifestyle in all its decadent and cushioned entitlement, the *Starship* and *Caesar's Chariot* also had a utilitarian function as loss leaders. Their operating expenses came to over $2,500 per flight hour, but the planes amounted to an aerial advertisement for their passengers' success and prestige. Other acts had flown by private plane—borne by a Lockheed Electra L-188A propeller-driven liner, nicknamed the *Lapping Tongue*, the Rolling Stones undertook a 1972 North American tour that overshadowed Led Zeppelin's—but Zeppelin upped the ante with the *Starship.* Featured in *The Song Remains the Same* as police escorts whisked the band in and out of American cities, the private airplane only added to the allure of mysterious, powerful performers who floated down to earth for a little while before winging skyward once more on a jet-set stairway to heaven. Both the *Starship* and *Caesar's Chariot* were eventually sold by their owners as rising gas prices and a changing music business reduced their viability. The airplanes were decommissioned in 1982 and 1987, respectively, and broken up for parts.

14

How the West Was Won

Led Zeppelin Around the World

Going to California: Zeppelin's Most Important Sites Worldwide

he most faithful and intrepid Led Zeppelin fans might design their own pilgrimage tour, where the required stops would be as follows.

39 Gerrard Street, Soho, London

The group's first formal rehearsals took place in a small room at this address (now said to be a restaurant) circa August 19, 1968. By all accounts it went very well and they decided to keep at it.

Bron-yr-Aur Cottage, Outside Machynlleth, Wales

Jimmy Page and Robert Plant together made two 1970 visits to this ramshackle country home where Plant had holidayed as a boy. The first, in May, cemented their personal friendship after a nonstop round of transatlantic and transcontinental touring; it also yielded material for *Led Zeppelin III*, such as "Friends," "That's the Way," and "Bron-y-Aur Stomp," as well as "Bron-yr-Aur" and "Poor Tom," shelved until *Physical Graffiti* and *Coda*, respectively. Page's first child, Scarlet, was also conceived there with his then-partner Charlotte Martin. A second visit in October–November also heard the inception of work destined for *Led Zeppelin IV, Houses of the Holy*, and *Physical Graffiti*, including "Going to California," "The Rover," "Down by the Seaside," "Over the Hills and Far Away," and the immortal "Stairway to Heaven." Isolated, without electricity, and nestled in the mystical Cambrian Mountains, Bron-yr-Aur helped Led Zeppelin diversify their repertoire from hard psychedelic blues to the unplugged light and shade that made them special. The home is now a private residence and visitors are asked to be considerate.

The Boleskine House, Off B852, Foyers, Scotland

Jimmy Page's Scottish retreat from 1970 to its sale in the early 1990s, the Boleskine House is chiefly remembered for its connection to the guitarist's spiritual inspiration, Aleister Crowley. The Boleskine House is neither a mansion nor a castle but, in Crowley's words, "a long, low building" over-looking Foyers Bay on the southeast side of Loch Ness. Built of stone in the late 1700s, it contains five bedrooms, three bathrooms, plus dining, draw-ing, and family rooms, and is situated on forty-seven acres of land. Page's "Hermit" sequence for *The Song Remains the Same* was filmed there, and the residence is often assumed by fans and fanatics to be where he practiced his own magic rituals; he and others discussed the house's strange history of suicides and insanity among residents and the unexplained sounds heard within. Page told William S. Burroughs that the Boleskine House "has very good vibes for anyone who is relaxed and receptive," and also expressed his belief that Loch Ness was indeed home to a mysterious monster.

Crowley owned the Boleskine House from 1899 to 1913 but only lived there between worldwide travels, and Page himself reported in 1976 that "I bought Crowley's house to go up and write in. The thing is I just never get up that way. Friends live there now." The remote location and spooky background of the dwelling have imbued it with an aura perhaps inflated beyond its place in Jimmy Page's career. No other members of Led Zeppelin ever visited the Boleskine House, and it has since been a bed-and-breakfast establishment and is now a private residence.

Earl's Court, Warwick Road, London

This 19,000-seat arena was the scene of Led Zeppelin's English farewell before commencing a period of tax exile—the five shows played to sellout audiences at in May 1975 are considered among the band's best. As of 2010 there were plans to raze the site and replace it with housing or retail developments, though not until after the 2012 London Olympics.

N1 Road Between Tan-Tan and Guelmim, Morocco

At the foot of Africa's Atlas Mountains near the country's southern border along the Sahara Desert, a long drive between these two small cities in 1973 provided Robert Plant with the lyrical impetus for Led Zeppelin's great

"Kashmir." "It was a single-track road which cut neatly through the desert," Plant told Cameron Crowe in 1990. "Two miles to the east and west were ridges of sand rock. It basically looked like you were driving down a channel, this dilapidated road, and there was seemingly no end to it."

Raglan Castle, Castle Road, Raglan, Monmouthshire, Wales

Scene of Robert Plant's fantasy sequence in *The Song Remains the Same*, this dilapidated medieval structure in southeast Wales was a good setting in which to depict the haunted visions of "The Rain Song."

Madison Square Garden, 4 Pennsylvania Ave., New York City

Led Zeppelin performed a total of fifteen shows at the legendary MSG between 1970 and 1977, among them the ones filmed in July 1973 for *The Song Remains the Same* and a staggering six full houses (the venue seats 20,000) in June 1977. The enthusiastic receptions won here in the 1970s proved the band to be one of the most popular in the nation. The Atlantic Records fortieth-anniversary show was also staged here, where a reunited Led Zeppelin (with Jason Bonham on drums) played several songs.

The Continental Hyatt House, 8401 Sunset Boulevard, Los Angeles

When touring southern California in the early 1970s, Led Zeppelin and their entourage set up camp at this twelve-story hotel, inaugurated in 1956 as Gene Autry's Continental. Management at the lodgings, which were not as ritzy as others in LA, made a point of tolerating the eccentric and sometimes destructive antics of celebrity guests, especially rock stars. Zeppelin's stays at the "Riot House" were marked by defenestrated furniture and appliances, wild parties that took up several floors, and countless groupie overnights. Civilians can still check in to the Hyatt House (now called the Andaz West Hollywood) but are advised to leave the motorcycles outside.

The Rainbow Bar & Grill, 9015 Sunset Boulevard, Los Angeles

Just down from the Riot House was the preferred drinking establishment of Led Zeppelin and other rock 'n' rollers when in Los Angeles. Many female hearts were won and broken at the Rainbow by members of the band, and John Bonham and various Zeppelin bodyguards committed some more physical breakages there. The open decadence of the Sunset scene stood in contrast to the more idealistic spirit of nearby Laurel Canyon and its singing-songwriting inhabitants. Visitors can still eat and drink at the Rainbow, and music and movie stars can still be spotted there; adorned with rock 'n' roll memorabilia, the walls, unfortunately, cannot talk.

Rodney Bingenheimer's English Disco, 7561 Sunset Boulevard, Los Angeles

Rodney Bingenheimer was a Los Angeles fan and hustler who established his own party scene here in 1972, which, like the Rainbow, also catered to visiting English rock royalty, not least of all Led Zeppelin. Jimmy Page joked about groupie feuds fought at Rodney's, "down to razor blade sandwiches," although his visibility there made him uncomfortable—"I mean you walk in and the next thing you know there are cameras everywhere and you're ducking under the bar to get away." One legend has it that Zeppelin paid Bingenheimer's medical bills after sex and partying combined to give him a heart attack in his thirties. Though its proprietor is the subject of a documentary film, *The Mayor of Sunset Strip*, Bingenheimer's Disco is no longer.

The Equinox Bookshop, 4 Holland Street, Kensington, London

From 1974 to 1979 Jimmy Page owned this small bookstore and printing house, which specialized in rare editions of occult volumes. As a business venture it was unsuccessful and although Page managed to build his personal library through the store, he clearly had no interest in maintaining it; after disagreements with the manager it was shut down. A tea shop stands on the location today.

The Mill House, Mill Lane, Clewer, England

Jimmy Page purchased this Berkshire home in 1980 for £900,000 from actor Michael Caine and owned it until the early 2000s. A spacious Georgian structure with a working water mill on the Thames River, it's significant in Led Zeppelin lore in that it was the scene of John Bonham's demise.

To Sing a Song for You: Bootleg Led Zeppelin

Despite manager Peter Grant's sometimes brutal crackdowns on audience members who were spotted with microphones or recording gear, probably more than half of Led Zeppelin's concerts between 1968 and 1980 were put on someone's tape machine. Before the Internet, a well-stocked record store or comprehensive mail-order house could provide fans with a good bootleg selection from many artists: professionally manufactured vinyl discs of live shows which captured a "real" performance that would otherwise be edited or overdubbed if released officially. All the major acts of the time, including the Beatles, the Rolling Stones, and Bob Dylan, were bootlegged. Today more than one thousand different bootleg editions of Led Zeppelin are available on CD, and many more single songs or fragments thereof can be heard online.

Among the most popular of the original bootleg records were *Live on Blueberry Hill* (Inglewood Forum in Los Angeles, September 4, 1970), *In the Light* (BBC radio performances, 1969–70), *Going to California* (Berkeley Community Theater, September 14, 1971), *Bonzo's Birthday Party* (Inglewood Forum, May 31, 1973), *The Destroyer* (Richfield Coliseum, Cleveland, April 27, 1977), and *Listen to This Eddie* (Inglewood Forum, June 1977). Other bootlegs were named for the location in which they originated, like *Ottawa Sunshine, Brussels Affair, Royal Albert Hall, Second City Showdown,* and *Return to Paris Theatre.* As might be imagined, the quality of these varies, sourced as they are from concertgoers with professional (reel-to-reel) or amateur (cassette) tape machines, situated at different points in the venue. On many bootlegs the sound of the nearby attendees cheering, clapping, or talking comes in and out between or during songs.

Another category of bootlegs that document Led Zeppelin is sound-board recordings of concerts—unmixed tapes fed directly from the in-house mixing deck that controlled the sound levels. These are generally better than the random captures of music from the floor or the bleachers. *Flying Circus*, taken from a Madison Square Garden show on February 12, 1975, is one of many Zeppelin examples. A third and legally most serious species of bootleg consists of master tapes stolen from studios where the artists made their official records; again, Led Zeppelin has had their work lifted this way, with alternate or discarded takes of material from *Led Zeppelin III* and *IV, Physical Graffiti,* and other authorized albums turning up to intrigue collectors (e.g., *1970 Studio Works, Studio Daze*). Sometimes the recordings find the band in a playful mood, enjoying themselves going over Chuck Berry's "Reelin' and Rockin'," Johnny Kidd and the Pirates' "Shakin' All Over," and other favorites of their youth (e.g., *The Cover Versions, The Lost Sessions Volume 5*).

Because of the illicit nature of all bootlegs—at least all Led Zeppelin bootlegs—many small or clandestine labels have issued differing versions of the same material, and buyers do not have the assurance of high reproduction standards and accurate notes that would come with sanctioned music. The members of Led Zeppelin have expressed mixed views of bootlegging. Revenues generated by the audience recordings have never put much of a dent in their own earnings as performers and songwriters, and in some cases the musicians have been pleased to hear themselves in their prime as fans did. On the other hand, the private or studio tapes that found their way into the bootleggers' markets are definitely taboo. "If it's someone with a microphone at a gig, that's one thing," Jimmy Page defined in 1998.

Magical Sound Boogie and *Long Beach Arena Complete* are just two of many Zeppelin bootlegs.   *Courtesy of Duane Roy*

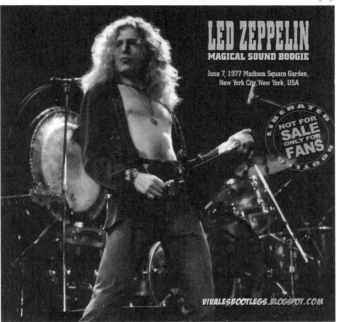

"They paid for a ticket, so it's fair game. But things that are stolen out of the studio—works in progress, rehearsal tapes, and things like that—are quite another. I'm totally against that. It's theft. It's like someone stealing your personal journal and printing it." Some of the Led Zeppelin studio and soundboard takes sold and traded are known to have been taken from Page's Mill House home in the 1980s: "[W]e did record a lot of shows, but many of the board tapes were stolen from me. . . . All that stuff, along with the recordings of our rehearsals, were stolen and have surfaced as bootlegs, and it's a drag. . . . Someone who was pretending to be a friend stole the tapes." In 2007 Page testified at the trial of a Scottish bootlegger who had produced and sold CDs and DVDs from Zeppelin performances and sound checks. "The legitimate part is where fans trade music, but once you start packaging up and you do not know what you are getting, you are breaking the rules legally and morally," he said under oath. "There are some of these recordings where it is just a whirring and you cannot hear the music."

Given the volume of what is freely available on the Internet, as well as preemptive Led Zeppelin releases such as *Coda*, *BBC Sessions*, *How the West Was Won* and the *Led Zeppelin* DVD, the contemporary reception for the pirated tracks of the group has likely dwindled to a small number of extreme specialists. For those interested, however, there is definitely an extensive body of live and studio music from Led Zeppelin that gives a dimension to their art not heard anywhere else.

How Many More Times: Zeppelin's Most- and Least-Performed Music

Over some five hundred–plus concerts a complete run of the songs the quartet played has been carefully assembled from audience recordings, reviews, printed set lists, and other data. Numbers frequently included were early warhorses like "Dazed and Confused" (210 performances), "Whole Lotta Love" (198 performances), and "Moby Dick" (158 performances). A mandatory "Stairway to Heaven" was played at every Zeppelin concert since before its record was released, amounting to 193 performances from 1971 to 1980, while "Since I've Been Loving You" figured in 191 shows, "Rock and Roll" in 166, and "Out On the Tiles" (either in its entirety or as an intro) in 163 gigs. The long, improvised passages of "Dazed and Confused" incorporated Gustav Holst's "Mars: The Bringer of War" in many versions (165 performances).

A few Led Zeppelin tunes were very rarely played live, or only played in part ("The Rover," "When the Levee Breaks," "Good Times Bad Times," "The Wanton Song") or never played live at all ("Custard Pie," "Houses of the Holy," "Night Flight," "Royal Orleans," "Tea for One," and some others). "Wearing and Tearing" was first played live when Jimmy Page made a guest appearance at Robert Plant's Knebworth gig in 1990, and "For Your Life" was not performed by the band until their 2007 O2 reunion.

The Dark Side of the Globe: Led Zeppelin's Following in the Non-English-Speaking World

Though the band originated in Britain, sang songs in English, and concentrated their concert events in the United Kingdom and the United States, they won fans all over the globe. Led Zeppelin received strong reactions to their shows in Japan, West Germany, and Holland, and they made their debut as the New Yardbirds in the Scandinavian lands of Denmark and Sweden. Subsidiaries of Atlantic Records released singles from their albums in Japan, Italy ("Muchismo Amor" b/w "Ruptura de Comunicaciones"), the Spanish world ("Sobra Las Colinas y Muy Lejos," "El Emigrante"), Germany ("Whole Lotta Love" reached number one there), Thailand, Sweden, the Netherlands, and elsewhere. The 1990s tours of the reunited Jimmy Page and Robert Plant, playing mostly Led Zeppelin material, traveled to big shows in the previously virgin territories of Brazil, Chile, Argentina, Mexico,

A rare Turkish edition of *Led Zeppelin II*.   *Courtesy of Robert Rodriguez*

Led Zeppelin's international popularity extended as far afield as Japan.
Courtesy of Robert Rodriguez

Croatia, Hungary, Poland, Romania, Bulgaria, Spain, the Czech Republic, Liechtenstein, and Turkey.

Many Americans, however, would be surprised to find that Zeppelin was less popular in Europe, Asia, and South America than in their own country. The United States provided by far the act's largest and most responsive audience, whereas other nations showed more interest in worldwide figures like Elton John, Pink Floyd, Abba, Queen, the Beatles, and homegrown talent. Rock outfits like Deep Purple and Cheap Trick became "big in Japan" even as they lagged behind Zeppelin in Britain or America. Well over half of Led Zeppelin's performances took place in the US, a deliberate strategy that corresponded with the home base of their record label, the intentions of their manager Peter Grant, and the country's network of supportive radio stations, concert promoters, and youth publications. Rock 'n' roll began in the States, and Led Zeppelin was nothing if not a rock 'n' roll group. The Englishness that made them seem remote and exotic in Pittsburgh and Minneapolis was less striking in Paris and Munich. Gigs in continental Europe were sometimes considered warm-ups for later North American shows (where some of the punters would have been US servicemen or their families), and an evaluation of Zeppelin's total record sales reveals that a disproportionate quantity of product was purchased in America. While Led Zeppelin is rightly thought of as an international phenomenon, their fame and influence is only moderate outside the Anglophone nations, is impressive but not dominant in Britain, and is greatest in the USA.

I Know Where That Jive Is At: Led Zeppelin's Following Among African Americans

While the band clearly drew on black blues influences like Robert Johnson, Howlin' Wolf, and Willie Dixon, and had a knack for funk rhythms rare in their genre, any cross-section of Led Zeppelin's concertgoers and record buyers would indicate that the majority of them were white people. Judging by photos of their audiences in the 1970s, "The Ocean" that Robert Plant sang to was mostly monochromatic. The same divide probably obtains with most stars of pop music, whose fan bases generally break down along racial lines; perhaps the most notable exception in rock 'n' roll would be Jimi Hendrix, who, to his own discomfort, was accepted by a bigger white audience than black and was once called "a psychedelic Uncle Tom" by white critic Robert Christgau.

Individual black musicians have certainly appreciated and adapted Led Zeppelin's music for themselves. Lenny Kravitz, Vernon Reid of Living Color, and Prince have all spoken of their youthful admiration for Zeppelin and their absorption of guitar-based heavy rock into their own work, and Zeppelin's drums and riffs have been sampled by many hip-hop acts of all backgrounds. To the extent that music is or should be color-blind and that anyone can enjoy any song by anyone else, African-American listeners have gotten into Led Zeppelin as much as whites have gotten into Billie Holiday, Funkadelic, the Supremes, Run-DMC, or Michael Jackson.

But black writer and critic Marcus Reeves, author of *Somebody Scream!: Rap Music's Rise to Prominence in the Aftershock of Black Power*, comments that "I know of no hard-core African-American Zep fans. . . . I knew a couple of Black folks, when I was in high school, who really dug the music and possessed an LZ LP or two. I even had my favorites like 'Levee Break' [*sic*] and 'Whole Lotta Love.' And for a few weeks in Eleventh grade I borrowed a classmate's Zep tape as an alternative to the hip-hop I was listening to. I also heard about hip-hop's connection to the band, but mostly from old school DJ's who played 'Levee' because of that big-ass beat in the beginning. Other than that, I never knew of any Black devotees who were fans like the white ones."

1974

February 23: Newspaper heiress Patty Hearst abducted.

May 4: Duke Ellington dies, age 75.

May: Led Zeppelin launches Swan Song label.

May–September: Led Zeppelin record *Physical Graffiti*.

June 17: IRA bomb explodes in UK Parliament.

August 8: Richard Nixon resigns US presidency.

September 8: Daredevil Evel Knievel attempts Snake River Canyon jump.

October 29: Muhammad Ali defeats George Foreman for heavyweight boxing title.

Movies: *Chinatown*; *The Godfather II*; *The Towering Inferno*.

Music: Eric Clapton, *461 Ocean Boulevard*; Lynryd Skynyrd, *Second Helping*; Joni Mitchell, *Court and Spark*; Steely Dan, "Rikki Don't Lose That Number"; Bachman-Turner Overdrive, "You Ain't Seen Nothin' Yet"; Barbara Streisand, "The Way We Were."

15

If You Can Clarify, Please Do

Led Zeppelin's Lurid Lifestyle

What the Little Fish Are Sayin': The Shark Incident

Even people who don't know much about rock stars' lives or rock stars' music have heard of this one: something about Led Zeppelin, a hotel room, a groupie, and a fish. The Shark Incident is a more-or-less authenticated episode of the band's tour exploits that has been widely cited as a pinnacle (or nadir) of rock 'n' roll debauchery. It's the punch line to many Led Zeppelin jokes, and the premise behind unauthorized T-shirts promoting the "Led Zeppelin Fishing Academy." Soon after it occurred, Frank Zappa commemorated it in a song, "Mud Shark," performed as part of the Mothers of Invention's live concept album *Fillmore East—June 1971*, and in 2000 it was named by *Spin* magazine as the Number One Sleaziest Moment in Rock. The honor is not as richly deserved as it seems.

The scenario is one in which the one most crucial participant—the groupie—has never come forward, so its pertinent details have been pieced together from several sources. Most accounts put the date of the Shark Incident at July 28, 1969, the day after Led Zeppelin had played at the Seattle Pop Festival at Woodinville, Washington's Gold Creek Park (the Doors, the Byrds, the Guess Who, the Flying Burrito Brothers, Spirit, Chuck Berry, and Bo Diddley also appeared), although they had also performed at Seattle's Green Lake Aqua Theater in May of the same year, and later at the Paramount Theater in October. The important point is that during an early tour of America the band and its retinue were staying at Seattle's Edgewater Inn on Puget Sound, a lodging where the guest suites overlooked the sea and it was possible to fish directly from windows on the lower floors.

Another significant factor in the Shark Incident is that this was a time before Led Zeppelin were the chart-topping, high-flying superstars of 1975 or 1977. In 1969 they were just one of many rock groups traveling North America in a ragtag crew of musicians, roadies, label or radio associates, friends, and local hangers-on. Indiscriminate or unorthodox sex among these groups and their admirers was common. Few fans could have named every member of the bands or distinguished between onstage performers, road managers, and buddies from other acts, and this is how the Shark Incident has been tied to the world-famous Led Zeppelin rather than the less-renowned Vanilla Fudge. At the Edgewater after the Pop Festival, an all-night party of performers, their attendants, and young women extended into the next day, and some of the fish (allegedly small mud sharks or red snappers, no more than three feet long) caught by John Bonham and Zeppelin tour manager Richard Cole had accumulated in the closet of the room they shared. Others hanging around included Jimmy Page, Robert Plant, and singer-keyboardist Mark Stein and drummer Carmine Appice of Vanilla Fudge (who'd also been billed at the Seattle Pop Festival), though on the periphery rather than at the center of the action.

At some point during the day's festivities one of the women—she's been named as a Jackie from San Francisco, but no one has confirmed it—may have mentioned bondage, and at any rate she disrobed and sprawled on a bed, whereupon Cole grabbed a fish and introduced it into her nether orifices. She may or may not have been tied to the bed, and Bonham, Cole, or the Fudge's Stein and Appice may or may not have also had conventional sex with her. Most versions of the story (including his own in *Hammer of the Gods* and *Stairway to Heaven*) place Cole as the ringleader. All those involved were either drunk or stoned or both. A supposed bystander, photographer Michael Zagaris, recalled for *Spin* that there were also live partridges in the room, and that as well as the Edgewater catch there were fish entrails from a Seattle market tossed into the mix. "Everybody was just going along with it," he was quoted. "They were pretending they were bored. When weird shit is happening, you don't want to be the guy who says, 'What the fuck is going on?'"

Aside from being some obviously very weird shit, the Shark Incident is notable for its factual fuzziness. Apparently Mark Stein filmed it with a Super 8 movie camera, but even with today's online depositories of embarrassing sex videos and amateur exposés, no footage has ever been shown in public. Pressed for explicit descriptions, Stein, Appice, and Cole have all either dodged the questions or embellished the tale ("That girl must have come twenty times," Cole has boasted), while Plant has shrugged it off by referring to the Zappa song and Page has never acknowledged it. The common threads of the differing accounts are that a) some kind of small saltwater marine life was used as a sexual device on a female, b) this

was in full view of several spectators, c) everyone was intoxicated, d) it happened quickly and was over as soon as it began, and e) it was a consensual
act. Kinky? Indeed. Sleazy? Sure. Worth all the fuss over forty years later?
Probably not.

It may be that even stranger things happened in Led Zeppelin's private
quarters when no one but those directly involved were watching, but the
relative openness of the Shark Incident has established its notoriety. It took
place in broad daylight, in the middle of a party, with bemused onlookers
standing around. There's also a possibility that other acts from the same
era got up to comparable backstage orgies yet never scored any number one
albums or wrote several all-time rock anthems, and so never had their own
"incidents" publicized. From today's viewpoint, the relevant issues are that
the groupie was not forced or coerced into something she obviously didn't
want to do, and that at the time it was repeated among the band's circle
as an amusing story but was otherwise no big deal. In hindsight it became
more and more outrageous, but in July 1969 it was business (or pleasure)
as usual for young entertainers and liberated women. Reported in several
biographies and circulated as a classic anecdote of sex, drugs, and rock
'n' roll, the Shark Incident has been magnified out of all proportion to its
drunken, spontaneous, and very brief essentials.

Wearing and Tearing: Led Zeppelin Versus Hotel Rooms

The wanton vandalism of their tour accommodations by rock stars is one of
the clichés of the genre. Songs like Lynryd Skynyrd's "What's Your Name,"
Grand Funk Railroad's "We're an American Band," the Rolling Stones'
"Memory Motel," Creedence Clearwater Revival's "Travelin' Band," and
others all allude to the stir-crazy sensation of endless road work that could
only be alleviated by pointless yet somehow satisfying destruction of their
lodgings. Members of the Led Zeppelin entourage were as guilty as anyone
of this—but no more guilty than anyone, either.

There are many stories of Zeppelin hotel and backstage havoc wrought
all over the world. In 1969 John Bonham splattered two cans of baked beans
over Richard Cole and a girl he was bedding in Los Angeles's Chateau
Marmont. Bonham laid waste to a Vancouver dressing room in 1970.
Bonham once flooded John Paul Jones's Hawaiian hotel room with a fire
hose. Bonham and Cole took samurai swords to Jones's suite in the Tokyo
Hilton in 1971. Bonham smashed up three dressing room trailers in Nantes,
France, in 1973. Jones's New Orleans hotel room caught fire after he passed
out with a lit joint and a transvestite friend. "When I woke up it was full
of firemen," the bassist admitted. The same year, Cole brought a Honda

motorcycle to the band's floor of LA's Continental Hyatt House, where it was raced up and down the hallways at all hours; Bonham is said to have done the same with a Harley-Davidson. In 1977 journalist Steven Rosen noticed that the phone in Page's Chicago suite had been forcibly pulled out of the wall. The ringing disturbed him, Page said. On the '77 tour, the aftermath of a Zeppelin–Bad Company hotel party in Fort Worth, Texas, was compared to a nuclear holocaust. At numerous stops, drinks, clothes, water balloons, furniture, and appliances were tossed out of hotel windows.

For all these confirmed instances—there are more apocryphal ones where the culprits and location are unnamed—the surviving members of Led Zeppelin have shrugged them off as wildly exaggerated or merely routine. Even while the quartet was still functioning, they dismissed the mayhem as something they outgrew after their first few circuits of North America. "Look, we were young then, but we're not like that anymore," Robert Plant explained to publicist Danny Goldberg no later than 1973. A few years on he looked back on those days as a lost era. "There was good fun to be had, you know, it's just that in those days there were more people to have good fun with than there are now. . . . People were genuinely welcoming us to the country and we started out on a path of positive enjoyment. Throwing eggs from floor to floor and really silly water battles that a nineteen-year-old boy should have."

"Sitting in this hotel for a week is no picnic," said Page to Cameron Crowe during the Zeppelin US tour of 1975. "That's when the road fever starts and that's when the breakages begin." "On the surface it seems moronic," pointed out publicist B. P. Fallon, "but it has to do with the pent-up energies after a gig. One minute you're ruling the world, and the next, if the girls haven't arrived yet, you're in a hotel room alone." "If it was fun you joined in, if it wasn't you didn't," Jones recalled for Dave Lewis in 1997. "But that sort of stuff got a bit tedious after a while. . . . I just avoided it because I disliked all that violence stuff. I know Robert never liked it. . . . In fact, Robert and I used to go out walking a lot to try and get a daytime existence." Plant himself has been particularly forthright about the matter. "Yeah, there were wild times, without having to go into the names of the recipients or the makes of televisions that went out the window," he told *Rolling Stone* in 1988. "I don't deny it. A lot I can't remember, unless someone brings it up to me. . . . I can remember a stream of carpenters walking into a room as we were checking out. We'd be going out one way, and they'd be going in the other way, with a sign, 'Closed for Remodeling,' being put on the door. It's kind of embarrassing."

Two qualifiers apply to these eventual admissions. One is that anywhere young men gather to let off steam after work, plenty of alcohol gets consumed and the parties usually turn boisterous; sometimes somebody gets hurt or something gets broken. All the personalities involved have spoken of the heavy boozing of Led Zeppelin's first frantic, economy-class treks around Britain, Europe, or North America, and the "I can't remember" line is not an excuse but an honest testimony of being blotto every night. The second factor to remember is that Zeppelin traveled with a road crew who were also males in their twenties, also doing heavy physical labor far from home. The four musicians in the act could cause trouble on their own, but add to them a complement of low-paid, anonymous chauffeurs, riggers, and bodyguards with less to lose (and fewer willing women to distract them) and the potential for destruction was multiplied many times.

Again, the hotel-wrecking reputation was hardly unique to Led Zeppelin, any more than the sense of psychological dislocation that inspired it. Guitar hero Randy Rhoads, who accompanied the solo Ozzy Osbourne on his first albums in the early 1980s, confided to a friend what life in a popular touring rock 'n' roll show was really like: "It was really grueling and . . . there's a lot of weird people out there," he said. AC/DC's Angus Young, meanwhile, explained that the song "Highway to Hell" wasn't a homage to Satan but a record of existence on the arena circuit. "All we'd done is describe what it's like to be on the road for four years. When you're sleeping with the lead singer's socks two inches from your nose, believe me, that's pretty close to hell." "Imagine being revered on stage for that golden hour and then rushed back to your hotel cell," remembered veteran keyboardist and producer Al Kooper. "You felt like some talented animal in a zoo on temporary leave." The trails of devastation left by Led Zeppelin were blazed by many other performers.

"It's strange how success and room-wrecking seem to go together," said Bev Bevan of the Electric Light Orchestra. "For years we never destroyed so much as a toothbrush holder and it was only when we were playing every night to sellout crowds of anything from 20,000 to 72,000 did we get in trouble." The ELO drummer articulated one of the hidden reasons for all the defenestrated TV sets: They could get away with it. For bands who toured as extensively as Led Zeppelin, the damage incurred by hotels was no more than overhead, paid for out of the nightly concert revenues. Like any professionals who travel for a living, the musicians and their crews became acclimatized to the itinerant lifestyle, becoming as well versed as any salesmen or executives in the amenities and regulations of various hotel chains (Keith Richards once commented that his toddler son Marlon's first words were "room service"). The hotels, for their part, were insured and prepared for occasional disruption from guests, and depraved rock 'n' rollers were actually getting more of their money's worth than the quiet family of vacationers on the next floor. Knowing that any liabilities were soon covered and that they would be five hundred miles away the next day anyway, the musicians and their friends had few qualms about messy pranks, lost furnishings, or flooded hallways. One familiar story has Zeppelin manager Peter Grant handing a five-hundred-dollar bill to a hotel clerk who'd expressed a longing to toss a television out a window himself. "Here, have one on us," he laughed.

"I think there was an enormous amount of adrenaline that we were building up onstage," Jimmy Page reflected in 2003, "and we were just taking it offstage into the land of mondo bizarro. You know, you'd have someone riding a motorcycle through a hotel hall, but that would only be exciting for fifteen minutes, then it would be next and next and next." He also told biographer Mick Wall, "There's a climax at the end of each show and the audience goes away, but you're still buzzing and you don't really come down. . . . There are different ways of releasing that surplus adrenaline. You can smash up hotel rooms—it can get to that state." "It was like a traveling football team, really," said Robert Plant. "But without being too facetious, that's what people *wanted*. Once the seed had been sown, it would be terrible if it was just once a week. It had to be all the time." Together the singer and guitarist point to the main drivers of Led Zeppelin's barbarism—releasing tensions and living up to expectations—that, many years after all the damages have been repaired, seem understandable if not quite forgivable. Yes, Led Zeppelin smashed up hotel rooms. They were young rock stars going from town to town and country to country: Why wouldn't they?

Dazed and Confused: Led Zeppelin and Drugs

Heavy substance abuse is another stereotype of rock 'n' roll, and one that well applied to Led Zeppelin. Several of their songs make lyrical nods to cannabis ("Going to California," "Misty Mountain Hop," "Over the Hills and Far Away"), cocaine ("For Your Life"), or unspecified dependency ("Nobody's Fault but Mine"). There are plainly druggy motifs to the abstract effects of "Dazed and Confused" and "Whole Lotta Love," while Robert Plant ad-libs a suspiciously energized *"I can't stop talkin'. . . . I can't stop talkin'. . . . I can't stop talkin'"* over the coda of "Trampled Underfoot." In concert Plant made occasional spoken acknowledgments of pot smoking, and even explicated the "pocket full of gold" as "Acapulco Gold!" in "Over the Hills and Far Away"; he introduced "Misty Mountain Hop" with "This is a song about . . . walking in the park and you've got a packet of cigarette papers in your pocket and you've got some good stuff to put in it. . . ." At other shows the singer prefaced "Dazed and Confused" with a story of the band's genesis (". . . as soon as we lit up our first joint, this was it") and later spoke of how the group would deliver fans ". . . a little taste of that, a little toot of this, a little blow of that . . ."

Most reports identify Jimmy Page as a heroin user from about 1975 to 1983, while John Bonham and Richard Cole are also implicated, and Peter Grant developed a severe cocaine habit that lasted from his Zeppelin years into the mid-1980s. Plant and John Paul Jones were, by the making of *In Through the Out Door* in 1978, "relatively clean" (Jones's words), although both had taken marijuana and cocaine throughout the band's career. Jones himself looks pretty glazed in photos taken at 1970's Bath Festival, and Plant is seen puffing a joint as he walks offstage in *The Song Remains the Same.* The nineteen-year-old Plant was photographed leading a small pro-pot rally in his native Birmingham in 1967, and Page blamed a stoned camera crew for inadequate footage of their 1973 Madison Square Garden gigs: "Everyone was stoned at the time, but at least we did *our* job." Richard Cole told Peter Grant's biographer Chris Welch of a main reason for the band's declining morale after 1975: "Well, basically everyone was doing coke," he said. In Cole's own *Stairway to Heaven* he wrote that Page admitted to him that he was "hooked" on heroin, and Eric Clapton, who performed with Page

Neal Preston's classic 1975 backstage shot has come to symbolize Led Zeppelin's rock 'n' roll indulgence.

Courtesy of Duane Roy

during the Action Research into Multiple Sclerosis (ARMS) shows of 1983, hinted that Page was "very frail" for the gigs. Other accounts state that members of Zeppelin were taking cocaine on their tour planes, just before hitting the stage (which would partly explain their athletic running and jumping around during "Rock and Roll"), and, in the case of John Bonham in 1977, right at his drums while performing.

Drug use and drug addiction have been an occupational hazard of pop musicians for decades. Louis Armstrong, Gene Krupa, Charlie Parker, Billie Holiday, Chet Baker, Charles Mingus, Stan Getz, Ray Charles, Johnny Cash, and Hank Williams are just some of the artists known to have taken, been arrested for possession of, or died from illicit drugs, before rock music ever existed. The rock revolution of the 1960s and '70s came along with—and was abetted by—the rising drug culture of the same period, during which virtually all the performers were occasional or regular takers of one kind of drug or another: marijuana, amphetamines, barbiturates, LSD, mescaline, cocaine, or heroin. The musicians in Led Zeppelin were as swept up in the drug tide as anyone, and paid the price for it.

"I can't speak for the others," Jimmy Page said in 2003, "but for me drugs were an integral part of the whole thing, right from the beginning, right to the end." Though others have reported that Page was fairly abstentious in the first years of Zeppelin, by the end of the 1970s he was visibly and audibly affected by his intakes. "It was totally reckless behavior. I mean, it's great that I'm still here to have a laugh about it, but it was totally irresponsible. I could've died and left a lot of people I love. I've seen so many casualties." To journalist Lisa Robinson he defended, "We were doing three-and-a-half-hour concerts. . . . By the end of that, you come offstage and you're not going back to the hotel to have a cup of cocoa. Of course it was crazy; of course it was a mad life." To rock writer Nick Kent he again made no apologies for his drugging: "I don't regret it at all because when we needed to be really focused, I was really focused." In 1988 Robert Plant told an interviewer, "The real lame thing is, and it has to be said, the singer went to bed. Not necessarily alone. But there was a lot to be said for trying to keep the voice in shape. . . . At a certain point, I had to say, 'Oh, the sun's coming up, I'm off.'" (In spite of such conscientiousness, many fans say Plant's voice did wear down over his Zeppelin career.) "I guess we all got messed up," the vocalist clarified in 2005. "The drugs did kick in and out. . . . And I had enough of what I'd had enough of quite early in the adventure." In 1997 John Paul Jones said to Dave Lewis that by 1977, "Every band was doing the drugs thing at the time—we didn't really worry much about it—but by then it was getting a bit out of control." Later the bassist admitted regret over John Bonham's death by alcoholic misadventure: "You always think, 'If

I'd have done this or that it might not have happened,' but, in those days, people knew less about helping other people with those kinds of problems. And besides, none of us were in much of a position to tell other people how to live their lives. We all partied all the time." In another interview Jones confessed, "I did more drugs than I care to remember—I just did it quietly." "We never had anybody checking us up saying, 'Oh, man, the blood test shows you're really low in minerals," said Plant, and Peter Grant conceded in a 1993 conversation, again with Dave Lewis, that by 1976, "Jimmy's health was suffering. There were definite drug problems with one or two people, including myself."

Clinically, Page, Bonham, Cole, and Grant may not have been as addicted as any street junkie. There are no accounts of them using needles for their fixes, and as rich musicians and well-connected managers they never had to steal or prostitute themselves to score. Bonham's death was not caused by an overdose, while both Page and Cole have survived into ostensibly healthy middle age, and Grant managed to trim his massive weight and clean his own system of all but tobacco before dying of a heart attack at age sixty. Led Zeppelin's contemporaries in rock 'n' roll, like the members of the Grateful Dead, Aerosmith, Black Sabbath, and Eric Clapton, David Bowie, and Keith Richards, were just as far if not further gone into their own drug excesses, let alone the confirmed drug casualties of Jim Morrison, Janis Joplin, Gram Parsons, Sid Vicious, and so many others. Pink Floyd, the Rolling Stones, and even the Beatles were far more identified by the public with drug use by members and fans than were Led Zeppelin, and individual performers Bob Marley, Lou Reed, Keith Moon, Neil Young, and Iggy Pop were far more open consumers of marijuana, speed, or heroin (Reed even mimed shooting up onstage). And what of the obvious drug connotations of Doobie Brothers, Cheech and Chong, and the New Riders of the Purple Sage's "Panama Red"?

Because of their huge record sales and cash intakes from concerts, the Led Zeppelin organization could *afford* ample supplies of premium substances, especially cocaine, but in the lucrative rock world of the 1970s such indulgence was a status symbol; any habits formed were unforeseen side effects of silver-spoon luxury. Similar problems took hold with high flyers the Eagles and Fleetwood Mac, whose platinum albums guaranteed steady rewards of quality blow. But spending lots of money on drugs—promoter Bill Graham recalled facilitating a $25,000 cash advance that went straight to Zeppelin's connection—does not necessarily imply physiological need. The members of Led Zeppelin took copious amounts of drugs and were in different ways debilitated by them, but they were not the only such offenders in their scene, nor even the worst.

You Need Coolin': Led Zeppelin's Arrest Records

Long-haired rowdies bringing rock music to the provincial towns of Europe and North America, crossing borders and surrounded by hordes of hopped-up kids, were in the 1960s and '70s (and today, for that matter) prize targets for police. The security around Led Zeppelin, however, was such that they rarely fell afoul of law enforcement and, unlike other acts, were not constantly dodging charges and court appearances. Ironically, the most serious trouble any of them got into was because of rather than despite the personal protection they brought with them.

The Zeppelin touring party often met with police hassles in their early years, particularly with John Bonham's and Richard Cole's drunken revelry, but they usually managed to avoid formal charges or permanent convictions. Bonham slept off a 1969 Kansas City binge in a jail cell; the same year he had to be restrained from taking off his clothes onstage during a Long Island jam with the Jeff Beck Group, before the cops stepped in. In the American south the band encountered vigilante and police resistance to their hippie looks and foreign origins, though no actual busts went down. A 1970 post-gig limo ride from Ottawa to Montreal had Page and John Paul Jones racing into Quebec to keep their joints out of the jurisdiction of the Ontario Provincial Police. In Perth, Australia, in 1972 the band's hotel was raided by the local law, but miraculously no drugs were found and the entourage made it out of the country. On the same antipodean tour Zeppelin were refused entry into Singapore due to their long hair. Jones has also told a story of being arrested for jaywalking in Los Angeles sometime in the 1970s and paying a $25 fine when he couldn't produce a passport (the police had never heard of Led Zeppelin). In France in 1973 most of the act, including Bonham, Jimmy Page, and Robert Plant, along with most of the road crew, were tossed into jail overnight for hotel and vehicular destruction. No arrests were made following the theft of the band's cash deposit from New York's Drake hotel in 1973, but Peter Grant was charged with assault for smashing an inquisitive reporter's camera after the robbery. In Monte Carlo in 1976, Bonham, Richard Cole, and roadie Mick Hinton were arrested after a nightclub fracas but were released the next day.

All of these would have been no more than misdemeanors or minor drug offenses had they been followed through, but in 1977 Zeppelin's most damaging run-in with the law took place, the one that would affect the rest of their career. Since the Drake heist, their hired muscle had grown more aggressive and even paranoid. Backstage at Oakland Coliseum during a show on July 23, West Coast heavyweight Bill Graham's staff member Jim Matzorkis was confronted by John Bonham, Peter Grant, Richard Cole, and Zeppelin bodyguard John Bindon after sharply refusing Grant's son, Warren, a Led Zeppelin placard from a dressing room trailer door. Full of cocaine-induced anger and agitation, Bonham booted Matzorkis in the groin, then Cole kept Graham at bay as the equally wired Grant and Bindon laid into Matzorkis inside the trailer. The hapless employee was pummeled mercilessly by Grant and Bindon, and the Zeppelin drummer and his three henchmen were arrested, charged with assault, and released on bail the next day. Later, through lawyer Jeffrey Hoffman, the four pleaded nolo contendere (a legal sidestep requiring proof of neither guilt nor innocence), then paid out $50,000 and received suspended sentences.

This last condition hung over Bonham until his death: any further Led Zeppelin visits to the United States meant he would be subject to criminal prosecution should he have any more problems with the American police. His anxiety over such a prospect may have driven him to drink even more heavily than usual as the band began rehearsals for a subsequent US tour, which is what finally caused his expiry on September 25, 1980. In later decades charges of murder and other violent crimes would circulate around hip-hop artists and their posses, but in 1977 the Oakland bust was one of the first times a rock 'n' roll group was at the center of something much heavier than a bust for drug possession, indecency, public drunkenness, or other petty crime. It was the bitter culmination of Bonham's years of aggressive antics and the logical consequence of the coked-out arrogance that had infiltrated the Zeppelin operation. "I had to sing ['Stairway to Heaven'] in the shadow of the fact that the artillery we carried around with us was prowling around backstage with a hell of an attitude," Robert Plant remembered the Oakland debacle. As the Rolling Stones learned after hiring the Hells Angels as crowd control at the Altamont Speedway near San Francisco in 1969, private security teams can end up being more dangerous to their employers than the outsiders they are paid to fend off. After Led Zeppelin's disbandment following Bonham's fatal bender, Jimmy Page himself went through two British court cases after he was found with cocaine, but the guitarist was let off with a conditional discharge in 1982 and a fine in 1984; he was also caught smoking and "visibly intoxicated" aboard a commercial jet during the Page-Plant tour of 1995 and faced a $1,000 fine.

Other than these instances, though, the band and its associates were entirely upright, peaceable, law-abiding citizens.

16

Mama It Ain't No Sin

Led Zeppelin and Groupies

Mrs. Cool Rides Around: The Girls of Zeppelin

Casual relations between male musicians and female fans were the third component in the great triumvirate of sex, drugs, and rock 'n' roll that dominated Led Zeppelin's glory years. Throughout the Western world, the advent of the oral contraception pill, the women's liberation movement, the relaxation of divorce and abortion laws, and a general sense of enhanced personal freedoms among young people led to a generational shift in long-standing standards of courtship, marriage, and morality. The upshot of all this was a widespread increase in premarital liaisons that became known as the sexual revolution. While there had always been a licentiousness to show business based on the aphrodisiac effects of fame, money, and mobility, in the culture of rock music in the 1960s and '70s the opportunities grew exponentially. The members of Led Zeppelin took full advantage of them.

As were their drug-taking and hotel-wrecking reputations, though, the groupie-enjoying legends around the quartet have been stereotyped and embellished past their rather mundane actuality. Names of conquests more connected to other acts have been tied in with Zeppelin, and anomalies like the Shark Incident portrayed as regular occurrences. Almost every rock performer of the period was having casual sex with his fans; security teams and other gatekeepers were getting their fair share too. The difference with Led Zeppelin is that the band was enormously successful and their critical stature has risen since their disbandment, so their enthusiastic but not unusual partaking of carnal pleasures has become remade as a superlative to match their other professional accomplishments. "The record industry was fuelled by cocaine, sex, and music," B. P. Fallon asserted to Brad Tolinski in 2007. "That was the norm. Except in the world of Led Zeppelin, the norm was magnified a million times."

For rock 'n' rollers on the road, sex at every stop was a given. It was no-strings, almost anonymous, sometimes even cruelly cavalier. "You won't make much money," Ronnie Hawkins famously told the Hawks (later the Band) when he hired them as his backup. "But you'll get more pussy than Frank Sinatra." Rolling Stones bassist Bill Wyman is said to have reached a tally of partners that extended into four figures, while Jimi Hendrix looked on the plentiful women he and his friends encountered as just "Band-Aids." Reporter Bob Greene once overheard a member of Alice Cooper's tour party recounting his exploits from town to town: "Let's see, Nashville yes, Greensboro no—wait, Nashville yes, Greensboro no, Madison yes, Ann Arbor yes, Toledo, let me think, I'm trying to remember what my room looked like, Toledo I got blown, Toronto yes . . ." "There are times when [women] come around after something and you're after something, too, so you get it together and everybody's happy," recalled Country Joe McDonald of Country Joe and the Fish. "My personal record is five chicks at once," recounted Van Halen's David Lee Roth. Songs like Steppenwolf's "Hey Lawdy Mama," Lynyrd Skynyrd's "On the Hunt," Kiss's "Room Service," Styx's "Midnight Ride," Motörhead's "Jailbait," or the Stones' "Starfucker" (live versions of which name-dropped Jimmy Page) were documents of the Dionysian lives led by peripatetic musicians during the most fervid years of the sexual revolution. Led Zeppelin's own "Living Loving Maid (She's Just a Woman)," "Sick Again," "Royal Orleans," and "Hot Dog" offer more firsthand accounts.

Overlooked in the annals of these rock 'n' roll sexcapades is that the groupies of Zeppelin's day were no longer the small-town, starstruck bobby-soxers who'd swooned for Sinatra or Elvis Presley. They had designs of their own. Some of them were determined young women who'd come of age just when free love and guiltless affairs were being touted as healthy and natural outlets for a society too long repressed by the old constraints of marriage, fidelity, and propriety; others were affluent and sophisticated girls who had already been initiated into sex, drugs, and rock music before ever meeting any rock musician in the flesh. Several of the groupies linked to Led Zeppelin aspired to celebrity themselves, and parlayed their relationships into a Warholian fifteen minutes of fame. The women based in Los Angeles, where stars from all media were familiar figures in a city whose main industry manufactured them by the hundreds, were especially calculating in their pursuits of both publicity and rock 'n' roll performers. None of them, anywhere, were attracted to the men only for their great personalities, as if their eminence as professional entertainers was incidental. Jimmy Page himself was quoted as saying that groupies from the metropolises of New York and LA "make a religion out of how many pop stars they can fuck." As crass or as opportunistic as the men could be, the women were not much more innocent.

Still, though there are several tell-all accounts by ex-paramours of Page and other rockers, it says something about the anonymity of most groupies that there are not more memoirs titled "My Night of Love with Led Zeppelin." Outside of the big cities, the old dynamic still held: The band showed up for a concert, a few local hopefuls found their way backstage or to the hotel suite, and the next morning it was all over and mostly forgotten, certainly by the band. As Robert Plant recalled for *Rolling Stone*, "[S]ometimes I'll meet somebody in New York or whatever, and they go, 'Hey, do you remember Swingo's, in Cleveland, on such-and-such a night?' And I remember, uh, romps." Page asked that Pamela Miller allow him to "do things" throughout the smaller burgs of America after he left their Los Angeles love nest, since it got "so bloody boring" otherwise. Even in their dressing rooms during Bonham's "Moby Dick" drum solo, the other players might get a quick service from a lady with a backstage pass. "Those were the days of pure hedonism," the guitarist said in 2003. "LA in particular was like Sodom and Gomorrah. . . . You just ate it up and drank it down. Why not?" To the Englishmen, the abundance of *everything* in America shaped and distorted all other considerations. As Zeppelin protégé Michael Des Barres explained to author Michael Walker in the cultural history *Laurel Canyon: The Inside Story of Rock and Roll's Legendary Neighborhood*, "The young girls represented to me the absolute change of being in America, where after my whole life of living in this archaic, sort of regimented country where I could have been speaking Latin, I come to America and the sandwiches are this thick and the girls are this thin."

In hindsight, the sex—like so much else with Led Zeppelin—may have been overstated. For one thing, the musicians sometimes found it easier to cohabit with one lover over a single time frame, or when in a single location, rather than go to bed with a complete stranger night after night. Plant, John Paul Jones, and John Bonham were all married men with children when the group was formed, and Page was in a long-term relationship after 1970, which was sometimes enough for him to resist temptation. In other settings they contented themselves with sex shows (strippers or duo acts) rather than the real thing. Road manager Richard Cole and his team of roadies also screened many an applicant before they could get to the four players in the group, leading to tales of "Led Zeppelin sleaze" that involved no one from the actual Led Zeppelin, and friends like Roy Harper likewise benefited from what Plant called "some of the Led Zeppelin by-products, like the occasional blow job." "While we had a reputation as rampaging sexual vandals," Plant said in a 1985 interview, "the truth is that most of the time we were looking for nothing [more] at bedtime than a good paperback." Well, maybe. To *Rolling Stone* in 1990 he went into considerably more detail: "Yeah, that era, the whole thing of the GTOs . . . Yeah, shoving the Plaster Casters' cast of Jimi Hendrix's penis in one of the girls' assholes at some hotel in Detroit was . . . quite fun, actually. I don't remember who did it, but I remember I was in the hotel at the time. It was . . . free love." In 2005 he was more up-front, saying, "Well, it depended on whose room key you had. There was a certain amount of youthful splendor in the grass, but it was pretty overblown." In the 2004 documentary *The Mayor of the Sunset Strip* it's remarked that Plant felt the title subject, LA superfan Rodney Bingenheimer, was more popular with women than he was. "With the females, sexually it was a very liberal scenario—loose as a goose," said B. P. Fallon. "You could say a bit of third-leg boogie went on." Just a bit.

Today, a list of the most confirmed Led Zeppelin conquests can be assembled from interviews, autobiographies, and other reminiscences, some of these tales a bit too tall to be taken at face value. Prominent figures would include, but are by no means restricted to, the following.

Pamela Miller

Jimmy Page's main squeeze in Los Angeles for a few months in 1969 and sporadically thereafter, "Miss P" later described her adventures with various, um, members of Led Zeppelin, the Doors, the Stones, the Flying Burrito Brothers, the Who, and the Jimi Hendrix Experience in the entertaining book *I'm with the Band*. (Her chronicle also discusses heavy flirting with Robert Plant and mentions a girlfriend named Mickey who was, in her words, "hanging on" to John Paul Jones.) Miller, who now goes by the name Pamela Des Barres after her marriage to the aforementioned Michael, was one of Frank Zappa's Girls Together Outrageously, a clique of Angeleno girls the acerbic Zappa cultivated as a kind of performance art complement to the all-male musical acts that were springing up throughout southern California in the late 1960s. Previously interviewed for Stephen Davis's *Hammer of the Gods*, she mentioned in passing that Page used whips on her GTO friend Miss Cinderella (Cynthia Sue Wells): "She loved it!" Said to be the partial inspiration for the character Penny Lane in Cameron Crowe's 2000 film *Almost Famous*, Miss Pamela was a member of one of the first idealistic groupie groups (she disdained the term herself) who genuinely believed themselves to be muses of the musicians they slept with: In their own minds, the GTOs were devoted fans first, artistic inspirations second, and sexual playthings third. Perhaps the most famous groupie to survive the era of serial partners and widespread drug use, Pamela Des Barres has gone on to author several honest and funny volumes compiling her very intimate history of rock 'n' roll.

Lori Mattix

A Page girlfriend whose existence was unknown until the publication of *Hammer of the Gods* in 1985, the celebrated "Lori Lightning" was involved with the guitarist from 1972 to about 1974. Not one of the GTOs but a later arrival on the Sunset Strip, she was notorious for her age when swept up into the Zeppelin scene—only fourteen years old—and for emerging after the hippie conceits of the 1960s groupie pioneers had faded. Page's romantic interest in a juvenile was questionable, to say the least, but unlike other infamous cradle-robbers like actor Rob Lowe, singer R. Kelly, or filmmaker Roman Polanski, he never saw his dalliance blow up in his face: he met Lori's mother, took the girl to the Disneyland amusement park, and sternly made her smoke an entire pack of cigarettes when he caught her lighting up.

Today the adult mother Lori Mattix has spoken fondly of her days and nights with Page, and Cameron Crowe has remembered a wistful latter-day meeting with an unidentified rock star who asked him, "Have you seen Lori?" It was Lori Mattix who Page was playing to when performing the 1972 Led Zeppelin concerts in Los Angeles and Long Beach, captured in the powerhouse *How the West Was Won* CDs of 2003. For all her status as Zeppelin's underage angel, however, Lori had already been modeling and haunting the rock 'n' roll hangouts of Hollywood when she met Page, and was not shy about being photographed with famous musicians in glamorous poses. She has also claimed (in Pamela Des Barres's *Let's Spend the Night Together*) that it was none other than David Bowie who deflowered her, though the chronology is problematic, since her Page affair likely began in June of 1972 and Bowie's first tour of the US was not until later that year. In that book she also discusses subsequent hookups with Ron Wood and Keith Emerson of Emerson, Lake and Palmer. Though perhaps more mercenary than the older groupies whose place in the hearts and bedrooms of English guitar heroes she usurped, Lori Mattix and her teenage peers were still products of the same blissfully permissive time and place of southern California in the early 1970s.

Lynn Collins

Collins was named as a Page fling from his Yardbirds gigs in the US (a photograph of her appears in Richard Cole's *Stairway to Heaven*) who may have still been around when the Zeppelin rose.

Bebe Buell

A *Playboy* model and girlfriend of guitarist Todd Rundgren, she had a short-lived relationship with Jimmy Page in 1974. She too authored a book of her wild life in the 1970s, *Rebel Heart*, which also describes her romances with Elvis Costello, Mick Jagger, and Steve Tyler of Aerosmith, who fathered her child, actress Liv Tyler.

Audrey Hamilton

A Texan brunette linked to Robert Plant in 1977, Hamilton was reportedly the inspiration for Led Zeppelin's "Hot Dog."

Krissy Wood

Wife of Ron Wood of the Faces and the Rolling Stones, she was seen off and on with Jimmy Page in the later years of Led Zeppelin after some bizarre partner-swapping at Wood's English home in 1974 (*Ronnie*, Wood's 2007 autobiography, makes no mention of this). Though she also was said to have had relationships with Eric Clapton, George Harrison, and John Lennon, the English Krissy (nee Findlay) was not really a groupie in the conventional camp-following sense. Her participation in the sex-drugs-and-rock-'n'-roll lifestyle, which she shared with Page during his most strung-out years, took its toll. Divorced from Wood in 1978, she died in poverty at age fifty-seven in 2005.

Linda Aldretti

Named as an American girlfriend of John Bonham in Pamela Des Barres's *Rock Bottom*.

"Little Rock" Connie Hamzy

The infamous "Sweet Sweet Connie" of Grand Funk Railroad's "We're an American Band," and one of the most brazen groupies of her era, Connie Hamzy claimed affairs with both Jimmy Page in 1971 and John Bonham the next year; she later included Arkansas governor Bill Clinton as a notch on her bedpost. She was with Page and Bonham in New Orleans, as Led Zeppelin never performed in Little Rock. Unashamedly promiscuous when it came to visiting rock stars, her other brushes with greatness were Alice Cooper, Keith Moon, Joe Walsh, Carlos Santana, and (by her own estimate) a literal cast of thousands. As with many of the most active groupies, her encounters usually extended only as far as a perfunctory BJ rather than anything more personal. She recorded her accomplishments in a book, *Rock Groupie.*

Cynthia "Plaster Caster" Albritton

Albritton was a mainstay of the Plaster Casters sculptress group, a Chicago trio who made models of rock stars' erections, taken from life. For the sheer kinkiness of their method, the Plaster Casters received a lot of attention in their day (and recognition in an eponymous Kiss song), though a complete list of their trophies is difficult to come by. The Casters' most famous sample is of Jimi Hendrix, but at some point around 1969–70, it seems likely that one or more of the men in Led Zeppelin posed for them—see the previous "quite fun" comment by Robert Plant.

Sable Starr

Starr was a friend of Lori Mattix who elbowed her way into the Zeppelin circle in 1972, and a reported Page conquest. Born Sable Shields, she went on to longer relationships with Iggy Pop and Johnny Thunders of the New York Dolls, and died of a brain tumor in 2009 at age fifty-one.

Morgana Welch

Slightly older than Lori Mattix and Sable Starr, Morgana frequented the Rainbow Bar & Grill on the Sunset Strip and cited both Robert Plant and the less rakish John Paul Jones as encounters in the early 1970s. Apparently Roy Harper was even in on one session, with more than his hat off. Morgana and her friend Tyla (last name unknown) led the LA Queens, a set of teenage groupies who placed themselves at the center of wherever British rockers congregated—they are immortalized in Zeppelin's "Sick Again," from *Physical Graffiti.* Of the attraction between Led Zeppelin and their Angeleno groupies, "There was definitely a mutual thing happening," she told Michael Walker in *Laurel Canyon.* "The California-Girl-blond-hair-suntan was very appealing to them; conversely, the English-dark-hair-never-see-the-sunshine thing was very interesting to us." Morgana Welch's own book—were you surprised she has one?—is *Hollywood Diaries,* published in 2007.

Queenie

Known only by her nickname (some sources call her Lynn), Queenie hung out with Lori Mattix and Sable Starr in LA and reputedly was one of Jimmy

Page's groupies in 1972. Other of her special friends are said to have been David Bowie, Marc Bolan, Rod Stewart, and David Johansen of the New York Dolls.

Michele Overman

Overman was mentioned in Des Barres's *I'm with the Band* as a Robert Plant amour in 1969.

Catherine James

A Los Angeles friend of Jimmy Page who was jettisoned for Miss Pamela in 1969 but had occasional rendezvous with the guitarist later, she described her romance with Page and others, including Mick Jagger, Jackson Browne, and Denny Laine of the Moody Blues, in a 2007 book, *Dandelion: Memoir of a Free Spirit*. "The silhouette of Jimmy cloaked in shimmery velvet, moons and stars, and the haunting, abandoned sound of the bow gliding across his guitar were enchantingly sensual," she writes. As late as 1995, she accompanied Page to Led Zeppelin's induction in the Rock and Roll Hall of Fame.

Barbara the Butter Queen

The Butter Queen was known in the 1970s for her liberal use of the dairy product as a lubricant, and mentioned by Robert Plant at a Fort Worth, Texas, concert in '73. At least one meeting with someone in the Led Zeppelin party may be conjectured, although details are slippery.

1975

January–March: Led Zeppelin tour North America.

February 24: *Physical Graffiti* released.

April 30: Saigon falls to North Vietnamese troops.

May: Led Zeppelin performs five sold-out shows at Earl's Court, London.

June 13: Inflation in UK reaches 25 percent.

August 4: Robert Plant and family injured in car accident, Greece.

September 27: Parents of comatose Karen Ann Quinlan make court request to disconnect her respirator.

October 29: New York City in financial crisis.

November–December: Led Zeppelin record *Presence*, Munich.

Movies: *Jaws*; *One Flew over the Cuckoo's Nest*; *Nashville*.

Music: Aerosmith, *Toys in the Attic*; Queen, *A Night at the Opera*; Kiss, *Alive!*; Bruce Springsteen, *Born to Run*; Sweet, "Ballroom Blitz"; The Captain and Tennille, "Love Will Keep Us Together"; The Eagles, "One of These Nights."

17

Love Some Other Man Too

Led Zeppelin as Song Swipers

Made Me Mad Mad Mad: Zeppelin and Other People's Songs

Some of the accusations directed against Led Zeppelin are far-fetched calumnies whose origins, wherever they lie, are well removed from anything the band actually said or did, but the charges of plagiarism are not among them. These go back to the group's first two albums in 1969 and have multiplied ever after, fed both by full-time critics suspicious of the quartet's apparently instant fame and by more mature or more knowledgeable listeners recognizing other artists' lyrics or riffs in Zeppelin material. The "blues thievery" allegations have snowballed until, by today, a disturbing portion of the whole Led Zeppelin catalogue (including their most celebrated work) is said to have been copied without due courtesy from elsewhere. In courts of law and public opinion, the controversy continues.

Two schools of thought have arisen out of this. The lenient one maintains that any misappropriation of older music by the members of Led Zeppelin was either accidental or inadvertent: something that had always been done, as an accepted and necessary recourse, with long chains of performers commonly putting their personal stamp on traditional work until someone—the "songwriter"—got around to applying for copyright. Delving into an extensive library of folk and blues tunes and updating them with new electronic technology, Led Zeppelin only popularized pieces that had hitherto languished in obscurity, and then were blamed by elitist reviewers for their success. In this reading, Zeppelin was actually the victim of jealous, pedantic, and self-righteous outsiders with cynical, exclusionary agendas of their own.

The less sympathetic interpretation holds that the cynicism was Led Zeppelin's, and Jimmy Page's in particular. Young and handsome white

Englishmen, backed by a major record label and extremely protective management, knowingly lifted words, music, and ideas from middle-aged, vulnerable, or uncommercial acts that lacked the legal means to defend their own intellectual property. That some of the acts were African American added implications of racism to the thievery indictment. Thus Led Zeppelin were guilty of exploitation on two levels: First they ripped off poor black people's songs, then they took advantage of their middle-class white audience, feeding counterfeit sounds to a ripe market too crass and too gullible to distinguish them from the real thing.

The truth, as it so often does, lies somewhere in between. Many of Led Zeppelin's "steals" were discerned only in retrospect, as musicologists or the musicians themselves reexamined the sources of hit tunes and connected them with some lesser-known predecessor the singer or the instrumentalists had only vaguely recalled when laying the tracks down in the studio. "You only get caught when you're successful—that's the game," Robert Plant has shrugged. Sometimes the supposedly plagiarized song was itself a composite of several prior inspirations that had floated around decades before pop music or even recorded sound. In other instances a hurried ad lib was used in lieu of an eventual (it was hoped) substitution, as John Paul Jones explained to Susan Fast: "Songs attributed to all four members were usually worked out in the studio in the 'writing period' before recording began. . . . Robert would sing along lyrics from blues songs that he already knew in order to get a melody and/or phrasing and would rewrite them later (or not!)."

Both Jones and Jimmy Page have been quick to point to Plant as the main culprit in Zeppelin's perceived royalty robberies. "I always tried to bring something fresh to anything that I used," Page claimed to *Guitar World*'s Brad Tolinski. "I think in most cases you would never know what the original source would be. . . . So most of the comparisons rest on the lyrics." Page has added that it was only upon the 1997 release of the group's *BBC Sessions* (featuring Zeppelin radio performances from 1969 and 1971) that he discovered that their hard rock run-through of "The Girl I Love She Got Long Black Wavy Hair" took its title and lyrics from a song of some forty years before by Sleepy John Estes (1899–1977). Certainly Plant was prone to using his almost unconscious absorption of blues lines as convenient fodder for his vocals, as detected on "How Many More Times," "Custard Pie," "The Lemon Song," and others, with little regard for verbal coherence; "Misty Mountain Hop" even has a bit of "The Teddy Bears' Picnic" in it, and during the fadeout of "Gallows Pole" he throws in some of the Mother Goose rhyme "See-Saw, Margery Daw."

So far, this sounds innocent. For the youthful auditors and spectators of Led Zeppelin's first performances, Plant's Mississippi wails and moans would have only signified the band's genre as "electric blues"—punters could spot their general style but not any specific song from which they were taken. Plenty of other acts of the day were doing something similar, from Cream ("Crossroads"), Hendrix ("Red House"), the Rolling Stones ("Parachute Woman"), and the Beatles ("Yer Blues") through Canned Heat, the original Fleetwood Mac, and Johnny Winter. These offerings might have been clumsy imitations or coarsened reductions, but to fans they still sounded more authentic than most other pop songs of the decade. (The 2001 film *Ghost World* has a scene where a country blues nerd is reluctantly taken to see a "blues band," which turns out to be a group of glam white players screaming how they've been "picking cotton all day" between distorted electric guitar solos.) The difficulty emerges when numerous Zeppelin cuts appear to derive not from a distant tradition but recent or even contemporaneous music.

It may be helpful to point out that none of the Led Zeppelin musicians were considered songwriters when the band formed, and even the Page-Plant composing partnership only took shape after the two had been recording and touring together for some time. In the pop music scene of the late 1960s, independent players who both wrote and performed their own music were still a rarity, albeit an expanding one—for every Bob Dylan, Pete Townshend, Brian Wilson, or Lennon & McCartney, there were considerably more acts scoring with ready-made tunes by professional tunesmiths or putting their own twists on already popular songs. Robert Plant and John Bonham had paid their dues in what we would call cover bands, doing sets of hip but not overexposed American and British numbers from varying eras, and as session men Jimmy Page and John Paul Jones had been responsible for backing up or enhancing arrangements put before them more or less completed. Led Zeppelin was not initially designed to be a vehicle for original songs—much less deep poetry or provocative political messages—but original *sounds*, and with the hectic traveling and recording itineraries of their first thirty-six months their scramble for new material was a haphazard one.

More contentiously, Page and Peter Grant had built Zeppelin around the premise of financial and creative security: "I wanted artistic control in a vice grip," the guitarist was to remember. Both had seen other acts break down or lose out through sloppy management or careless production, and both were determined not to miss any potential revenues as had the Yardbirds or the one-hit wonders of Page's many session jobs. Attaching his or his bandmates' names to a Zeppelin publishing credit may have been no more than a precautionary move—a way to ensure that whatever royalties were earned from their records (whose huge long-term sales they would not have foreseen in '68 or '69) were sent to them first. "If something was derived from the blues, I tried to split the credit between band members," he has added. Robert Plant, for his part, has joked that Page met his objections to Led Zeppelin's authorship claims with a conspiratorial "Shut up and keep walking." Again, the motivation behind these seems to be not to deprive others of legitimate income but to assert a legal stake in a given Zeppelin song for the players who had changed or added to whatever framework previously existed.

Page's definition of "derived from the blues" is the touchy one. Most major Led Zeppelin plagiarism complaints, including the formally litigated ones, are over electric or country blues songs sourced as far back as four decades or as recently as a few years: "How Many More Times," "Whole Lotta Love," "The Lemon Song," "Bring It On Home," "Hats Off to (Roy) Harper," "Custard Pie," "In My Time of Dying," and "Nobody's Fault but Mine." Page, as producer of the records and filer of songwriting information, either thought the quartet was getting away with something, or was truly ignorant of the various literal and musical components that went into the Zeppelin cuts. Both scenarios are plausible. Jimmy Page was no sucker and known to be tight with his money—why would he give away royalties if no one caught on that he wasn't entitled to them? However, though Page and Plant were blues fans and collectors of blues records, they were perhaps too young and too busy to be very careful blues scholars. Armchair music historians may piece together the bases of the material well after the fact, but working musicians didn't have the luxury of transcribing every fragment of lyric or lick down to its inception. Note too that the searing covers of "You Shook Me" and "I Can't Quit You Baby," on Led Zeppelin's very first album, were from the beginning properly cited as Willie Dixon originals, an unlikely step by people bent on poaching every last dime from black blues singers.

This is at the heart of the Zeppelin plagiarism issue: What if the provenance of every disputed track *was* scrupulously referenced? What if "Black Mountain Side" was put down to Bert Jansch, and what if Bobby Parker's name was attached to "Moby Dick"? In that case, instead of complaining that the hyped pretty boys in Led Zeppelin shamelessly pilfered money from homely but more genuine artists, critics would say either that Zeppelin bastardized others' work while borrowing their folk or blues credibility with unjustified name-checks, or that Zeppelin foolishly gave away credits to musicians who were at most vaguely responsible for the final results. It was, and to some extent remains, a no-win situation. In reality, sometimes Page and his mates seemed to be operating out of ignorance or amnesia, other times out of haste, and other times out of sheer chutzpah, none of which make them very attractive but which are neither equally incriminating. The following analyses of the most hotly contested Led Zeppelin tracks—and a few of the least—may at last put the matter in perspective, with the band's initial composers' attribution listed alongside a final verdict.

Led Zeppelin

Right from the start the accusations flew. Arriving on the scene with an impressive advance from Atlantic Records and led by an ex-Yardbird with a cult following, Zeppelin soon saw their debut record—not just its individual songs but the entire album—dismissed as a mere duplicate of the Jeff Beck Group's *Truth*, released in October 1968. *Rolling Stone* magazine's review, from a time when its reviews were highly relevant to the youth market, called *Led Zeppelin* a "twin" of the earlier disc, and elsewhere the album has been dismissed as "recycled Jeff Beck Group." Beck himself recalled listening with barely controlled fury when Page played him an acetate of the new record: "This is a piss-take, it's got to be."

The Jeff Beck Group's 1968 album was said by critics to be the obvious model for *Led Zeppelin*.   *Author's Collection*

There are certainly parallels between the two LPs, and Page in all likelihood would have heard and studied Beck's when preparing his own. *Truth* is a premier album from a talented English electric blues guitarist, constructed to show off the artist's skills with extended solos and a crunching overall feel; Beck's own liner notes suggest, "This must be played at maximum volume whatever phonograph you use," and characterize his playing as "[p]robably the rudest sounds ever recorded, intended for listening to whilst angry or stoned." Sound familiar? The Jeff Beck Group was a four-piece lineup, with Rod Stewart on raspy vocals, Ron Wood on bass, and Mick Waller on drums; *Truth* consisted of heavy blues numbers ("Let Me Love You," "Blues Deluxe," "I Ain't Superstitious"), covers and standards rearranged for hard rock ("Morning Dew," "Ol' Man River"), and even a traditional acoustic guitar instrumental ("Greensleeves"). A standout is the slow blues "You Shook Me." On first listen, comparing those to *Led Zeppelin*'s "How Many More Times," "I Can't Quit You Baby," "Babe I'm Gonna Leave You," "Black Mountain Side," and, well, "You Shook Me" requires no great critical insight.

Led Zeppelin were of course playing the same styles of music as the Jeff Beck Group and loads of other late-'60s rock acts, with their drawn-out dirty blues, psychedelic guitar, howling vocals, and extended instrumental jams. Beck and Jimmy Page had been chums since their teen years, sharing a love for the rockabilly licks of James Burton and Cliff Gallup, and as young men in the Yardbirds they had been the star attractions of a popular touring and recording act. Both of them knew and worked with John Paul Jones, who even contributed keyboard to some of the Beck cuts. "If you've got things you enjoy, then you want to do them," Page said of his and Beck's musical correspondence. The *Truth*-versus–*Led Zeppelin* argument was perhaps a foreseeable conflict between two players of the same age and background with similar tastes and at the same points in their respective careers, responding to the same trends in pop music.

Their differences, though, are just as significant. Jimmy Page produced his record, while Beck's was overseen by the erstwhile Yardbirds director Mickie Most. *Led Zeppelin* benefits from what have been described as its "terraced dynamics" (jarring cuts and segues whereby each song comes in sharp contrast to those on either side of it), whereas *Truth* is more of a meandering selection of pieces harder to distinguish from one another. (And for what it's worth, *Truth*'s "Rock My Plimsoul," "Blues Deluxe," and "Let Me Love You" have been heard as unlawful rips of B. B. King's "Rock Me Baby" and "Gambler's Blues," and Buddy Guy's "Let Me Love You Baby," respectively.) Led Zeppelin was a self-contained act whose first collection required an outsider, tabla player Viram Jasani, for but a single cut, while the Jeff Beck Group brought in John Paul Jones, keyboardist Nicky Hopkins, and, on "Beck's Bolero," Jimmy Page himself. Ron Wood and Mick Waller were a good though unspectacular rhythm section, but John Bonham's opening fills on "Good Times Bad Times" announced the coming of one of the most influential rock drummers ever.

As much as anything, Led Zeppelin were a quartet to which each member was expected to contribute equally, yet the very name "Jeff Beck Group" implies that there was room for only one person at the top of the bill. Indeed, Beck went on to play with a variety of accompanists through-out the '70s, including Stewart, Wood, Waller, Hopkins, and later bassist Tim Bogert, drummers Aynsley Dunbar and Carmine Appice, and key-boardist Jan Hammer. For all his talent, Beck spread himself too thin as a bandleader, while Page shrewdly shared the spotlight with a consistent lineup of individuals who all blossomed in the next few years. *Truth* is a fine album with a sonic template recognizable in subsequent work by other artists, but *Led Zeppelin* represents that model concentrated, intensified, and perfected.

"Good Times Bad Times" (Page-Jones-Bonham)

Though the song is an original first sketched by John Paul Jones, the title of this hard-hitting leadoff is the same as a 1964 album cut by the Rolling Stones.

"Babe I'm Gonna Leave You" (Traditional, arranged by Jimmy Page)

The first of Zeppelin's great "light and shade" hybrids, whose later editions included "Ramble On," "Over the Hills and Far Away," "Ten Years Gone," and "Stairway to Heaven," "Babe I'm Gonna Leave You" was planned as one of the group's hallmark numbers from at least Page and Plant's first get-together in the summer of 1968. Page was intrigued by the idea of merging soft folk or pop songs into hard rock, perhaps thinking of the Beatles' "A Day in the Life," the Moody Blues' "Nights in White Satin," or Vanilla Fudge's outrageous take on the Supremes' "You Keep Me Hangin' On." The guitarist heard Joan Baez do the piece and rebuilt it around overdubbed acoustic and electric guitars, Plant's soaring vocals, and John Bonham's mighty drum work. More than ten years later, the American Anne Bredon (née Ann Loeb), possibly through one of her grown children, was made aware that one of the biggest rock 'n' roll acts in the world had done one of her songs on their premier album. By then the singer-songwriter was no longer active in the folk music scene, and in fact she is primarily remembered today for her convoluted connection to Led Zeppelin.

It turned out that Joan Baez had indirectly heard, through the coffee-house circuit, Bredon's "Babe I'm Gonna Leave You," and then performed it on her own 1962 album *Joan Baez in Concert*, assuming Bredon's tune to be a public-domain standard and citing it as such (Baez and Page, coincidentally, share a birthday). So Led Zeppelin's "Babe" of 1969 only repeated the "Traditional" credit first noted by Baez; subsequently both the Baez and Zeppelin track listings have been corrected to name Bredon as the composer or cocomposer of the new arrangement, and Bredon herself now earns royalties from the song. Many Zeppelin analysts have unquestioningly described "Babe I'm Gonna Leave You" as the group's version of "a traditional folk song," as unaware as Baez or Page that it was in fact written by a living performer in the middle of the twentieth century. In other places the obscure Bredon is misidentified as British folksinger Anne Briggs.

The confusion around "Babe I'm Gonna Leave You" underscores the glibness of the Zeppelin plagiarism accusations, if even a musician as respected for her ideals as Joan Baez could mistake a copyrighted work for a preindustrial archetype. Players and listeners of the US and British folk music movement of the 1950s and 60s were devoted to the notion of rustic realism, to music that belonged "to the people," rather than the commercial assembly lines of Tin Pan Alley. Occasionally, as in this case, they chose to believe that their songs were old ballads or spirituals rather than actually confirming it. In its plaintive minor chords and themes of rambling, seasons, and *"I can hear it callin' me,"* "Babe I'm Gonna Leave You" *does* sound like something from the 1800s, and it is heard on the Baez album alongside actual folk standards such as "Kumbaya" and "Streets of Laredo." Other old songs with similar moods include "I'm A-Leavin' Cheyenne," "The Girl I Left Behind," and "Oh, Babe, It Ain't No Lie." Though in retrospect it is easy to point out misstated authorship once a song is featured on a hit record, the matter is far less transparent in the active lives of gigging and recording musicians selecting an eclectic body of material.

"You Shook Me" (Willie Dixon)

Although the blues bassist and songwriter is rightly named as the author of this track—and later said it was one of the works he was "proudest to be associated with," alongside Foghat's recital of his "I Just Want to Make Love to You" and the Rolling Stones' rendering of "Little Red Rooster" —"You Shook Me" is not a note-for-note, word-for-word cover. Robert Plant can't resist sneaking in some of Robert Johnson's "Stones in My Passway," in the lines *"I have a bird that whistles / And I have a bird that sings . . ."* That few of Zeppelin's vociferous detractors have picked up on the addition implies that, to them, it's okay to "borrow" material from a venerable black performer if another one is getting the credit. Recent credits of the song add J. B. Lenoir's name to Dixon's.

"Dazed and Confused" (Jimmy Page)

Arguably the most egregious of Led Zeppelin's infringements, the climax of *Led Zeppelin*'s first side was a direct remake of American folk singer Jake Holmes's "Dazed and Confused," which the Yardbirds had seen performed in 1967. The Yardbirds put the number into their own final sets, designated

Legendary bluesman Robert Johnson's lyrics and music occasionally turned up in Zeppelin material.   *Author's Collection*

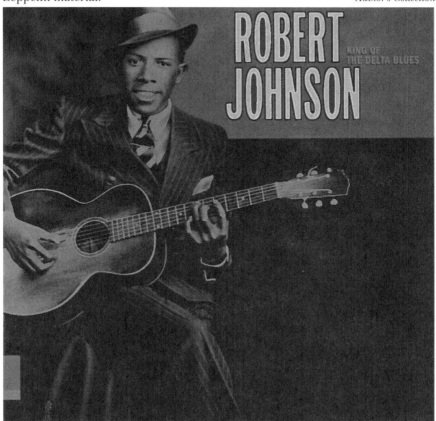

"I'm Confused," and by the time of its inclusion on the Zeppelin album it had reverted to "Dazed and Confused" but gained different lyrics, a bowed guitar solo from Jimmy Page, and then a fast passage that utilized the Yardbirds' old "Think About It" instrumental break. A regular part of the group's concerts for several years, it was, despite its new electrification, Gothic vocals, and special effects, still recognizably the Jake Holmes song.

If Page had kept the title but changed the music, or changed the title but kept the music, the steal would be less obvious and more tolerable, but Zeppelin's "Dazed and Confused" is the guitarist at his guiltiest. In later years he dodged the issue of Holmes's authorship ("What's he got, the riff or whatever?"), reasonably pointing to the hard rock makeover he gave it in 1968; it's true that, as a Led Zeppelin set piece, "Dazed and Confused" became longer and darker than anything Holmes had created. Holmes himself was first quoted as saying, "What the hell, let him have it," upon first learning of the grab, but told Zeppelin biographer Mick Wall in 2008, "I've written letters saying, 'Jesus, man, you don't have to give it all to me. Keep half! Keep two-thirds! Just give me credit for having originated it.'" Yet even Holmes admits that by now "Dazed and Confused" is so closely tied to Led Zeppelin and Jimmy Page that it has become more their song than his. Between Page's sonic elaboration and the audience's experience, through hundreds of live performances and millions of records sold, he is probably right. Still, for Page to take up as his own a song by a fellow artist—not a long-dead itinerant folk singer but someone working the same stages he was—ranks as a definite black mark on his career. As of June 2010, Jake Holmes had formally filed a lawsuit in a California court for his share of the song's royalties.

"Your Time Is Gonna Come" (Page-Jones)

Both the Zeppelin ballad and Ray Charles's "I Believe to My Soul" contain the lyric *"One of these days and it won't be long . . . Look for me and I'll be gone."* The rhymes are so obvious that the intersection may be a coincidence, but considering the rest of the evidence, and Jones's professed love of Charles's music, a suspicion lingers.

"Black Mountain Side (Jimmy Page)

A raga-like acoustic guitar solo (accompanied by Viram Jasani's tabla), this was the first indication of Led Zeppelin's great stylistic range, and Page's guitar tuning of D-A-D-G-A-D (as opposed to the conventional E-A-D-G-B-E) marks an early herald of the epic "Kashmir," done in the same configuration. But "Black Mountain Side" is noticeably like Bert Jansch's "Black Waterside," released on his album *Jack Orion* in 1966, where it was credited as a traditional song, arranged by the guitarist. "I wasn't totally original on that," Page conceded in a *Guitar Player* interview from 1977. "It had been done in the folk clubs a lot; Annie Briggs was the first one that I heard do that riff. I was playing it as well, and then there was Bert Jansch's version."

Like "Dazed and Confused," the song might have attracted less criticism had the title not been identical or nearly identical to its model (blues singer Bessie Smith did a "Black Mountain Blues" and country picker Doc Watson a "Black Mountain Rag"). Both the Briggs and Jansch takes on "Black Waterside" have verses sung over droning chords played slower than the Led Zeppelin track, while "Black Mountain Side" sounds more like a conscious exercise in six-string virtuosity. Bert Jansch, who Page has always named as a major influence, has wryly commented on the closeness of the two pieces but refrained from pursuing any legal action. "Black Waterside" was, as Page attested, a mainstay of the British folk repertoire, and in his mind the *Led Zeppelin* remake may have been removed enough—faster, unaccompanied by lyrics, and with its sitar-like sonority emphasized—to justify listing himself as the composer.

"Communication Breakdown" (Bonham-Jones-Page)

Some listeners have claimed the blistering, trailblazing riff of this cut was patterned after rockabilly hero Eddie Cochran's "Nervous Breakdown," but nothing in the Cochran song is reminiscent of Led Zeppelin. Although Jimmy Page was definitely influenced by Cochran and other early rock 'n' rollers like Cliff Gallup and James Burton, he had already been playing fast, distorted, and bass-heavy guitar lines before "Communication Breakdown" took shape—e.g., "Train Kept A-Rollin'," "Think About It," his and Jeff Beck's workouts on Freddie King's "I'm Going Down"—and the song's title was probably a gesture toward other uptempo precedents, such as the Rolling Stones' "19th Nervous Breakdown" or the bluegrass favorite "Foggy Mountain Breakdown."

"I Can't Quit You Baby" (Willie Dixon)

Confirmed as Dixon's, like "You Shook Me," Zeppelin's effort has been described as hewing more to Otis Rush's 1966 remake of his own 1950s cover, rather than to the previous Little Milton adaptation. Not a lift, then, but a roundabout homage.

"How Many More Times" (Bonham-Jones-Page)

An early sign that Led Zeppelin were playing fast and loose with blues songs came in this nominal original whose lyrics were manifestly indebted to Howlin' Wolf's "How Many More Years," from 1951. Robert Plant, improvising over the band's psychedelic jam session, also throws in lines from "Steal Away," Albert King's "The Hunter," and pop-country icon Jimmy Rodgers's "Kisses Sweeter than Wine." "That has the kitchen sink on it, doesn't it?" Page asked rhetorically about "How Many More Times." "It was made up of little pieces I developed when I was in the Yardbirds. . . . It was played live in the studio with cues and nods." The "little pieces" were a welter of influences, among them the Yardbirds' essays of "Good Morning Little Schoolgirl" and Howlin' Wolf's "Smokestack Lightning," and a previous "How Many More Times" by Gary Farr and the T-Bones; both Plant and John Bonham had performed Howlin' Wolf's "How Many More Years" together in their Birmingham years. The long, multipart Zeppelin rendition of the Howlin' Wolf precedent figured prominently in the band's concerts of 1968 and 1969, but on the album, away from the free-form live performances where Page would again stroke his guitar with a violin bow, the various words and music cobbled together to make "How Many More Times" were not difficult to trace.

"Whole Lotta Love" (Bonham-Jones-Page-Plant)

Led Zeppelin's first big hit and still one of their two most famous songs, the *Led Zeppelin II* starter is also their most confirmed case of plagiarism—the one purists gloat over when insisting that the group were no more than spoiled, selfish white guys who got rich robbing the gritty, grizzled authors of real blues. In 1987 an out-of-court settlement was reached with Willie Dixon (1915–1992), who wrote the "You Need Love" that Muddy Waters recorded in 1962, for an estimated $200,000; Dixon's name is now attached to issues of "Whole Lotta Love," and royalties are collected by his estate.

The "Whole Lotta Love" dispute is centered entirely around its lyrics: Waters sings, *"I ain't foolin' / You need schoolin',"* while Robert Plant begins, *"You need coolin' / Woman I'm not foolin'."* By the end of the track he further quotes the Dixon songs "Shake for Me" and "Back Door Man." Though the lift is apparent, Plant actually came by his words through a little-heard 1966 cover of "You Need Love" by England's the Small Faces, only there it was credited to singer Steve Marriott (ironically Jimmy Page's first choice as singer when forming Zeppelin) and bassist Ronnie Lane (whose battle with multiple sclerosis spurred Page to play a series of benefit dates in the

The original credits of "Whole Lotta Love" made no acknowledgment of "You Need Love," composed by Willie Dixon.   *Author's Collection*

early 1980s). The title itself could be a nod to Jerry Lee Lewis's "Whole Lotta Shakin' Goin' On" or Fats Domino's "Whole Lotta Lovin'."

John Paul Jones has speculated that "Whole Lotta Love" first took shape during an onstage jam in 1969, when the quartet would stretch out for lengthy boogies around "Dazed and Confused" or Garnet Mimms's "As Long as I Have You"—certainly Page's simple E-based riff is something he might have hit on spontaneously—forcing Plant to quickly dip into his mental stock of blues lines. On the other hand, in 1977 Page insisted, "I had ["Whole Lotta Love"] worked out already, that one, before entering the studio. I had rehearsed it." Though "Whole Lotta Love" has the same unvarying key as "You Need Love," there's little doubt that Plant was thinking of Muddy Waters's piece more than Page was when they recorded the Led Zeppelin version.

The distorted, echoed, and stereophonic treatment Page and his group gave "You Need Love" only angered the cognoscenti more, as they accused Zeppelin of reducing the subtleties of Chicago blues to a heavy metal overload. Rock journalist and Jimi Hendrix scholar Charles Shaar Murray has decried Zeppelin's adaptation of "You Need Love" as something "come through crass exaggeration of surface impressions, and the intoxicated egos of posturing ninnies who appear not to realize that they have someone else's dick stuffed down their trousers. . . ." He summarizes "Whole Lotta Love" as "thermonuclear gang rape." Yet the huge scale of "Whole Lotta Love," with its canyons of reverberation and the sonic nightmare of its surreal interlude, is exactly what separates it from the down-home funk of its prototype. Musicologist Susan Fast has countered that criticisms such as Murray's are themselves a simplistic formula: i.e., "Black blues musicians are the 'real thing,' not only the inventors of the genre but also those who lived the stories they were telling. White rockers appropriate the surface but can never match the 'depth' of black blues performers."

"They couldn't get us on the guitar parts or the music," Page has concluded, "so they nailed us on the lyrics. . . . If you took the lyric out and listened to the track instrumentally, it's clearly something new and different." Not different enough for Willie Dixon, though. The battle over "Whole Lotta Love" sums up the divisions engendered by the popularization of blues-based rock 'n' roll in the 1960s and after: black versus white, old versus young, mono versus stereo, bar bands versus stadium acts, stern curators versus gleeful experimenters, and a narrow clique of connoisseurs versus a broad, sensation-hungry demographic. Where the assessment rests is conditional on where the assessor sits.

"The Lemon Song" (Bonham-Jones-Page-Plant)

Together with "Whole Lotta Love" and "Bring It On Home," "The Lemon Song" gave Led Zeppelin's doubters of the early 1970s their choicest ammunition. A number one album by an upstart, corporate-backed assemblage of former studio hacks and long-haired nobodies was found to be rife with unauthorized reproductions of blues stalwarts—every good rock critic of 1969 knew The Blues was where it's at, and who did these foppish Brit pretenders think they were, daring to pass off the legendary Howlin' Wolf's "Killing Floor" as their own?

Through his publisher, Chester "Howlin' Wolf" Burnett (1910–1976) did sue Led Zeppelin for "The Lemon Song," resulting in an out-of-court settlement reached in 1972 that put his name on subsequent editions of Zeppelin's track (including the live version from 1997's *BBC Sessions*). Like most of the group's blues-based material, "The Lemon Song" relies on several older songs for its music and words, and only the most obvious of these was highlighted by the plaintiff and his advocates. As well as 1964's "Killing Floor" (which featured sterling guitar performances from Wolf regular Hubert Sumlin and a young Buddy Guy), "The Lemon Song" reflects Albert King's "Crosscut Saw" and quotes the infamous citric line from Robert Johnson's "Traveling Riverside Blues": *"Squeeze my lemon 'til the juice runs down my leg. . . ."* As usual, Led Zeppelin's cover was less a reverent study than a starting point for their own soloing, in this case a very groovy John Paul Jones bass showcase and some tight boogie between Jimmy Page and the rhythm section. Given that "The Lemon Song" was dashed off between gigs in their hard-driving circuits of 1969, registering the track as a joint effort by all four members may have seemed like either a lark or a forgettable oversight, but with the album's eventual blockbuster status the tune became a prime example of Zeppelin's musical misallocations.

"Thank You" (Page-Plant)

The opening verse of this ballad—*"If the sun refuse to shine, I would still be lovin' you / When mountains crumble to the sea, there will still be you and me"*—is reminiscent of that for Jimi Hendrix's "If 6 Was 9," released two years earlier in 1967—*"If the sun refuse to shine, I don't mind. . . . / If the mountains fell in the sea, let it be, it ain't me. . . ."* "Thank You" has been noted as one of Plant's first lyrical contributions to Led Zeppelin, a love song to his wife Maureen, and it sounds like he had Hendrix in mind when he began writing. On the other hand, the imagery of suns losing their shine and mountains crumbling has often been used to signify "forever" in song (the Everly Brothers' "Devoted to You" and Ben E. King's "Stand by Me" are just two examples, and not the earliest), so if Plant had cribbed the couplet from Hendrix its sun-and-mountains premise seems to have been fair game.

"Moby Dick" (Bonham-Jones-Page)

John Bonham's concert percussion showcase was sometimes introduced as "Pat's Delight" (after his wife), but on *Led Zeppelin II* it was renamed "Moby Dick," perhaps in allusion to drummer Ginger Baker of Cream's comparably leviathan "Toad." However, while the drum solo itself is pure Bonzo, the opening and closing guitar riffs strongly resemble those in Bobby Parker's R&B gem from 1961, "Watch Your Step."

Given that the drum solo rose out of onstage jams, it may have been that Page and Jones spontaneously gave it a launch pad based around a simple figure they could both master quickly, and Parker's "Watch Your Step" was the one they unconsciously settled on. The "Moby Dick" guitar line, which Page punctuates with devastating solo licks heard nowhere on "Watch Your Step," is one of those primal boogie runs that have more to do with the layout of the instrument than any planned execution—countless rock and blues songs are based on this I-IV-V structure, where the player simply transposes the same fingering patterns to different strings or different frets to achieve an expansion and then resolution of an initial sequence. Page had already tried a precursor of this riff in "The Girl I Love She Got Long Black Wavy Hair" on BBC Radio, and an echo can be detected in the Jeff Beck–era Yardbirds' "I Wish You Would," a number credited to Billy Boy Arnold. Even the Beatles' "I Feel Fine" and "Day Tripper" have been mentioned as takeoffs of "Watch Your Step" (John Lennon was a fan of the Parker single), while "Watch Your Step" is said to have been based in turn on jazzman Dizzie Gillespie's "Manteca"—all of which suggests how nebulous the influence of a simple guitar hook repeated in a blues progression can be.

"Bring It On Home" (Page-Plant)

The third brazen blues binge on *Led Zeppelin II*, "Bring It On Home" is actually a good example of how innovative the foursome were when putting their own marks on other people's songs, in this case Rice Miller's (aka Sonny Boy Williamson) performance of Willie Dixon's number. This too became part of the financial settlement between the band and Dixon, whose name has once more been restored to the particulars of Zeppelin publishing entries.

The 1969 performance begins with what Page later defended as "a tribute" to Sonny Boy Williamson (c. 1910–1965)—a direct imitation of his 1963 recording for the Chess label of Chicago—then opens up with a deliberate boost in volume level into a heavy rock riff whose bluesy origins are nearly drowned out in decibels. Ironically, this was not the first time the members of Led Zeppelin had run afoul of Sonny Boy Williamson. Jimmy Page and other young English players had recorded with the crusty singer and harmonica player when he crossed the Atlantic in 1964–65 (uncomfortable takes of "I See a Man Downstairs" and "It's a Bloody Life" surfaced afterward), and a blues-besotted teen named Robert Plant even claimed to have walked away with one of Williamson's mouth organs after seeing the bluesman play in Birmingham around the same time. The lyrics of the Led Zeppelin version are not far from Williamson's, and the faithful opening segment is certainly a giveaway, but their metallic take serves to underscore how differently they played the blues from the men they were allegedly copying.

"Since I've Been Loving You" (Page-Plant-Jones)

A magnificently tragic slow blues, "Since I've Been Loving You" is in essence the usual three-chord progression redone in a minor key, augmented by Jones's soulful keyboards and one of Page's most expressive guitar solos. Though a common device untraceable to any one author, the minor blues arrangement was recognizable from such earlier songs as B. B. King's "The Thrill Is Gone" and Big Mama Thornton's "Ball and Chain," as covered by Janis Joplin.

Lyrically, "Since I've Been Loving You" is one of Robert Plant's lazier efforts, with its first line, *"Workin' from seven to eleven every night / Really makes life a drag, I don't think that's right,"* plainly appropriated from "Never," done in 1968 by Moby Grape, one of the singer's beloved West Coast hippie groups: *"Working from eleven to seven every night / Ought to make life a drag, yeah, and I know that ain't right. . . ."* Likewise, his evocation of losing his worried mind and tears that fell like rain are veritable clichés of blues and pop wording, long established in such numbers as "Worried Man Blues" and "Crying in the Rain." The Zeppelin title could even be an amalgam of Ivory Joe Hunter's "Since I Met You Baby" and Otis Redding's "I've Been Loving You Too Long." Though one of the band's best-known and most powerful cuts, boasting superb performances from each member, "Since I've Been Loving You" exemplifies how the foursome could sometimes lean far too heavily on a hodgepodge of other people's work when constructing their own (admittedly very striking) material.

"Gallows Pole" (Traditional, arranged by Page and Plant)

This really is a traditional song and therefore properly designated as one, although just how Led Zeppelin came by their heavy folk variation is open to conjecture. Jimmy Page has pointed to American Fred Gerlach's 1950s version as his model, but it has also been heard as taken from Dorris Henderson's "Hangman," recorded in 1965. It's possible that both Gerlach and Henderson were working from "Gallis Tree," issued by the great American folk singer Huddie "Leadbelly" Ledbetter (1885–1949), but many lyrical modifications on the song have been transcribed in "The Gallows Pole," "Penitentiary Blues," "The Maid Freed from the Gallows," "Poor Boy," and others. Whatever the source, Page must have known the song was familiar enough not to try to claim it as his own.

"Tangerine" (Page)

One of Led Zeppelin's prettiest ballads was begun two years prior to its 1970 release on *Led Zeppelin III*, when Jimmy Page and his fellow Yardbirds recorded a very similar demo called "Knowing That I'm Losing You" with different words. Along with "Dazed and Confused" (also begun under the Yardbirds), this is one of the two Zeppelin non-instrumentals that credit Page as the sole songwriter. Yet the 'Birds' vocalist, Keith Relf, must surely have had a hand in "Knowing That I'm Losing You," so why wouldn't he have been included in a share of "Tangerine"?

From *Led Zeppelin III*, "Tangerine" had its roots in an earlier song jointly composed by Page and Yardbird Keith Relf.   *Author's Collection*

Relf died of electric shock in 1976, so it's impossible to get his side of the story. The strummed A minor–G-D guitar figure and pedal steel licks are doubtless all Page's invention, but where the new lyrics came from is uncertain. (There was already a Johnny Mercer swing number from the 1940s called "Tangerine," bearing no relation to either the Yardbirds or Led Zeppelin.) Remaining Yardbirds Jim McCarty and Chris Dreja, as well as Keith Relf's sister, Jane, have all complained that some of Relf's original lines can be heard in "Tangerine" (the verse beginning *"Measuring a summer's day . . ."* is common to both songs) and that Relf could have used the resultant royalties as his career declined. Page may have sincerely believed that the unfinished state of "Knowing That I'm Losing You" made it eligible for him to claim the remake as completely his, or he may have walked away with another man's work with the confidence of a rising rock star against the diminished clout of a fading one. It's been speculated that the lost love of "Tangerine" is Page's mid-'60s girlfriend, American singer-songwriter Jackie DeShannon (which might coincide with the song's inception in early 1968), although there is no firm evidence to support this.

"That's the Way" (Page-Plant)

Though the lyrics of this plaintive ballad are Plant's, the chords were very loosely inspired by the folk perennial "The Waggoner's Lad," as performed by the premier British folk guitarists of the 1960s, John Renbourn and Bert Jansch. "That's the Way" is one of the few instances of a Led Zeppelin piece whose music is more derivative than its words, although only the most attentive musicologists would spot the kinship of "That's the Way" and "The Waggoner's Lad."

"Hats Off to (Roy) Harper" (Traditional, arranged by Charles Obscure)

Another mix of blues storylines dominates this *Led Zeppelin III* oddity. Most of the verses are from "Shake 'Em On Down," by Booker T. Washington, aka Bukka White (1909–1977), but there's also input from Mississippi Fred McDowell (1904–1972), Oscar Woods's "Lone Wolf Blues," and Howlin' Wolf's "Brown-Skin Woman." The "Charles Obscure" tag may be Page's nudge at the sensibilities of archivists who duly tracked down every possible root of such songs—his way of saying that the ultimate author was forever lost in the mists of time—although it turns out there's not as much obscurity as he may have thought. The title echoes Del Shannon's 1961 hit "Hats Off to Larry."

"Black Dog" (Jones-Page-Plant)

Nothing on this spiraling and excruciatingly tricky riff-based track could be construed as stolen from elsewhere, but chief songwriter John Paul Jones has acknowledged that the intricacy of the signature run first came to him after listening to Muddy Waters's *Electric Mud* album of 1969, with songs like "Tom Cat" and "She's Alright": "I wanted to write an original riff that had that same type of busy, yet plodding, feel." Others have suggested Jones was in fact recalling *This Is Howlin' Wolf's New Album*, a similarly psychedelicized treatment of a veteran bluesman from the same time. Jimmy Page, for his part, admits that the structure of "Black Dog"—unaccompanied singing interspersed with electric guitar boogie—was based on Fleetwood Mac's "Oh Well," by Peter Green: "I wanted to create a call and response between Robert's vocal and the band." The Who's treatment of Mose Allison's "Young Man Blues," from 1970's *Live at Leeds*, is built on the same alternating pattern. As with so much rock and pop, the distinction between following a successful but malleable formula and merely copying someone else's specific ideas depends on the judgment of the listener.

"Black Dog" is also notable for its dense clusters of blues diction, as recited by Plant in a sort of pre-digital sampling technique: glancing off traditional songs like "I Got to Roll," plus "Nobody Knows You When You're Down and Out"; Big Bill Broonzy's "Hey Hey"; Slim Harpo's "I'm a King Bee"; Robert Johnson's "Steady Rollin' Man"; Big Joe Turner's "Shake, Rattle and Roll"; Chan Romero's "The Hippy Hippy Shake"; and even a couplet that hints at the Beatles' "Drive My Car," his use of terminology such as *"baby," "mama," "shake that thing," "I don't know but I been told," "big-leg woman,"* et cetera, makes the song less reliant on any one source—as could be said of "Whole Lotta Love" or "Since I've Been Loving You"—and more of a collage of imagery whose various origins are impossible to pin down. "Black Dog" is thus one of Led Zeppelin's smartest blues "thefts," if it is a theft at all, in that its allusions are so brief, so scattered, and so self-evidently hark back to a trove of earlier music.

"Rock and Roll" (Bonham-Jones-Page-Plant)

Like "Black Dog," "Rock and Roll" makes no apologies for sounding like a resuscitated nugget from decades previous. Indeed, the number was first played as an ad-lib studio laugh, while the four musicians were struggling to nail the time of "Four Sticks" when a frustrated John Bonham moved to his hi-hat cymbal to bash out Earl Palmer's intro to Little Richard's "Keep A-Knockin'," from 1957. "If something really magical is coming through," Jimmy Page looked back, "then you follow it." The rest of the session dropped "Four Sticks" and polished "Rock and Roll." Page's riff sounds a little like Roy Orbison's "Oh, Pretty Woman" sped up and turned inside out, although he was more likely winging a conventional Chuck Berry–style twelve-bar progression, and Robert Plant seems to draw on the Diamonds' "The Stroll," the Monotones' "The Book of Love," and Jackie Wilson's "Lonely Teardrops" for his verses—all so openly as to moot any question of underhandedness.

"Stairway to Heaven" (Page-Plant)

Uh-oh. Is the masterpiece a forgery? A cottage industry of analysis, exegesis, and skepticism has sprouted around Led Zeppelin's single most celebrated title, perhaps an inevitable by-product of the song's endless radio airplay and air guitar performances. Yet all the smoke emanating from the alleged plagiarism of "Stairway to Heaven" is generated by a surprisingly small fire. Whereas the cases of "Dazed and Confused" or "Whole Lotta Love" have fairly substantial evidence connecting them to prior songs, the link between "Stairway" and Spirit's "Taurus" lies in just a few notes—but since they're among the most instantly identifiable notes in popular music, there is some explaining to do.

In the years following the release of "Stairway to Heaven" in late 1971 and its gradual rise to prominence as an all-time rock 'n' roll anthem, a few listeners began to connect the song's quasi-classical descending introduction to a similar progression heard on the acoustic instrumental from Spirit's self-titled 1968 debut record. The California-based Spirit, whose biggest hit was "I Got a Line on You" (also 1968), had appeared together with Led Zeppelin several times in 1969, and along with covering Spirit's "Fresh Garbage" on stage, the Englishmen had also adapted Spirit guitarist Randy California's electronic device of a theremin for their own sets. If Page and his bandmates had been impressed with Spirit enough to play one of their songs and take up one of their most distinctive instruments, it stood to reason that they had also heard "Taurus" and later incorporated its chords into their own work. Or did it?

To properly compare "Taurus" and "Stairway to Heaven," a little bit of musicology and a basic knowledge of guitar playing are required. "Taurus" is an eerie, quietly psychedelic piece in which an open A minor chord repeatedly cycles down to F major seventh in single steps—the player's middle and pinkie fingers move one fret with each arpeggio (where the individual notes of a chord are plucked) until the shape changes to the open F major seventh, and then back to the adjacent fingering of A minor.

It's a hypnotic part that sounds more complicated to execute than it is, and—adding to the controversy—the official sheet music for "Stairway" presents chord boxes (fingering diagrams for guitarists) that show the Led Zeppelin song played in the same way. It isn't. Jimmy Page's introduction begins up the neck of the guitar where the notes are higher, again beginning in A minor and going down to F, only with a completely different chord shape that brings in an ascending B and then a C note played on the high E string. The bass notes of both "Taurus" and "Stairway" share a chromatic descent of A to G-sharp to G to F-sharp to F, but Page's line has an almost jazzy construction, whereas California's is more of a folk method that slightly recalls the techniques of Donovan or other minstrels.

On initial hearing, of course, the parallels between the two movements are plain, and it could well be that Page was thinking of "Taurus" when he began to put "Stairway to Heaven" together on acoustic guitar in 1970. Then again, as with any number of other musical passages, some chord shifts and changes practically write themselves, in that it would be harmonically difficult *not* to follow one with another to make emotional sense. Willie Nelson's rendition of the Hoagy Carmichael chestnut "Stardust," for example, has a similar lead-in from a minor chord that goes down one fret at a time for a similarly wistful effect. If Page was copying California, he did so with the skills of a more proficient musician, redoing an interesting but unremarkable arrangement in a more elaborate way. Page's onetime collaborator and girlfriend Jackie DeShannon was to recollect showing a part she had written to the guitarist, then (1964) a busy session player. "Jimmy played it back to me, of course ten times better, and it was perfect." Something analogous may have happened when Page decided he liked the inherent theme of "Taurus" but wanted to make it more ornate.

Not everyone may buy this, certainly—Randy California has commented with some bitterness on the resemblance of the opening of "Stairway" to that of "Taurus"—but the connection between the two songs seems to derive more from the ubiquity of Led Zeppelin's classic than from any planned appropriation. In other words, it's probably a coincidence that one very famous piece of music sounds, for a few seconds of its eight minutes, like a mostly forgotten one. The same goes for "And She's Lonely" by the 1960s group the Chocolate Watchband, another purported "Stairway" foundation. Meanwhile, guitarist Randy Bachman (the Guess Who, Bachman-Turner Overdrive) has opined that the Robert Plant's vocal melody in "Stairway" was inspired by the blind Irish harpist Turlough O'Carolan's "Carolan's Dream," from the eighteenth century. Others have compared Bob Dylan and Jimi Hendrix's "All Along the Watchtower" to the final electric minutes of "Stairway to Heaven" (the songs are once more structured on the same descending chords repeated over and over), but Page himself said the same segment reminded him of Ray Charles's "Hit the Road, Jack." Who's to say? Though for some Zeppelin cuts the charges of plagiarism are pretty pointed, those aimed at the most enduring Zeppelin number of all are far less persuasive.

"When the Levee Breaks" (Bonham-Jones-Page-Plant-Memphis Minnie)

Though Led Zeppelin's hugest blues explosion is today listed as a shared creation with the blues singer Memphis Minnie (Lizzie Douglas, 1897–1973), the first pressings of the album on which it appeared left the influential Delta vocalist-guitarist's name off the credits. In fact, a more accurate acknowledgment might name Minnie's husband and musical partner at the time of her recording, Kansas Joe McCoy (1905–1950), as a sixth cowriter, since their 1929 song described the recent Mississippi River floods of 1927 and the subsequent migration of impoverished black farm workers to the industrial hub of Chicago. By the band's fourth record the opposing cases for formal purism against spontaneous evolution were being felt: The version of "When the Levee Breaks" on *Led Zeppelin IV* owes as much to the 1971 performance of the four young Britons, plus Page and Andy John's recording techniques, as it does to the forty-year-old original, and the "Memphis Minnie" tacked on to the Bonham-Jones-Page-Plant citation reads a little grudgingly.

"Custard Pie" (Page-Plant)

The funky intro to *Physical Graffiti* is yet another of Robert Plant's simmering stews of blues, whose lines are dominated by Bukka White's "Shake 'Em On Down," plus Sleepy John Estes and Hammie Nixon's "Drop Down Mama" from 1935, Sonny Boy Williamson's "Help Me," and Blind Boy Fuller's "I Want Some of Your Pie." Here it's worth considering again what the self-proclaimed composers were thinking when they put their names to this— did they imagine their quotations were stitched together so randomly as to constitute a new work, did Plant forget where exactly his verses came from and not bother looking them up, or did Page assume rich white superstars had better lawyers than any poor black troubadour could ever enlist against them? "Custard Pie" isn't as disjointed as, say, "Black Dog" in its lyrical premises, but nor is it descended from one immediate forerunner, like "Dazed and Confused" or "The Lemon Song." The Page-Plant credit here must be put down to the now-typical Led Zeppelin muddle of carelessness, opportunism, and indifference.

"The Rover" (Page-Plant)

Pure speculation, but this *Physical Graffiti* grinder has a similar descending chord passage to Elvis Presley's "Burning Love," slowed down and distorted. Page and Plant were firm Elvis fans, and the entire band even met the King on one occasion. However, "The Rover" was first essayed in 1970 as an acoustic song and remade in its final version by 1974, while "Burning Love" was released in 1972. Probably a curious overlap rather than a studied imitation.

"In My Time of Dying" (Bonham-Jones-Page-Plant)

Led Zeppelin's longest piece clocks in at over eleven minutes, and, with Page's Danelectro electric guitar tuned to a bluesy open A, it is also one of his most compelling slide demonstrations. Much of the song's authenticity, of course, is owed to its predecessor, "Jesus Make Up My Dying Bed," recorded by Texan religious preacher and street performer Blind Willie Johnson (c.1890–1947) in 1927. The Zeppelin take was probably inspired by Bob Dylan's cover (titled "In My Time of Dyin'") from his 1962 debut album, which later figured in some of the teenage Robert Plant's 1960s sets. Another candidate could be folk-blues artist Josh White's rendition from the early 1930s. But the song may even predate Blind Willie Johnson's version: A 1942 collection, *Songs of American Folks*, notes "We have never heard this song except from Wallace House, the most versatile guitarist and Folk Singer we know, who in turn got it from [folklorist] Zora Hurston," where it's called "Jesus Goin' to Make Up My Dyin' Bed." Any number of African-American spirituals call on Jesus ("Soon I Will Be Done," "Wade in the Water," "When I'm Gone"), and the scorching blues-rock of Led Zeppelin's cut, while clearly descended from Blind Willie Johnson, is a pretty extreme elaboration on a standard thematic premise. "It was just being put together when we recorded it," Page has said of his "In My Time of Dying." "It's jammed at the end and we didn't even have a proper way to stop the thing. . . . I liked it because we really sounded like a working group."

"Boogie with Stu" (Bonham-Jones-Page-Plant-Ian Stewart-Mrs. Valens)

The credits of this jaunty cut, a lighthearted vamp taped in 1971 with Rolling Stones keyboardist Ian Stewart (who also played on "Rock and Roll"), may have been Page's rejoinder to the critics who had been tossing the thievery labels around from day one. "Curiously enough, the one time we tried to do the right thing, it blew up in our faces," he told *Guitar World* magazine in 1998. The song, he said, "was obviously a variation

Blind Willie Johnson's "Jesus Make Up My Dying Bed" was an obvious forerunner of Zeppelin's "In My Time of Dying."   *Archive Photos/Getty Images*

on 'Ooh! My Head' by the late Ritchie Valens, which itself was actually a variation of Little Richard's 'Ooh! My Soul.' What we tried to do was give Ritchie's mother credit, because we heard she never received any royalties from any of her son's hits, and Robert did lean on that lyric a bit. So what happens? They tried to sue us for all of the song! We had to say bugger off." How conscientious Page really intended to be is difficult to say. "Mrs.

Valens" reads like an inside joke more than a genuine recognition (Ritchie Valens, killed in the 1959 plane crash that took Buddy Holly, was born Richard Valenzuela), and it's questionable how much income actually went to Concepcion "Connie" Valenzuela—or why Little Richard (Richard Penniman) didn't get anything from either Valens or Led Zeppelin.

"Nobody's Fault but Mine" (Page-Plant)

By the time of 1976's *Presence*, Led Zeppelin were one of the biggest rock groups in the world, and Jimmy Page must have known the album would be a massive seller whose fourth song would soon be noted for its resemblance to Blind Willie Johnson's "It's Nobody's Fault but Mine" from 1928. Page was likely more mindful of John Renbourn's 1966 acoustic take (credited to Renbourn) than Johnson's, and Robert Plant added cryptic and despairing lyrics about having a monkey on his back and having to change his ways, relevant to the Zeppelin lifestyle of the day. The *Presence* version, done as a hard rock number with sinuous phasing effects and a titanic rhythmic underlay, was another electronic update where the advanced stereophonic medium was presumed to displace the Texas gutbucket message.

With "Custard Pie" and "In My Time of Dying," "Nobody's Fault but Mine" reveals the offhand manner in which Led Zeppelin observed their late-period legal niceties. Once more, the issue comes down to whether Page, Peter Grant, and the rest of the musicians really considered themselves above the publishing laws as they applied to dead or elderly African-American blues artists, or whether they merely supposed the sonic sophistication of their performances amounted to original songs, no matter what previous examples they'd drawn on. Their invulnerable commercial stature of the mid-1970s would argue the former, but their frenetic schedules and compromised mental health of the same era weighs in favor of the latter.

"Tea for One" (Page-Plant)

Led Zeppelin's one obvious case of self-plagiarism, "Tea for One" uses the same basic chord progression (C minor, F minor, G minor) as the Page-Plant-Jones opus "Since I've Been Loving You" and probably derived from jams around the older song. However, "Tea for One" features a more mature lyric, unlike the blues formulae of "Since I've Been Loving You," and its instrumentation is driven by Page's tasty guitars without the keyboard flourishes of the prototype.

"In the Evening" (Jones-Page-Plant)

Long after its release on 1979's *In Through the Out Door*, Robert Plant admitted that the first line of this intro track was taken from the obscure "Tomorrow's Clown," by early English rock 'n' roller Marty Wilde.

"South Bound Saurez" (Jones-Plant)

The "sha-la-la-las" toward the end of this catchy groove are almost identical to the backing vocals in Roy Orbison's "Mean Woman Blues." Of course, there is no way to copyright such phrases, which are as basic to the language of pop music as "baby," "ooh wah," "hoochie-koo," and "wang dang."

"Poor Tom" (Page-Plant)

First recorded in 1970 but not released until 1982's *Coda*, "Poor Tom" uses Page's quirky guitar tuning and Bonham's rat-a-tat drumming to illustrate an ancient story of jealousy, murder, and punishment. Both the title and the narrative seem to date back to the seventeenth century, around such British folk lyrics as "Poor Tom hath been imprison'd," "Poor Tom the Taylor [sic] His Lamentation," and "Poor Tom's Progress." Others point out that the instrumentation suggests Robert Wilkins's "Prodigal Sun," an acoustic blues number later played by the Rolling Stones. Near the end of the song Plant also quotes the hippie maxim "Keep on truckin'," either from the famous R. Crumb poster of 1968 or Blind Boy Fuller's "Truckin' My Blues Away," from 1937.

18

Steal Away

Other Musicians' Borrowing from Led Zeppelin

Many Many Men: Zeppelin Songs Imitated

A part from Zeppelin's broad sonic influence on all of rock—heavy electric riffs, gentle acoustic ballads that turn into headbanging anthems, squealing blues guitar solos, mystical lyrics, and so on—there are a few specific cases where one or more of their own songs can be heard underneath new tracks by later players. This doesn't even take into account the many hard rock or metal acts that used the Led Zeppelin "look" (four-piece groups with big hair, open shirts, sensitive singers, and brooding guitar heroes) for their own video or live appearances.

Because Zeppelin was so popular few artists have thought they could do with "Whole Lotta Love" or "The Lemon Song" what Page and Company did with "You Need Love" and "Killing Floor," but nevertheless the following titles are instances where it is not hard to hear Led Zeppelin's music used, inadvertently or not, as the basis for nominally original material.

Kingdom Come: "What Love Can Be"

Dubbed "Kingdom Clone" by Jimmy Page and many fans, the late-'80s German-American hair metal act used the Plant-like vocal timbres of singer Lenny Wolf to pull off this hit, which sounds a lot like "Since I've Been Loving You" as heard in a parallel universe.

Kingdom Come: "Get It On"

Less traceable to a single Zeppelin cut, "Get It On" incorporates the stuttering riffs of "The Ocean" and "Black Dog" and the ascending progression of "Kashmir," while Wolf's vocals are highly reminiscent of those on "What Is and What Should Never Be."

Lynryd Skynyrd: "Sweet Home Alabama"

Though the song is an undisputed rock 'n' roll classic in its own right, the opening three chords and guitar lick of the Dixie anthem are almost identical to the intro of "Your Time Is Gonna Come." It's hard to patent something as simple as the D-C-G arrangement, but play the two songs back-to-back and the (likely accidental) similarity is obvious.

Whitesnake: "Still of the Night"

By another 1980s metal outfit that took advantage of Led Zeppelin's ongoing status as a favorite disbanded band, this hard rocker plainly borrows the same call-and-response pattern of "Black Dog"—unaccompanied vocals alternating with a twisty blues-based riff. Both live and on TV, guitarist Adrian Vandenberg was even seen bowing his guitars à la Jimmy Page. Whitesnake's brazen reproduction of Zeppelin's music and showmanship bothered Robert Plant, whose pouting and posing stage moves singer David Coverdale had down to perfection, but Page ended up working with Coverdale on a collaborative 1993 album and Japanese tour. "Still of the Night" went full circle when it was played by Page himself in Japan. Another Whitesnake number, "Judgement Day," could be the unholy union of Zep's "Kashmir" and "Babe I'm Gonna Leave You."

Heart: "Barracuda"

A longtime FM radio essential, this number, with its hard-driving, stop-and-start thud, is very derivative of Zeppelin's "Achilles Last Stand." Drummer Denny Carmassi was later recruited into the Coverdale-Page band, flattering the late John Bonham with his very sincere imitation.

Heart: "Sylvan Song"

This lovely instrumental of guitars and mandolins from the 1977 *Little Queen* album could well be guitarist Nancy Wilson's approximation of Zeppelin's "The Battle of Evermore," "Going to California," or "Bron-yr-Aur," similar to all three without directly quoting any one.

Black Sabbath: "Paranoid"

Like the Heart and Skynyrd cuts, this founding text of heavy metal from 1970 is a sidelong tribute to Zeppelin's inescapable redefinition of rock 'n' roll orchestration. The timeless worldwide hit was recorded almost as an afterthought while the quartet were making their second album. Bassist-lyricist Geezer Butler reportedly worried over the opening riff's resemblance to "Communication Breakdown" (there's also a hint of "Dazed and Confused" there as well). Both "Paranoid" and "Communication Breakdown" are fast and heavily distorted guitar progressions in the key of E; both are played with the chording hand deadening the strings enough to give them a chunky, almost percussive texture; and both are short: "Paranoid" is timed at 2:50, while "Communication Breakdown" runs 2:26. Though not a deliberate copy of any Zeppelin song, "Paranoid," like many other well-known rock tracks, would not have been possible without the audio precedents established by Page, Plant, Jones, and Bonham in 1969.

Eric Clapton: "Let It Grow"

Clapton himself has admitted to unknowingly ripping off the introduction to "Stairway to Heaven" for inclusion in this number from his album *461 Ocean Boulevard*, released in 1974. In his 2007 autobiography the guitarist confesses that this was "a cruel justice," since, as a devoted blues purist himself, he had often been critical of Led Zeppelin's liberal takes on the Delta and Chicago canons. "Let It Grow" is still a nice tune, however, and the listener has to attend carefully for the "Stairway" snippet.

Billy Squier: "Lonely Is the Night"

Here and on his other famous songs from 1981–82 including "The Stroke," "My Kinda Lover," and "Everybody Wants You," the American singer-guitarist's voice and playing had a very Zeppelin-esque feel, emphasized by his high vocal range, stammering guitar lines, and record production that seemed to reproduce the reverberating audio stamp of *Presence* or *In Through the Out Door*. As with most of the titles listed here, there is no real plagiarism involved on "Lonely Is the Night," but rather something between slavish tribute and subconscious mimicry.

Aerosmith: "Train Kept A-Rollin'"

Justly credited to songwriters "Tiny" Bradshaw, Lois Mann, and Howard Kay, the Aerosmith version (from 1974's *Get Your Wings*) is nonetheless heavily indebted to that played by the Yardbirds, as heard on their 1965 record *Having a Rave-Up* and on their US tours. The members of Aerosmith were all bowled over by the Yardbirds and were equally impressed by the first American Led Zeppelin concerts of 1969, which also featured a forceful cover of the song. In London in 1990, Jimmy Page accompanied Aerosmith in some onstage jams of "Train Kept A-Rollin'." Aerosmith leaders Steve Tyler and Joe Perry have struck up personal relationships with Page, and Aerosmith's sound and songwriting, particularly during their 1970s heyday, was highly shaped by Led Zeppelin. "We learned a lot [from Zeppelin] in terms of playing big places with the echo," Perry has said. "And they knew how that kind of music, if you played it a certain way with certain rhythms, was going to work better." Other Aerosmith tunes with a strong Zeppelin flavor include "Nobody's Fault" and "Round and Round."

Rush: "Working Man"

The 1974 debut album by this great Canadian power trio, then with original drummer John Rutsey, first gained notice with its aural resemblance to Led Zeppelin. "Working Man," boasting singer-bassist Geddy Lee's piercing vocals and guitarist Alex Lifeson's fat guitar tone, certainly recalls long Zeppelin improvisations like "How Many More Times" and "The Lemon Song," while other Rush tracks from the LP, such as "In the Mood" and "Finding My Way," also harked back to the loose blues workouts of *Led Zeppelin* or *Led Zeppelin II*. "Jimmy Page was my favorite guitarist," Lifeson has looked back. "I wanted to look like him and play like him. And judging from our first record, you can see the influence there."

 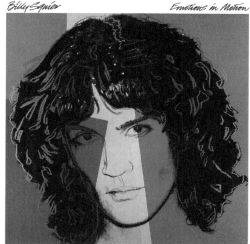

Rush and Billy Squier were among many artists clearly influenced by the Led Zeppelin sound.
Author's Collection

The Cult: "Lil' Devil"

Ian Astbury and Billy Duffy, singer and guitarist of this group, always acknowledged their love of Led Zeppelin, and during their peak years of the late 1980s and early 1990s the influence was conspicuous. "Lil' Devil," from 1987's *Electric*, is based on a guitar line loosely adapted from "Heartbreaker." Later their "Edie (Ciao Baby)," off *Sonic Temple* in 1989, alluded to "an angel with a broken wing," quoted from a Jimmy Page interview of the 1970s as well as a chapter title in *Hammer of the Gods*.

The Mission (UK): "Black Mountain Mist"

Another British act from the period of the Cult, who also blended the droning aura of goth music with the traditional elements of hard rock, the Mission too were noted Zeppelin acolytes. "Black Mountain Mist" does not so much copy any Zeppelin music as borrow its title from two tracks, "Black Mountain Side" and "Misty Mountain Hop." The Mission's hewing to the Led Zeppelin style on *Children*, the 1988 album on which this was featured, may be forgiven: The record was produced by John Paul Jones.

1976

March 31: *Presence* released

April 5: Billionaire Howard Hughes dies, age 70.

April 5: James Callaghan replaces Harold Wilson as British prime minister.

June 19: Soweto Uprising, South Africa.

July 4: US Bicentennial celebrations.

August: Montreal Olympics.

September–October: *The Song Remains the Same* album and movie released.

September 18: Chinese premier Mao Tse-tung dies, age 82.

November 2: Jimmy Carter defeats Gerald Ford in US presidential election.

Movies: *Taxi Driver*; *Rocky*.

Music: Boston, *Boston*; Kiss, *Destroyer*; Steve Miller Band, *Fly like an Eagle*; Bob Seger and the Silver Bullet Band, *Live Bullet*; Blue Öyster Cult, *Agents of Fortune*; Eagles, *Hotel California*; Tom Waits, *Small Change*; the Ramones, *The Ramones*; Bob Marley and the Wailers, *Live!*; Fleetwood Mac, "Rhiannon"; Roxy Music, "Love Is the Drug"; Hot Chocolate, "You Sexy Thing"; Elton John and Kiki Dee, "Don't Go Breaking My Heart."

19

Lots of People Talkin', Few of Them Know

Led Zeppelin and the Occult

Devil Mocks Their Every Step: The Soul-Selling Legend

Probably the most enduring—and most fantastic—legend pertaining to the group is the one that claims Jimmy Page made a pact with Satan to ensure his band's popularity. Newcomers Robert Plant and John Bonham went along with the deal, goes the story, but the more seasoned and savvier John Paul Jones refused, and thereby was spared the personal misfortunes and fatalities that befell the three signatories.

This is a great yarn that has added immensely to Led Zeppelin's mystique, but it is on its face ridiculous. "We never made a pact with the Devil," an exasperated Plant said in a post-Zeppelin interview. "The only deal I think we ever made was with some of the girls' high schools in the San Fernando Valley." The deadpan Jones, for his part, confirmed he'd backed out of the diabolical contract: "I'd run out of ink or blood or something. My old dad said, 'Never sign anything without first talking to a lawyer.'" Page's comments on Zeppelin's alleged Satanism have ranged from the oblique to the annoyed. "I don't want to get into too many backlashes from Christian fundamentalist groups," the guitarist demurred around the time of his 1994 reunion with Plant. "I've given those people too much mileage already." Stephen Davis's *Hammer of the Gods* repeated the tale as heard by his various sources (Page girlfriend Pamela Miller and French promo man Benoit Gautier are quoted), and the soul-selling stigma has become a permanent part of the Led Zeppelin biography.

Why the story should be attached to the band is the more relevant issue. Part of the countercultural movement of the 1960s involved the exploration of non-Western religious traditions, including Buddhism and Hinduism, and the rediscovery of pagan or animist belief systems that had been nearly obliterated by the prevailing Judeo-Christian orthodoxies of several centuries. At the fringes of this proto–New Age philosophy were the truly occult (from the Latin for "covered" or "hidden") practices that had long been actively suppressed by conventional authority but which were now ripe for revival: witchcraft, astrology, crystals, the *I Ching*, fertility cults, and other "alternative" spiritualities. Young, curious, and rendered impressionable by psychedelic drugs, the hippies and their various offshoots took to the occult in large numbers. The mass media reflected the changes, in books and films like *Rosemary's Baby, The Exorcist, Chariots of the Gods,* and newly fashionable authors like H. P. Lovecraft, Edgar Allan Poe, and J. R. R. Tolkien. UFOs, Bigfoot, the Loch Ness monster, tarot cards, Ouija boards, and similar subjects were embraced by a wide public. A *Time* magazine cover story of June 1972 alerted readers to "The Occult Revival" sweeping across America.

Coinciding with this was the primacy of rock music. Inevitably, these two big interests of a generation would overlap, whether it was the Rolling Stones singing "Sympathy for the Devil" (1968) following their previous album *Their Satanic Majesties Request,* or Black Sabbath singing "Black Sabbath" on their eponymous debut record (1970), in addition to the gender-bending shock rock of Alice Cooper and David Bowie, and the sacrificial stage shows of long-forgotten acts like Black Widow, which featured numbers titled "Come to the Sabbat" and "Conjuration." In the years before MTV, home video, and the Internet, there was far more speculation than fact surrounding even the most successful performers, since the sheer breadth of the market for rock 'n' roll permitted healthy sales of records and tickets with a minimum of authorized publicity; rock stars lived lives of such unrivaled wealth and mystery that almost anything could be credibly said of them. Was Paul McCartney really dead? Did Bob Dylan really pose in drag on the cover of his *Bringing It All Back Home?* Did Frank Zappa and Alice Cooper really have an onstage "gross-out" contest? Did Peter, Paul and Mary's "Puff the Magic Dragon" really encourage pot smoking? Did Donovan's "Mellow Yellow" really refer to the hallucinogenic properties of smoked banana peels? Did Led Zeppelin make a bargain with the devil? Who could authoritatively deny it?

The selling of one's soul in exchange for worldly gain is an ancient myth. The Gospel of Luke tells of Christ tempted by Satan during his forty days of wandering in the wilderness: "And the devil said unto him, All this power I will give thee, and the glory of them: for that is delivered unto me; and to whomsoever I will give it. If thou therefore wilt worship me, all shall be thine" (Luke 4: 6-7). English playwright Christopher Marlowe's *Doctor*

Faustus (1604) was based on a German tract, *The History of the Damnable Life and Deserved Death of Doctor John Faustus*, a purportedly true account of a sixteenth-century personage who experimented in magic and sorcery. Marlowe's Faust sells his soul to the devil but is ultimately dragged off to hell after partaking of the forbidden knowledge and experience granted to him by Lucifer's servant Mephistopheles. The German account was also the basis for several adaptations, among them Johann Wolfgang von Goethe's 1806 play and Charles-François Gounod's 1859 opera. Several medieval narratives concern magicians who unlocked dangerous secrets from rare books known as *grimoires*, including a student of Cornelius Agrippa who was killed by a demon he had inadvertently summoned after reciting the text of one such volume. English occultist MacGregor Mathers (1854–1918) wrote of a contemporary, Antony of Prague, who had given up his soul for forty years' worth of supernatural powers, only to be found murdered. Stephen Vincent Benét's famous short story "The Devil and Daniel Webster" (1937) situated the Faustian scenario in pioneer America. Nineteenth-century violin virtuoso Niccolò Paganini was said to have sold his soul for musical proficiency (his technique was called "Mephistophelean" and "bewitching"), and the same accusations circulated around twentieth-century bluesman Robert Johnson. Schoolyard whispers insisted the theatrical hard rockers Kiss picked a band name that was an acronym for *Knights In Satan's Service*, and Black Sabbath's 1976 compilation album was titled *We Sold Our Soul for Rock 'n' Roll*.

The first oral reports of Led Zeppelin's devilish transaction probably surfaced sometime in the 1970s but were so transparently nonsensical they were not taken up in any other medium. They would have been rooted in the basic facts of the group's fame and riches; leader Page's guarded admissions of his interest in magic and the unknown; the obscure symbolism on several of their album covers; their unashamed (if not then publicized) enjoyment of sexual and chemical indulgences while on tour; and eventually the death and injuries that struck Plant's family and the band's dissolution following John Bonham's death. Few have noticed the logical inconsistency in the premise: If John Paul Jones refused to sell his soul, how come he still got rich and famous? Wouldn't Mephistopheles have requested a more amenable bass player? Printed references to the Zeppelin "curse" began to crop up in the more sensational rock publications after 1975 and especially after the tragically curtailed 1977 American tour. Combine these with the general atmosphere of innuendo, supposition, and superstition that affected both the pop music industry and the pop culture of the decade, and it would only require the fantasizing aloud of a single disc jockey, journalist, or hanger-on to ripple into the urban legend remembered today. Contemporary discussion of the Satanic pact rumor, indeed, cites it as an example of the credulity of rock fans rather than the debauchery of rock stars.

Prayer Won't Do You No Good: The Zeppelin Curse

The reports of a jinx on Led Zeppelin, as suggested by the 1975 car accident that severely injured Robert Plant and his wife, the 1977 death by viral infection of Plant's young son, and the 1980 death of John Bonham, were never more than cheap headlines for British tabloid newspapers and their American equivalents in the rock press. "The comments about it at the time all connected it to Jimmy's dalliances and preoccupations with the dark side and whatever," Plant observed. "I've never shared those with him and I don't really know anything about it." While the *Presence* album (with the regretful "Nobody's Fault but Mine," "For Your Life," and "Tea for One") conveyed a theme of unease, and though Plant was said to be unwilling to sing "In My Time of Dying" or, following the collapse of a Californian beachside residence, "The Ocean," much more of the bad luck was played up by the press. The London *Evening News* ran a story titled "Zeppelin's 'Black Magic' Mystery" shortly after Bonham died, while the English trade paper *New Musical Express* featured "Bonzo's Last Bash." Eventually rock magazine covers featured blurbs like "Led Zeppelin: The Evil Curse That Haunts Them" and "Jimmy Page: Will Black Magic Kill Him?" Even the thoughtful commentator Gary Herman in his 1982 *Rock 'n' Roll Babylon* wrote that "it is certainly true that Led Zeppelin as a group have had a peculiarly tragic record of untimely death and severe accident associated with themselves and their entourage."

Is this true? Consider first the confirmed fatalities, misadventures, arrests, and assaults associated with Led Zeppelin:

- **John Bonham**: Died of a pulmonary edema following a drinking binge at Jimmy Page's house, 1980.

- **Phillip Hale**: A young photographer friend of Jimmy Page died in Page's Sussex home in October 1979. An inquest attributed the death to an accidental overdose.

- **Sandy Denny**: Guest vocalist on "The Battle of Evermore" died after a domestic fall, 1978.

- **Karac Plant**: Died of a respiratory virus in 1977, age five.

- **Jim Matzorkis**: Employee of promoter Bill Graham, severely beaten by John Bonham, Peter Grant, Richard Cole, and Zeppelin security man

John Bindon backstage at an Oakland concert, 1977. Bonham, Grant, Cole, and Bindon were arrested and charged with assault.

◆ **Stanley Blair**: Concertgoer, injured in a melee outside Cincinnati's Riverfront Coliseum, 1977; one fan died in this same episode, although whether or not it was Blair himself is unknown.

◆ **Keith Harwood**: Engineer on several Zeppelin albums, killed in an auto accident in 1976.

◆ **Robert Plant, Maureen Plant**: Severely injured in car crash on the Greek island of Rhodes, 1975.

◆ **Unnamed *Starship* stewardess**: Assaulted by John Bonham, 1975.

◆ **Michelle Myer**: Los Angeles PR agent, assaulted by John Bonham, 1975.

◆ **Jimmy Page**: Injured his left ring finger in a train door in Britain preceding the US tour, 1975.

◆ **Danny Markus**: Promo man, had eyeglasses smashed by John Bonham, 1973.

◆ **Les Harvey**: Guitarist with Stone the Crows, managed by Peter Grant, electrocuted and died onstage, 1972.

◆ **Mac Nelson**: Student at Vancouver's Simon Fraser University, recording a Zeppelin concert for the Scientific Pollution and Environmental Control Society, assaulted by the band's road crew, August 1971.

◆ **Joe Baldwin**: Father of John Paul Jones, died suddenly during a Zeppelin tour, August 1970.

◆ **Jason Bonham**: Slightly injured in a childhood accident, necessitating his father's temporary departure from a US tour, 1969.

◆ **Ellen Sander**: Journalist, assaulted by unnamed band members, 1969.

◆ **Assorted concert attendees, venue staff, bystanders, and hangers-on**: Injured or assaulted in the vicinity of individual band members, Led Zeppelin live appearances, and/or the group's management and security team, 1969–80.

This is a serious tally of trouble that lends credence to the curse theory—until it is compared to the history of other groups and soloists from the same era. The Beatles lost their manager Brian Epstein to a drug overdose in 1967; chief roadie Mal Evans was killed in a Los Angeles police shootout in 1976; leader John Lennon was gunned down by a deranged fan in 1980 at just forty years of age; and lead guitarist George Harrison succumbed to cancer in 2001 at age fifty-eight, following another fan attack he had sustained the previous year. The Rolling Stones, who also were linked to occult specialists including Kenneth Anger and artist Donald Cammell, had their founder Brian Jones drown in his swimming pool in 1969; played their disastrous Altamont concert the same year in which one fan was murdered by Hells Angels; and suffered several years through Keith Richards' crippling heroin addiction, while numerous associates, wives, and girlfriends themselves fell victim to drug dependency. The Who have lost half their original lineup to drug fatality—drummer Keith Moon in 1978 and bassist John Entwistle in 2002—and themselves played a Cincinnati concert in 1979 where no fewer than eleven punters were trampled to death. After enduring the unwanted interest of the Charles Manson family, the Beach Boys have been affected by producer Brian Wilson's drug-induced mental illness and the premature deaths of his two brothers Dennis (drowning, 1983) and Carl (cancer, 1998). Pete Ham and Tom Evans, the two principal members of the chart-topping Badfinger, committed suicide in 1975 and 1983, respectively. Of more recent vintage, Def Leppard drummer Rick Allen's left arm was amputated after Allen's 1984 car crash, while the band's guitarist Steve Clark died of an overdose in 1991. Nor were members of Led Zeppelin the only rockers to have been shattered by the death of a child: Jerry Lee Lewis, Roy Orbison, Keith Richards, Eric Clapton, Joe Walsh, Rush drummer Neil Peart, and Mötley Crüe singer Vince Neil have all experienced similar heartbreak. There are no reputed "curses" around any of these performers, leading to a conclusion that contentions of a Led Zeppelin curse are what Jimmy Page condemned as "a horrible, tasteless thing to say."

Heed the Master's Call: Was Jimmy Page a Satanist?

Someone once said that if you are a celebrity and want to be known as an art lover, be seen once at a gallery; if you are a celebrity and want a reputation as a fitness buff, be seen once jogging. Jimmy Page has been subject to the same typecasting. While he has been publicly associated with a variety of figures prominent in the field of the occult—underground filmmaker Kenneth Anger, Beat novelist William Burroughs, and especially Aleister Crowley—in retrospect his rumored affiliations and activities seem less and less central to his life and career. "I mean, asking me about black magic and Aleister Crowley and whatnot . . . Give me a break," he said in 1991. "It's all so stupid. I'd rather talk about the music, you know?" "It's unfortunate that my studies of mysticism and Eastern and Western traditions of magick and tantricism have all come under the umbrella of Crowley," he added in 2003. "Yeah, sure, I read a lot of Crowley and I was fascinated by his techniques and ideas. But I was reading across the board. . . . It wasn't unusual [in the

1960s] to be interested in comparative religions and magic. And that's it."
In 2007 he went further, explaining, "There's no point in saying more about
it, because the more you discuss it, the more eccentric you appear to be."
What he first spoke about with some enthusiasm in the early years of Led
Zeppelin's ascendancy he later took pains to downplay, in the face of fan
gossip and tabloid sensationalism.

"I do *not* worship the Devil," Page declared as far back as a 1976 *Rolling
Stone* interview with Cameron Crowe. "But magic does intrigue me. Magic
of all kinds." In the same conversation he conceded, "I'm not about to deny
any of the stories. . . . I'm no fool. I know how much the mystique matters.
Why should I blow it now?" It's noteworthy that the other members of Led
Zeppelin neither shared Page's interests nor appeared to regard them as
excitedly as fans did. Robert Plant was always offhand about Page's supposed persuasions. "Jimmy had his moments when he played his games,"
he said in 1985, "but none of them with a great deal of seriousness, and
through his own choice, he never really tried to put the story straight. . . .
He got some kind of enjoyment out of people having the wrong impression
of him." On Page's infatuation with Aleister Crowley, the singer shrugged,
"I think Page just collected the works of an English eccentric." "There was a
lot of humor in the group, a lot of humor in the music," corroborated John
Paul Jones. "Not all this glowering, Satanic crap." So the question is how
an intelligent and mild-mannered pop musician preoccupied with his craft
could have become "the Dark Lord of Hard Rock," slandered as some sort
of wizard obsessed with ritual, sorcery, and the supernatural.

Jimmy Page later admitted to have read Aleister Crowley's major work,
Magic in Theory and Practice, at the age of eleven (Crowley wrote volumi-
nously, and this and other of his treatises have been published individually
and within other collections). Fellow session musicians have recalled Page's
workplace chats encompassing "all sorts of odd cult things," while Yardbirds
drummer Jim McCarty remembered that "Jimmy seemed very interested in
perversions. . . . Every now and then he'd start talking about instruments of
perversion and the Marquis de Sade." The Yardbirds' Chris Dreja has told of
meeting Page in the mid-1960s as a keeper of exotic aquarium fish. "He was
a strange guy, even then." None of these quirks, however, add up to anything
suggesting devil worship; mostly they reveal a bright and well-read young
man with esoteric interests outside the cliché rock 'n' roller's fixations of
electric guitars, fast cars, and faster girls.

By the end of the 1960s, having earned some money as a studio player
and a Yardbird—and with substantial revenues from Led Zeppelin in the
offing—the aesthete and former art student Page began to seriously collect paintings, manuscripts, and other antiques, some related to Aleister

Crowley but others as innocuous as Pre-Raphaelite furniture and prints by Dutch lithographer M. C. Escher. His 1970 purchase of the Boleskine House in Scotland, a former abode of Crowley's, and his taking ownership of London's fantastic Tower House and the Equinox specialty bookshop in 1974, sealed his reputation as a dedicated scholar of the occult, and in interviews promoting Led Zeppelin records or tours he freely spoke of his research into the subject. Sitting for the climactic shot of his "Dazed and Confused" sequence in *The Song Remains the Same* (where he had to remain still while his "Hermit" makeup was altered between takes), Page revealed that he drew on yoga training to hold his position. He was even said to have been contracted to contribute articles to the British *Man, Myth and Magic* publication, but none of these have ever turned up. Yet again none of this connoisseurship should be equated with Satanism. Like others who have ventured into the science and history of magic and fringe religions (including Crowley), Page was perhaps guilty of playing on outsiders' ignorance of the distinctions between out-and-out devil worship and the far more nuanced and arcane principles he was actually attending to. "[Y]ou can't ignore evil if you study the supernatural as I do," he hinted in 1973. "I have many books on the subject and I've also attended a number of séances. I want to go on studying it." *The Song Remains the Same* also showed Page sitting alone on the grounds of his Sussex home as optical effects made his eyes radiate a demonic glow. It was this sort of teasing, maybe-I-am, maybe-I'm-not obfuscation that eventually came back to haunt him.

"Satanism" itself, so far as it can be understood, is a rather confused system that can mean different things to different people. Some have described it as at bottom a psychological disorder in which its victims cannot achieve any sexual pleasure unless through transgressive or blasphemous acts. Others claim it is merely reverence for a very different being than Christian theology's arch-villain, who they say has been unjustly blamed for human suffering. Not true, say these Satanists: Their deity is one of self-fulfillment and personal autonomy, a healthy contrast to the guilt and denial espoused by centuries of religious indoctrination. Anton LaVey (1930–1997), American founder of the Church of Satan, encapsulated his tenets as "the worship of life," maintaining that he and his disciples were "concerned with the fullest gratification of the ego on this plane of existence." Then why the pentagrams, black candles, and nude ceremonies of his organization? Groups like LaVey's typified the latter-day Satanism that reveled in creepy shock effects to titillate the squares, yet still pretended to be a serious philosophy that had somehow drawn the reproaches of the intolerant. The briefly popular 1980s metal performer King Diamond likewise denied anything aberrant in his messages—"Satan, for me, is not like the guy with two horns and a long tail. . . . Satan stands for the powers of the unknown, and that's what I'm writing about"—before putting on his skull makeup and going back to shriek numbers titled "The Possession" and "Black Horsemen."

The most extreme Satanism, whose rites and beliefs were first documented in France during the 1600s, consisted of active and often obscene parodies of the Catholic liturgy. Though authentic and objective accounts are hard to come by, covert rituals of defrocked priests, sexual desecrations of Christian figures (as statuary or human stand-ins), and animal or occasionally human sacrifice did take place from the early modern era right into the twentieth century. These seem to have arisen out of unconscious but deeply felt hostility toward an all-powerful Church, combined with a very disturbed erotomania that had no other outlet in pious society. By Jimmy Page's lifetime the emotional need to resort to such outlandish performances had become extinct, and this kind of Satanism had become fodder for horror fiction and movies rather than something still observed among reasonable people.

Page revealed in 1988 that he had no religious upbringing at the hands of his nonobservant parents ("They were baptized but they didn't go to church"), though in the mid-1990s he was seen wearing a "Recovering Catholic" T-shirt on a talk show with Robert Plant. Whatever his background, as an adult Page became a wealthy man able to afford and acquire many valuable items with occult connotations, and able to privately subscribe to the code of Thelema, as transcribed by Aleister Crowley in his capacity as head of the Ordo Templi Orientis (Order of the Temple of the East). It's been speculated that Page likely joined the OTO when a member of Led Zeppelin and is still involved, though the order is by its creed highly discreet and not open to the dilettante. Crowley's *Book of the Law* puts forward the famous decree "Do what thou wilt shall be the whole of the Law," going further to maintain:

> [E]ach of us stars is to move on our true orbit, as marked out by the nature of our position, the law of our growth, the impulse of our past experiences. All events are equally lawful—and every one necessary, in the long run—for all of us, in theory; but in practice, only one act is lawful for each one of us at any given moment. Therefore Duty consists in determining to experience the right event from one moment of consciousness to another.

This is not that far from the values upheld by Anton LaVey and in some respects even resembles the objectivism of author Ayn Rand (*The Virtue of Selfishness*). Thelema is centered around an exaltation of the Will—the adherent's fundamental life purpose and desire—as the most important element. As the determined leader of what became one of the most popular and profitable musical acts of the twentieth century, Jimmy Page appears to have been a devout and well-rewarded Thelemite. On the other hand, he has also been associated with a variety of charitable organizations, an altruistic gesture that would seem to contravene the "Do what thou wilt" instruction.

So how did Page's "Satanist" rep arise? Like many who preached a new religion, Aleister Crowley was outspoken in his denunciation of old ones. Raised (and probably warped) by a rigidly and narrowly Christian mother, Crowley adopted his title as "the Great Beast" from her own epithet for him and spent his life alternating quite sober explications of Asian or ancient spiritualities with scandalous bids to overturn the priggish Victorian and Edwardian moral conventions of his day. Thus *The Book of the Law,* which Crowley claimed had been dictated by the spirit Aiwass through his entranced wife in 1904, contains a passage exhorting:

> I am in a secret fourfold world, the blasphemy against all gods of men. Curse them! Curse them! Curse them! With my Hawk's head I peck at the eyes of Jesus as he hangs upon the cross. I flap my wings in the face of Mohammed & blind him. With my claws I tear out the flesh of the Indian and the Buddhist, Mongol and Din. Bahlasti! Ompehda! I spit on your crapulous creeds.

Defining and celebrating his own faith by reversing or at least realigning the biblical hierarchies of good and evil, Crowley virtually invited the condemnation of his peers—never mind his personal escapades of drug addiction, sodomy, spousal abuse and abandonment, and general irreverence. Ever since, many critics and journalists have used "Satanist" as a shorthand label for Crowley and by extension Jimmy Page, even though neither man meets the accurate description. Page, certainly, has never displayed in his art or life the cheap demonology of lesser, death metal bands, like Slayer or Lamb of God, and in interviews has sprinkled his remarks with pleasantries like "Good lord," "Crikey," and "My goodness gracious." In 2000 he went so far as to take legal action against a London magazine that had run an article attesting he had cast Satanic spells over the dying form of John Bonham; he won financial damages and the publishers were forced to apologize and deny the story.

From Aleister Crowley Page learned and applied the disciplines of intention, focus, and effort: "What I can relate to is Crowley's system of self-liberation in which repression is the greatest work of sin," he said in 1977. "Because his whole thing was liberation of the person, and that restriction would foul you up, lead to frustration which leads to violence, crime, mental breakdown, depending on what sort of makeup you have on underneath." Yet there was more to this than just diligence or self-gratification. Crowley transcribed and carried out numerous magical "operations" in order to secure his goals, using complex invocations and symbols, a substitution technique Jimmy Page was to borrow many years later. "Yes, I knew what I was doing," he responded to a query from *Guitar World*'s Brad Tolinski about the puzzling glyphs and sigils worn on his stage clothes and displayed on Led Zeppelin album sleeves. "But the fact is, as far as I was concerned, it was working, so I used it. But it's really no different than people who wear ribbons around their wrists: It's a talismanic approach to something. Well, let me amend that—it's not exactly the same thing, but it is in the same realm." Until he makes a candid confession to the contrary, it may be assumed that this was about as mysterious as the guitarist's efforts in magic got. If his Thelemite values helped him to do well at his chosen profession, they did not seem to have saved him from the ordinary human setbacks of ill health or other misfortune—any more than they did Aleister Crowley, who died broke and addicted to heroin at age seventy-two. Ultimately, Page's most lasting achievements can be attributed to the talent he displayed for the whole world rather than any hidden rituals or incantations he might have conducted out of the public eye. "I'll leave this subject by saying the four musical elements of Led Zeppelin making a fifth is magic unto itself," he concluded. "That's the alchemical process."

And If You Listen Very Hard: The Backward Messages on "Stairway to Heaven"

Yes, there are backward messages audible to anyone who wants to hear them, but no, they were not put there by Led Zeppelin.

The strangest of the various myths concerning the band, and one of the most publicized, the "Stairway to Heaven" smear has actually been addressed by the surviving members who have been pained to have their masterpiece tarred in such a fashion. "We were so proud of [the song]," Robert Plant told *Rolling Stone* in 1990, "and its intentions are so positive, that the last thing one would do would be . . . I find it foul, the whole idea." Elsewhere the vocalist stated, "You can't find anything if you play that song backward. I know because I've tried. There's nothing there." He said to *Musician* magazine in 1983, "The first time I heard [the rumor] it was early in the morning when I was living at home, and I heard it on a news program. I was absolutely drained all day." John Paul Jones was similarly dismissive: "Of course, it's fatal, you know, because you tend to wind these people up after a while. If you go around saying, 'Oh, yes, if you play track eight at 36 rpms, you'll definitely hear a message,' they'll say, 'All right,' and go right home and try it. . . . It's just sitting ducks, really." Jimmy Page has refused to dignify the allegations with any comments at all. Following Plant's dismissal, "I figure if backward masking really worked, every record in the store would have 'Buy this album!' hidden on it," Page summed up: "You've got it, you've hit the nail on the head. And that's all there is to say about it."

Backward masking stories are not unique to Led Zeppelin, and "Stairway to Heaven" is not the only rock song purported to contain them. At the heart of the notion is the occult fad that took hold in the youth culture of the 1960s and '70s, along with the professional and consumer record-ing technology in use at the time and the almost mystical significance attached by audiences to the private lives and commercially released music of the era's most popular performers. Led Zeppelin was caught up in the controversy through an unfortunate coincidence of factors, which, however implausible they seem separately, together made for a fascinating riddle; as with Charles Manson's murderous interpretations of the Beatles' lyrics on their 1968 "White Album," the imagined backward messages on "Stairway to Heaven" have nothing to do with the intentions of the group itself but nevertheless add an intriguing dimension to the work. Only in the rock 'n' roll heyday could anything like backward masking have been conceived, and only Led Zeppelin could be thought to have implanted Satanic adjurations in their most celebrated anthem.

Since the beginning of mechanically reproduced sound, engineers (including pioneer Thomas Edison) noticed that recording and playback machines could be run in reverse as well as forward; speech and music played backward did have a recognizable flow or rhythm, which made for an incidental curiosity to anyone who got to hear it. It was not until the advent of multitrack recording in the 1950s, where separate takes of perfected performances could be "mixed" into a single completed composition, that the possibilities of backward sounds were opened up. Blended into other-wise conventionally recorded material, an isolated backward track could have a striking effect. (The almost unlistenable B side of a 1966 novelty hit, Napoleon XIV's "They're Coming to Take Me Away, Ha-Haaa," was the same song entirely reversed.) Before the invention of electronic or digital phasing features and the sonic alterations made possible with computer technology, backward recordings were one of the few gimmicks available to recording professionals—and one of the simplest to achieve.

For rock 'n' rollers exploring the new psychedelic realm, incorporat-ing one or more backward tracks into their cuts was a very freaky device.

Jimi Hendrix used them (along with sped-up and slowed-down tapes) on "Are You Experienced," "Third Stone from the Sun," and other tunes, and the Beatles employed a variety of experimentations in "Tomorrow Never Knows," "Strawberry Fields Forever," "I'm Only Sleeping," "Rain," and elsewhere in their discography. "Rain," the B side of 1966's "Paperback Writer," heard John Lennon's voice played in reverse for an entire verse. "Before Hendrix, before the Who, before *any* fucker," Lennon said proudly in 1980. "I got home from the studio and I was stoned out of my mind on marijuana and, as I usually do, I listened to what I'd recorded that day. Somehow I got it on backward and I sat there, transfixed, with the earphones on, with a big hash joint. I ran in the next day and said, 'I know what to do with it, I know. . . . Listen to this!' So I made them all play it backward." During psychedelia's brief flowering, backward music became one of its trademark ornaments.

Though there are assuredly no "messages" in "Stairway to Heaven," some Led Zeppelin songs do utilize backward tracks. Jimmy Page was as alert to the studio innovations of mid-1960s rock music as anyone, and tried out some techniques while still in the Yardbirds. Rather than simply invert a tape of live instruments or vocals, Page hit upon the concept of reversing their *echo*—"bouncing it down" to another track—so that the reverberation, not the original sound, is heard back to front. "You turn the tape over," he explained later, "and then record the echo which is obviously after the signal; you turn the tape back and it precedes the signal." Reverse echo has a surreal, disorienting quality quite different from the plainer methodology of just turning a finished performance around; the closest a player can come to it without recording is to hit a chord or note on an amplified instrument with its volume turned down, then raise the volume while the initial resonance fades away. This very subtle trick was first used on the Yardbirds' folly "Ten Little Indians," but is better placed in Led Zeppelin's "You Shook Me," "Whole Lotta Love," "When the Levee Breaks" (backward music on *Led Zeppelin IV!*), and takes on a special potency in "The Wanton Song." Page noted that *Led Zeppelin*'s engineer Glyn Johns doubted reverse echo would even work until the guitarist-producer overruled him. "I had to scream, 'Push the bloody fader up!' And lo and behold, the effect worked perfectly. . . . [Johns] just couldn't accept that someone knew something that he didn't—especially a musician. . . . The funny thing is, Glyn did the next Stones album, and what was on it? Backward echo!" (Page probably refers to "You Got the Silver" from *Let It Bleed*.)

But though rock stars including Led Zeppelin were certainly putting inverted sounds onto their records, they never thought of using them to implant coded statements that could only be deciphered by listening to the discs rotated counterclockwise. That was the fans' idea. Some of the sharper or more attuned members of the audience must have deduced that the strange sounds on "Are You Experienced" or "Tomorrow Never Knows" were manipulated audio tracks, and, through trial and error and some damage to turntables and styli, started to uncover exactly what had gone into them. At the same time, as figures such as the members of the Beatles and Bob Dylan withdrew from public appearances, followers tried to detect more in their work than just the music. Millions of young record buyers felt such artists were so influential that no lack of accessibility could keep them from reading *something* into the albums—perhaps their heroes were trying to convey secrets too incriminating or revolutionary or upsetting to be spelled out as verses and choruses for anyone (including parents or police) to hear.

The most shocking of these secrets was the information that Beatle Paul McCartney had been killed in a car accident and replaced by a double. Rumors that "Paul is dead" were rife across American campuses in 1969, as the Beatles' album covers and songs were minutely analyzed for what turned out to be an impressive range of "clues" offered to the studious. One of the most persuasive of these was John Lennon's nonsense syllables muttered at the end of "I'm So Tired" from the "White Album": Played backward, they sounded like *Paul is dead, man, miss him, miss him.* Played backward, the sound collage "Revolution #9" also revealed something that sounded like *Turn me on, dead man.* From the rich apocrypha of "Paul is dead" it was not long before any popular rock 'n' roll outfit could be given the same treatment. Though the musicians involved sometimes denied any attempt to "hoax" the public—as did all the Beatles, including McCartney himself—there were simply too many listeners chasing too few musicians for every last rumor to be duly discredited. Then, in November 1971, Led Zeppelin released their untitled fourth album, including the standout "Stairway to Heaven."

Because it was never issued as a single, and because Led Zeppelin were not, for all their sold-out concerts and number one records, the most visible group of their decade, it was some time before anyone alleged that "Stairway to Heaven" carried its own program of backward messages. Perhaps this cult status helped engender the allegations in the first place—after all, if Led Zeppelin were hiding Satanic imprecations in their songs, they wouldn't have rushed to broadcast them to all and sundry, would they? It's possible that, in 1973 or 1978, some gathering of stoned teenagers somewhere in America put their favorite Led Zep epic on the turntable and, knowing the folklore of other rock artists' "signs," decided to spin the album the wrong way around. Not knowing what they were about to hear—with no preconceived results in mind—they might have been surprised, and a little spooked, to hear slurred phrases that almost sounded like *There is no escaping it. . . . Here's to my sweet Satan . . . for it makes me sad, whose power is Satan . . . I will sing because I live with Satan. . . .* Back in class the next day, the story was told and retold, and, to anyone who wanted to believe it, there was no turning back. Perhaps.

Led Zeppelin had been disbanded for almost two years before the backward-message rumor was aired in public. In 1982 a Louisiana pastor named Jacob Aranza had published a slim tract titled *Backward Masking Unmasked: Backward Satanic Messages of Rock and Roll Exposed*, which raised the issue of a Satanic subtext in "Stairway to Heaven" and other songs. The same year, the California State Assembly held a hearing of the Committee on Consumer Protection and Toxic Materials where, on April 27, legislators heard rock songs by Led Zeppelin, the Beatles, Styx, Electric Light Orchestra, and Black Oak Arkansas that were claimed by witness William H. Yarroll to contain backward messages. Colorado-based Yarroll, described as both a neuroscientist and a management consultant, told the committee that pro-Satan encryptions were obligatory duties on the part of musicians who had agreed to "perform certain things" in service of the devil. "The potential for manipulation of people completely unaware of what is going on here is truly staggering," said Assemblyman Phillip D. Wyman, a Republican, while Democrat Chairwoman Sally Tanner agreed that the messages were "a very serious matter. . . . I think we have to look a lot further in this." By June, federal representative Robert Dornan, another Republican from California, had introduced a bill in Congress providing for warning labels on records found to contain backward messages.

The anti-rock movement had been encouraged by the conservative swing in American politics (capped with Ronald Reagan's election to the presidency in 1980), and thus the hunting down of occult influences in pop music was part of a larger social reaction against the so-called moral permissiveness of the previous decades. Later in the 1980s, the Congressional Parents' Music Resource Center (PMRC) held hearings investigating "porn rock" as purveyed by a variety of acts, and a veritable Satanism scare swept the nation, leading to hysterical accusations of ritual abuse of children at day care centers, the diabolic undertones of the Dungeons & Dragons board game, and supposed Satanic motives in several murder cases. Backward masking in famous rock songs was noted as another symptom of the epidemic. Religious zealots led the crusade, as exampled by one preacher on a widely distributed "educational" tape titled *Satan's Secret Sabotage*:

> . . . These bands are singing about voodooism, the Occult, Satan, drugs and sex, and far more. . . . Led Zeppelin's Jimmy Page is a

devout follower of the teachings of Aleister Crowley and presently lives in the former Occultist's mansion, known as the Boleskine House, overlooking the lake where the Loch Ness monster lives. . . . This mansion features an underground passageway where Crowley held human sacrificial ceremonies to Satan. This is the same passageway that now leads to his grave. . . . Herein lies the connection in Aleister Crowley's *Book of Magic*: that one of his Occultic teachings should be that we should learn to talk backwards, write backwards, and play phonographic records backward, and this inspired and encouraged the use of back masking in the record industry and directly tied it to the Occult, and this was to become the channel for Satanically infiltrating the minds of unsuspecting people.

Musicians and the music business, for their part, reacted with incredulity to the backward-masking stigma. "Swan Song is in the business of making records that play in one direction," Lauren Siciliano of Led Zeppelin's private label was quoted. "We've never recorded anything backward intentionally." Another Swan Song official asked, "What's wrong with you people anyhow? Playing a record backward will blow your turntable." Bob Merlis of Warner Brothers called the indictments "a non-issue. . . . The fact that some fanatics are looking at it is amusing. To use state money to investigate the matter goes from amusing to ridiculous."

The irony was that all the attention put on backward masking, especially on the prime suspect of "Stairway to Heaven," actually promoted the search for hidden messages in rock songs among listeners to whom such fantasies would otherwise never have occurred. Just as the witch trials of medieval Europe likely introduced the concept of devil worship to those who might not otherwise have considered it while condemning the mostly innocent people who were accused of it, so did the likes of Jacob Aranza and William H. Yarroll inspire thousands of fans to go back to their copies of *Led Zeppelin IV* (or buy the record for the first time) and listen for the Satanic urgings said to be audible therein. In 1984 a clinical study conducted by the University of Texas at El Paso, "The Role of Suggestion in the Perception of Satanic Messages in Rock-and-Roll Recordings," was published, which concluded that subjects prompted to hear such messages disproportionately claimed that they did. "When large numbers of listeners report that they can indeed hear the demonic hymns, a reasonable hypothesis is that suggestion is playing an important role," the study's authors observed. "There is ample evidence to suggest that, when vague and unfamiliar stimuli are presented, [subjects] are highly likely to accept suggestions, particularly when the suggestions are presented by someone with prestige or authority." It was noted incidentally that rock opponents' use of the term "backward masking" was erroneous (it is applied in diagnoses of schizophrenia and has nothing to do with records or music). The songs selected for the University of Texas study were the Beatles' "Revolution," Black Sabbath's "Black Sabbath," and Led Zeppelin's "Stairway to Heaven," a pretty righteous rock block if heard on the radio.

An obvious objection to the backward-masking charge—that the messages could never be heard unless you took the trouble of spinning the disc the wrong way around—was ignored by proponents of the theory, who argued that the messages worked on a subconscious level and were "unscrambled" by the brain, which failed to register their phonetic content. This idea was itself a holdover from the subliminal-advertising accusations of the 1950s which were popularized in books like *The Hidden Persuaders*, claiming print and televised commercials were doctored to feature seductive or enticing text and pictures that bypassed consumers' rational resistance. Some rock groups, playing along with the controversy and the earlier "Paul is dead" fabrication, put deliberate backward messages on their records, including Pink Floyd on *The Wall* and ELO on *Face the Music*, but there was nothing Satanic in these spoofs. In time, lawsuits contending backward masking by Judas Priest and Ozzy Osbourne had encouraged teen suicides were thrown out of court and the topic became another instance of cultural myth in the age of mass communication, or a modern chapter of the 1841 treatise *Extraordinary Popular Delusions and the Madness of Crowds*. Priest singer Rob Halford testified that the backward lyrics *he* heard in his music ran to such absurdities as, "Hey look, Ma, my chair's broken" and "It's so fishy, personally I'll owe it."

So, what of the backward messages on "Stairway to Heaven"? Even today, long after vinyl albums and mechanical turntables have become obsolete, some die-hards refuse to disavow the rumor. Digital recording, in fact, now makes it more convenient to play *Led Zeppelin IV* in any direction or speed without the hassle of manually rotating a record player. Aleister Crowley's recommendations from *Magick in Theory and Practice* that daily activities, including talking, walking, and spinning phonographs, be conducted in reverse provided telling proof for those already convinced (e.g., the author of *Satan's Secret Sabotage*). "Let the Exempt Adept first train himself to think backwards by external means," Crowley wrote, adding, "Let him constantly watch, if convenient, cinematograph films, and listen to phonograph records, reversed, and let him so accustom himself to these that they appear natural and appreciable as a whole." But there were other pointers, notably the backward lettering of the album title on the inner sleeve of *Houses of the Holy* and the split-screen shots in *The Song Remains the Same*, whereby members of the band were seen in mirrored or reversed images in the same frame. Crucial to the legend was the belief that the "Stairway" messages were Satanic, so a song ostensibly about heaven would therefore have to be about hell in its sonic negative. A few Zeppelin songs do reference the devil or Satan ("No Quarter," "Houses of the Holy," "Achilles Last Stand," "Nobody's Fault but Mine"), hell ("Dazed and Confused"), "the Evil One" ("Ramble On"), the "Dragon of Darkness" ("The Battle of Evermore"), or heeding "the Master's call" ("Houses of the Holy"). The more elaborate interpretations of "Stairway"'s reversed lyrics, around the line *"If there's a bustle in your hedgerow,"* are transcribed as *"So here's to my sweet Satan, the one whose little path will make me sad, whose power is Satan / He'll give you 666 / There was a little tool shed where he made us suffer, sad Satan."* Reinforcing this tangent were the verified accounts of Black Masses where the Lord's Prayer was recited backward and crosses were hung upside down. There was also the sensational 1970s novel and movie *The Exorcist*, in which what first appears to be gibberish uttered by a disturbed child is revealed to be a demonic voice speaking backward, thus "Nowonmai" equaled "I am no one," et cetera. When all of these are implied to the typical Led Zeppelin audience, as they would have been in the years after the song's release, the reversed snippets of "Stairway to Heaven" do have an eerie tone, and there is a haunting melancholy in the depiction of a "sad Satan" whose "path will make me sad," but their resemblance to actual, premeditated vocalization is—once and for all—a complete and utter accident.

20

It's Not as Hard as It Seems

The Art of Led Zeppelin

Pictures of Eleven: Led Zeppelin's Album Covers

T hough the artistic value of rock music from the 1960s and '70s might still be debated, few would disagree that the decades were the high point of the record industry's use of photography and graphic design. This is because the twelve-inch LP album, with its larger "canvas," had taken over from the smaller 45-rpm single as the prime economic driver of the business, and also because of the relatively expansive budgets and creative license granted to performers and their packagers. Few rock stars were directly responsible for the imagery on their album jackets (exceptions being Bob Dylan for *Planet Waves*, Cat Stevens for *Teaser and the Firecat*, Joni Mitchell for *Ladies of the Canyon*, John Entwistle for *The Who by Numbers,* and a preteen John Lennon for *Walls and Bridges*), but the exterior presentations of the classic rock era were pinnacles of pop art as much as the music they showcased. *Dark Side of the Moon*'s prism; *Sticky Fingers'* denim-straining crotch; the pissed-on pillar of *Who's Next*; the crispness of Bruce Springsteen's *Born to Run* (photographer Eric Meola) and Aerosmith's *Draw the Line* (caricaturist Al Hirschfeld); the surrealism of Yes's *Tales from Topographic Oceans* (sci-fi illustrator Roger Dean) and the Grateful Dead's *Aoxomoxa* (Rick Griffin); the beauty of Derek and the Dominos' *Layla and Other Assorted Love Songs* (Frandsen De Schonberg) and Santana's *Abraxas* (Mati Klarwein)—all constitute some of the most recognizable visual emblems of the last century. The covers of all of Led Zeppelin's original albums belong in the same category.

If there is a common theme to the wonderfully diverse range of pictures and portraits from the record sleeves of Zeppelin and their contemporaries, it is that they were as far removed from the bland commercial motifs of older artists as it was possible to get. Almost anything could go onto the album covers, as long as it wasn't a traditional grinning publicity shot of the performers themselves. The resultant creativity—what did the Jeff Beck Group have to do with an apple? Or Black Sabbath with a greenish woman at dusk? Or Rush with a nude figure and a pentagram?—shaped the audience's opinion of the music inside. There was then a density and a depth to the records that was only partly about the tunes and the lyrics; aesthetically, the discs and their containers were inseparable (as well as useful platforms for joint-rolling). No performers from the period had a more consistent run of beautiful, haunting, and thought-provoking album covers than Led Zeppelin.

Led Zeppelin

An initial calling card whose stark black-and-white design has become an emblem for the band itself, the cover of Led Zeppelin's debut album got the band off to an explosive start even before the needle dropped on "Good Times Bad Times." Although it was an obvious choice to have a zeppelin of some kind pictured on the jacket, it was Jimmy Page's decision to use one of the most famous and disturbing news photographs of the previous thirty-odd years, from one of the first occasions when newsreels, still cameras, and radio broadcasters were on hand to capture an historic moment for rapid dissemination, as the basis for the artwork. Taken by a United Press cameraman in the first seconds after the Nazi dirigible *Hindenburg* exploded at Lakehurst New Jersey, following a transatlantic flight on May 6, 1937, the widely syndicated shot could fairly have been called "iconic" even before it was adopted by Led Zeppelin. According to Who bass player John Entwistle, a similar picture of the British R-101 airship's crash near Paris in 1930 was in mind when he and Page considered forming a band after their "Beck's Bolero" session with Jeff Beck in 1966 ("We'll go over like a lead zeppelin"), and there were certainly other stock photographs of airship wrecks from the same period to have chosen, but Page picked the best one.

To avoid licensing fees, it fell to Royal College of Art student George Hardie to render the copyrighted 1937 photograph into an original picture. Like Led Zeppelin, Hardie was young and looking for a break, and he had a connection with the band through a fellow student who knew Page. Hardie first submitted more imaginative (though less visually arresting) sketches of an airborne zeppelin, but Page, showing him a library book with the *Hindenburg* still, insisted that the stock image be simply re-created. This Hardie did, using tracing paper and a special Rapidograph ink pen. His fee was £60 (about $400 US). Look closely and the painstaking, dot-by-dot

George Hardie's rendering of the *Hindenburg* disaster became a Zeppelin trademark.   *Author's Collection*

detailing of the flames, the rupturing framework of the airship, and the looming dark of its underside can still be seen as they were initially illustrated. Stretched across the cover in a neat diagonal pointing straight at the band name in the upper left corner, with a phallic suggestiveness few punters could miss, the new record by the English heavy blues group would catch many an eye in the record bins of 1969. In a moment when most pop record jackets were splotched with a rainbow of colors and cliché psychedelic surrealism, *Led Zeppelin* was almost unique in its monochrome reproduction of an instantly recognizable press photo. The gambit paid off. Years later, comparably historic images were used for hard rockers Mr. Big's 1991 *Lean Into It* (a nineteenth-century Parisian train wreck) and Rage Against the Machine's self-titled debut in 1992 (a Vietnamese monk's self-immolation), but the Zeppelin artwork remains definitive.

On the back of *Led Zeppelin*, Page commissioned ex-Yardbird Chris Dreja—who had very nearly stayed on with the reformed act in 1968—to take the photo of the four band members. Unsmiling, posed in a circle around the song titles and (not completely truthful) author credits, the quartet stared out in serious black and white. All of them were barely into their twenties, wearing expressions of grim arrogance that would be borne out in the run of hit records they were to enjoy from this premier disc on. Though the soft-focus frame of Dreja's portrait is unexceptional, it looks like the photographer did (or was asked to do) a few touch-ups on Page's hair, where the waves in the guitarist-producer's tresses appear to have been given some doctored luster. Other info on the sleeve lists Glyn Johns as "Director of Engineering," a title given again only on the next Led Zeppelin album, and Peter Grant as "Executive Producer," a title to be used on all the rest. Interestingly, a Zeppelin "logo," based on George Hardie's first submissions and reused in various promotional releases and even the next album, was placed at the bottom of the back cover, an early example of rock

The back-sleeve photograph of *Led Zeppelin* was taken by ex-Yardbird Chris Dreja.
Author's Collection

branding that predated or was contemporaneous with the Rolling Stones' tongue, Aerosmith's wings, the Grateful Dead's "Steal Your Face" skull, and Zeppelin's own Swan Song angel.

Led Zeppelin II

The "Brown Bomber" was Zeppelin's breakthrough album. Though its cover is no match for the unforgettable symbolism of its predecessor, it did extend the Gothic, martial implications of *Led Zeppelin* with another zeppelin shape spread over both sides over both the inner and outer gatefold, and with the curious use of another often reproduced photograph, in this case a group portrait of flyers from Germany's Jasta 11 squadron, taken during World War I in March 1917. There were no doubt some listeners who would have vaguely understood the picture to be of some kind of military unit. With its white zeppelin outline splayed across the Germanic brown of the sleeve, *Led Zeppelin II* gave a first impression of more hard-hitting, take-no-prisoners music, which, containing as it did "Whole Lotta Love," "Heartbreaker," "Moby Dick," and "Bring It On Home," was a fair assessment.

Another young Londoner, art director David Juniper, illustrated the cover. Juniper was from Epsom, Surrey, along with Jimmy Page, and studied at art school around the same time as the future Zeppelin leader. "The music of *Led Zeppelin* had blown me away," he told Rockpopgallery.com in 2007, "and so, on spec, I mocked up a fold-out design for the second album and took it to Peter Grant and Mickey [*sic*] Most at RAK Records. . . . The combination of photography and airbrush illustration was very tricky, especially compared to today's digital equivalents. The cover imagery was completely experimental and I liked the combination of the abstract ghostly zeppelin shape along with a faded World War I photo of German aviators." Juniper took a publicity shot of the four Zeppelin members and fit their faces over those of the pilots, adding an odd, almost random collage of other heads (or just sunglasses, moustaches, and beards) to alter those of the Jasta fliers.

From left to right, the standing figures on the Zeppelin album are:

- ◆ Unknown Jasta pilot, with shades and facial hair added (not Richard Cole or Peter Grant)
- ◆ Miles Davis, with eyes altered and beard, over Jasta Leutnant Hintsch
- ◆ Vizefeldwebel Festner, with facial hair (resemblance to Charles Manson is accidental)
- ◆ Leutnant Emil Schaefer, with shades and facial hair (not Cole or Grant)

This photo of Manfred von Richthofen's World War I fighter squadron was altered by artist David Juniper for the cover of *Led Zeppelin II*.   *Author's Collection*

◆ Andy Warhol "Superstar" Ultra Violet, over Oberleutnant Kurt Wolff (not actress Glynis Johns as a joke on former engineer Glyn Johns)

◆ Astronaut Neil Armstrong, over Leutnant Georg Simon

◆ John Bonham, over Leutnant Otto Brauneck

Seated figures:

◆ Jimmy Page, over Leutnant Esser

◆ Robert Plant, over Leutnant Krefft

◆ John Paul Jones, over Leutnant Lothar von Richtofen (brother of "Red Baron" Manfred, who was omitted from the original photo)

It's possible some early viewers assumed the group to be a ten-piece Led Zeppelin band, including black and female personnel, making the portrait more puzzling than it already was. Inside, the more straightforward panorama of a spotlighted zeppelin cruising over a towering classical structure, with the album credits printed as if on marble, emphasized the oversize nature of the songs and the quartet itself. These too evoked a Wagnerian, Sturm und Drang aesthetic, like something out of Leni Riefenstahl's *Triumph of the Will*, that was perfectly appropriate for the bluesy bombast of Led Zeppelin. Though the conceit would seem cheesy when other acts took it on (see Deep Purple's *In Rock*, Boston's *Boston*, and countless heavy metal covers), it was in October 1969 an effective visualization of the group's sonic scale and ambition. Juniper's *Led Zeppelin II* was nominated for a Grammy Award for Best Album Cover in 1970 but lost to Gary McFarland's *America the Beautiful.*

Led Zeppelin III

"A disappointment," Jimmy Page called the cover of the third Zeppelin album in a 1998 interview. "I'll take responsibility for that. . . . I knew the artist and described what we wanted with this wheel that made things disappear and change. But he got very personal with his artwork and disappeared with it. . . . I thought it looked teeny-bopperish." With its rotating volvelle that utilized the principle of crop rotation calendars, *Led Zeppelin III* was the most elaborate of the band's album jackets to date, but graphically it was less successful: busy, cluttered, and, as Page complained, too "personal" for the message Led Zeppelin wanted to project. For what it's worth, John Paul Jones has volunteered that his own favorite Zeppelin cover is "the one with the wheel." The artist of the sleeve went by the name Zacron, but Page and others knew him as Richard Drew.

The strange cover of *III* was nevertheless congruent with the unexpectedly acoustic tones of its music. Prominent were birds, butterflies, and insects; geometrical shapes; Victorian-era illustrations of mechanical objects; old cars (one with the initials "JP"); and a variety of flying machines, including British airships that were cousin to the German zeppelins, a flight of Hawker Fury biplanes from the 1930s, a twin-boomed Luftwaffe Focke-Wulf Fw 189; and the Montgolfier brothers' hot-air balloon of 1783. A castle with the numeral 4 and the word *Private* superimposed may refer to Page's address of 4 Shooters Hill in Pangbourne, Berkshire. The entire hodgepodge of found imagery was strongly reminiscent of the pop art of Peter Blake (famous for the Beatles' *Sgt. Pepper*) and other British designers working in the same fashionable style of the period. In addition to the riotous colors and pictures from the rest of the jacket, the circular volvelle featured photos of the band members (lined up so the same player appeared in two or three cutouts at once), and even shots of what may be Robert Plant's dog Strider (subject of "Bron-y-Aur Stomp") and a young child, possibly one of John Paul Jones's daughters, or John Bonham's son Jason or Plant's daughter Carmen. The comparatively understated back cover showed only the quartet plotted in a geometric layout (for some reason, only Plant's picture is tinted), with the singer's necklace doctored to bear another of Zacron's ornamental shapes.

The most significant detail on the inside cover of *Led Zeppelin III* was not any of the artist's eccentric clippings, or even the bulbous font of the group name, but the acknowledgment of the location where Plant and Jimmy Page had first composed some of its material. Misspelled as "Bron-y-Aur," the Welsh retreat is given a very hippie credit—what exactly is "a somewhat forgotten picture of true completeness"?—that established its centrality in the Zeppelin legend. Though unmentioned there, it would be in the following album's "musical statements" that the greatest impact of the "small derelict cottage in Snowdonia" would be heard.

Untitled (Led Zeppelin IV)

As well as being one of the most popular records of all time, the fourth Led Zeppelin album came in the most enigmatic sleeve ever to contain an album of commercial pop music. The words *Led Zeppelin* were seen nowhere on the disc's packaging—not even on the record label itself—and to this day the mysteriously opaque cover's outer and inner designs are some of the key ones in the group's mythology.

It is true that the album was not as anonymous as has been claimed. By the year of its release in 1971 many progressive rock record jackets were stylized works that eschewed bold banner texts in favor of some or other talismanic visual: Blind Faith's self-titled debut of 1969 (bare-chested adolescent girl), King Crimson's *In the Court of the Crimson King* the same year (grotesque facial close-up) John Lennon's *Plastic Ono Band* from 1970 (Lennon and Yoko Ono reclining under a tree), Dylan's 1970 *Self-Portrait* (self-portrait), and others, were all practically barren of titles or artist names on their front covers. Led Zeppelin took this approach a step farther by putting *no* identity on either side of their album, yet in a sense they were only catching up to other star acts who were so big that they literally needed no introduction. Jimmy Page's reasons for the move were not just pride, though, but also resentment. "[T]he cover wasn't meant to antagonize the record company," he told Brad Tolinski in 2001. "It was designed as a response to the music critics who maintained that the success of our first three albums was driven by hype and not talent. . . . So we stripped everything away, and let the music do the talking." When the promotional department at Atlantic Records objected to the band's idea of an untitled release, "We said they couldn't have the master tape until they got the cover right," avowed Robert Plant. After some insistence by Peter Grant and the rest of the band, Atlantic gave in, but in any case, the LP arrived in stores shrink-wrapped with some wording on disposable stickers, and shipped in large quantities

BLACK·DOG·
ROCK·AND·ROLL·
THE·BATTLE·OF·EVERMORE·⚒
STAIRWAY·TO·HEAVEN·

MISTY·MOUNTAIN·HOP·
FOUR·STICKS·
GOING·TO·CALIFORNIA·
WHEN·THE·LEVEE·BREAKS·

⚒ SANDY·DENNY· APPEARS·BY·COURTESY·OF·ISLAND·RECORDS·

RECORDED·AT·
HEADLEY·GRANGE·HAMPSHIRE· ISLAND·STUDIOS·LONDON·
SUNSET·SOUND· LOS·ANGELES·CALIF·

INSIDE· ILLUSTRATION 'THE·HERMIT' BARRINGTON·COLBY· M·O·M·
DESIGN· CO·ORDINATION· GRAPHREAKS·

PRODUCED·BY·JIMMY·PAGE·
EXECUTIVE· PRODUCER· PETER·GRANT·

Since 1971, the four symbols from *Led Zeppelin IV* have been an enduring source of speculation for fans.   *Courtesy of Len Ward / The Rad Zone*

and with attendant promotion (posters, review copies, etc.) that clearly tied the product to the famous rock'n' roll group.

The cover of what most fans have come to call *Led Zeppelin IV* (a logical assumption after the numeric titles of its predecessors) was another gatefold edition, with both exterior and interior wraparound images. At first glance, the picture is of some sort of dilapidated wall with a battered painting of an old man carrying a bundle of sticks hanging askew—open the fold, and the wall is revealed to be a ruin, with a modern apartment tower looming over soulless low-income housing in the background. The photo was taken by rock lensman Keith Morris in the Eve Hill area of the West Midlands town of Dudley, near Robert Plant's home of Wolverton in the suburbs of Birmingham; the John Bonham family had only recently vacated the high-rise, known as Butterfield Court. Jimmy Page explained that the surprise juxtaposition of preindustrial decay with grim technocracy was intentional: "[W]e decided to contrast the modern skyscraper on the back with the old man with the sticks—you see the destruction of the old and the new coming forward."

Page has also said that the painting itself was a chance discovery he made while antiquing in the Berkshire municipality of Reading with Robert Plant. "Robert found the picture of the old man with the sticks and suggested we work it into our cover somehow." The guitarist was an enthusiastic collector of Art Nouveau artifacts and other pieces from the nineteenth century, and the unattributed painting fitted in with his personal tastes, but it has been speculated that the portrait was not the accidental find he made it out to be. Some have said that it depicts a George Pickingill, the so-called Wizard of Essex, who reportedly held a malefic sway over the farmers and townsfolk around the village of Canewdon in the late 1800s. According to rural hearsay, the notorious Pickingill practiced witchcraft in his district, had somehow resided there for over one hundred years, and cast terrible ancient spells against anyone who dared to

Pamela Colman Smith's tarot illustration of the Hermit was adapted by artist Barrington Colby for *Led Zeppelin IV*.   *Author's Collection*

cross him—with the aid of a carved wooden stick he always carried. If the "old man with sticks" is indeed a representation of Pickingill, Page has either deliberately misled interviewers on the subject, or by an amazing coincidence it has turned up on a work by artists long linked to the occult. It may be, in the end, just an unknown painter's picture of an elderly farmer, resuscitated for use on a rock album.

Inside was another old man with a stick, albeit a more recognizable one. Officially known as *View in Half or Varying Light* but better remembered as "The Hermit," the inner gatefold was a variation on Pamela Colman Smith's design for that card in a familiar 1910 edition of the tarot deck. "It's basically an illustration of a seeker aspiring to the light of truth," Page said, noting the young aspirant climbing the rocky crag toward the elderly robed figure with the lamp, as a medieval walled town stands in the distance. Nowadays any flip through a pack of Arthur Edward Waite tarot cards will soon trigger a flashback to Led Zeppelin wall hangings, T-shirts, and incense sticks. In 2007 Page clarified that "The Hermit" originated from an 1854 Pre-Raphaelite painting of Christ by William Holman Hunt, *The Light of the World*, where the subject holds a lamp at nighttime.

This picture was credited to a Barrington Colby (sometimes spelled Coleby), whom Page described as "a friend." The "MoM" after Colby's name may stand for Man of Mystery, since his works have rarely been seen elsewhere, and it's even been speculated that he was no more than an alias of the former art student Jimmy Page himself. *View in Half or Varying Light* is not an especially well-executed drawing—it's really a straight copy of the tarot card—although some have strained to see a scary face hidden in the rocks upon which the Hermit is perched. Colby is said to currently reside in Switzerland. The 1996 album *Shaman*, by British New Age guitarist Phil Thornton, has presented Colby paintings, and, coincidentally or not, Thornton has collaborated with Egyptian musician Hossam Ramzy, who directed the Arabic backing players for the 1994 Jimmy Page and Robert Plant *No Quarter* project. Ultimately Barrington Colby might have been just another art school connection of Jimmy Page's, like George Hardie, David Juniper, and Richard Drew/Zacron, who unlike those men has since staked out a more idiosyncratic career apart from the field of commercial art.

With this record, Led Zeppelin for the first time personalized even the inner dust jacket of the vinyl disc. Here things became very mysterious. On one side the lyrics for the album's undisputed highlight, "Stairway to Heaven," were printed in a font Page had seen and appreciated from an old edition of the English *Studio*, a journal of the Arts and Crafts movement of the nineteenth century; the lavish, almost calligraphic lettering made the words appear as if out of an antiquated past rather than the sterile 1970s, which (as with the contrasting architectures of the exterior cover) was exactly the point. Yet another unknowable image from a previous century, a small black-and-white engraving reproduced in one corner showed a Renaissance-era bearded man studying a book with a few runes inscribed on a background rock and what looks like the word "London." Like the scattering of clips that had turned up across *Led Zeppelin III*, this may have been just a copyright-free thumbnail appropriated for its ambiguity, although present-day English occultist Dave Dickson told Zeppelin biographer Mick Wall it could be a representation of Dr. John Dee. Dee, an authenticated astrologer and magician in the court of Queen Elizabeth I, had himself sometimes transcribed cryptic signs and symbols for his own rituals; these sigils are today still visible in his preserved works such as the *Tuba Veneris* and the tablet *Sigillum Dei Aemeth*. The odd marks visible in the *Led Zeppelin IV* etching of him (or whoever it is) corresponded with those printed across the top of the sleeve's obverse.

Magic Runes Are Writ in Gold: The *Led Zeppelin IV* Symbols

For many years after the release of the album in November 1971, the quartet of designs from *IV* were the subjects of fans' wild guesswork and elaborate attempts at decoding. They were displayed on the band members' equipment in concert, as well as in their personal jewelry and clothing, but while it was soon possible to tell which symbol was whose, the riddle of what they stood for remained unsolved. In later years, though, the surviving players in Led Zeppelin have come forward with limited explications of their origins and intention—the runes have still been employed by the performers in the course of their solo careers—and independent research has to a large extent settled the matter. However, in forty years the four symbols have lost little of their graphic impact, and they continue to be among the most unique and readily identified corporate signatures in the world. Not bad for a gimmick Jimmy Page once called "just another ruse to throw the media into chaos."

Page at first wanted to use only a single logo for the record, in lieu of a conventional title, but he soon decided it would fairer to let each of the band's musicians choose his own. Since it was his idea, of course, he ended up with the most elaborate and obscure design while the others' were more easily sourced—in retrospect it seems that John Bonham and John Paul Jones were not overly excited about the idea and soon acquiesced to Page's fait accompli. "He showed us *The Book of Signs*," recalled Jones, "and said we should each choose a symbol. So Bonzo and I did this, though later we discovered Jimmy and Robert had gone off and had their symbols specially designed, which was typical." *The Book of Signs*, a 1930 reference text by

German typographer Rudolf Koch, was a common work tracing a history of European Christian and pre-Christian pictograms and runes. "John Paul Jones's symbol . . . was found in a book about runes and was said to represent a person who is both confident and competent because it was difficult to draw accurately," said Page. Jones's choice was the circle with a trio of arcs intersecting in its center to form three ovals. Bonham, likewise, soon settled on another Koch talisman, the three interlocking circles. "I suppose it's the trilogy," Robert Plant interpreted afterward. "Man, woman, and child . . . At one point, though, in Pittsburgh, I think, we observed that it was also the emblem of Ballantine's beer." A variation on Bonham's mark was used in the logo for his son Jason's 1990's band, Bonham. The drummer and bassist's pick of symbols that were geometric echoes of each other implied both their musical synergy and their subordinate roles in the group. Guest vocalist Sandy Denny also received her own diminutive sign, three linked triangles, that was again taken from the Koch volume.

SIGILLUM DEI ÆMETH, A PANTACLE
MADE BY DR. JOHN DEE.

Some of the inscriptions on this design by occultist John Dee resemble the alchemical and astrological symbols later taken up by Jimmy Page for his "ZoSo" trademark.

Author's Collection

Robert Plant's insignia was a more personal decision. "It represents courage to many red Indian tribes," said the singer. "I like people to lay down the truth. No bullshit—that's what the feather in the circle is all about." This symbol was adapted from English author James Churchward's *The Sacred Symbols of Mu*, another book from the 1930s, which purported to summarize the culture and philosophy of a Pacific lost continent; his "research," like many of the Zeppelin intellectual influences, gained currency during the backlash against Darwin, Marx, and industrialism that drove many British eccentrics and dissenters around the turn of the twentieth century. "All sorts of things can be tied in with Mu civilization, even the Easter Island effigies," Plant asserted. "These Mu people left stone tablets with their symbols inscribed into them all over the place." Though few serious archaeologists have time for the Mu theory, studies like Churchward's were rediscovered by the 1960s counterculture and esteemed as correctives to an increasingly

Lettering and design from the nineteenth-century British journal *The Studio* influenced Zeppelin's graphic style.   *Author's Collection*

rational and secular society. The airy, delicate symbolism of Plant's ringed feather well captured his lyrical and spiritual outlook.

Jimmy Page's sign from *Led Zeppelin IV* is not an Icelandic rune, a pseudo-ancient glyph, nor the word "ZoSo," though many have deciphered it as those and more extreme solutions. John Paul Jones told an interviewer, "Jimmy got his [symbol] from who knows where," and recalled the guitarist revealing to him it "was something to do with Saturday." Essentially Page's design is an astrological stand-in for the planet Saturn, from the centuries when the language of astrology was an advanced discipline rather than the self-help shorthand of lions, fish, twins, and scales served up today. The "ZoSo" emblem has been found in a 1557 document, *Ars Magica Arteficii* by Jerome Cardan (c. 1490–1565) an Italian physician and mathematician, and later turned up in two nineteenth-century French occult manuals, *Le Triple Vocabulaire Infernal* and *Le Dragon Rouge* (the latter a reprint of a 1521 manuscript). Both these and similar works are filled with many twisty, stylized designs that almost resemble words but which were once used as cryptograms in a variety of alchemical and magical practices; in each case, "ZoSo" is some derivative of the planet Saturn, the ruler of Page's astrological sign of Capricorn. Jones's recollection of "something to do with Saturday" is accurate insofar as the word itself is from the Latin *Saturni dies*, day of Saturn.

It is possible to break down Page's sigil into both a signification of Saturn ("Z") and the 666 ("oSo") as transcribed by Aleister Crowley—some have even explained it as a reference to tantric sex or the three-headed hound Cerberus—but the bottom line is that Page probably intended "ZoSo" to be a kind of written mantra, a private ideogram that applied to his personal birth sign and his own sophisticated knowledge of the occult. Like "abracadabra" or "hocus pocus," it was an internalized term best understood only by the occultist himself. Aleister Crowley had stated that true magicians should devise numerous such terms, "and he should have quintessentialized them all into one Word, which last word, once he has formed it, he should never utter consciously even in thought, until perhaps with it he gives up the ghost." A simple horoscope symbol for Capricorn, or the more ordinary runes of Jones and Bonham or the feather of Plant, were either too general or too obvious for Page: "ZoSo" was intricate enough to stand out visually and esoteric enough to baffle most if not all Led Zeppelin listeners. As he said to Mick Wall, "My symbol was about invoking and being invocative. And that's all I'm going to say about it."

The only named credits on *IV* are for Page as producer, Peter Grant as executive producer, Barrington Colby for "The Hermit," and Sandy Denny.

A little-known firm registered in the very 1971 label of Graphreaks was listed as the design team (Bob Fell and Danny Halperin have been named as the proprietors); among their scant other achievements were the Who's *Live at Leeds*, the Move's *Looking On*, and the self-titled debut *T. Rex*, all from the same year. As Led Zeppelin's biggest-selling record, containing their most popular song and several other perennial favorites, the fathomless riddles of its presentation have become as legendary as the music in its grooves. The four symbols used instead of the players' real names certified the audience's view that their beloved artists were not just lineups of compatible musicians but personifications of greater forces, a view begun with the four Beatles' roles as mind, heart, soul and body, and extending to the Kiss foursome's as the Starchild, the Demon, the Spaceman and the Cat. In today's flux of downloading, iPods, ringtones, and other disposable culture, the rich layers of meaning hidden in the cover of *Led Zeppelin IV* make it not only a classic of rock 'n' roll album photography and graphics but a triumphant example of a lost art.

Houses of the Holy

If not Led Zeppelin's best album then certainly the one with the most attractive album cover, *Houses of the Holy* continued the wordlessness of its predecessor and extended the mystical allusions of its layout. Neither *Houses* nor *IV* have any zeppelins on their jackets. Here again another gatefold design was used inside and out, augmented with clever and painstaking use of hand-tinting to realize its luminous color effects. *Houses of the Holy* is one of the masterworks of album illustration credited to the London agency of Hipgnosis (cf. Graphreaks), perhaps the most successful of all the record jacket design houses from the 1970s, whose gallery of spectacular covers includes many of the best-known rock albums of all time, with clients such as Pink Floyd, Black Sabbath, Yes, Def Leppard, 10cc, and UFO. Founded by Storm Thorgerson and Aubrey "Po" Powell, Hipgnosis specialized in conceptual, subtly detailed vistas that combined photography and art in mind-warping combinations; one reason the craft practiced by Hipgnosis and its competitors declined in later decades was that record labels invested more of their promotional funds in videos, prohibiting all but the simplest execution of mere album covers. *Houses of the Holy* was Led Zeppelin's most complicated sleeve yet, but the results were worth the expense.

Jimmy Page first approached Hipgnosis after admiring their cover for Wishbone Ash's *Argus*. According to Page, Storm Thorgerson's initial suggestion of a cover concept for the new Zeppelin record was of a tennis

The ornate *Houses of the Holy* font showed Art Nouveau influences.

Courtesy of Robert Rodriguez

racket. "Racket—don't you get it?" asked the artist. "Are you trying to imply that our music is a racket?" Page retorted before dismissing him. "We never saw him again," said the guitarist. "He had some balls! Imagine—on a first meeting with a client." The job went to Thorgerson's partner Aubrey Powell instead, who proposed a photo of either the mysterious Nazca lines in distant Peru, or of the geological rock formation at Giant's Causeway in Northern Ireland. Page and Peter Grant opted for the latter (though costs were not really an issue for the band at this point), while Powell sought to create a picture that recalled the Arthur C. Clarke novel *Childhood's End.* By the climax of the science fiction classic, a final generation of Earth children is taken to merge with a cosmic "Overmind." "The island lay golden in the heartless, unfeeling sunlight . . . ," Clarke writes. "There was no sound or movement from the children. They stood in scattered groups along the sand, showing no more interest in one another than in the homes they were leaving forever. . . . The scattered, unutterably lonely figures began to converge. . . ."

Powell took two child models, siblings Stefan and Samantha Gates, to the Giant's Causeway location and took a series of photos of them over several early mornings in November 1972. The gatefold shot was taken at the ruin of nearby Dunluce Castle. Because of inclement weather the natural lighting Powell wanted was unavailable and so had to be fabricated in the studio, where Phil Crennell airbrushed in the glowing blues and oranges of the final image. "When I first saw it," Powell said, "I said, 'Oh my God.' Then we looked at it, and I said, 'Hang on a minute, this has an otherworldly quality." Page's recollection is more practical: "When the proofs for the album came back, they didn't look anything like the original artwork. Again, we were on a deadline and there wasn't much to be done. I suppose it doesn't matter now."

The nudity of the Gates kids—composite photography multiplied the pair into eleven bodies visible on both sides of the outside cover—has made the *Houses* cover Led Zeppelin's closest to a controversial one, and it was reportedly banned in Spain and some states of the US Bible Belt. Today a whiff of exploitation might be detected in the sacrificial pose of the gatefold, where a naked adult holds one of the children aloft, and as even Powell admitted in 2009, "This could never have been done now—we'd be accused of all sorts of horrible things. In those days there was a sort of hippie innocence." The grown man in the midst of the prepubescent brother and sister has never been identified (he may be the shoot's makeup artist, Tom Smith), but outtakes from the photo shoot show him on the Giant's Causeway rocks behind Samantha and Stefan. In a sequence from Zeppelin's *The Song Remains the Same*, Robert Plant's own children Carmen and Karac frolic naked in a brook, with the same sort of back-to-the-land, dawn-of-a-new-race spirit that informed the *Houses of the Holy* illustration.

Inside the jacket, the lyrics for all the LP's songs were printed, as well as the vocal and instrumental lineup of each track. These were done in a plainer style than the "Stairway to Heaven" typeface from *Led Zeppelin IV*, but on both sides the album title was inscribed (both frontward and reversed) in another Art Nouveau font, this one designed by freelance Hipgnosis hire Bush Hollyhead. Though adapted from any number of lettering motifs of the late nineteenth century, the curvy and elongated slopes of the characters became the unofficial print of subsequent Led Zeppelin promotions, with the old-fashioned hyphen between the words once more suggesting the band's affinity for a handcrafted Britannic golden age. This font continued to be employed right up to 2007's *Mothership* release. It was Peter Grant's idea to sell the album with a removable band naming the record and its author, "to shut Atlantic up," said the manager. Thanks to the powers of Hipgnosis, the surreal radiance of the *Houses of the Holy* cover makes it the Zeppelin disc that art lovers might enjoy even more than music fans.

Physical Graffiti

The sprawling stylistic range of this great double album is reflected in its cover, which contains the most textual and visual information visible on any Led Zeppelin record. In hindsight some of the graphic content here may be too haphazard to carry the heady insinuations of the group's other jackets, and the façade of miniature reproductions does not translate well to the smaller media of cassette tapes or CDs, but for sheer numbers of odd, revealing, suggestive, or confounding pictures on the sleeves, *Physical Graffiti* is unbeatable.

Though many two-record sets of the time came in foldout covers, *Physical Graffiti* bucked the trend by placing both LPs in a single outside envelope; inside was a wraparound bearing the track listings and production info, while inside *that* came the two jackets for the separate vinyl records. The brownstone whose windows and doorways are seen at day and night on both sides of the album was located at 96–98 St. Mark's Place in New York City's East Village (it's also seen in the Rolling Stones' 1981 video for "Waiting on a Friend"). For this project Led Zeppelin turned not to Hipgnosis but to London-based designer Mike Doud of Alliance Graphique Internationale (AGI) and New York's Peter Corriston, who together devised the print and photo containers of the record, the most notable element of which was the die-cut holes made in the brownstone's windows. "We walked around the city for a few weeks looking for the right building," Corriston told the *New York Times* in 2002. "I had come up with a concept for the band based on the tenement, people living there and moving in and out." The shot of the address was captured by Elliott Erwitt. In fact the real building has five stories but to properly fit onto the album cover it was reduced to four, and accidentally or not a two-story brick structure with similar window openings was used for José Feliciano's 1973 effort *Compartments*. Peter Corriston was the man behind several other familiar record jackets, among them the Stones' *Some Girls* (with its own cutouts), *Emotional Rescue*, and *Tattoo You*.

From a rich and celebrated act soon to be disparaged by the punk rock explosion, the 1975 release utilized the jumbled "ransom note" lettering style before the Sex Pistols on their influential *Never Mind the Bollocks* cover, whose DIY technique virtually created the entire punk alphabet: the fifteen songs on the Zeppelin record are titled in exactly the same manner. The foldout sheet that wraps around the inner sleeves had the St. Mark's Place window frames rendered by Dave Heffernan, topped by evil-looking gargoyles not present on the building. Individual track production notes were listed (the music was assembled from several years' and locations' worth of recording), with Page's dig at engineer Ron Nevison for accidentally erasing early tapes of "The Rover," which were "Salvaged by the grace of [Keith] Harwood."

The images on the inside covers are an incongruous range of subjects—movie stills, great paintings, stray clippings, and snapshots of the Led Zeppelin members and their associates—of which only the private pictures, taken by friends like Roy Harper and B. P. Fallon, likely bore much significance to the musicians. Some of the hokey old advertisements or editorial illustrations recall those dug up for use on *Led Zeppelin II* and *III* and anticipate the ones to be featured in *Presence*.

Record one, front cover

* *Top row, left to right:* Flight of RAF biplanes / Zeppelin manager Peter Grant / actress Carole Lombard / embracing couple / astronaut Buzz Aldrin
* *Second row:* Robert Plant / John Bonham / John Paul Jones / Jimmy Page—all during a previous Japanese tour
* *Third row:* Horse and dog portrait / Pears shaving soap advertisement / Parmigianino's *Vision of St. Jerome* altarpiece / bondage outfit
* *Fourth row:* Illustration of children / *Wizard of Oz* still / John Bonham / coronation of Queen Elizabeth II

Record one, back cover

* *Top row:* Jules Verne's *From the Earth to the Moon* / cat / woman crushed by giant foot / burlesque strip reel / Caravaggio's *Young Sick Bacchus*
* *Second row:* John Paul Jones / Dante Gabriel Rossetti's *Prosperine* / John Bonham / Robert Plant in drag
* *Third row:* Buster Crabbe in *Flash Gordon's Trip to Mars* / Robert Plant / da Vinci's *Woman with an Ermine* / angel
* *Fourth row:* Woman with stockings / John Bonham and Jimmy Page in drag / John Paul Jones and Jimmy Page / coronation of Queen Elizabeth II

Record two, front cover

* *Top row:* Nun with umbrella / Laurel and Hardy in *Wrong Again* / black youth with ice cream cone / Pope Leo XIII / Charles Atlas
* *Second row:* Embracing couple / Elizabeth Taylor in *Cleopatra* / hands-in-crotch close-up / Jimmy Page
* *Third row:* Zeppelin / designer Peter Corriston (?) / designer Mike Doud (?) / bodybuilder
* *Fourth row:* John Bonham and Robert Plant / woman on alligator / navy dive effect test photos / coronation of Queen Elizabeth II

Physical Graffiti contained the most imagery of all Zeppelin album covers.

Back cover

- *Top row:* King Kong / Robert Plant / man falling from building / explosion / harp woman
- *Second row:* Nude man at swimming pool (possibly Robert Plant) / *Undersea Kingdom* 1930s serial / Lee Harvey Oswald / John Bonham
- *Third row:* John Bonham (?) / Jimmy Page in drag / Native American woman / girl with dog
- *Fourth row:* Serial movie still / kitchen / devils / coronation of Queen Elizabeth II

There's an Angel on My Shoulder: The Swan Song Logo

Physical Graffiti was the first product from Led Zeppelin's private record label, operated under the umbrella of Atlantic Records but run by Peter Grant and jointly owned by Grant and the four band members. The operation lasted until the early 1980s. "Swan Song," usually defined as an artist's final output preceding death or retirement, had begun as an instrumental song sketch from Jimmy Page, then had been floated as an album title, and was finally picked as the name of the new business venture. The Swan Song picture that went on the LPs and which was minimized to an all-purpose Led Zeppelin logo for T-shirts, posters, and other merchandise was taken directly from artist William Rimmer's 1869 canvas *Evening (The Fall of Day)*, with slight modifications to the position of the winged figure's arm. Born in Liverpool in 1816 but raised in obscurity in New England, the self-taught Rimmer made sculptures and paintings and is respected by art scholars, although this piece alone has won him the attention of a far wider audience. With the *Hindenburg* explosion, the Hermit of the tarot, and the four *Led Zeppelin IV* symbols, the Swan Song image remains one of the most famous Zeppelin trademarks.

The 1974 logo was executed by Joe Petagno, an American graphic artist who had already done work for Alice Cooper and underground publications including the *LA Free Press* and *The Oracle*. "I contacted Storm from Hipgnosis and asked him if he would be interested in collaborating," Petagno recalls today. "He said my reputation preceded me and that I would be more than welcome." Through the English firm, he presented some original Swan Song designs to Led Zeppelin, but the band "had some reservations. . . . They asked if I could do a Rimmer copy for them, as they thought it suited their label, or identity, as it were . . . . I thought it would be best to create something new and original, but the client is always right and in the end I did a take on the Rimmer piece for them." Petagno's Swan Song was done in gouache and colored pencils on illustration board. He did several versions, and the "sunset" picture was finally selected by the band. "I think it took me about nine days to complete it," he says. "The Swan Song lettering was one hundred percent original and it's a piece I'm very proud of. . . . It was very satisfying to work with the mighty Zeppelin. They are one of my favorite bands of the day, so needless to say, I was very happy and proud to be involved on this level." Joe Petagno has continued a successful career as a rock illustrator, and is known especially for his Gothic covers for Motörhead.

Because of the Swan Song subject's ecstatic pose, long fair hair, and muscular build, fans at first took it as an idealized Robert Plant (minus genitalia), but deeper investigation suggested it was a representation of the mythical Icarus, or the Greek sun deity Apollo (patron of music and poetry), or even of the biblical Lucifer. The morning star, identified in Latin as "Lucifer," was associated by ancient Israelites with the rebel archangel cast out of heaven for challenging God, as described in the Old Testament's Isaiah 14: "How art thou fallen from heaven, O Lucifer, son of the morning! . . . For thou has said in thine heart, I will ascend into heaven, I will exalt my throne above the stars of God. . . . I will ascend above the heights of the clouds; I will be like the most High." Rimmer's *Fall of Day* may therefore be a depiction of Lucifer's ejection into hell—Jimmy Page was by 1975 working on a soundtrack for Kenneth Anger's *Lucifer Rising* film project. The original, done in crayon, oil, and graphite, is today housed in the Boston Museum of Fine Arts; for his heroic anatomical draftsmanship Rimmer himself has been called "a Yankee Michelangelo."

Presence

The cover to *Presence*, the second Led Zeppelin album cover to be composed by Hipgnosis, and the second to draw on the talents of George Hardie, may be the group's eeriest visual projection of itself. Though lacking the occult overtones of *Houses of the Holy* or the confounding wordlessness of *Led Zeppelin IV*, the sleeve still creates a haunting sense of uncertainty, with the unexplained purposes of its "Object" set into an otherwise banal gallery of domestic and outdoor scenes. Only the outside covers of the gatefold were photographed by Hipgnosis's Aubrey Powell and Peter Christopherson; the interior shots were taken from old *Life* and *Look* magazines. The family posed around the table on the front were photographed in a studio and then superimposed in front of a boat show at London's Earl's Court arena (scene of Zeppelin's last great run of English concerts), while the girl student on the back was none other than Samantha Gates, late of *Houses of the Holy*. A broad white border around the pictures mirrors that of another memorable Hardie-Hipgnosis arrangement, Pink Floyd's 1975 *Wish You Were Here*.

"We needed something so powerful, so huge, that it made you weak just to think of it," recalls Storm Thorgerson of the cover's conception. The dark little obelisk that is the focus of each *Presence* shot became known as "the Object," and appears to be the bearer of some kind of psycho-spiritual power—a presence. "Perhaps it was a cosmic battery, or a spiritual relic, or alien artifact, exposure to which seemed essential." There is something faintly sinister about the way it occupies such an important place in the routine settings of a golf course, a bank, a school, and a park, like some crucial centerpiece of an unnamable ritual or a plot twist in a David Lynch movie. The Object was illustrated onto the photos by Richard Manning, looking, in Thorgerson's words, "more a hole than a thing, an absence rather than a presence." After a first meeting with Led Zeppelin, Peter Grant, George Hardie, and the Hipgnosis team where the premise of the cover was discussed, it was Jimmy Page's idea to change the shape of the Object with a linear irrationality inspired by one of his own favorite artists, Dutch printmaker M. C. Escher. Physical promos of the Object were cast by Crispin Mellor and used for photo shoots and giveaways. "You can put a number of different interpretations on it," said Page, "so it's best to leave it as an open-book situation." The other group members were themselves evasive or undecided about the Object's meaning, Robert Plant comparing

The surreal images from the *Presence* gatefold were taken from old *Life* and *Look* magazines.   *Courtesy of Len Ward / The Rad Zone*

it to a religious symbol or the similarly transformative Object in Stanley Kubrick's 1968 film *2001: A Space Odyssey.* "The meaning behind it has been present throughout time, you know. . . . Its purpose has been there since time began."

Unlike *Physical Graffiti* or the later *In Through the Out Door,* the *Presence* cover is not bursting with pictorial trickery, but its very minimalism makes its point better than any wider array of gimmicks. Though subject to copyright, the Object has never attained the branded status of "ZoSo" or the Swan Song logo—relative to Zeppelin's other output, the record was not a big seller—but like the music it contained, the jacket, with its quiet inscrutability, is among the quartet's most entrancing statements.

The Song Remains the Same

Today remembered as a flawed and self-indulgent double-album soundtrack for a flawed and self-indulgent concert film, *The Song Remains the Same* was a multimedia representation of Led Zeppelin in all their imperial glory. The record cover and the movie poster used the same designs, both supplied by the art department of the releasing studio, Warner Brothers. This was a predictable collage of drawings based on scenes from the documentary; e.g., John Paul Jones on horseback, Jimmy Page with his bow, John Bonham in a drag racer, and the band's *Starship* jetliner. Most notable on the two-disc record (reissued in a lavish update in 2007) was the illustration depicting a ruined movie theater, placed over a second one of the same venue, intact this time, where the name "Led Zeppelin" can be partly discerned on the marquee. Inside was a booklet offering stills from the film and a suitably flattering essay, in this case not quite deserved, from rock journalist Cameron Crowe.

In Through the Out Door

Again the work of Hipgnosis and with a rich well of varied effects, designs, and photographs, the series of *In Through the Out Door* packages were perhaps compensation for the artistic thinness of the album itself. Here the surprise was in which of six available covers would be available to buyers, an enticement heightened by literally presenting the record under cover of a plain brown wrapper, stamped with a matter-of-fact title and author credit. The brown-bag idea was inspired by Peter Grant's boast that Led Zeppelin records would sell truckloads no matter what was on the cover, although the conceit had previously been demonstrated by the Beatles' *The Beatles* (the "White Album") and the Who's *Live at Leeds.* Even the multiple

Nineteen seventy-nine's *In Through the Out Door* was made available in several different sleeves.

Author's Collection

sleeves were not unheard of, as the Zones' *Under Influence* and a three-song Damned EP were also issued with several jackets in 1979, the same year as *In Through the Out Door*.

But the Zeppelin record was the most conceptualized of these: The scenario of the cover was centered around a lonely patron at closing time in a seedy bar, as seen from the differing perspectives of the bartender, a piano player, a female barfly, a seen-it-all private eye, and a pair of shady B-girls. A complete sextet would thus show an almost 360-degree view of the solitary drinker of Jim Beam as he burns his Dear John letter (in fact there are additional variants of the six covers where the models' poses are very slightly altered). According to Storm Thorgerson, the bar was a London set based on Aubrey Powell's "personally researched" watering holes in New Orleans, although it's also said to be a recreation of that city's Absinthe Bar on Bourbon Street, a hangout of the band on their later visits to the Crescent City. Jimmy Page supposedly selected the original location, a bar he knew on the Caribbean resort of Martinique, but this could not be replicated. Given a sepia-toned tint by Richard Manning that emphasized its bluesy, world-weary mood, the portrait also had a swash of brighter color across it, as if observed through a dusty window. This device also provided a clue to the possibilities of the black-and-white inner dust jacket, whose first printings (i.e., the million or so copies scooped up by fans in '79) could be moistened to bring out their own colors. When a damp tissue was dabbed on the close-ups of the ashtray, glass, bottle. and coins—and the embers of the breakup letter that was the key to the whole scene—a rainbow of pigment would emerge, an idea suggested by Jimmy Page from a coloring book owned by his young daughter Scarlet.

Though the *In Through the Out Door* cover is one of Hipgnosis's most elaborate, there is little on it besides its track and production info that actually connects with Led Zeppelin. No single element in the picture can stand alongside the *Hindenburg*, the Hermit, or the Object in the four-some's iconography. Just as the disc's title promised a comeback of sorts for the band, it could be that the watercolor effect was meant to show that the battered Zeppelin now had been given what Thorgerson called "a lick of fresh paint across a faded surface." The evocative cast of drinkers and other seedy characters might be listening to the album's torch song "I'm Gonna Crawl" on the jukebox, but beyond that it would seem to be a case where the creativity of the illustrators and the musicians had diverged. *In Through the Out Door* was the fourth Led Zeppelin studio record in a row to be nominated for a Best Album Cover Grammy award, but neither it nor *Houses of the Holy*, *Physical Graffiti*, or *Presence* was a winner in the category.

Coda

The last complete album of unreleased music put out by Led Zeppelin, 1982's *Coda* was a contractual obligation owed by the band to Atlantic Records. Jimmy Page complained that the duty of assembling the outtakes and nuggets of a band broken up over the death of their drummer was "disgusting," but the record served as an adequate close to their career. The collage of group and individual pictures on the gatefold, a lesser Hipgnosis production, was actually one of the best things on the effort: The individual Zeppelin players had only occasionally been depicted on their records, and *Coda* nicely rectified the general public's vagueness as to what Page, Robert Plant, John Paul Jones, and John Bonham really looked like. So here were the four men at differing moments of the previous twelve years, showing the telescoped effects of the rock star experience. There are a few unexpectedly light snaps of Page dressed as a cricketer (using a guitar for a bat), the laughing quartet assembled behind what may be a urinal, and Led Zeppelin in rehearsal in 1977, hamming it up as a nightclub act circa 1955. Note how the shots of Bonham especially belie the late percussionist's reputation as the ravaging "Beast" of hotel suites and dressing rooms—instead he appears a cheerful, smiling man signing an autograph, hoisting his mate and boss Page up off the boards after a show, and tenderly sitting his daughter, Zoë, on his knee. Strangely, it is Page's daughter Scarlet who's airbrushed out of the center shot of Bonham and Page at an awards dinner. Ditto the original Knebworth background of the 1979 portrait of the band applauding some unseen activity (reportedly a strip act), as a brighter setting was superimposed behind. The back cover of *Coda* showed an aerial shot of huge circular tailing ponds, standing for Led Zeppelin's now-complete sequence of ten albums.

Led Zeppelin (Box Set)

This highly successful 1990 compilation, while standing apart from the original Zeppelin LPs, fit in well with the band's history of inventive and allusive visuals. By a firm called Mission Control, each CD or cassette of the four-piece collection was packaged within one of the four *Led Zeppelin IV* symbols cleverly worked into a natural scene: Plant's feather was a (winter) ice formation, Page's "ZoSo" a (spring) sundial, Bonham's rune an actual rune inscribed on a (summer) rock, and Jones's on an (autumnal) shoreline. The box set cover was an ingenious reference to the group's imposing legacy, portraying the vast shadow of an unseen zeppelin over a field inscribed with alien crop circles. A quartet of apparent printers' marks at each corner were numbered 54, 69, 79, and ∞ (infinity), perhaps standing for the *54* songs in the anthology, the first of which were released in 19*69* by an act whose last album as an active unit came out in 19*79*, but all of which will last *forever*.

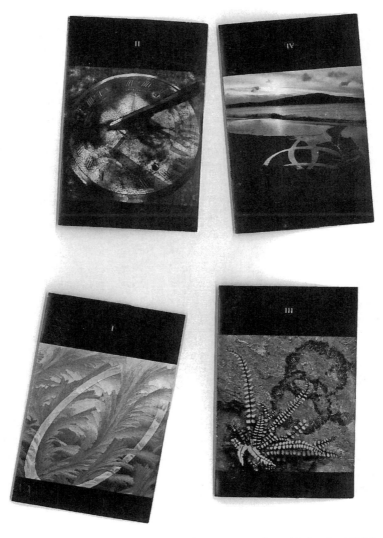

Led Zeppelin's four symbols were adapted into seasonal motifs for the 1990 box set.

Author's Collection

1977

March 28: 574 dead in jumbo jet collision, Canary Islands.

April–July: Led Zeppelin tour US.

June: CB radio fad takes off, US.

July 24: Peter Grant, Richard Cole, John Bindon, and John Bonham charged with assault after beating of Bill Graham employee Jim Matzorkis, Oakland, California.

July 27: Led Zeppelin's tour is cancelled following death of Robert Plant's son.

August 16: Elvis Presley dies, age 42.

Movies: *Star Wars*; *Close Encounters of the Third Kind*; *Saturday Night Fever*; *Annie Hall.*

Music: Fleetwood Mac, *Rumours*; the Sex Pistols, *Never Mind the Bollocks*; Meat Loaf, *Bat out of Hell*; Debbie Boone, "You Light Up My Life"; Ted Nugent, "Cat Scratch Fever"; Abba, "Dancing Queen."

21

The Story Was Quite Clear

Led Zeppelin in Literature and Film

Inspiration's What You Are: Literary and Artistic Figures Who Influenced Led Zeppelin

For the most part, the ensemble was four rock 'n' roll musicians whose main motivation was the joy of creating and performing together, but their development was also shaped by a variety of external social and cultural movements from their own and earlier times. Jimmy Page, as the founder and leader of the band, was particularly affected by his months as an art student in the early 1960s. On Led Zeppelin's album covers and logos, and in the overall evolution of their work, the aesthetic effects of some of this training can be discerned.

The Pre-Raphaelite Brotherhood

Formed in London in 1848 among a small group of British painters and students, the Pre-Raphaelites sought to make a new, more naturalistic national art that drew on scenes from biblical, medieval, or Renaissance literature for its subjects. They disdained the nineteenth century's static and sanitized portraits of contemporary nobility—dukes on horseback, duchesses in their drawing rooms—in favor of emotionally stirring images that spoke to deeper and more spiritual matters of life; their title was meant to assert an allegiance to the style of Italian painting that preceded the advances represented by Raphael (1483–1520). Some of the most famous Pre-Raphaelite pieces include William Holman Hunt's *The Awakening Conscience*, John Everett Millais' *Ophelia*, and John William Waterhouse's

The Lady of Shalott and *A Mermaid*. Architect William Burges's 1881 Tower House, owned by Jimmy Page since the early 1970s, also derives from the same neo-Gothic sensibility. When Page spoke to interviewers expressing his "affinity for the ideals of the pre-Raphaelites," he was probably referring to the painters' inclinations toward outdoor settings, rustic characters, and an imagined Elizabethan purity. Led Zeppelin's lovely acoustic ballads, like "That's the Way," "Friends," "Tangerine," and "Going to California," as well as the idyllic introduction to "Stairway to Heaven," convey something of a Pre-Raphaelite mood. Page is known to possess valuable works of art by Pre-Raphaelite figures like Edward Burne-Jones, and in the group's 1970s prime the leonine Robert Plant was described in London's *Financial Times* as "a painfully thin pre-Raphaelite heroine."

The Arts and Crafts Movement

Emerging around the same epoch and within the same intellectual circles as the Pre-Raphaelites, leading Arts and Crafts figures such as William Morris rejected Victorian Britain's growing trends of mass production and industrialism. Instead they called for a return to—and made for themselves—personal, less replicable motifs of design and ornamentation, away from the standardized products whose abundant manufacture and consumption determined a soulless, class-stratified society. The Arts and Crafts journal *Studio* was where Jimmy Page found the font used for the "Stairway to Heaven" lyrics printed in *Led Zeppelin IV*, and the bucolic and idiosyncratic sounds of "Black Mountain Side," "Thank You," "Down by the Seaside," and "Bron-yr-Aur" evince the movement's same celebration of unplugged, cottage-industry naivety. To a journalist around the time of *IV's* release, Page explained the album cover: "[T]he old man carrying the wood is in harmony with nature. . . . His old cottage gets pulled down and they put him in these urban slums, old slums—terrible places." The painting itself, he later said in *Guitar World*, was found by him and Robert Plant on an antiquing expedition. "I used to spend a lot of time going to junk shops looking for things other people might've missed. You know, I'd find all these great pieces of furniture, really fine Arts and Crafts things that people would just throw out." Of course, Led Zeppelin existed in the late twentieth entury, traveled by jet aircraft, and used advanced recording and amplification equipment of which William Morris could never have dreamed, but Page's nostalgia for a distant, pre-technocratic simplicity was similar.

J. R. R. Tolkien

"Robert was into all that fairy stuff," John Paul Jones opined of his vocalist's lyrical inspirations. It is true that, like thousands of his fellow hippies in the Britain and North America of the 1960s and '70s, Robert Plant did read and enjoy *The Lord of the Rings* and other fantastic literature by John Ronald Reuel Tolkien (1892–1973), and several of the author's invented people and places found their way into Led Zeppelin songs. The evil Gollum and the wasteland of Mordor are mentioned in "Ramble On," while the Dark Lord, the Queen of Light, and ringwraiths turn up in "The Battle of Evermore." The titular peaks of "Misty Mountain Hop" refer to *The Lord of the Rings'* geography, while Plant's dog Strider, to whom he dedicated "Bron-y-Aur Stomp," was named for a Tolkien character. Some listeners also detect allusions to Tolkien's world in "Over the Hills and Far Away," "Four Sticks," "No Quarter," and "Stairway to Heaven." Though none of these references are especially complex or serious, his layperson's interest in mythology both real (Norse, Celtic) and fictional (*The Lord of the Rings*) informed much of Plant's most original verses. Led Zeppelin's popular association with the vague medievalism of wizards, runes, dragons, forests, Vikings, castles, and the like—and its subsequent appropriation by dozens of sword-and-sorcery heavy metal acts—are an indirect by-product of J. R. R. Tolkien's broad and devoted international readership.

William S. Burroughs

The Beat Generation author of *Junky* and *Naked Lunch* held an unusual interview with Jimmy Page in 1975, published as a cover story in the US rock and culture magazine *Crawdaddy*. Titled "Led Zeppelin, Jimmy Page & Rock Magic," the conversation is a rather awkward one, as two heavyweights of cult literature and pop music strain to find much in common. While Burroughs (1914–1997) did his research in attending a Zeppelin concert, probably at Madison Square Garden on February 7, the middle-aged gay American author and the young straight British guitarist seemed most comfortable discussing their shared interests in magic, the trance rhythms of North Africa, and their mutual associates Kenneth Anger, Donald Cammell, and Mick Jagger. (It's also possible that, out of print, they found another joint taste in narcotics, a subject with which both men were familiar.) Though nothing of Burroughs's fiction is perceptible in Led Zeppelin's songs, he and his Beat peers certainly prefigured the counterculture's fascination with the occult, drugs, and sexual experimentation. It was in Burroughs's 1964 work *Nova Express* that the characters of "the Heavy Metal kid" and "the Heavy Metal people of Uranus" first introduced the term *heavy metal*, a phrase later used to define the music of Led Zeppelin, to a youthful audience.

Aleister Crowley

The short answer is: The influence was less than many suppose. Unlike the Beatles, Led Zeppelin never put a picture of Crowley on one of their albums; unlike Ozzy Osbourne, the group never wrote a song about him; and unlike Iron Maiden singer Bruce Dickinson, no one of the quartet ever wrote a movie screenplay (Dickinson's was called *Chemical Wedding*) loosely based on Crowley's life. Edward Alexander Crowley (1875–1947) relates to Zeppelin only via his latter-day aficionado Jimmy Page, who openly talked of studying the occultist's magical doctrines and who became a famous collector of Crowley artifacts, including a former residence. "That was his business," John Paul Jones told *Uncut* magazine in 2009 of Page's Crowley research. "It was not an interest of mine." Robert Plant and John Bonham took the same position.

A few obsessive analysts have attempted to frame all of Led Zeppelin's music as a coded homage to Crowley. Thomas Friend's 2004 study *Fallen Angel: The Untold Story of Jimmy Page and Led Zeppelin*, for example, claims that the structure and lyrics of "Stairway to Heaven" represent "a worship of Lucifer" based on Crowley's teachings—never mind the extremists who hold that the anthem is woven with backward messages in praise of Satan. Others have pointed to Page's "deitic" hand gestures between concert strums or solos, as if he were summoning some invisible spirit while performing. The "oSo" in Page's "ZoSo" sigil is also said to be in some way connected with either Crowley or one of his disciples, Austin Osman Spare. Even if these theories were partially accurate, they would still place Crowley well down the scale of Zeppelin's inspirations.

In fact, the one tangible link between Led Zeppelin's music and Aleister Crowley was literally embedded in the vinyl of *Led Zeppelin III*. For the first pressings of the record in 1970, Page and American engineer Terry Manning inscribed Crowley's dictum "Do what thou wilt" on one side of the master disc's runoff groove, and continued "Shall be the whole of the law" on the other. Jimmy Page was a conscientious producer and, in the days when the physical transfer of the primary acetate onto vinyl was a last, crucial step in the recording process, he was on hand to oversee the job. Usually masters had ordinary serial numbers inscribed, but Page and Manning together hit on the idea of carefully imprinting some Aleister Crowley philosophy; Manning has also recollected etching "So mote it be"

Aleister Crowley (1875–1947), whose name and exploits have been inextricably linked with Led Zeppelin.   *Hulton/Getty Images*

and "Love under will" on both sides of an alternate master. "We joked that with the different things written on different lacquers, real fans would have to buy two or more records to complete the set," Manning told *Whole Lotta Led Zeppelin* author Jon Bream in 2007. "This was absurdly funny to us, as we couldn't imagine anything like that might really happen." "Do what thou wilt" was also printed on flyers announcing parties for the launch of the Swan Song label in 1974.

Any more speculative interpretations of Crowley's influence on the recorded output of Led Zeppelin are just hearing things. Jimmy Page's fantasy scene in *The Song Remains the Same* was shot on the grounds of Scotland's Boleskine House, where Crowley had lived long before, but, as Page himself admitted in a Zeppelin-era interview, his interest was ultimately "a personal thing and isn't in relation to anything I do as a musician, apart from that I've employed his system in my own day-to-day life."

Can I Take You to the Show: Led Zeppelin on Film

A significant factor in the band's long-term success was their low-key media presence during the 1970s. They diligently sat for interviews, posed for publicity shots, and employed press liaisons to spread word of their achievements to reporters, but they never sought the blanket television and tabloid coverage upon which some of their contemporaries relied. As a consequence there are numerous unrelated programs and movies where the group is seen or mentioned, without keeping track of taped talk show or promotional appearances and occasional po-mo references on series like *The Simpsons* or *That '70s Show*. Today a scattering of official and unofficial TV and cinematic releases are available that present the Led Zeppelin story from several angles. Some of this material has been posted in short clips on the Internet, but the best of them are recommended for viewing in their entirety.

All Your Own

In 1958 a segment of this British youth talent show presented a four-piece group from Epsom, Surrey, as the youngsters busked their way through Leadbelly's "Cotton Fields" and "Mama Don't Allow No Skiffle Around Here." One of the two guitarists was a shy fourteen-year-old named Jim Page, but it was not until many years later that the clip was discovered and featured in the 1995 documentary series *Rock 'n' Roll: An Unruly History*. Widely seen since, it's a charming peek into the very early career of an artist who was never again as innocent as he appears here: there's a lot of mileage to be got out of his reply to host Huw Wheldon that, if he couldn't make a vocation out of playing skiffle, he hoped to enter the field of biological research.

Blow-Up

The Yardbirds appear in a segment of Michelangelo Antonioni's influential mod murder mystery set in Swinging London, performing "Stroll On," a legal rewrite of their staple "Train Kept A-Rollin'." New recruit Jimmy Page is seen in medium shot while co-lead guitarist Jeff Beck smashes his guitar, as instructed by the director. Decades after *Blow-Up*'s 1966 premiere, the Yardbirds' rockin' interlude is one of the best things in the film, which has otherwise aged poorly.

Groupies

Though no one from Led Zeppelin participated in this sleazy 1970 exploitation documentary (Joe Cocker, Ten Years After, and Zeppelin's almost-singer Terry Reid were the musical highlights), it contains a short scene where an unidentified female discusses Jimmy Page's proficiency with whips.

The Song Remains the Same

For many years the band's sole and best cinematic effort was a mix of Madison Square Garden concert footage from 1973, studio re-creations of the same gig shot in London in 1974, and private scenes of the members' home lives interspersed with staged dramatizations of their songs. *The Song Remains the Same* has been must-viewing in theaters or on video for Zeppelin fans, but impartial spectators have found it overlong and pretentious, and some of the performances are not as good as those heard on bootlegs from the same period. Today it has been displaced as a live document by later material—notwithstanding an updated 2007 edition—although it still merits a look for providing a glimpse of the quartet at the summit of their rock star hubris.

Lucifer Rising

Underground filmmaker Kenneth Anger's unearthly collage of occult imagery continues to disturb decades after its 1980 release. Jimmy Page was first commissioned to create the soundtrack for Anger's erratic production schedule in 1972, but the director "fired" him in 1976 for failing to provide useful music. The official version of the film credits Charles Manson family member and convicted murderer Bobby Beausoleil as the composer, although Page's weird synthesized tones have been heard on a bootleg album, and the bearded guitarist himself is briefly seen in a single panning shot from the finished work.

The Song Remains the Same (1976) offered an imperfect portrait of Zeppelin's live act.
Courtesy of Robert Rodriguez

Son of Dracula

John Bonham can be seen drumming for "Count Downe"'s band, in this 1974 mess conceived and produced by boozy buddies Harry Nilsson and Ringo Starr.

Concert for the People of Kampuchea

An early example of star-studded rock 'n' roll benefit shows, this one, put on by UNICEF in London in December 1979 for victims of the Pol Pot regime in Cambodia, featured Robert Plant singing with Rockpile, and the ad hoc "Rockestra," including John Paul Jones and John Bonham. A DVD condensation of these concerts, also with Queen, the Clash, the Pretenders, and Elvis Costello, is available.

Death Wish II

Jimmy Page's first recorded outing after the disbandment of Led Zeppelin was the soundtrack for a 1982 Charles Bronson movie, a sequel to the 1974 vigilante classic. The film itself is an average shoot-'em-up, but Page's suspenseful score, made in collaboration with vocalist Chris Farlowe and Fairport Convention drummer Dave Mattacks, among others, is a compelling and underrated gem from his oeuvre.

Scream for Help

John Paul Jones also wrote and performed a soundtrack for *Death Wish II* director Michael Winner, in this case a pedestrian thriller from 1984. "It was a horrible film," Jones admitted to Dave Lewis. "A bit of a disaster all around, really." As with the earlier Winner project, the music is more interesting than the movie—Jimmy Page plays on "Crackback" and "Spaghetti Junction." Both the *Death Wish II* and *Scream for Help* soundtracks are worth locating on album.

Give My Regards to Broad Street

It says something about John Paul Jones's professional reputation that the most famous rock 'n' roll bassist of all, Paul McCartney, picked him to play backup in the "Ballroom Dancing" sequence from his 1984 film.

No Quarter: Jimmy Page and Robert Plant Unledded

The landmark 1994 reunion of Led Zeppelin's two most visible personalities began as an episode of the MTV network's *Unplugged* program, which put electric rock 'n' rollers into a more acoustic setting. Page and Plant were captured on video performing with Western and Egyptian backing musicians in a London TV studio, a small band in Wales, and local Moroccan instrumentalists in Marrakech. Mixing matured versions of Zeppelin classics such as "Thank You," "Kashmir," "Since I've Been Loving You" and "Nobody's Fault but Mine" with the intriguing African explorations of "Yallah," "City Don't Cry," and "Wonderful One," the collection was a classy comeback for two superstars not content to replicate past glories.

Led Zeppelin (DVD)

A blockbuster release in 2003 that clinched Led Zeppelin's entry into the highest reaches of rock aristocracy, this career retrospective was the long-awaited revelation of the band's live prowess that *The Song Remains the Same* wasn't. Spanning the concert triumphs of the Royal Albert Hall in 1970, Madison Square Garden in 1973, Earl's Court in 1975, and Knebworth in 1979, as well as rare TV appearances and interviews, the two-disc package is the best available Zeppelin visual chronicle and a mandatory intro for newcomers to the legend.

A to Zeppelin: The Unauthorized Story of Led Zeppelin

As per the title, this documentary features interviews with such Zep associates as Richard Cole, Chris Dreja, and Lori Mattix, but no actual Zeppelin music is heard and the biographical content is cursory. There are a few comparable products on the market, using unlicensed footage and bland commentary from marginal figures to capitalize on Led Zeppelin's enduring allure.

Led Zeppelin: Physical Graffiti—A Classic Album Under Review

Another unauthorized production, this one offers in-depth analyses of the music, benefiting from the close scrutiny of musicologists, Zeppelin experts Dave Lewis and Nigel Williamson, and the memories of *Physical Graffiti* engineer Ron Nevison. *Led Zeppelin: Physical Graffiti* is more substantial than the usual quickie bios.

Released in 2003, the Led Zeppelin DVD was the authorized visual document of the band that fans had been waiting for.   *Author's Collection*

Led Zeppelin—The First Album

Similar to the above, this documentary covers the seminal 1969 debut.

It Might Get Loud

This 2008 documentary on the art and history of the electric guitar featured the Edge of U2, Jack White of the White Stripes, and Jimmy Page separately and together conversing on their lifelong explorations of the instrument. Zeppelin fans were thrilled to share Page's candid reminiscences about first discovering the rumble of Link Wray, and to accompany him on his nostalgic visit back to Headley Grange. Great viewing for guitar buffs, and good to see the Sorcerer in contented middle age.

Like a Leaf Is to a Tree: Books About Led Zeppelin

With the rock biography an industry unto itself in the publishing business, generating thousands of titles on acts of all periods and styles, it's no surprise that a small library's worth of Zeppelin-related volumes have been issued over the years—four books alone have been written on the making and meaning of *Led Zeppelin IV*. Depending on the reader's interest, he or she can choose from various formats (picture book, chronology, critical study) and authorial approaches (tell-all, interview collection, annotated guide), but with so much selection some books have garnered more respect than others. The following is not a complete list of every single Led Zeppelin work ever released but a general introduction to the most popular, most accurate, and most entertaining editions to cover the band.

Biographies

Hammer of the Gods: The Led Zeppelin Saga, by Stephen Davis

First published in 1985 and updated in several later versions, this best-selling account has remained a standard course in Led Zep 101 for thousands of new fans. This success has come despite (or because of) the surviving members' adamant rejection of it. "I think I opened it up in the middle somewhere and started to read, and I just threw it out the window," Jimmy Page told *Rolling Stone* in 1990. "I mean, I couldn't bother to wade through that sort of stuff." John Paul Jones muttered that the book "made us out to be sad little people. . . . [Davis] ruined a lot of good, funny stories." And Robert Plant has likewise dismissed *Hammer* as any kind of truthful document: "If you get stuck into denying it, you're prey to these people. . . . The guy who wrote that book knew nothing about that band. He got all his information from a guy who had a heroin problem who happened to be associated with us." For these and other comments, many hard-core Zeppelin followers have likewise refused to countenance Davis's story.

But the real problem with *Hammer of the Gods* is not its accuracy but its emphasis. Journalist Davis was actually in the Zeppelin entourage on the

1975 US tour, and seems to have witnessed Plant's infamous "I'm a Golden God" boast as well as other behind-the-scenes embarrassments; no one has ever disproved his assertions that Page was a heroin addict engaged in a relationship with a minor female, that John Bonham was a violent and uncontrollable drunk, or that a Zeppelin groupie was once sexually serviced with a dead fish. On the other hand, Davis relied extensively on details from prior biographer Ritchie Yorke and from reporter Ellen Sander, and especially on the very personal and subjective memories of Lori Mattix (misspelled in the book) and tour manager Richard Cole, who even the writer admits was then "drinking away the $200,000 he had left over from Zeppelin." *Hammer of the Gods* is thus a great read for anyone sniffing out the group's most sordid episodes, but its perspective is limited and subsequent writers have painted a far more realistic picture.

Led Zeppelin: The Story of a Band and Their Music, 1968–1980, by Keith Shadwick

British music critic Shadwick's study focuses on Led Zeppelin's songwriting, recording, and performing history, and is a thoughtful and balanced work for average punters. Though die-hards might quibble with some of the author's musical judgments, the title is a welcome counterweight to the scandalizing of *Hammer of the Gods.*

When Giants Walked the Earth: A Biography of Led Zeppelin, by Mick Wall

The longest narrative biography to date, by an English rock journalist who has known and spoken with Page, Plant, and Jones regarding their time in the foursome, *Giants* is distinguished by Wall's very thorough research into Page's occult secrets. Like many Zeppelin scholars, though, he does recycle much material from other sources, and his italicized "first person" passages, purporting to be the inward thoughts of the band members and Peter Grant, feel awkward and arbitrary.

Stairway to Heaven: Led Zeppelin Uncensored, by Richard Cole and Richard Trubo

Avoid. The ex-Zeppelin road manager's best inside dirt was already dished to Stephen Davis, leaving him to assemble this sleazy rehash of his adventures with the band. *Uncensored* unintentionally reveals how peripheral Cole was in the Led Zeppelin career arc, and its patently made-up dialogue ("We're working like maniacs, and you put us in a hotel that's like a battlefield!") is cheesy. Page later said he considered suing Cole over this, "but it would be so painful to read that it wouldn't be worth it."

Led Zeppelin: The Definitive Biography, by Ritchie Yorke

This reasonably thorough account was revised in the 1990s from a Zeppelin-era sanitized edition. Yorke's was the first responsible bio from someone who had covered the band firsthand in their early years, but Page's reaction in 1976 was that it was "a classic case of someone abusing their access to us."

Peter Grant: The Man Who Led Zeppelin, by Chris Welch

A candid and even poignant life story of Zeppelin's indomitable manager serves as well as any other book to trace the act's course from the 1960s to the 1980s. Welch's book contains valuable anecdotes from such fringe players as Mickie Most and filmmaker Peter Clifton, who nevertheless understood what was going down.

John Bonham: A Thunder of Drums, by Chris Welch and Geoff Nichols

Welch and drummer Nichols do justice to Bonzo's personal and musical legacy, not shying away from his alcoholic excesses but at the same time dissecting the nuts and bolts of his technique. Useful for Zeppelin fans and drum enthusiasts alike.

Jimmy Page: Magus, Musician, Man, by George Case

Full disclosure: I wrote this. Though the book was hampered by Page's lack of direct input, most fans and reviewers found it to be a fair chronicle of the guitarist's growth before, during, and after Led Zeppelin, with special attention paid to instruments and musical development.

Robert Plant: Led Zeppelin, Jimmy Page, and the Solo Years, by Neil Daniels

This shaky, unauthorized bio teems with factual errors and pointless opinions from people wholly uninvolved with the subject.

LZ-'75: The Lost Chronicles of Led Zeppelin's 1975 American Tour, by Stephen Davis

LZ-'75 is more inside dirt from the author of *Hammer of the Gods,* dug up from his brief accompaniment of their US circuit back in the day. The book contains a few new insights that couldn't be printed in *HOTG,* but is mostly rehash.

Scholarly

In the Houses of the Holy: Led Zeppelin and the Power of Rock Music, by Susan Fast

This *extremely* academic treatise on Zeppelin's music and showmanship can be valued for giving the group the serious consideration it rarely was accorded during the 1970s. It does, however, contain many sentences like "The fluid approach to text in Led Zeppelin . . . requires an equally fluid, polysemous approach to analysis, one that shuns unities or fixed homologies" and "Just underneath the surface of the melodic and rhythmic squareness is a harmonic and formal openness and irregularity that is highly significant in terms of the semiotics of the piece," so be warned.

Led Zeppelin and Philosophy, by Scott Calef

From a series of titles exploring the deeper meanings of famous rock groups' lives and art, this one puts the Zeppelin canon on the couch. Good fun for Zep-heads, but perhaps baffling to newbies.

Compendia

Led Zeppelin: A Celebration and *Celebration II: The Tight but Loose Files*, by Dave Lewis

These are great reference texts by the founder and editor of the band's original fan magazine, *Tight but Loose*. Lewis has long enjoyed special access to the Zeppelin circle and has been exceedingly conscientious in his research. Both books provide timelines, discographies, concert dates, and other data, as well as key interviews with the principals.

Led Zeppelin: The Concert File, by Dave Lewis with Simon Pallett

Exhaustive gig-by-gig examination of Zeppelin's live work from beginning to end, including set lists, local reviews, and memories from attendees and fellow performers. Not essential for casual fans, but a bounty of info for the committed.

Led Zeppelin: The Press Reports, by Robert Godwin

A gold mine of contemporary newspaper and magazine articles on Zeppelin from the late 1960s to 1980. Many of the reviews and quotations dispel the myths of the ensemble's absolute resistance to media contacts, and some show the players as mere mortals trying to sell records and concert tickets before they became untouchable rock gods.

The Rough Guide to Led Zeppelin, by Nigel Williamson

Passable but hardly explosive factoids won't impress most serious listeners.

Picture Books

Whole Lotta Led Zeppelin: The Illustrated History of the Heaviest Band of All Time, by Jon Bream

Whole Lotta Led Zeppelin is a lavish collection of stage shots, backstage passes, and other promo paraphernalia with all-star sidebars from friends, admirers, and critics. Full disclosure: I contributed two essays to this.

Led Zeppelin: Shadows Taller Than Our Souls, by Charles R. Cross

Another gorgeously illustrated coffee-table book, distinguished by pullout facsimiles of tickets and assorted handouts, though the textual filler is less spectacular.

Led Zeppelin: Good Times, Bad Times: A Visual Biography, by Jerry Prochnicky and Ralph Hulett

Though Zeppelin's staple photographic record has been reproduced in many places, this collection manages to bring out some refreshingly little-seen and private shots to flesh out the usual pictorial evidence.

Led Zeppelin: In the Light, by Howard Mylett and Richard Bunton

This very early (1981) photo compilation set the bar high for subsequent illustrated volumes. Author Mylett also pioneered with a fine Jimmy Page picture book, *Tangents Within a Framework*.

Jimmy Page, by Jimmy Page

Not the autobiography many fans were hoping for but a limited-edition scrapbook of Page's personal photos, from specialty publishers Genesis Publications. The book retailed in 2010 at over £300 a pop, but future mass-market pressings are anticipated.

22

And It Makes Me Wonder

Led Zeppelin's Greatest Song

To Be a Rock and Not to Roll: The Making of "Stairway to Heaven"

he genesis of Led Zeppelin's most famous work precedes the formation of the band. Rock music's sophistication had snowballed with the ascendancies of Bob Dylan and the Beatles from 1964 on. Increasingly personal or "poetic" lyrics, more elaborate orchestrations of tunes, more involved utilization of studio technology, and the commercial dominance of the long-playing album against that of the 45-rpm single—all set precedents for "Stairway." One obvious change that affected the entire medium was the acceptance of pop songs longer than the prescribed three minutes. Dylan's "Like a Rolling Stone" (1965) was just under six minutes in duration, and the Beatles' global hit "Hey Jude" (1968) clocked in at 7:11. The Doors' album cut "The End" (1967) was over eleven minutes long. Before this time most pop tracks either started fast and loud and stayed fast and loud, or started slow and quiet and stayed slow and quiet, but by the late 1960s the arrangements were becoming more ambitious, with the climactic structures of the Beach Boys' "Good Vibrations," Procol Harum's "A Whiter Shade of Pale," or the Moody Blues' "Nights in White Satin" (all 1967), the Rolling Stones' "Gimme Shelter" (1969), the Who's "Pinball Wizard" (1969), the Beatles' "Let It Be" (1970), and Simon & Garfunkel's "The Sounds of Silence" (1965) and "Bridge over Troubled Water" (1970). Perhaps the most triumphant of these new epics was the Beatles' "A Day in the Life," which brought their 1967 landmark *Sgt. Pepper's Lonely Hearts Club Band* to its shattering finale.

Though "Stairway to Heaven" is ultimately the achievement of all four Led Zeppelin members, the song's basic premise was first conceived by

Jimmy Page. Hearing other acts expand their sound fired his competitive spirit, and by 1970 he was moved to plan his own effort in the field. Already he had premiered his beloved "light and shade" constructions with *Led Zeppelin*'s "Babe I'm Gonna Leave You," "Your Time Is Gonna Come," and the lengthy "Dazed and Confused," as well as *Led Zeppelin II*'s "Ramble On," "What Is and What Should Never Be," and "Thank You." All of these were either acoustic-electric hybrids or long explorations of contrasting dynamics, where the volume, tempo, and instrumentation were built up and toned down as the songs played out. In April of that year Page told a reporter, "Insomuch as 'Dazed and Confused' and all those things went into sections, well, we want to try something new with the organ and acoustic guitar building up and building up to the electric thing." As the album that became *Led Zeppelin IV* was prepared at Headley Grange, following his and Robert Plant's second visit to the Welsh cottage of Bron-yr-Aur, the opening chords of "Stairway" were tried and perfected on Page's New Vista home studio tape deck. "I'd been fooling around with the acoustic guitar and come up with different sections, which I married together," recalled the guitarist. "But what I wanted was something that would have the drums come in at the middle, and then we'd build up to a huge crescendo. Also, I wanted it to speed up, which is against all musical—I mean, that's what a musician *doesn't* do, you see." Although the song was performed on a guitar tuned to the standard E–A–D–G–B–E, Page later said that the droning modalities of "White Summer" and "Black Mountain Side" formed "Stairway to Heaven"'s bottom steps.

The next stage in the song's creation was to bring it to Led Zeppelin's other players. At Headley Grange John Paul Jones was the first after Page to work on the piece, and he quickly grasped its structure. Armed with the cache of acoustic instruments he always brought to studio sessions, he pulled out a bass recorder—something never played before or since on a Zeppelin track—and accompanied Page's trial runs. Considering how it is this wooden pipe that imbues the song with its unforgettably archaic mood, it's interesting that neither Jones nor John Bonham received any songwriting credit on "Stairway to Heaven," but the final ascription somehow suits its soft-heavy, light-shade, rural-urban duality: man-made *Page* coupled with the organic *Plant*.

The work was rehearsed and demoed at Headley Grange but conclusively recorded at Island Studios, with the probable date of its taping sometime in January 1971. "I was very much into doing tracks that built, and you would add extra layers to the song, and it reached a crescendo at the end," recalled engineer Andy Johns. "I mentioned that to [Page]. 'I've got a song that does that. . . . Wait 'til you hear it.'" In addition to Page's Harmony acoustic guitar

"Stairway to Heaven" remains Led Zeppelin's greatest and most famous statement.
Author's Collection

and Jones's double-tracked recorders, there is also Jones's Hohner electric piano underlying the middle portions of the track, and Page brings in a Fender XII electric twelve-string guitar, directly injected into the mixing deck without amplification for a chiming texture, from 2:14 on. The two other key components of "Stairway"'s music, Bonham's drums and Page's electric guitar solo, were put down at Island. "We really couldn't have done the acoustic guitar and drums at Headley—we needed a nice big studio," Page explained.

John Bonham's entry at the song's 4:19 mark is a simple fill by his standards, but resounds with such force after such suspenseful absence in the previous verses, that "Stairway to Heaven" turns into a heavy rock 'n' roll cut from the instant he appears. Other classic tunes benefit from dramatic percussive fanfares—Ringo Starr's in the Beatles' "A Day in the Life" and "Hey Jude," Charlie Watts's in the Stones' "Wild Horses" and "Sister Morphine," Nick Mason's in Pink Floyd's "Time"—but Bonham's is absolutely volcanic. According to assistant engineer Richard Digby-Smith, Page requested a retake of the drummer's first attempts, to Bonham's annoyance. "This always happens," he complained. "We get a great take and then you want to do it again." But the master version hears him taking out his impatience on the snare and toms, with spectacular results. "And when they play it back," Digby-Smith said, "Bonham looks at Jimmy like, 'You're always right, you bastard.'"

Then came Page's turn. The descending rhythmic base underneath the guitar solo and final verses, a simplified arrangement of the same A-minor pattern with which "Stairway" starts, was played on his Gibson Les Paul in tandem with Jones's Fender bass. But Page's climactic lead lines were played on his Fender Telecaster, which he'd put aside after the 1969 *Led Zeppelin II* sessions. This was a wise move, as the Telecaster had a distinctly piercing tone that could cut through the fatter riffs of the Gibson. Plugged into either his Supro or Marshall amplifier, Page first sketched a basic outline of his solo while listening to the playback, warmed up, then taped three in quick succession. "I remember sitting in the control room with Jimmy," said Andy Johns. "He's standing there next to me, and he'd done quite a few passes, and it wasn't going anywhere. I could see he was getting a bit paranoid, and so I was getting paranoid. . . . It was a silly circle of paranoia. Then bang! On the next take or two, he ripped it out." Richard Digby-Smith likewise recollected Page slouched on a speaker as he played his part. "I had the first phrase worked out, and a link phrase here and there, but on the whole that solo was improvised," Page reported.

Beginning at 5:54, Page mainly uses a pentatonic blues scale for the part (the notes A, C, D, E, and G), but he also incorporates the additional notes of F and B that impart a minor or classical feel. The resultant Aeolian implications of the solo make it more melodic than his leads for "Good Times Bad Times," "Since I've Been Loving You," or his other Chicago and Delta tributes; though other guitarists would do even more baroque solos in the future, the trend toward quasi-Romantic electric guitar runs took a giant leap forward from "Stairway to Heaven." A cyclical set of fast bluesy licks in the middle of the sequence makes more tension, a Hendrix-like device done to perfection here by Page and soon a standard move in long rock guitar exhibitions. The repeated four-note "sighing" fills at 6:24, 6:28, 6:33, and 6:38 were punched into the solo after Page's completed take (the overlapped sounds of two separate guitars are audible), but in concert, Page was able to replicate all tracks of the studio solo almost exactly. Listen, too, for how the descending A minor-G–F progression (which reminded Page of that for Ray Charles's "Hit the Road, Jack") becomes more syncopated when the vocal line returns after the Wagnerian blast of E–C–A sextuplets that concludes the solo.

From a musical standpoint, what makes "Stairway to Heaven" so effective is the seamlessness of its sonic expansion. Note how the opening acoustic guitar and Robert Plant's first verses are recorded with an almost "dry" intimacy, but then more and more echo is added throughout the song, so that by Plant's octave-jumping declamations from 6:43 he seems to be singing from atop a mountain in a thunderstorm. Because the fundamental key of A minor is maintained from beginning to end, it is impossible to dissect "Stairway" as merely two or more compositions stuck together, as might be said of "Dazed and Confused"; instead the listener is forced to reexamine any preconceptions of folk versus rock or acoustic versus electric, since each different section blends so subtly into the next. Young people whose parents or teachers derided their music as "noise" could play them "Stairway" with no introduction and watch as their elders slowly realized the peaceful, poetic ballad was in fact the work of long-haired rock 'n' rollers. When mass-marketed pop records seemed to be indistinguishable from traditional Celtic madrigals, the grown-ups might think, Maybe these kids have better taste than we assumed.

If this was not the first rock song to rise to a resounding crescendo— even Zeppelin's "Babe I'm Gonna Leave You" does that pretty powerfully— "Stairway to Heaven" contains the broadest sweep of styles, in its nearly eight-minute journey from quiet pastoral to screaming hard rock, or from the year 1500 to 1971. Musicologist Robert Walser has written, "Musically, 'Stairway' fuses powerful 'authenticities,' which are really ideologies. . . . The narrative juxtaposition of the sensitive (acoustic guitar, etc.) and the aggressive (distorted electric guitar, etc.) has continued to show up in heavy metal, from Ozzy Osbourne to Metallica." According to a 1986 analysis of the song in *Guitar for the Practicing Musician* magazine, no less a figure than Herbert Von Karajan, conductor of the Berlin Philharmonic Orchestra, was exposed to "Stairway" and described its structure as "almost perfect," enthusing, "Even if I were to rearrange it for the Berlin Philharmonic, I would do it like the record."

Sometimes All of Our Thoughts: What "Stairway to Heaven" Means

The great mystery that has befuddled millions of Led Zeppelin fans lies in the open-ended allusions of Robert Plant's words for "Stairway." The song *seems* to carry some kind of inner secret that can be understood if the right connections are made between the various scenes depicted in its verses, but its real attraction is in the way each different passage suggests a new direction only to be confounded by the next one, like an insoluble maze of symbolism and evocation. In *Rock of Ages: The Rolling Stone History of Rock and Roll*, "Stairway to Heaven" is described as "an unknowable song, but one that nonetheless exerts a terrible, beautiful allure." Rock scholar Greil Marcus has compared the Zeppelin work to Dylan's "Like a Rolling Stone," "both in the grandeur of its sound and in its call for an escape from the Kingdom of Mammon in its words—an escape into a daydream of Druidic forests while riding the escalator up to the lingerie floor of Harrod's." In *Hammer of the Gods* Stephen Davis describes it as "an invitation to abandon the new traditions and follow the old gods," and in *When Giants Walked the Earth* Mick Wall writes that "Stairway" is simply "the grandest, certainly most affecting musical statement of [Jimmy Page's] generation."

Page himself could make no input but could only marvel at Robert Plant's lyrical inventiveness. "When one listens to records they always come up with their own concepts and visions, and 'Stairway' really allows for that. The fact that we printed them on the inner sleeve demonstrates what we thought of the song. But even with the lyrics printed on the sleeve of each album and CD, people still came up with their own interpretations. That's wonderful. . . . I didn't really get involved, but I do remember [Plant] asking me about the 'bustle in your hedgerow,' and saying, 'Well, that'll get people thinking,' but other than that . . ."

The irony here, of course, is that Plant famously wrote the lines for "Stairway" in, depending on who you listen to, either a fit of genius or a burst of let's-get-it-over-with obligation. "It was really intense," recalled Page. "And by the time we came up with the fanfare at the end and could play it all the way through, Robert had eighty percent of the lyrics done." Andy Johns remembered saying to Plant at Island Studios, "Hey Percy, it's your turn to sing," to which Plant responded, "Oh, God, really? Hang on for a sec. Play me the track again." "He's sitting in the back of the control room scribbling away," the engineer recounted. "He hasn't finished the lyrics yet. . . . I think there was one run-through to warm up and two takes and then he was done." "It was done very quickly," Plant confirmed to Cameron Crowe for Crowe's essay in the 1990 Led Zeppelin box set. "It took a little working out, but it was a very fluid, unnaturally easy track. . . . There was something pushing it, saying, 'You guys are okay, but if you want to do something *timeless*, here's a wedding song for you.'" "It's a nice, pleasant, well-meaning, naïve little song, very English" he told *Rolling Stone* in 1988. "It was some cynical aside about a woman getting everything she wanted all the time without giving back any thought or consideration . . . and then it softened up after that. I think it was the Moroccan dope."

Given that Plant spent his formative years idolizing American music and American culture, the subjects of his songs seemed to become *less* American after he'd actually discovered the country as a twenty-year-old member of Led Zeppelin. The Tolkien references in "Ramble On" and the Viking saga of "Immigrant Song" presage the haunted meadows and woodlands of "Stairway to Heaven" more than anything in Robert Johnson or Moby Grape; the jaundiced portrait of "a Lady who's sure" in the opening lines may have come after the songwriter had made several trips to the US and seen just how spoiled by affluence real Americans could be. At least as she's characterized in the first verse, the heroine of "Stairway" is a descendant of the "Living Loving Maid," in her materialism and vanity. Her description as a "Lady" might derive from the hippie term *old lady*, for a female partner of any age, and from such songs as Dylan's "Sad-Eyed Lady of the Lowlands" and the Beatles' "Lady Madonna," and Joni Mitchell's *Ladies of the Canyon* album. The phrase "stairway to heaven," indeed, had been used before, as the title of a 1946 British fantasy film starring David Niven; there were also the songs "Stairway to the Stars" and George and Ira Gershwin's "I'll Build a Stairway to Paradise" that dated from the swing era, as well as a peppy Neil Sedaka effort of 1960, "Stairway to Heaven."

After the Lady is introduced, Plant then turns to a collection of nature portraits for the next verses, all prefaced in the ballad form: There's a sign on the wall; there's a songbird who sings; there's a feeling I get; if there's a bustle; yes, there are two paths; there's still time; and finally, there walks a Lady. The reappearance of the Lady in the song's torrential final minute is the only resolution offered, and the alternate characters of the Piper and the May Queen rival her as enigmas. (The Piper himself may be Plant's unconscious nod to Pink Floyd's 1967 album *The Piper at the Gates of Dawn*, named after a chapter in Kenneth Graham's children's fable *The Wind in the Willows*.) Following the instrumentation of Page, Jones, and Bonham, Plant starts off somewhere in the Elizabethan era—"all that glitters is gold" is from Shakespeare's *The Merchant of Venice*—then ends up with the very contemporary juxtaposition of "to be a rock and not to roll." Any spiritual or philosophical message here is extremely vague: Instead Plant establishes a timeless mood of a preindustrial landscape where traditional pagan beliefs still have validity in the physical world. Thus the songbird conveys an intelligible message about words having two meanings; looking westward stirs his inward longing for escape; his mind's eye shows him rings of smoke and (somehow) voices; the mysterious Piper will "lead us to reason"; the bustling hedgerow is merely the May Queen's spring clean; your humming head merely the Piper's call; and so on. Another aspect of the song's setting is how it begins in a still morning where the stores are all closed, then promises that "a new day will dawn," and concludes with shadows grown "taller than our souls," as if the story has unfolded over the course of a day and into the evening. "Stairway to Heaven" cannot be reduced to a basic moral or idea, but Plant's vivid pictures of a countryside epiphany seem to promote a human reintegration with the natural kingdom and a modern rediscovery of pre-Enlightenment superstition.

"Stairway to Heaven" does not carry the deep literary echoes of Bob Dylan's most complex songs, or even the obvious tributes of the Jefferson Airplane's "White Rabbit" (Lewis Carroll), the Doors' "Alabama Song" (Bertolt Brecht), and eventually Rush's "Anthem" (Ayn Rand) and the Police's "Don't Stand So Close to Me" (Vladimir Nabokov), but it was, even so, influenced by Robert Plant's reading. Though there are no open references to the vocalist's favorite, J. R. R. Tolkien, the lyrics' visions of forests, a brook, rings of smoke, two paths, and the whispering wind could come straight from Middle Earth. Others have interpreted the Lady as a distant homage to Edmund Spenser's epic poem of 1590, *The Faerie Queene*, an allegorical quest where a labyrinthine forest has "So many pathes, so many turnings seene / That which of them to take, in diverse doubt they been," and "Now soft, now loud, unto the wind did call: / The gentle warbling wind low answerèd to all." Even Plant's interjection, "I got some good news," before Bonham's drum entry in live versions of the song, suggests the biblical "Good News" delivered by Jesus Christ.

In interviews, Plant spoke of Scottish folklorist Lewis Spence's 1949 book *The Magic Arts in Celtic Britain* as a recent study of his whose details later seeped into "Stairway." Spence, an eccentric who also took seriously Atlantis legends and those of other lost civilizations, was a conscientious historian of the occult, and *The Magic Arts* is an impressive catalogue of mythology from Scotland, Wales, and Ireland. In it, he writes of the dragons once believed to dwell underneath the Welsh Mount Eryri (Snowdon), near where the cottage of Bron-yr-Aur was later constructed. As well, he notes that an Irish manuscript of the twelfth century, *The Book of the Dun Cow*, tells of the fort of Scatha, a Caledonian sorceress, which held a magical cauldron and gold and silver treasures, and of how various Balkan, Norse, and Celtic stories describe glass heavens accessible only by steep mountains or hillsides. Spence also comments on a long-ago "Battle of the Trees" as told in poems from the fourteenth-century Welsh *Book of Taliesin*—a title Plant may have connected with Deep Purple's 1968 album *The Book of Taliesyn*. Plant told critic Robert Palmer that his upbringing in the English Midlands affected his poetics as much as any other influence. "You don't have to have too much of an imagination or a library full of books if you live there. It's *still* there. On a murky October evening, with the watery sun looking down on those hills over some old castle and unto the river, you have to be a real bimbo not to flash occasionally."

There is no key to unlocking the puzzle, but a puzzle it will always remain. If "Stairway to Heaven" had shorter or simpler music, or if its lyrics took on the more typical rock 'n' roll topics of love or sex, it would have had little of its eventual impact. Plant's words for the song, however randomly scrawled down from a jumble of pop-folk stereotypes, perfectly complement the stateliness of Page's slow orchestration. The "meaning" of the track is elusive and, according to the author, wasn't written with one in mind, but it is delivered with such sincerity it can only convince the audience of a deeper purpose. Likewise, the disjointed conjurations of medieval and pastoral idioms make little sense when read literally, but are expressed as if they carry a vital message for an entire generation. As it turned out, they did.

The Forests Will Echo: How "Stairway to Heaven" Has Affected Led Zeppelin's Reputation

You don't have to be a fan of Led Zeppelin to know the band's most popular song. "Stairway" has taken on a life of its own since its appearance on *Led Zeppelin IV* in November 1971, and is now one of the most significant documents of the rock 'n' roll era: timeless hymn or overblown embarrassment, classic or cliché, love it or hate it, "Stairway to Heaven" is Zeppelin's unchallenged magnum opus and a milestone of popular culture.

"Every musician wants to do something of lasting quality," Jimmy Page told Cameron Crowe in 1975, "something which will hold up for years, and I guess we did it with 'Stairway.'" "I think that song is great," said Robert Plant thirty years later. "If I listen to it objectively, from a distance, I really enjoy it." "'Stairway' embodies a lot of what Led Zeppelin was about," confirmed John Paul Jones in 1990. "It's a good tune, for a start." Indeed, "Stairway to Heaven" is Zeppelin's signature, inextricably identified with the four musicians and with the rock music of the period. *Rolling Stone* magazine has listed it as number thirty-one in its "500 Greatest Songs of All Time"; it is included in the Rock and Roll Hall of Fame's "500 Songs that Shaped Rock and Roll"; it has earned a place in the Grammy Awards Hall of Fame; and Page's guitar solo itself has been cited as the number one best in rock 'n' roll in *Guitar World*. The song's opening arpeggios are a mandatory hurdle for beginning pickers, and FM radio listeners in North America have regularly voted "Stairway" as the Greatest Rock Song Ever through countless on-air request lines for over three decades. It has been respectfully covered by artists as diverse as jazz guitar maestro Stanley Jordan, country queen Dolly Parton, and soul diva Mary J. Blige, translated into a symphonic edition by the London Symphony Orchestra, and given a tongue-in-cheek treatment by artists such as Dread Zeppelin, Pat Boone, and Tiny Tim. Never released as a single, "Stairway to Heaven" is nonetheless estimated to have been broadcast over three million times on radio stations around the world. The record it highlighted has sold almost 40 million copies internationally. The total value of its earnings in royalties from all sources has been estimated at $562 million US.

"Stairway" was first performed live by Led Zeppelin on March 5, 1971, in Belfast, Northern Ireland, and was played in every single completed Zeppelin concert thereafter. In Berlin on July 7, 1980, a fourteen-minute rendition was the final song (before encores) of the intact Led Zeppelin's last show. Its US debut during the 1971 summer tour of North America quickly alerted the band to the significance of what they'd come up with. At Los Angeles's Inglewood Forum on August 21, more than two months before *Led Zeppelin IV* was released, Jimmy Page remembered a "sizeable" standing ovation after the piece was premiered. "I thought, 'This is incredible, because no one's heard this number yet. This is the first time they're hearing it!' It obviously touched them, you know." The unique qualities of "Stairway to Heaven" were made manifest by the double-neck Gibson EDS 1275 six- and twelve-string guitar Page had acquired to play it, giving the performances a memorable visual as well as musical component. A live version was highlighted in the *Song Remains the Same* film and album, and the solo artist Page played an instrumental rendition for his 1983 ARMS concerts and his 1988 *Outrider* tour. The song was also heard at Led Zeppelin's Live Aid and Atlantic Records anniversary reunion shows in 1985 and 1988, respectively, although Robert Plant had become leery of singing it and at the latter event almost refused to do so. By Zeppelin's one-off 2007 gig "Stairway to Heaven" had nearly worn out its welcome as a touchstone for musicians and audience alike.

Indeed, the very familiarity of "Stairway" has become the biggest strike against it. Plant has said that "there's only so many times you can sing it and mean it," adding that "in all honesty, there are songs, and there are books, and there are moments, and there are people that belong to particular times in your life, and then it's gone. . . . Some good things just go so far round and round and round that in the end you lose perspective of what they really have." Since it became an FM radio standard, comedians have poked fun at its high regard among pot-smoking suburbanites endlessly requesting it on their local stations: "Yeah, could you play 'Stairway to Heaven' by Led Zeppelin? Like, I have every one of their albums, but I'm too stoned to put it on the turntable." Others have dismissed it as the worst example of rock 'n' rollers' sophomoric attempts at philosophy, a banal confusion of obscurity for intellectual depth. In 1992 a special edition of *Life* magazine, "Forty Years of Rock 'n' Roll," named "Stairway to Heaven" as four of the top five worst songs of the 1970s (the other was "Muskrat Love" by the Captain and Tennille). Humorist Dave Barry has written that "I seriously believe that 'Stairway to Heaven' would be a much better song if they cut maybe 45 minutes out of it," and that, along with "Hey Jude," Lynyrd Skynyrd's "Free Bird," and Eric Clapton's "Layla," "I know these are great rock classics; I'm just saying that after a while they get to be really *boring* rock classics whose primary musical value seems to be that they give radio DJs time to go to the bathroom." Barry also quotes musician Tim Rooney's list of the ten requests Top 40 cover bands hate most: "Stairway" occupied five spots, while Creedence Clearwater Revival's "Proud Mary" took two, and "Louie Louie," "Free Bird," and "Feelings" filled out the rest. The *New York Times*'s Howard Hampton has described "Stairway" as "stunningly ubiquitous . . . a colossus of drug-inspired kitsch, melding the ethereal with the histrionic." In a *Rolling Stone* review of U2's 1984 live album *Under a Blood Red Sky*, the "bone-crushing arena-rock riff" of "Sunday Bloody Sunday," a song with a similar A-minor chord progression to the Zeppelin classic, was praised by Christopher Connelly as "'Stairway to Heaven' for smart people."

The overexposure of "Stairway to Heaven" has meant that, ultimately, too many listeners hear its reputation rather than its music. In the same way that *The Godfather* is shown on late-night commercial TV, Beethoven's *Ode to Joy* adapted for ad jingles, George Orwell's *Animal Farm* taught to bored high school students, and van Gogh's *Sunflowers* reproduced on coffee mugs, "Stairway" has been taken far out of its original context and has suffered the indignity of being received as a golden oldie rather than as a serious work of art. It is easy to joke about reverent radio broadcasters and awestruck, lighter-flicking teenagers, but harder to return to the work's actual content and consider it as a performance rather than a punch line.

Like many well-known rock songs, too, the Led Zeppelin anthem has been freighted with more importance than it was originally intended to bear. Robert Plant's hasty stream-of-consciousness transcription of its lines is now one of those Rock Legends that have been far more greatly venerated by fans than by their creator. According to Mick Jagger, Keith Richards first considered the Stones' "(I Can't Get No) Satisfaction" as "just a silly kind of riff," while Eddie Van Halen said of his pivotal "Eruption" guitar solo that "I just didn't think it would be something we'd put on a record," and Paul McCartney's "Yesterday" began life with a working title of "Scrambled Eggs." John Lennon once confessed, "I suppose I'm so indifferent about [the Beatles'] music because most other people take it so seriously. . . . It's nice when people like it, but when they start 'appreciating' it, getting great deep things out of it, making a thing of it, then it's a lot of shit. . . . It just takes a few people to get going, and they con themselves into thinking it's important."

Yet "Stairway to Heaven" can still stand as Led Zeppelin's masterpiece. It challenges its fans and foes alike with questions of brilliant inspiration versus seat-of-the-pants expediency, of the intentions of the artist versus the expectations of the audience, and of longevity versus familiarity. The song's power to move and thrill forty years since its release is an impressive quality in the arena of popular music, where the majority of output is valued for its instant commercialism or "catchiness" rather than any social durability—let alone any potential elevation into something like a secular hymn to be played at weddings and funerals. Like other institutions, "Stairway" may have become vulnerable to resistance and resentment, but the fundamental fact of institutions is that they command respect. "Stairway to Heaven" continues to deserve it.

Yes, There Are Two Paths: Other Rock Songs That Follow the "Stairway" Model

The success of *Led Zeppelin IV* throughout the 1970s and beyond inspired many artists to craft their own epics. Recurring themes and styles included the gentle opening that gradually increased in volume and bombast; the questing, proclamatory lyrics; and the soaring, virtuoso guitar solo. They've been called rock anthems, at first with irony and in time in acknowledgment that their words and melodies truly did seem to serve as quasi-official music for large segments of the youth population—pop songs whose cultural impact could not be measured by record sales or chart positions alone. Ann Powers in the *New York Times* commented in 1998 how the typical such track, also known as a "power ballad," "offered a sense of profundity to fans who craved it . . . low culture insisting on its right to mimic high art." Among the most revered rock anthems that clearly adopted the "Stairway to Heaven" template are the following.

AC/DC: "Hell's Bells"

As close as the Thunder from Down Under come to a power ballad, their 1980 *Back in Black* monster opens with a solemnly tolling bell and an ominous A-minor guitar figure, then grows in intensity. There aren't any acoustic guitars or recorders here, but the song still captures the suspense of the Led Zeppelin prototype.

Aerosmith: "Dream On"

Although the Boston badasses' anthem took shape before *Led Zeppelin IV* was released in 1971, it wasn't in record stores until their 1973 debut. Like "Stairway," this starts with a quiet solo guitar progression and then lumbers awake with a massive drum roll, and by the end Steve Tyler is wailing a stirring message of self-belief over the band's cycle of ascending chords. For all its familiarity, still a great moment.

Blue Öyster Cult: "(Don't Fear) the Reaper"

Ghostly, sinister, and morbidly beautiful, the BÖC standard uses the A-minor, G, and F chords of "Stairway to Heaven," at first with arpeggios and finally in a furious distorted climax. Raise your fist and kill yourself.

Boston: "More Than a Feeling"

A very pretty guitar figure intros this exuberant memoir of the mystical Mary Ann, and then a crushing minor chord run pounds the song home. Producer Tom Scholz's melodic, expertly structured guitar spotlight is a quintessential hold-your-Zippos-high acme of classic rock.

The Eagles: "Hotel California"

The cocaine cowboys' greatest song is a close rival to "Stairway," with Don Felder's immortal Spanish-style guitar intro, the memorable visuals of Don Henley's lyrics, and the Tiffany-twisted electric soloing of Felder and Joe Walsh (like Page, Felder used a Gibson EDS 1275 double-neck to play the song onstage). This too was accused by idiots of carrying Satanic messages, in lines about steely knives that just can't kill the beast. The song has has also received egregious FM radio overplay since its 1976 release, but justly so.

Both Boston's "More Than a Feeling" and U2's "Sunday Bloody Sunday" borrowed from the "Stairway to Heaven" light-and-shade musical template.

Author's Collection

Guns N' Roses: "November Rain"

The Gunners' patent bid for a rock anthem is almost a parody of the style, throwing in every cliché of the arena showstopper: the tender piano intro, the gradual accumulation of electric instruments, the ecstatic guitar solo, and finally the "Layla"-like coda with a heavenly choir of voices. With a song-writing credit going alone to the inimitable Axl Rose, the 1991 video for this track (from the much-hyped *Use Your Illusion* double release) made its pretensions even more obvious, especially when guitarist Slash wails alone on his Les Paul at the edge of a windswept cliff. Still, the sheer sincerity and production polish of Guns N' Roses on "November Rain" allows them to pull off the attempt with flying colors.

Journey: "Wheel in the Sky," "Don't Stop Believin'"

Both of these cuts became requisite concert pieces for Journey. "Wheel in the Sky" opens with a neatly done D-minor acoustic guitar figure and then becomes a heavy rocker, while "Don't Stop Believin'" offers a positive theme of faith and confidence. Vocalist Steve Perry's range was as majestic as Robert Plant's, and employed with great gusto on these two.

Judas Priest: "Beyond the Realms of Death"

Singer Rob Halford has admitted that the song, from *Stained Class* in 1978, is "a bit like our 'Stairway to Heaven.'" It alternates between gentle acoustic lament and heavy metal paean to suicide. Gotta love the Priest.

Kiss: "Black Diamond"

From the band's 1974 self-titled debut album, this number starts with a sad A-minor arpeggio and then morphs into a punchy ode to a street-walker. "The tag at the end reminds me of early Neil Young or 'Stairway to Heaven,'" opined Kiss's Paul Stanley.

Led Zeppelin: "Over the Hills and Far Away"

Though Zeppelin never really tried to hit on a formula, the exploratory material from *Houses of the Holy* was plainly riding on momentum from the previous *Led Zeppelin IV*. The intricate acoustic guitar commencement that segues into a full rock show echoes "Stairway to Heaven," and the vague lyrics that invoke a lady, the open road, wondering, and gold seem to have evolved out of the earlier cut.

Lynyrd Skynyrd: "Free Bird," "Simple Man"

Along with "Hotel California" and Queen's "Bohemian Rhapsody," "Free Bird" is one of the only songs to challenge "Stairway to Heaven" in FM radio overplay and repeated popular demand. The comic stereotype of the rock-loving yahoo yelling out for "Free Bird" at any musical performance—of polka, reggae, techno, or a string quartet—is an indication of how loved the 1973 Skynyrd jam has become. According to guitarist Gary Rossington, singer Ronnie Van Zant wrote his lyrics to the track in less than five minutes, beating Robert Plant's time for the "Stairway" transcription by a good half hour. "Initially it was just a slow ballad," Rossington recalled. "Then Ronnie said, 'Why don't you do something at the end of that so I can take a break for a few minutes. . . .' Ronnie kept saying, 'It's not long enough, make it longer.'" Live versions of "Free Bird" could go almost fifteen minutes. "Simple Man," also from '73's *Pronounced Leh-nerd Skin-nerd*, is arguably a better work. Like "Stairway" it is built around an A-minor key and slowly rises from quiet arpeggios to vast power chords, while Van Zant lays down one of his most compelling lessons of integrity and heartland authenticity.

Metallica: "Fade to Black," "One"

These two early successes from the thrash gods can't be called power ballads, but they do employ the acoustic-electric light-and-shade construction of "Stairway." As in the Zeppelin song, their juxtaposition of solo classical guitar with amplified rock makes both styles all the heavier.

Mötley Crüe: "Home Sweet Home"

The Crüe's big live sing-along number has a Queen-like piano intro that then grows into full power ballad mode with a screaming guitar solo from Mick Mars. Somewhat cheesy, but still moving if heard without irony.

Queen: "Bohemian Rhapsody"

Though "Stairway" often tops radio polls regarding the Greatest Songs of All Time, this epic hit has sometimes beat the Zeppelin opus to the number one spot. Indeed, Freddie Mercury's masterpiece may have even done Page and Plant's light-and-shade structure one better, by skillfully blending rock with not the simpler sounds of folk but the extravagance of opera. The result was that "Bohemian Rhapsody," from 1975's *A Night at the Opera*, became as grand a statement as anything in popular music—daring listeners to decide whether it was a bastardization of an established highbrow art form or the logical maturing of a newer, crasser medium. While "Stairway to Heaven" certainly set the precedent for the Queen spectacular (and is the longer song by a couple of minutes), it seems almost humble by comparison. According to Queen guitarist Brian May, Mercury scored "Bohemian Rhapsody" with his private notational system that "looked like buses zooming all over his bits of paper," and that the amount of overdubbing required to complete the work on a sixteen-track recorder nearly wore the oxide off the master track, to a point where the tape became almost transparent.

Rush: "The Trees"

The Canadian power trio have always acknowledged their musical debt to Zeppelin, and any number of their songs hark back to heavy blues style of the four Englishmen. Drummer Neil Peart's lyrics are often literate to a fault, based on complex poetic structures and long, multipart movements that offer some deep social allegory or sci-fi dystopian vision. Both qualities owed something to *Led Zeppelin IV*, and this well-known song, from 1978's *Hemispheres*, has the pastoral intro, hard rock launch, and sylvan imagery of "Stairway to Heaven." The entire Rush album *2112* has much of the same soft-loud, intimate-huge, rustic-futuristic philosophical affectations.

Styx: "Come Sail Away"

From 1977's *The Grand Illusion*, this remains the most popular song from the oft-derided AOR kings, getting under way with some very pretty piano runs and sensitive lyrics about being free, then blasting into outer space with aliens. Their earlier "Suite Madame Blue" is another FM anthem that was doubtless inspired by the enigmatic female of "Stairway to Heaven."

Tesla: "Love Song"

The highly underrated Tesla always stood apart from their era's pack of spandex hair metal bands, and produced this beautiful power ballad, heard on 1989's *The Great Radio Controversy*. Guitarist Frank Hannon's heroic solo is as impressively lyrical as Page's on "Stairway," and he even performed it on a Gibson double-neck for some live shows.

U2: "Sunday Bloody Sunday"

Though U2 were not a band to copy anything in the Zeppelin format, they still came up with a stadium-rousing powerhouse that had the same effect on audiences as "Stairway to Heaven"—and with the same benefit to their long-term career.

Remember Laughter? "Stairway to Heaven" Banned from Guitar Shops

This urban legend got a wide airing in the 1992 comedy *Wayne's World*, where Mike Myers's title character attempts to play the song on a display Stratocaster but is quickly stopped by a sales clerk. Shown the "No Stairway to Heaven" sign, Wayne is bummed out: "No 'Stairway'! Denied!" (Copyright rules prevented even Myers's fragmentary "Stairway to Heaven" from being heard in most TV and video releases of the movie.)

Though fictionalized in *Wayne's World*, the scene is based on the real saturation of music store employees by countless amateur versions of well-known rock songs. Anyone who has worked around guitars has heard untrained people, mostly young males, try to play at rock stardom with valuable instruments and other professional equipment that they aren't really qualified to handle. "Customers" ask to try Gibsons or Fenders they have no intention of purchasing, and then proceed to regale bystanders and staff with what little they know of "Stairway to Heaven," Deep Purple's "Smoke on the Water," Black Sabbath's "Iron Man," the Beatles' "Blackbird," or Van Halen's "Eruption." The problem is that, as familiar as such pieces are to the rock audience, most neophyte guitarists have no idea how the songs are accurately played, and their faltering approximations are difficult to listen to—especially for the twentieth time in a shift.

"Stairway" in particular was a pretty advanced guitar sequence in 1971 and still requires some preliminary experience. For players whose repertoire consisted of three-chord songs like "Twist and Shout" or "Louie Louie," the leap to Jimmy Page's A minor (V position), then A minor (add 9) / G-sharp, C/G, D/F-sharp and then F major 7 was almost impossible to finger and pick with a natural, confident rhythm; consequently most guitar shop performances of the famous intro were painfully awkward. But because guitar heroics look and sound so cool to newbies, many youthful guitarists have attempted to musically run before they can walk, distracted by the range of instructional materials that teach simplified or tablature notation for tunes first played by talented pros with solid groundings in fingerboard theory and mechanics—e.g., the members of Led Zeppelin. The "No Stairway" rule, though hardly enforceable by law, was a common joke for patrons and personnel of music retailers who just wanted to discourage untutored wanna-bes from getting in over their heads, embarrassing themselves and annoying everyone else. In February 2005 *Guitar World* magazine's regular "Dear Guitar Hero" column presented Page himself with a variety of readers' questions, one of which was "Have you ever gone into a guitar shop and played 'Stairway to Heaven'?" This drew a laugh from the Magus, at least. "No, I haven't," he said. He may be the only guitarist who hasn't.

1978

March 15: Massive oil spill off French coast.

May: Led Zeppelin rehearse in Clearwell Castle.

July 25: First test-tube baby born, London.

September 18: Camp David peace talks between Israel and Egypt.

October 13: Sex Pistol Sid Vicious charged in death of girlfriend Nancy Spungen.

October 23: Pope John Paul II inaugurated.

November 29: More than 900 die in mass suicide in Jonestown, Guyana.

November–December: Led Zeppelin record *In Through the Out Door*, Stockholm.

December–January: "Winter of Discontent" in UK as strikes cripple the country.

Movies: *Grease*; *National Lampoon's Animal House*; *The Deer Hunter*; *Midnight Express*.

Music: Van Halen, *Van Halen*; Rush, *Hemispheres*; the Rolling Stones, *Some Girls*; Willie Nelson, *Stardust*; Paul Simon, "Slip Slidin' Away"; the Bee Gees, "Stayin' Alive"; Alicia Bridges, "I Love the Nightlife."

23

I Got Something I Think You Oughta Know

Led Zeppelin Behind the Scenes

Friends: The Personal Dynamics of Led Zeppelin

Sting of the Police once admitted to an interviewer that "a band is an artificial alliance most of the time." A few rock groups are comprised of friends who became musicians, but most are musicians first and only grow companionable once they have been working successfully together for a while. In the case of Led Zeppelin, the four men all genuinely liked each other, and they are the rare group whose ultimate breakup was due to the death of one member rather than personal estrangement between several. That said, the players' relationships were based more on their musical compatibility and professional respect than on any natural affinity between them.

"Jimmy and I got along well with Jonesy and Bonzo," Robert Plant told *Rolling Stone* in 1988, but Jimmy Page has qualified that, "We all lived in different parts of the country, so when we came off the road we didn't really see each other. . . . We really only socialized when we were on the road." John Paul Jones has added, "We were never a band that socialized. We wouldn't see each other after we got off the road until we'd start recording again." "We got together when we needed to and then did our own thing," Peter Grant said to Dave Lewis in 1993. "We didn't live in each other's pockets." Part of Zeppelin's strength, indeed, was in the four musicians' independence from each other and their freedom from the forced fishbowl intimacy that frustrated more publicity-hungry acts.

Robert Plant and John Bonham were buddies from their teenage years, having grown up in the same city and played with many of the same people;

they were even bandmates in the Band of Joy before they shared a stage in Led Zeppelin. These two were probably the closest members of the group. They were guys from England's Black Country taken up into an international rock 'n' roll sensation when they were both only twenty years old, and the adventure made their bond secure. "It was a bit like being on a space shuttle, in a way," Plant said to Mick Wall. "So we did grow together, although we were never really particularly similar. But we had common ground which we began to share and we realized as time went on that we had to make this thing work." It was Bonham who came to support Plant after the death of his son in 1977 (neither Page nor Jones attended the boy's funeral), and it was Bonham who could best bring the singer down to earth. "It was an honest relationship, where he would say, 'Look, you can't sing, but just go out and look good and I'll look after everything else behind you,'" Plant remembered in his 1988 *Rolling Stone* chat. "We always had this antagonistic relationship—and I miss that. . . . Every time I got a bit like, 'Hey, I'm the star,' he'd be back there in the middle of a concert growling, 'You're fucking hopeless! But don't forget, I'm here.'"

Page and Jones, by contrast, were slightly older Londoners who'd already reached the higher levels of the pop music industry, Page as a session vet and member of the hit-making Yardbirds, and Jones also as a studio whiz who'd rubbed shoulders with the likes of the Rolling Stones, Dusty Springfield, and Donovan. "Jonesy was a bit . . . not *withdrawn*," Plant looked back on their first meeting in 1968, "but he stands back a little and shoots the odd bit of dialogue into the air. It's good stuff, but an acquired taste, really. . . . [Page] had a demeanor which you had to adjust to; it certainly wasn't very casual to start with." The guitarist and bassist-keyboardist had known and occasionally worked with each other for years, but were not ones to hang out together. They were colleagues, not pals. "I knew [Page] well from the session scene, of course," Jones confirmed to Dave Lewis. "He was a very respected name." For this pair Led Zeppelin was not an adventure but a project, a creative and commercial undertaking that they began with clear ideas and no illusions. "My reasons for joining up with Led Zeppelin were purely musical," said Jones. He admired Bonham's drum work ("He was just such an exciting musician to work with. . . . He really kept you on your toes as a musician and a listener") and was usually on good terms with his rhythm section partner. "Sometimes you'd say the wrong thing and he'd take it the wrong way, but we were still pretty close," Jones told Chris Welch, author of *John Bonham: A Thunder of Drums*. The most musically disciplined man of the act, Jones took a while to gravitate to Robert Plant. ("He never knew what to make of me," Jones was quoted in *When Giants Walked the Earth*.) He did reveal to Dave Lewis that by 1978 he and Plant were the two "relatively clean" Zeppelin players, and their mutual more-or-less healthy condition brought them closer together. "Led Zeppelin was a very strange, four-quadrant marriage," Plant told Chuck Klosterman. "When we were kids, Bonham and I were the toughest guys around. . . . So when he passed, I really didn't want to stay with the southern guys—the two guys from London."

Jimmy Page, as Zeppelin's instigator and final authority, had a different connection to the others. Pressed by interviewer Charles Young in 1988 as to whether he thought Bonham was an alcoholic, Page could only stammer, "I wasn't close enough to him to know that." During the band's early period of steady touring and recording he shared with Plant, Jones, and Bonham the camaraderie of establishing Led Zeppelin's name and fortune in the face of resentful press and a daunting workload, but fame, power, and especially drug abuse would isolate him as the 1970s wore on. He and Plant grew tight during their 1970 visits to Bron-yr-Aur cottage, where they began to seriously write songs together, and they both formed an exclusive empathy as the two most visible performers of the act, onstage and off. "The more you get into the bloke, although he seems to be quite shy, he's not, really," Plant told a reporter at the time. "He's got a lot of good ideas for songwriting and he's proved to be a really nice guy." But by the end of Zeppelin, Plant conceded that "the relationship deteriorated," and into the 2000s he characterized their dynamic as "like [that of] Walter Matthau and Jack Lemmon. . . . Page is a very clever, talented guy who has a particular slant on music, and I was always his sidekick who had a different slant on music."

For John Paul Jones, his exclusion from the Page-Plant reunions of the 1990s strained ties that were already distant. "It was a great shame, particularly after all we'd been through together," he said to Dave Lewis. Plant's offhand press conference joke that Jones was "parking the car," when asked about the absence of Led Zeppelin's third survivor from the *No Quarter* album and tour, caused a rift that took some time to heal. "It's just so banal, and I imagine that he's feasted with acrimony for years on the fact that I said that, but I did apologize to him," the vocalist said in 2005. "So I think we carry all this stuff and really, we should just get together and count all our blessings and say, 'Hey, I loved you a long time ago. What's going on now?'" Today the three remaining members seem to have the same mixture of affection and exasperation for one another as any middle-aged former college roommates, sports teammates, soldiers, or coworkers. Considering the emotional extremities of what they have lived through together—adulation and exhilaration; celebration and addiction; triumph and disaster; rural England and metropolitan America; love, birth, and death; sex, drugs, and rock 'n' roll—their continued rapport should be valued by them and appreciated by their fans.

I Don't Care What the Neighbors Say: Where Led Zeppelin Lived

Inclined to return to the bosoms of home and family while between concert travels, each Led Zeppelin player resided well apart from the others. Their abodes were suited to their situations as newly rich men with young families, who could afford luxurious, even extravagant, properties that would have otherwise been well beyond the means of struggling musicians. The suburban estates, city addresses, or country seats of the four from 1968 to 1980 were:

Jimmy Page
 ◆ Pangbourne Boathouse (4 Shooters Hill, Pangbourne, Berkshire)
 ◆ Plumpton Place (Ditchling Road, Lewes, East Sussex)
 ◆ Tower House (29 Melbury Road, Kensington, London)
 ◆ Mill House (Mill Lane, Clewer, Berkshire)

Robert Plant
 ◆ Jennings Farm (Blakeshall, Wolverley, Kidderminster, Worcestershire)
 ◆ Cwm Einion Sheep Farm (near Artists Valley, Wales)

John Paul Jones
 ◆ The Straw Hat (Private residence, Chorleywood, Hertfordshire)
 ◆ Farm (Crowborough, Sussex)

John Bonham
 ◆ Butterfield Court (Dudley, Worcestershire)
 ◆ Old Hyde Farm (Cutnall Green, Worcestershire)

Physical Graffiti: Led Zeppelin's Parents, Spouses, Siblings, and Children

Unlike other British and American acts of their period, the musicians of Led Zeppelin were not tabloid celebrities whose biographies were regularly splashed across the gossip columns. In fact during the early 1970s even many fans would have been hard-pressed to name the wives or other family ties of anyone in the band. Where Mick Jagger, Rod Stewart, David Bowie, or Elton John were subject to enormous media intrusion into their personal lives (some of which, it should be said, they invited upon themselves), Zeppelin's personnel were almost anonymous. Only in the ensuing decades have more detailed background portraits emerged, pieced together from published interviews, books, and other anecdotal reports. Other than their involvement in one of the biggest and best rock 'n' roll groups ever, Page, Plant, Jones, and Bonham experienced upbringings and adulthoods notable mainly for their ordinary English middle- or working-class characteristics: the modest, common-sense values of people who enjoyed tea, cricket, snooker, pints of ale, Rolls-Royce cars, the *Carry On* comedy series, and gardening. The Seattle mud sharks, New Orleans transvestites, and Bangkok brothels were incidental.

Jimmy Page

The Dark Lord of Hard Rock was the only child born to James Patrick and Patricia (Gaffikin) Page, and was raised in Epsom, Surrey. James Senior was described by his son as an industrial personnel officer, and Patricia, Page said, did "various things," although his birth registration listed her as a doctor's secretary. Jimmy Page was in a long-term relationship with French model Charlotte Martin, with whom he had a daughter, Scarlet Lilith Eleida Page, born in 1971 (she was conceived at Bron-yr-Aur cottage). He was married to American Patricia Ecker in the 1980s and early 90s and his son with her, James Patrick, was born in 1988. He has three more children, Jana, Zofia, and Ashen, by a later partner, Brazilian Jimena Gomez-Paratcha.

Robert Plant

Zeppelin's Golden God was the first of two children born to Robert and Annie (Cain) Plant; his sister, Alison, followed nine years later. The senior Plant was a civil engineer in Halesowen, a suburb of Birmingham, while Mrs. Plant was a homemaker. In 1968 young Plant married Maureen Wilson, with whom he had three children, Carmen Jayne (1968), Karac (1972–1977), and Logan Romero (1979). Plant and Maureen divorced in the early 1980s and he has never remarried, although he has had several relationships since, including with singers Alannah Myles and Najma Akhtar, who participated in the *No Quarter* project. Another son, Jesse Lee, was born in 1991 to Shirley Wilson.

Robert Plant and wife Maureen in the mid-1970s.   *Courtesy of Robert Rodriguez*

John Paul Jones

Christened just John Baldwin, the future Jonesy was also an only child, born to musician Joe Baldwin and his wife Marjorie, née Little. He grew up in the County of Kent, southeast of London. For many years Joe had played piano and arranged scores on the British band circuit, even getting some recording gigs in the 1930s as part of an act called Baldwin and Howard. By John's childhood Joe and Marjorie were performing as a musical comedy duo and their son sometimes accompanied them on English tours. "She was the singer," Jones reminisced to Zeppelin expert Steve Sauer in 2001, "and she had a really incompetent accompanist or willfully difficult accompanist. . . . He goes to the piano, he'd pull out an alarm clock, and the audience gags. So she'd never really get through a song." Known professionally as John Paul Jones since 1964, he married Maureen Hegarty in 1966 and three daughters followed: Tamara Nicola (1967), Jacinda Melody (1968), and Kiera Loveday (1971).

John Bonham

The eldest of three children, Bonzo was named after his father John Henry (Jack) Bonham, who was married to Joan, née Sargent. Bonham Senior was a carpenter and building contractor in Redditch, outside Birmingham, while Joan operated a neighborhood shop. The drummer had two younger siblings, Michael (Mick) and Deborah. Bonham married Pat Phillips in 1965, and had two children with her: Jason Paul (born in 1966) and Zoë Louise (born 1975).

Call Me Another Guy's Name: Zeppelin Nicknames and Pseudonyms

Working, playing, traveling, and partying together for twelve years, the foursome naturally developed or repeated familiar terms for each other, not always of endearment. Managers and roadies also earned their own sobriquets, including Peter "G" Grant, Richard "Ricardo" Cole, Joe "Jammer" Wright, Kenny "Pissquick" Pickett, and Ian "Iggy" Knight.

The most widely heard diminutives and handles given to the Zeppelin players were as follows.

Jimmy Page

"Nelson Storm"
Occasionally used in the early 1960s while a playing guitar for Neil Christian (true name Chris Tidmarsh) and the Crusaders.

"Little Jim"
From his session musician stint, distinguishing him from his older guitarist colleague "Big Jim" Sullivan.

"Pagey"
Obvious, preceding and outlasting his Zeppelin years.

"Led Wallet"
Once Page was successful in Led Zeppelin, roadies and other outsiders made cracks about his purported cheapness; he always denied the label and no one in the group used the appellation. Peter Grant, though, did once say that "if you want to bump off Jimmy Page, all you have to do is throw tuppence in front of a London bus."

"The Old Girl"
A private joke between Grant and road manager Richard Cole, around the guitarist's lengthy costume and hair routines while preparing for gigs.

"Hoover Nose"
Quoted by Angela Bowie and used by security goon John Bindon in 1977, when Page showed up at a cocaine party.

"S. Flavius Mercurius"
Page guested on his friend Roy Harper's 1971 album *Stormcock* under this Romanesque alias.

"James MacGregor"
In at least one instance, Page registered into hotels using this name, possibly an allusion to Aleister Crowley associate S. L. MacGregor Mathers.

Robert Plant

"Percy"
Often substituted by associates and other Zeppelin members as the singer's first name but still something of a mystery in its origins. Plant himself said, "It was something to do with my anatomy. . . . Maybe they wouldn't call me that now." Another explanation traces the nickname to English horticulturalist and broadcaster Percy Thrower, whose low-key gardening programs amused the Zeppelin generation as "watching plants grow," which they then connected to their own budding Plant.

"Planty"
See "Pagey," above, and "Jonesy," below.

"The Golden God"
Never addressed this way by others but claimed by Plant himself in a much-quoted moment of vainglory (probably drug-related). His classical features and flowing blond hair made the title an apt one.

"The Wolverhampton Wanderer"
Plant used a football (soccer) alias when producing a 1978 record by Birmingham locals Dansette Damage.

John Paul Jones

"Jonesy"
Another obvious variation, and the only one regularly stuck on the bassist. The name "John Paul Jones" was itself, of course, a pseudonym of John Baldwin.

John Bonham

"Bonzo"
The best-known Zeppelin nickname is how friends, bandmates, and most average fans identify the drummer. It was given to Bonham as a teenager in Birmingham, in reference to a long-running British cartoon character created by George Studdy. The fictional Bonzo was a loveable puppy pictured in a variety of innocent misadventures, and the similarity of his name and disposition to the young percussionist made the moniker inevitable. Bonham's tag may also have echoed the cult Bonzo Dog Doo-Dah Band comedy group.

"The Big B"
Hailed as such by Robert Plant at some concerts following his "Moby Dick" drum solo.

"The Beast"
A less generous title applied to Bonham in the later 1970s, when his unpredictable and violent behavior on tour made him an intimidating figure within the band's entourage.

Led Zeppelin

"The New Yardbirds"
The first of the group's public appearances in September 1968 employed this or a variant in press releases and publicity handouts.

"The Nobs"
Often alleged but never confirmed, the band are said to have been billed under this name in Cophenhagen, Denmark, on February 28 1970, after an aristocrat descendant of the von Zeppelin family took offense to the quartet's title and incendiary cover of their first album. Surviving ticket stubs for this concert are printed with "Led Zeppelin," so the story is a dubious one.

Little Drops of Rain: The Members' Favorite and Least Favorite Led Zeppelin Songs

The complete Zeppelin catalogue has its high and low points in the eyes and ears of its listeners—and its makers. There are no real clunkers put out against the musicians' wishes, and most material had their unanimous approval, but they each had some tracks they preferred over others.

Jimmy Page

Page was definitely proudest of "Stairway to Heaven" and has said so many times. "To me, I thought it crystallized the essence of the band. It had everything there and showed us at our best as a band and as a unit," he said in 1975. "We knew it was really something" upon recording it, the guitarist told *Guitar World* in 1991. "It was certainly a milestone along one of the many avenues of Zeppelin," he said to Mick Wall. The one cut Page has admitted to having reservations over is "All My Love" from *In Through the Out Door*. "I wasn't really very keen on 'All My Love,'" he was quoted as saying in *Guitar World*. "I could just imagine people doing the wave and all of that. And I thought, 'That's not us.'" Elsewhere, he said the song "sort of felt like the Rod Stewart sort of songs of the time with the scarf-waving." There's also a story that Page was none too fond of "Living Loving Maid (She's Just a Woman)," the only song from *Led Zeppelin II* the band never performed in concert.

Robert Plant

The vocalist has come out in favor of "Kashmir" as "the definitive Led Zeppelin song." "It's the quest, the travels and explorations that Page and I went on to far climes well off the beaten track. . . . That, really, to me is the Zeppelin feel." Plant also said in the same *Rolling Stone* interview that *Physical Graffiti*, the album containing the tune, was his preferred Zeppelin collection. "It sounded very tough, but it was also restrained, exhibiting a certain amount of control, as well." He estimated other of the best Zeppelin moments to be "In the Light" and his singing on "The Rain Song." Though Plant has sometimes made snide remarks about "Stairway to Heaven" he does not *hate* it—"I was a kid, you know?"—but he too is known to have no love for "Living Loving Maid."

John Paul Jones

Jonesy told Dave Lewis that his personal picks of the Zeppelin canon are "Kashmir," "The Ocean," "The Crunge," "Over the Hills and Far Away," "When the Levee Breaks," and "In My Time of Dying." He's also praised "Stairway to Heaven," but told Chris Welch that he "hated" "D'yer Mak'er." "It would have been all right if [Bonham] had worked at the part—the whole point of reggae is that the drums and the bass really have to be very strict about what they play. And he wouldn't, so it sounded dreadful." Not a few Zeppelin fans would disagree.

John Bonham

Bonzo was enthusiastic about most of Zeppelin's work: His driving beats reflect the physical and emotional energy he brought to every song he played on. His solo showcase "Moby Dick" was an obvious leaning, but his strong contributions to "Out On the Tiles," "Kashmir," and "When the Levee Breaks" ranked them high on his list as well. But John Paul Jones has noted that Bonham, who found reggae "boring," likewise couldn't stand "D'yer Mak'er." Too bad for him.

Throw Me a Line: Why Robert Plant Received No Songwriting Credits on *Led Zeppelin*

On most Zeppelin albums, authorship of original material was divided variously among the four members of the group: Page-Plant, Page-Plant-Jones, Page-Plant-Jones-Bonham, Page-Plant-Bonham, and even Plant-Jones. On the first record, however, Plant was excluded from any composers' credits, even though he was part of the act from the beginning and even though his improvisatory vocal style was a distinct component of Led Zeppelin's sound. The reason usually given for this is that the young singer was still under contract with CBS Records, who'd released his and Listen's soon-forgotten records of 1966 and 1967, and was therefore ineligible to be signed to Atlantic Records as a member of Led Zeppelin. Once the CBS contract expired (or, just as likely, was bought out by Peter Grant), Plant's name could be attached to subsequent Zeppelin creations. Post-Zeppelin issues from the *Led Zeppelin* period do list Plant as cocomposer, as on "Traveling Riverside Blues" and "The Girl I Love She Got Long Black Wavy Hair," and he now shares credit with Jimmy Page and Anne Bredon for "Babe I'm Gonna Leave You."

There may be other factors here. "I contributed to the lyrics on the first three albums," Page recalled, "but I was always hoping that Robert would eventually take care of that aspect of the band." Most accounts claim that "Thank You" from *Led Zeppelin II* was the first song for which Plant actually sat down and wrote words, suggesting he had no part of any earlier work. On the debut record, only "Good Times Bad Times," "Your Time Is Gonna Come," and "Communication Breakdown" were really new material; Page's

"Dazed and Confused" had evolved out of the Yardbirds' "I'm Confused" and, before that, Jake Holmes's "Dazed and Confused," while the remainder of the songs were Willie Dixon numbers, the instrumental "Black Mountain Side," and the obvious blues adaptation "How Many More Times." Aside from singing these, Plant's input must have been negligible. Of the three recruits to Page's New Yardbirds, Plant was the one most on probation, whereas the producer was more confident of John Bonham and John Paul Jones's talents. In *Hammer of the Gods*, road manager Richard Cole even asserted that Plant might have even been fired by Page after Led Zeppelin's first US tour, a charge Page evaded in a 1988 interview in *Musician* magazine. Between his inexperience, his legal obligations to a rival record label and his shaky status in the band's first few months, Plant's songwriting, such as it was, had to go unacknowledged.

Kinda Makes Life a Drag: The 1973 Led Zeppelin Robbery

Following their three-night engagement at New York's Madison Square Garden in July 1973, the band was robbed of some $200,000 in private cash holdings while staying at the Drake Hotel. This supplied the unexpected twist in *The Song Remains the Same*, which documented the concerts and the following press coverage of the crime, but no arrests have ever been made.

Led Zeppelin on tour in the 1970s was awash in money. The '73 American shows alone were estimated to gross $4 million for the band, based on ticket sales multiplied by an average price of $7, so the problem of handling and securing all that revenue (kept mostly in hundred-dollar bills) was a real one. In 1973 such sums were kept on hand to pay for amenities like the *Starship* airliner, the *Song Remains the Same* film crew, and assorted purchases by band members of instruments, cars, records, antiques, or drugs. The theft was discovered by Richard Cole on July 29, just before the last show, when he looked into the safety deposit box of the Drake Hotel where Zeppelin were staying. "I gazed blankly at the box for a few seconds and could feel an uncomfortable chill sweeping through my body," Cole recalled in his overheated memoir, *Stairway to Heaven*. Responsible for the only key to the deposit, Cole was the prime suspect and questioned by police, but was released without charges. Local headlines put the missing figure at a cool $203,000. According to Cole, the band eventually won a settlement with the Drake for the lost money.

So where did it go? It's fair to assume Cole was not the culprit, having reliably handled Led Zeppelin's personal safety and concert takes for four years of almost nonstop performing. In his *When Giants Walked the Earth*

Mick Wall raises the possibility that someone in the group's inner circle smuggled it out of the US himself to avoid tax burdens (while crying robbery as a distraction), although again the question is why such a ruse would be played then and only then. A hotel employee or someone in cahoots with one or more of the hotel's staff may have secretly had access to the money;

"Led Zeppelin was a very strange, four-quadrant marriage," recalled Robert Plant.
Courtesy of Robert Rodriguez

Wall also notes the organized crime element that was then entering many areas of the music business, where tempting piles of loot were left lying around by stoned guitarists and their friends. The publicity surrounding Zeppelin's record-breaking 1973 shows may have been enough to entice some sharp New York B&E artists to make a quick and easy score off of some long-haired limeys naïve enough to carry two hundred grand with them. A 2009 comic novel by Jason Buhrmester, *Black Dogs: The Possibly True Story of Classic Rock's Greatest Robbery*, speculates that the steal was achieved by a youthful gang of rock-loving misfits—a far-fetched but entertaining prospect. For now, the Drake robbery remains in the cold case files.

Good Times Bad Times: Swan Song

Zeppelin's private record label was born with great hopes in 1974 and died a sad death in 1983. Not only did the company put out *Physical Graffiti, Presence, In Through the Out Door,* and *Coda* but it also released also some respectable work by other artists, including Bad Company's *Bad Company* and *Straight Shooter,* the Pretty Things' *Silk Torpedo,* and eventually Jimmy Page's *Death Wish II* and Robert Plant's *Pictures at Eleven.* Rocker Dave Edmunds and blues mistress Maggie Bell were also signed to Swan Song. Like other such enterprises in the lavish rock scene of the 1970s, Swan Song was begun as an exercise in hubris, on rock stars' vague ideals of subverting corporate capitalism from within: to get as big and as rich as Led Zeppelin (or the Beatles, the Rolling Stones, the Grateful Dead, the Jefferson Airplane, or Earth, Wind & Fire, who also founded their own labels) seemed to mark some sort of vindication for the youth counterculture, so the next logical step was from the boards to the boardroom. "It's a lube job for the ego," Swan Song president Peter Grant admitted to the *New York Times* in 1992.

Artist-owned labels also had the added satisfaction of freeing the principals from the oversights and second guesses of older, straighter executives—even though Zeppelin's real bosses at Atlantic Records had given them almost complete artistic control from the beginning of their contract, and even though the suits at other labels such as Casablanca and Asylum were as profligate with employee perks as any of their guitar-playing, coke-snorting clients. Swan Song's chief advantage for Led Zeppelin was as a tax shelter, a means to reinvest some of the massive amounts of money coming to the band rather than merely hand most of it over to Britain's Inland Revenue. Some of the band's collective earnings had gone into the 1975 film *Monty Python and the Holy Grail* (Zeppelin were fans of the Flying Circus and partied with some of the Pythons in LA), and the Sussex mansion Hammerwood Park was purchased in their name in 1973 as a possible recording room, but was never used. Finding and producing rock 'n' roll talent, then, seemed to be the best business for Swan Song to pursue. It didn't work out that way.

As president of Swan Song, Peter Grant afterward reflected to Dave Lewis, "What I regret is not getting someone in to run it properly. We kept getting it wrong, or I did." Grant and his staff had one huge asset—Led Zeppelin—and several considerably smaller ones, and as Zeppelin declined and fell, so did the company. Grant's own drug problems from the mid-1970s on hastened the end of an already untenable situation. Had the organization been able to take on a wider range of successful artists it might have diversified to its benefit, but, as Grant said, "There were just not enough hours in the day. . . . [E]ven to do Zep justice was a twenty-four-hour job." He also admitted to turning down an offer to manage Queen in 1975, and the defunct Swan Song offices were cluttered with ignored demo tapes from future prospects Iron Maiden and Paul Young.

A rundown of Swan Song's executive, legal, and administrative staff would name:

- Peter Grant, president 1974–83
- Phil Carson, liaison to Atlantic Records
- Danny Goldberg, US vice-president 1974–76
- Abe Hoch, UK vice-president 1974–76
- Alan Callan, vice-president 1976–83
- Steven Weiss, US attorney
- Shelley Kaye, legal assistant
- Joan Hudson, UK accountant
- Mark London, security
- Sam Aizer, Lauren Siciliano, Janine Safer, US publicists
- Nancy Gurskik, Mitchell Fox, US assistants
- Fiya Hunt, Carole Brown, Unity MacLean, Sian Meredith, Daniel Treacey, UK assistants

A Little Silver, a Little Gold: Superhype, Joaneline, and Flames of Albion

Led Zeppelin's original songs were published by companies registered in these names. Superhype covered the material from *Led Zeppelin* to *Houses of the Holy*; Joaneline covered *Physical Graffiti*; and *Presence, In Through the Out Door,* and *Coda* were published by Flames of Albion.

Music publishing—the license to transcribe, notate, or otherwise disseminate the words and music of copyrighted tunes—has been a hidden driver of the music business for decades. Before recorded sound was the dominant musical medium, sheet music sales were the most lucrative aspects of the industry, as upright pianos and sight reading skills were common in middle-class households. While performances and record sales can net the artists considerable sums, the long-term investment represented by a songwriting credit can be far more remunerative in the long run; this is why (say) composers Paul McCartney or Keith Richards have bigger personal fortunes than their bandmates Ringo Starr or Charlie Watts. Because authorship of Led Zeppelin's music was often shared among three or four members of the band, all the players, and the inheritors of John Bonham, have done very well by their association with the group. The dominant partnership of Jimmy Page and Robert Plant (they alone are named as the writers of "Thank You," "Ramble On," "Immigrant Song," "Stairway to Heaven," "Going to California," "The Rain Song," "Houses of the Holy" and "Achilles Last Stand") has given them the edge in annual royalty income; both men have made the 2009 London *Times* annual Rich List with holdings valued at £75 million (Plant) and £70 million (Page), while John Paul Jones ekes out a living with his meager £35 million.

Superhype Publishing Incorporated was registered by Peter Grant and Jimmy Page as Led Zeppelin was getting off the ground in 1968, as part of Grant's everything-to-the-artist managerial strategy. It guaranteed from the outset that any popular songs to be composed by one or all of the group's members would earn money for them and not some Svengali (the Lennon-McCartney songbook originally got the two Beatles twenty percent each, their manager Brian Epstein ten percent, and the remaining half went to publisher Dick James). According to Grant, Superhype was the production company through which the act was signed to Atlantic Records, rather than as the four individual musicians and their manager. The offhand joke of a name likely became an embarrassment to Grant and his clients as the money started rolling in, along with charges that Zeppelin was a "hype band," so the Joaneline title was tried before the classier-sounding Flames of Albion Music Incorporated was launched. "We sold off the publishing company some years later," Grant revealed of Superhype to Dave Lewis. "The whole deal with Atlantic gave us various clauses that we were able to use in our favor." Each company, part of the American Society of Composers, Authors, and Publishers (ASCAP) organization, was simply the vehicle through which Led Zeppelin's creators collected their royalties from reproductions of their songs, whether broadcast on radio or written down in whole or in part. Actual sales of Zeppelin albums, as well as fees for live appearances, were a different revenue stream. Today Joaneline does not exist, but both Superhype and Flames of Albion are administered through Led Zeppelin's parent company of Warner Music.

24

These Things Are Clear to All

Led Zeppelin and Their Peers

In the Eyes of Other Men: Before, During, and After Zeppelin

Regarded now as one of the all-time best rock 'n' roll artists, it's instructive to consider how Zeppelin has been compared and contrasted with a gallery of other performers who've been subject at different times to as much or more acclaim. Many of these acts have a fan base that overlaps with Led Zeppelin's, but others are usually categorized well apart from the Zeppelin league, and our understanding of the band expands after it's placed alongside various predecessors, competitors, and inheritors.

Elvis Presley

Calculating the influence of the King of Rock 'n' Roll on an entire generation of musicians is impossible—the music might not even exist today if not for the success of Tupelo, Mississippi's most famous son. Presley was not the first white artist to make black sounds palatable to a white audience, but he was the one whose persona and performing style conveyed a smoldering sexuality and youthful insolence that were to pervade all of Western culture from his time onward. Elvis could never have foreseen descendants like Led Zeppelin, but descendants they nonetheless were.

Jimmy Page has said that his first inclinations to seriously play guitar arose after hearing a 1955 Presley B side, "Baby Let's Play House." "I heard that record and I wanted to be a part of it; I knew something was going on," he reflected. Robert Plant, likewise, cited Elvis as the central figure in his teenage explorations of the blues and its offshoots: the good-looking, honey-voiced American white boy who made the raw performances of Sonny

Boy, Muddy, Big Boy, Sleepy John, and Howlin' comprehensible to a good-looking, honey-voiced English white boy. The Led Zeppelin lineup—singer, guitarist, bassist, and drummer—was prefigured by Presley's 1950s band of himself, guitarist Scotty Moore, bassist Bill Black, and drummer D. J. Fontana.

Led Zeppelin performed, or at least vamped through, many songs popularized by Elvis in concert, usually in a long medley in the middle of "Whole Lotta Love." Among them were "That's All Right, Mama," "I Need Your Love Tonight," "I'm Moving On," "Heartbreak Hotel," "Mystery Train," and "A Mess o' Blues." In 1969 Jimmy Page took his girlfriend Pamela Miller to see an Elvis show in Las Vegas, although he declined an offer to meet the King that time; Page was already friendly with Presley's guitarist James Burton, a rockabilly ace who'd also played on classics by Ricky Nelson. "We sat around with acoustic guitars and just played whenever we could fit a jam in between recording sessions," Burton recalled. From 1973 on, Zeppelin and Elvis also had concert promoter Jerry Weintraub in common. *Houses of the Holy* took the number one album spot away from Presley's *Aloha from Hawaii* in early '73.

Led Zeppelin actually did meet Elvis Presley on two memorable occasions, a summit of rock heavies awesome to imagine today but relatively low-key at the time. Presley had heard Zeppelin's music and, through Weintraub, knew of the English act's popularity and, through a stepbrother, of "Stairway to Heaven" and their musical chops. "We're gonna do that again," he told an LA audience in May 1974 after cutting one number short, "because we've got *Led Zeppelin* in the audience and we want to look like we know what we're doing up here." Later that night, the band and Peter Grant were taken to Elvis's hotel room and held a friendly get-together that ran two hours over the planned twenty minutes. "We went up to his suite and his girlfriend Ginger was there with just a few other people," said Jimmy Page. "I can tell you, we were really nervous. When he came in the door, he started doing his famous twitch. You know, he didn't put that on—that was something he really did." Presley and John Bonham broke the ice to discuss a mutual love of hot rod cars, while Robert Plant remembered, "We all stood in a circle and discussed this whole phenomenon, this lunacy. . . . [Elvis] was very focused, very different to what you now read." "Is it true, those stories about you boys on the road?" Elvis asked, to innocent denial. The literal heavyweight Peter Grant accidentally sat on Elvis's father, Vernon. As the musicians parted, Plant and Elvis harmonized on Presley's "Love Me." The next year John Paul Jones and Zeppelin tour manager Richard Cole dropped in on Presley's Los Angeles home and hung out. By then Presley, with only a couple of more years to live, was clearly becoming divorced from reality as he insisted on trading wristwatches with the men of Zeppelin. "The evening continued like this for the next half hour," Cole recalled, "with an orgy of gift-giving that Elvis seemed to find exciting." Afterward, Presley's chief bodyguard Jerry Schilling informed Cole, "We haven't seen the Boss have such a good time in years."

The Beatles

They were at the epicenter of popular music in the last half of the twentieth century, and every rock 'n' roll group that came afterward was in their debt and in their shadow. Led Zeppelin have sold hundreds of millions of records and influenced countless numbers of musicians and ordinary listeners, but their achievement is still less than the Beatles'.

Zeppelin's foursome certainly bettered the professional landmarks established by the earlier quartet. They had a tougher manager who made sure his "boys" got every bit of earnings that were owed them, wealth the earnest Brian Epstein could never win for his own clients. Zep's live gigs were marked by non-shrieking audiences and a more than adequate sound system, two things which the Beatles sorely missed after they became an international sensation in 1963–64 and whose absence drove them from the touring circuit after 1966. Measured by straight chops if not intuitive flair, the Zeppelin personnel could outplay the Beatles: John Lennon and George Harrison never attempted twenty-minute guitar solos, and Ringo Starr would have been swallowed alive by "Moby Dick." On their 1973 American outing Zeppelin broke attendance records set by the Beatles in 1965—Zeppelin's appearance in Tampa, Florida, on May 5 drew more fans than the Beatles' legendary Shea Stadium show—and it was *Led Zeppelin II* that displaced *Abbey Road* from the pinnacle of the album charts in late 1969. There was also a symbolism in Led Zeppelin's finally wresting the title of "Best Group" from the Beatles in the British *Melody Maker* readers' poll in September 1970, the first time in eight years the Fab Four had not won the vote.

Though the Beatles were and remain the most famous rockers ever, they knew Led Zeppelin was around. "Oh, I can just tell where the groups came from, and all that, any of them now," John Lennon told *Rolling Stone*'s Jann Wenner in his illuminating 1970 interview. "I can tell, you know, like Zeppelin and Fleetwood Mac, where everything came from." As Zeppelin rose through the 1970s, ex-Beatles George Harrison and Ringo Starr were sometimes seen in company with one or more of the band members, and John Bonham threw a drunken Harrison into the swimming pool at an LA party in 1973. Bonham and John Paul Jones played at Paul McCartney's

Zeppelin broke the Beatles' 1965 attendance record with this 1973 Tampa gig.

Courtesy of Duane Roy

benefit concerts for Kampuchea in 1979; Jones appeared in McCartney's *Give My Regards to Broad Street* vanity project in the early 1980s; and Robert Plant and Jimmy Page had a memorable reunion at a 1990 Knebworth show headlined by McCartney.

Led Zeppelin's players, conversely, respected the Beatles' music and public impact; they even improvised some of their songs in concert, including "I Saw Her Standing There" and their standard "Some Other Guy." As studio musicians in the 1960s, Jones and Jimmy Page knew the Beatles as industry leaders (McCartney's praise of Jones's arrangements on a Donovan session won the future Zeppelin bassist Donovan's confidence), although they recognized that the Beatles were not the invulnerable Fab Four the press made them out to be. Page went to a Beatles show in early 1963 and recollected, "They didn't go down too well and I actually heard John Lennon going past saying, 'Fuck these London audiences.'" At a 1970 New York press conference, included on 2003's *Led Zeppelin* DVD, Page and Plant were quizzed by reporters whose only reference point was the Beatles: "I think they're great, they've done some fantastic statements," said Page in the rock-speak of the day. "The fact that they got through to so many millions and millions of people has been an inspiration for every performing group in England," added Plant, "and I should imagine the world." Huge though Led Zeppelin became, the Beatles' place at the top of the pops is secure.

The Rolling Stones

Unlike the Beatles, the Rolling Stones were operational over the same decade as Led Zeppelin, and both felt each other as competition. Zeppelin's players were annoyed that the Stones drew far more publicity when the two acts played North America in 1972: "All we read was the Stones this, the Stones that, and it pissed us off," John Bonham was quoted afterward. "Here we are, flogging our guts out and for all the notice being given to us, we might as well be playing in bloody Ceylon." Indeed, during the 1970s and early 1980s the Stones were by far the more visible group, between Mick Jagger's regular blurbs in the society columns and Keith Richards's in the police bulletin, and the Stones managed to artistically and commercially come back from a mid-decade slump with a run of excellent albums including 1978's *Some Girls*, 1980's *Emotional Rescue*, and 1981's *Tattoo You*, followed by a triumphant 1981 American tour. By then Led Zeppelin had already declined and fallen. As their '81 shows commenced in his city to enormous fanfare, a *Philadelphia Journal* reporter declared, "There's no other band I know, not the Who, not Led Zeppelin, not the Grateful Dead, can do this. So maybe the Stones really are the best rock band in the world."

Yet the Zeppelin-Stones rivalry did not end there, and its beginnings went way back. As teenagers, Jagger and Richards actually renewed their childhood acquaintance on a train platform in John Paul Jones's home of Sidcup, a London suburb, and the first formations of the group they would lead together began then. Even more fateful was a shared expedition between Jagger, Richards, their new accomplice Brian Jones, and

Jimmy Page in October 1962, as the young Londoners took a van ride up to Manchester to see American bluesmen including T-Bone Walker and John Lee Hooker at a folk festival there: a tiny cult of earnest fans and collectors, none of them yet twenty years old, who became four of the most pivotal figures in world popular music of the next two decades. "I remember them vividly because Keith said he played guitar and Mick said he played harp," Page looked back. This episode has been noted in a memoir by Page's Epsom friend David Williams, in his 2009 book *First Time We Met the Blues: A Journey of Discovery with Jimmy Page, Brian Jones, Mick Jagger and Keith Richards.*

As the Rolling Stones gained notoriety in the mid-1960s, Jimmy Page was admitted to the group's inner circle and recording studios, as were neighborhood friends like tea-boys and tape operators Glyn and Andy Johns. Page demonstrated for Richards a guitar solo used in their 1964 hit "Heart of Stone," was prominent on sessions overseen by the Stones' manager and producer Andrew Loog Oldham, and played on Brian Jones's 1966 soundtrack for the movie *A Degree of Murder.* Home jams between Page and another suburban boy, Eric Clapton, were later released by Oldham's Immediate label after being overdubbed with drums, bass, and harmonica via Rolling Stones Jagger, Charlie Watts, and Bill Wyman. Some tracks on a 1975 album of '60s Stones rarities, *Metamorphosis,* featured Page and were noted thusly. According to Wyman, Page was even a candidate to replace the troubled Brian Jones before his 1969 death. John Paul Jones, too, was one of Oldham's go-to session players—it's said Oldham himself suggested Jones adopt his stage name after seeing a marquee for the 1959 movie about the American naval hero—and was given credit for his arrangement of "She's a Rainbow" on the Stones' 1967 psychedelic album, *Their Satanic Majesties Request.* Robert Plant was singing with the Stones' old friend Alexis Korner when Page tapped him for the New Yardbirds.

Throughout the 1970s, Page, at least, remained close to various Rolling Stones. They had sex, drugs, and rock 'n' roll in common, not necessarily in that order. Underground filmmaker Kenneth Anger had been toyed with by the Stones before hiring Page to compose the music for his *Lucifer Rising* opus. The head Zeppelin and Keith Richards were both taking heroin in the middle years of the decade, and Page, Richards, new recruit Ron Wood and ex–Blind Faith bassist Rick Grech reportedly taped a late-night jam named for Page's daughter, "Scarlet," around the same time Page began his affair with Wood's wife, Krissy. She wasn't the only female to be passed between the rockers—Pamela Miller and Bebe Buell also got to know both the Rolling Stones and Led Zeppelin from very private perspectives. "Didn't I tell you he's a devil?" Buell quoted Jagger after her dalliance with Page fell through. "You're just not kinky enough for him, not weird enough."

Richards and Wood's sideline band, the New Barbarians, were an opening act at Zeppelin's 1979 Knebworth performances. In 1985 Page provided a guitar solo for "One Hit (To the Body)" from the Stones' so-so *Dirty Work*, and by 2007 Wood and former bassist Wyman were billed as opening acts at Led Zeppelin's O2 reunion concert. The art school dropouts and blues-loving adolescents from the bedroom communities of south London had traveled a long way together.

In that long run, it appears that Led Zeppelin may have surpassed the Rolling Stones as rock music's second most influential band. The Stones certainly were aware of the newer band's ascendancy from 1968, and their rejection of Led Zeppelin as a guest act on their *Rock and Roll Circus* film that year (they picked Jethro Tull instead) may well have been driven by a perceived threat that Jimmy Page and John Paul Jones's new assembly would steal their show. Drummer Charlie Watts has acknowledged that the Stones' entry into the stadium circuits of 1969 was affected by Zeppelin: "[I]n '69 you really had to be on top of it to play. That's how Hendrix and bands like Led Zeppelin came about. . . . I call that tour the Led Zeppelin tour, because it was the first time we had to go on and play for an hour and a half. . . . Led Zeppelin had come to the States, and they would do a twenty-minute drum solo and endless guitar solos."

Although Robert Plant has spoken in the 2000s of maintaining a friendship with "the singer in that band," the Stones themselves have made the odd crack at Zeppelin's expense, Ron Wood in his autobiography recalling his first impression of John Bonham's resemblance to "a farmer," and Keith Richards commenting in 1986, "Now, I don't like Led Zeppelin at all, piss on 'em," and characterizing Plant and Bonham as "a pair of clueless Ernies from the Midlands." Though the Stones have lasted considerably longer than Zeppelin and have a deeper catalogue of instantly recognizable hit songs, they have sold fewer records and have a less consistent history, which now includes appearances on *The Simpsons* and in the *Pirates of the Caribbean* movie franchise, and at the Super Bowl halftime show, plus the licensing of their music to the Hallmark greeting card company along with Windows and Starbucks. The first of the English blues-rock bands to find international fame, the Stones made a deeper impression on the social movements of the 1960s and '70s, with their historic sexual, racial, and pharmaceutical provocations, and they set the precedent of the debauched vocalist-and-guitarist duo that became a classic stage pose with Zeppelin and so many other groups. But Zeppelin's *music* has probably shaped the subsequent course of the recording and performing businesses to a greater degree: The Rolling Stones are the one and only Rolling Stones, whereas Led Zeppelin are often named as the true instigators of a whole hard rock genre. Barring a surprising reinvention as they approach their seventies, the Rolling Stones now have to take a backseat to the briefer but therefore less diluted accomplishments of Led Zeppelin.

Bob Dylan

The former Robert Zimmerman was, with the Beatles, one of the two most important rock artists of the 1960s, and his innovative lyrical experiments opened up the possibilities for every songwriter that came later—it's unlikely Robert Plant could have penned such personal or imaginative songs as "That's the Way," "Over the Hills and Far Away," "The Rover," "Tea for One," or "All My Love" if not for Dylan's example. Though Plant and Page both expressed admiration for Dylan's work his most conspicuous link with Led Zeppelin is his version of "In My Time of Dyin'," from his self-titled 1962 debut album. The song was credited as "Traditional, arranged by Dylan," unlike the *Physical Graffiti* take that was down to "Bonham-J. P. Jones-Page-Plant." Dylan's unvarnished blues and folk covers of the early '60s popularized two styles that were later to be given the distinctive Zeppelin treatment. The other anecdotes of the Dylan-Zeppelin connection are Peter Grant's flummoxed reaction circa 1974 when he introduced himself to the singer as Led Zeppelin's manager ("I don't come to you with *my* problems, do I?" Dylan snorted), and a 1969 tale of the up-and-coming British band bumping into "Bobby" Dylan's proud mother in Florida.

The Who

In some ways, the Who almost *were* Led Zeppelin. The group was one of the very first whose aural assault was an integral part of their music, and drummer Keith Moon and bassist John Entwistle were to be the rhythm section for an ensemble conjectured in 1966 by Jimmy Page and Jeff Beck, the one both Who members expected to go down like the world's biggest lead balloon. Studio musician Page played on some of the Who's first tracks, Richard Cole had been a Who roadie, and guitarist Pete Townshend later said he and Page had known the same girlfriend in the mid-'60s. "She'd obviously fucked him to death, and then proceeded to fuck me to death," he said. Moon sat in at one of Zeppelin's last American concerts in 1977. Into the 1970s the Who were known for their extreme volume in concert, for Moon's wild behavior offstage and unstoppable drum work onstage, for Entwistle's quiet demeanor and expert musicianship, for singer Roger Daltrey's flowing curly hair, bare chest, and macho postures, and for Townshend's obsessive spiritual interests and idiosyncratic leadership of the band. Substitute those names for John Bonham, John Paul Jones, Robert Plant, and Jimmy Page, and the descriptions would still apply.

In fact, for most of the decade the Who were thought to be the superior quartet, one of rock's reigning triumvirate (along with the Beatles and the Stones) who'd led the original British Invasion. Led Zeppelin, on the other hand, were seen as money-mad upstarts purveying the reductive formula of heavy metal. The Who had already amassed several classic rock songs to their name, among them "I Can't Explain," "Magic Bus," "I Can See for Miles," "Substitute," and the anthemic "My Generation." They'd played at the 1967 Monterey Pop Festival with Jimi Hendrix; their ambitious 1969 rock opera *Tommy* was heard as rock's most compelling bid yet for artistic sophistication; and they reliably filled stadiums and sold albums in quantity, among them such superb discs as *Who's Next*, *Quadrophenia*, and *The Who by Numbers*. It was not until Moon's death from a drug overdose in 1978 and his replacement by Kenney Jones that the Who's status began to slip, as Townshend battled his own demons. At this point the band's continued output could only pale next to their older records. They staged a supposed farewell tour in 1982, a second one in 1989, and Daltrey and Townshend are still performing as the Who even after Entwistle's 2002 death. From sharing a single bill in Columbia, Maryland, with Led Zeppelin in 1969, the Who co-headlined a joint American tour with Jimmy Page and the Black Crowes in 2000. While Townshend's chordal electric guitar work has won him many admirers, his technique is less advanced than Page's, and although the Who (like the Rolling Stones) have a deserved place among the rock 'n' roll immortals, time and public opinion have given Led Zeppelin the edge.

Cream

This great power trio was a direct forerunner of Led Zeppelin, one specifically cited by reviewers and Atlantic Records publicity when the New Yardbirds were taking flight. Jimmy Page and Eric Clapton, both ex-Yardbirds, had been friends since the early 1960s after jamming at London's Marquee Club, and John Bonham was in awe of drummer Ginger Baker's abilities. Clapton was a guitar hero before most listeners had ever heard of Page, and Bonham's "Moby Dick" was likely conceived as the successor to Baker's "Toad." Instrumentally, Cream's virtuosity was emulated by many acts, including Zeppelin; for years afterward, serious rock groups were expected to be very skilled musicians who played imposing racks of equipment at high volumes. Man for man, Clapton, Baker, and vocalist-bassist Jack Bruce were all as good or better on their instruments as Page, Bonham, and John Paul Jones.

Where Led Zeppelin differed from Cream was in their personal cohesion, which carried the four players together over ten years, while the fractious Clapton, Baker, and Bruce barely held on from 1966 to 1968. The result was a deeper and more diverse collection of material, much stronger managerial authority maintaining a more loyal fan base, and a more lucrative recording and performing career. Eric Clapton sounded a little jealous in later complaining that Zeppelin were "unnecessarily loud. . . . They overemphasized whatever point they were making." Jack Bruce sounded a *lot* jealous (and maybe a bit loaded?) at a 2008 awards ceremony hosted by *Classic Rock* magazine, where he was quoted as saying, "Fuck off, Zeppelin, you're crap. You've always been crap and you'll never be anything else. The worst thing is that people believe the crap that they're sold. Cream is ten times the band that Led Zeppelin is. . . . You're gonna compare Eric Clapton with fucking Jimmy Page?" No sunshine in his love.

In fairness to Clapton, Slowhand has had a more productive and diverse career since 1980 than Jimmy Page, and is still performing and recording new material. As of 2010 he had embarked on a shared concert tour with another ex-Yardbird, Jeff Beck. Though neither Clapton nor Beck has racked up the drawing power or record sales of Led Zeppelin, both men have put themselves and their work before audiences more often than Page, whose halting output as a solo artist has left his Zeppelin years to stand as his defining musical achievement. Of the three star Yardbirds, Page went on to form the biggest sequel, but Clapton and Beck have enjoyed the more durable professional lives.

Jimi Hendrix

Hendrix, like Cream, was a definite commercial and musical model for Led Zeppelin: distorted electric blues for the sex, drugs, and protest generation. James Marshall Hendrix is debatably a more crucial rock 'n' roll figure than Zeppelin. His technological innovations of amplification and effects; his firm straddling of the rock, blues, funk and jazz genres; and his tragic, drug-related death at age twenty-seven are as iconic as anything in the four Englishmen's mythology. Jimmy Page himself believed Hendrix to be "the best guitarist any of us ever had," and millions would agree that Hendrix's command of his Stratocasters was superior to Page's of his Les Pauls. Page never saw Hendrix perform, due to their conflicting schedules of the late 1960s and early '70s, although there's a story that the two guitarists were introduced at a New York bar when Hendrix was completely out of it, as he often was.

Hendrix was said to have praised John Bonham's bass drum footwork, but he, like his friend Eric Clapton, found Led Zeppelin's extremely heavy riffs too far from authentic blues for his tastes. Asked about Zeppelin in one interview, he only rolled his eyes. "When you have the once-in-a-lifetime chance to work with an artist whose stature is so huge and overwhelming, it kind of overshadows everything else," recalled engineer Eddie Kramer of his Hendrix collaborations, "even though I loved working with Zeppelin, the Stones, Traffic, and, in fact, everyone." Page paid tribute to Hendrix with a version of the Woodstock "Star-Spangled Banner" at some 1977 American shows, while Hendrix's death the previous day was acknowledged by Robert Plant from the stage at Madison Square Garden on September 19, 1970. "A great loss came about for the whole of the music world," he told the fans. "And we would like to think that you, as well as us, are very sorry that Jimi Hendrix went." If Led Zeppelin collectively was a stronger band than Hendrix's Experience, Hendrix himself—singer, guitarist, songwriter, producer, showman—was closer to an individual rock 'n' roll genius.

Janis Joplin

The tragic blues mistress shared billing at festivals in Atlanta and Dallas with Led Zeppelin in the summer of 1969, when she was the bigger name. Robert Plant later told US television interviewer Charlie Rose of a backstage meeting with Pearl, "She was just kind and knew I was quite naïve," adding that she gave him tips on vocal maintenance and control. Many listeners have commented on how Plant's singing style was reminiscent of Joplin's, in his stream-of-consciousness flows of blues expressions and inflections sourced from a scattering of older tunes. If he did not directly copy her, audiences would have been prepared for his work on *Led Zeppelin* and *Led Zeppelin II* by hearing Joplin's performances on *Cheap Thrills* and *I Got Dem Ol' Kozmic Blues Again Mama!*.

Joni Mitchell

"Find a queen without a king / They say she plays guitar, and cries, and sings"—the lyric from Zeppelin's "Going to California" honored the ethereal Canadian singer-songwriter who was considered second only to Bob Dylan as rock's most personal and profound soloist. Both Jimmy Page and Robert Plant were big fans of Mitchell's, Page saying her music "brings tears to my eyes," and confiding to Richard Cole, "My dream is to find a young Joni Mitchell lookalike—thin, angular features, long blond hair. . . ." Led Zeppelin often played their take on Mitchell's triumphant "Woodstock" in their onstage

jams of 1975. Her adoption of quirky alternate acoustic guitar tunings echoed and encouraged Page's. Speaking of Los Angeles's Laurel Canyon neighborhood, where Mitchell presided with partner Graham Nash and many other sensitive folk artists, Plant said, "The canyon scene was a continuation of the artistic will to continue some sort of aesthetic and respectable role for pop music, so that there was an intention beyond 'Rock-a-Hula Baby.'" He explained "Going to California" thusly: "When you're in love with Joni Mitchell you've really go to write about it now and again." Page and Plant did manage to meet Mitchell during the 1970s Zeppelin years, but only for small talk.

Neil Young

Another Canadian legend whose music alone and with Buffalo Springfield influenced Led Zeppelin's quieter moments, the singer sometimes known as Bernard Shakey was, with compatriot Joni Mitchell, an example of a mellow, introspective composer for Page and Plant to follow. "Going to California," *Led Zeppelin III*'s "Friends" and "That's the Way," and *Physical Graffiti*'s "Down by the Seaside" all hark back to Young's vibe from his eponymous debut, *Everybody Knows This Is Nowhere*, and *After the Gold Rush*. Led Zeppelin quoted his tunes "Cinnamon Girl," "Cowgirl in the Sand," and "Down by the River" in concert, as well as the Springfield's "For What It's Worth." Young, for his part, has praised Jimmy Page as one of his favorite guitarists, and mentioned him in his 1995 song "Downtown," from his *Mirror Ball* album. Young was also inducted into the Rock and Roll Hall of Fame with the surviving members of Led Zeppelin in 1995, participating in an all-star jam on "When the Levee Breaks" with Page, Plant, and John Paul Jones.

The Doors

Though their trippy keyboards and Jim Morrison's poetic ramblings were representative of the 1960s "acid rock" genre, the dark and sometimes dangerous mood of the Doors was a predecessor of the hard rock developed by Led Zeppelin. Zeppelin and the Doors were on the same bill at the Seattle Pop Festival in July 1969 (Richard Cole perpetrated the Shark Incident back at the hotel), where Morrison's onstage behavior was subdued following his Miami arrest for indecent exposure. The Doors were much the better-known group in 1969, but they were already on a decline as their singer sank further into alcoholism and an alienation from the experience of rock stardom; Zeppelin's brutal blasts of riffs and blues themes was an exciting contrast to the Doors' vague "happenings." Nevertheless, Morrison

Led Zeppelin were among many classic artists who emerged at the height of the rock era in the 1960s and '70s.   *Courtesy of Robert Rodriguez*

at his best boasted a powerful stage presence that was the equal of Robert Plant's, and the Doors' long, mesmeric performances paved the way for Led Zeppelin's. On the 1995 Jimmy Page and Robert Plant tour, the Doors classic "Break On Through" was played in a medley with other numbers.

Alice Cooper

Led Zeppelin played some important early US dates at the Whisky a Go Go club in Los Angeles in 1969, sharing the bill with this up-and-coming band, whose name was then that of the whole group rather than just the creepy lead singer. By the mid-1970s it was the theatrical "shock rock" of Alice Cooper that was getting more publicity in America, but that was the way Led Zeppelin liked it. The grotesqueries of Cooper's stage act (boa constrictors, guillotines, dead baby dolls, et cetera) made the band one of the very few to draw criticism from Zeppelin's players. Robert Plant said to *New Musical Express* in 1973, "Alice Cooper's weirdnesses must really make these kids feel violent. . . . So you put things like that in front of them, and I don't think it's right." Jimmy Page told William S. Burroughs in 1975, "Our crowds, the people that come to see us, are very orderly. It's not the sort of Alice Cooper style, where you actually *try* to get them into a state where they've got to go like that, so that you can get reports of this, that, and the other."

Pentangle

Along with comparable acts like Fairport Convention and the Incredible String Band, this group, with its Elizabethan English folk, was a major, if seldom recognized, influence on Led Zeppelin. Founded by guitarists John Renbourn and Bert Jansch—both acoustic heroes for Jimmy Page—the band boasted a complex blend of baroque instrumental styles and a rock sensibility that inspired Zeppelin's pastoral sounds of "Black Mountain Side," "Going to California," "The Battle of Evermore" (sung with Sandy Denny of Fairport Convention), "Over the Hills and Far Away," "Bron-yr-Aur," and "Stairway to Heaven." If not for the Celtic, quasi-Renaissance musical example set by the British folk movement of the 1960s, Led Zeppelin would have lacked the treed, idyllic dimension that stood in such contrast to the heavy electric blues at which they more obviously excelled. In 1979 Zeppelin did Fairport Convention the favor of having them open one of their Knebworth shows, and Page's 1980s work with his friend Roy Harper also has a strong English folk flavor.

Black Sabbath

The sloppy, sleazy Rolling Stones to Led Zeppelin's polished and positive Beatles, Sabbath are sometimes considered the only real rivals for Zeppelin's title of heavy metal heavyweights. Sharing the same four-piece lineup and the same emphasis on fat electric guitar riffs and thudding drums, both groups are claimed as favorites by many listeners today; in the early 1970s Black Sabbath was close behind Led Zeppelin as an American concert attraction and in international record sales. Indeed, fans who couldn't get enough of *Led Zeppelin, II, III,* and *IV* happily turned to *Black Sabbath, Paranoid, Master of Reality, Vol 4,* and *Sabbath Bloody Sabbath* for even harder rock and even more overt references to drugs and the occult. Sabbath guitarist Tony Iommi was as accomplished an electric soloist as Jimmy Page, and his dissonant guitar lines on "Black Sabbath," "Iron Man," "War

Pigs," "Sweet Leaf," "Snowblind," and other cuts are as lethal as Page's on "Dazed and Confused," "Communication Breakdown," "Whole Lotta Love," "Heartbreaker," "Immigrant Song," "Black Dog," and "Rock and Roll."

Black Sabbath's personnel all came from around Birmingham, England, and had known John Bonham and Robert Plant as local hopefuls like themselves. "I grew up with John, and me and him had traded licks and played together since we were fifteen," said Sabbath drummer Bill Ward. Bonham was best man at Tony Iommi's wedding and invested in a short-lived Birmingham record shop with Iommi and Sabbath singer Ozzy Osbourne. There's little doubt that Black Sabbath's acquisition by the US Warner Brothers label was an attempt to capitalize on the previous success of Led Zeppelin, by appealing to the young masses of America with the same heavy blues. Rumors of a Los Angeles jam between Led Zeppelin and Black Sabbath around 1972 have tantalized many fans, and a smiling, middle-aged Iommi and Page have been photographed together in the 2000s as two exemplars of British guitar heroics.

But while Bonham, for one, appreciated Ward's playing on Sabbath's "Supernaut" and envied Ward's use of two bass drums, the rest of Led Zeppelin had less respect for the foursome. Zeppelin were doing dramatic distorted boogie before them, and soon enough branched out into folk, funk, and raga departures, whereas Sabbath have little in their repertoire to compare with "Kashmir," "Bron-y-Aur Stomp," "The Battle of Evermore," "Trampled Underfoot," or "D'yer Mak'er." In interviews of the 1970s Robert Plant dismissed "groups in England who still rely on riff after riff after riff. . . . Some audiences can shake and bang their heads on the stage to riffs all night long, but subtlety is an art that must be mastered if you're to be remembered." After Osbourne's firing in 1979, Sabbath soldiered on well past Zeppelin's own demise, but thereby made their own formula more apparent—riff after riff after riff. Black Sabbath's music of 1970 to 1975 still stands as a credible complement to Led Zeppelin's and is in some respects more compelling, but since then their legacy has fallen farther and farther behind.

Deep Purple

Along with Black Sabbath the next best thing to Zeppelin as the leading British hard rockers of the 1970s, Deep Purple compare well with Zeppelin for instrumental and vocal wallop, but less favorably as a consistent band. Purple's great records *In Rock*, *Machine Head*, and *Made in Japan* are nearly as influential as Led Zeppelin's in defining the heavy metal state of the art, and arguably more so in inspiring later generations of electric guitar virtuosi in the "neoclassical" mold. A run of such FM staples as "Lazy," "Burn," "Highway Star," "Space Truckin'," and the monolithic "Smoke on the Water" are close rivals to "Stairway to Heaven" and "Whole Lotta Love" in radio rotation. Like Jimmy Page, guitarist Ritchie Blackmore had earlier done time with Neil Christian and the Crusaders and the London session scene, and unlike Page he was known for the razor-sharp precision of his soloing. Onetime Purple singer David Coverdale later joined forces with Page for a coolly received 1993 album.

Deep Purple also rented the *Starship* for their US concert tours, but their internal differences and fluctuating membership kept them from reaching Zeppelin's financial—and ultimately artistic—heights. The group's first records, released in 1968, actually predated those of Led Zeppelin, though they had yet to hit upon a durable lineup or musical direction. "If Purple had stayed together," recalled keyboardist Jon Lord, "we might have achieved the same mid-seventies status that they did. They embraced the arena rock 'n' roll show with open arms, whereas we didn't embrace it quite so completely." A much-modified version of Deep Purple is still performing, with American pro Steve Morse filling Blackmore's shoes, and Blackmore now plays in an unusual medieval act, Blackmore's Night, that takes the Celtic motif farther than Zeppelin ever did.

Pink Floyd

The champion psychedelic artists of the rock era, Floyd released their first records before Led Zeppelin (in 1967) and were still drawing huge crowds decades after Zeppelin's 1980 disbandment. Unlike Black Sabbath or Deep Purple, Pink Floyd had staked out different turf than heavy metal, and so offered a dreamy, druggy contrast to the electric blues and wooden folk of Zeppelin. When the later band exploded out of the gate in 1969, Floyd were already suffering from the LSD-driven mental breakdown of founder and guitarist Syd Barrett, replaced by David Gilmour by the time of the albums *A Saucerful of Secrets* and *Ummagumma*, and were seeking to establish a new sound. Appearing alongside Zeppelin at 1970's Bath Festival, drummer Nick Mason recalled that the complex studio instrumentation of *Atom Heart Mother* was to be recreated onstage, in "an attempt to keep up with the John Paul Joneses." Pink Floyd became a significant US concert attraction after their 1973 classic *Dark Side of the Moon*, a record whose worldwide sales exceed those of *Led Zeppelin IV*, and David Gilmour played along with John Bonham and John Paul Jones in Paul McCartney's Rockestra shows of 1979. With both Zeppelin and Floyd disparaged as dinosaur acts by punk rockers and their journalistic boosters in the late 1970s, it was ironic that the huge popular demand for *In Through the Out Door* and *The Wall* were credited with saving a moribund record industry. The latter-day Floyd has replaced departed bassist Roger Waters with Guy Pratt, a versatile session player who also performed as part of the David Coverdale–Jimmy Page band in 1993.

David Bowie

As studio musicians, both Jimmy Page and John Paul Jones worked on songs for the struggling David Jones in the 1960s, and Page renewed his acquaintance with the rechristened David Bowie in the 1970s. It was Bowie whom Page outbid to buy his sumptuous Tower House in 1974, by which time Ziggy Stardust, alias Aladdin Sane, was in the vanguard of the new "glam rock" that was sweeping the pop scenes of Britain and America. (In 1973, however, *Melody Maker* reviewer Roy Hollingworth had commented, "If you wanna hear a rock and roll band, wipe off that bloody silly makeup and go see Zeppelin.") David Bowie's unique and literate music was of a different order than Led Zeppelin's, but, like Jimmy Page, he had fallen under the twin spells of Aleister Crowley and cocaine. There are accounts of Page and Bowie sharing mounds of white powder together while viewing footage from Kenneth Anger's *Lucifer Rising*, of Bowie being so far gone into cocaine-induced paranoia he felt that his Los Angeles swimming pool was possessed by Satan, and of a strung-out Bowie being fearful of Page's enigmatic presence and allegedly demonic powers. Angela Bowie, the singer's wife during the 1970s, has also documented her participation in a 1977 hotel room party with members of Led Zeppelin where Page was kidded as "Hoover nose," and lived up to the name.

AC/DC

Led Zeppelin took the majestic "Stairway to Heaven," but AC/DC were careening down the "Highway to Hell." Led Zeppelin demanded a "Whole Lotta Love," but AC/DC were satisfied with a "Whole Lotta Rosie." Though many would say Zeppelin were the masters of hard rock, the Australian quintet, on the same Atlantic record label, has proven nearly as successful with their own outback roadhouse interpretations of the genre. More than the punk rockers who emerged around the same time, AC/DC seemed to dislodge the complacent English rock aristocracy to win the hearts of the headbanging masses: they topped *Sounds* magazine's "New Order Top 20" list of 1976, ahead of the Sex Pistols, the Damned, and Motörhead, while Zeppelin was on the "Boring Old Farts Top 20," in company with the Rolling Stones and Rod Stewart. A useful quote from the Marquee Club's

Jack Barry cited AC/DC as the most exciting act he'd seen perform in that venue since Led Zeppelin. With the brilliant double entendres of original singer and lyricist Bon Scott and the combined guitar attack of brothers Angus and Malcolm Young, AC/DC eschewed the profundities of "Kashmir" and the acoustic delicacy of "The Battle of Evermore" for predictable, crowd-pleasing, straight-on rock 'n' roll. Zeppelin's veteran engineer Eddie Kramer was called upon by Atlantic to produce the album that became *Highway to Hell* in early 1979 but his professional methodology clashed with the Australians'. "They were different from Zeppelin, for obvious reasons," he said. "I think that band required a specific type of handling which I had no idea how to do at that moment in my career." "It turns out the guy was full of bullshit and couldn't produce a healthy fart," was Bon Scott's take on the Kramer episode. Scott died from alcohol poisoning in 1980—the same year and in the same way as John Bonham—but the group survived and thrived with *Back in Black* and beyond; drummer Chris Slade, late of Jimmy Page's the Firm, was even part of their lineup for a short period. Like other of Zeppelin's hard rock rivals, AC/DC have outlived their originality, but in their heyday they made some excellent records that compare well to Zeppelin's best.

Van Halen

Until the advent of these flamboyant Californian rockers, Led Zeppelin's Gothic style was the model for all the heavy guitar-based pop music of the 1970s. When Eddie Van Halen first laid down his two-handed "Eruption" guitar solo on the 1978 debut album, however, six-string heroics were defined a few steps upward, and when David Lee Roth first belted out "Ain't Talkin' 'bout Love," rock showmanship was redefined by the spandex standards of Hollywood rather than the misty atmosphere of Boleskine House. Hugely popular and influential in the following decade, Van Halen were the first of a new generation of rock 'n' rollers for whom Zeppelin were inspiration, not competition. Eddie Van Halen himself admitted that his innovative "tapping" technique came to him watching Jimmy Page do the same thing on an LA "Heartbreaker" solo circa 1972: "I'm going, 'Wait a minute—I can do that! Use that finger up here, and use this as the nut and move it around.' That's how I first thought of it." Page, in turn, has complimented the younger player on his fretboard dexterity: "You know, you talk about what I've done on the guitar and that's what *he's* done on guitar. . . . I must say that I can't do it." With Roth on vocals, Van Halen has essayed Zeppelin's "The Rover," and with Sammy Hagar at the mic they've done a solid "Rock and Roll."

U2

The house band of the United Nations, fronted by a Nobel laureate, may be the last of the true classic rock groups. Though U2's minimalist, punk-derived style was initially far different from the larger-than-life productions of Led Zeppelin, the Anglo-Irish foursome did maintain the same instrumental configuration, and singer Bono and guitarist Dave "the Edge" Evans have approximated the Plant-Page performance dichotomy of exuberant showman paired with introverted musician. It was the Edge who graciously inducted the Yardbirds into the Rock and Roll Hall of Fame in 1992 and admitted that the blues abilities of guitarists like Page, Jeff Beck, and Eric Clapton were so intimidating he could only seek out a personal sound completely distinct from them. "I was never really interested in heavy metal or that sort of thing," the Edge told *Rolling Stone* in 1988, "but Zeppelin, of all those groups, really had something." Along with Jack White of the White Stripes, the Edge finally dared to play with Page for revealing scenes in the 2008 documentary *It Might Get Loud*.

Nirvana

The polar opposite of Sunset Strip party rockers Van Halen, Nirvana too reconfigured the music scene over their short career. After Nirvana, the blinding guitar runs and godlike pretensions of Led Zeppelin and their many imitators seemed well and truly passé, but hindsight shows the Seattle trio were more enthralled by the Zeppelin legacy than they or their fans may have wanted to believe. With the pathetic Kurt Cobain on guitar and vocals the group tried a painful "Heartbreaker" and "Immigrant Song" at very early gigs, and had a song called "Aero Zeppelin" on the 1992 compilation *Insecticide*; in 2008 ex-Nirvana drummer Dave Grohl's Foo Fighters invited Jimmy Page and John Paul Jones onstage at London's Wembley Stadium to play "Ramble On" and "Rock and Roll" in front of 86,000 fans. By 2010 Grohl was playing in Them Crooked Vultures with John Paul Jones.

Pearl Jam

Another of the 1990s "grunge" bands whose introverted songwriting and performance styles came as a welcome contrast to the hair-gel histrionics of Guns N' Roses or Mötley Crüe, Pearl Jam have now maintained respectable career for over two decades. In a surprise duet at Chicago's House of Blues in 2005, the group performed with Robert Plant, doing "Fool in the Rain" with the singer and melding their band's "Given to Fly" with the very similar "Going to California." Bassist Jeff Ament has said that "Pearl Jam's goal every night is, 'Let's try to be Zep in '73, Madison Square Garden.' They changed it up with every record. When we made *Ten,* we wanted to be as diverse as possible so we could go any direction we wanted after that, the way they did."

The Black Crowes

In 2000 the southern rockers revived themselves with a joint album and US tour project that had them teaming up with Jimmy Page. Their combined document, *Live at the Greek,* was a popular Internet-only release when first retailed and offered fans a satisfying selection of such Zeppelin highlights as "Heartbreaker," "The Lemon Song," and "Custard Pie," as well as the Yardbirds' "Shapes of Things," Fleetwood Mac's "Oh Well," and the Black Crowes' own "Remedy." For Page, being onstage with two other guitar players was a rare treat: "When we did 'Ten Years Gone' with Led Zeppelin, there's all these guitars on the record, and I used to do my best to try to get through it with just one guitar. . . . [W]hen we did 'Ten Years Gone' with the Crowes it was quite fantastic—they had obviously done their homework." "I think the Jimmy Page thing just helped us home in on who we really are," guitarist Rich Robinson looked back. "And that was a great thing for me—a confidence builder." His singer brother Chris took an even longer view of his association with Led Zeppelin's leader. "They're part of the vocabulary of rock 'n' roll. . . . They're another example of how much inspiration there is in the things that have come before us."

1979

January 30: Shah of Iran deposed in Islamic Revolution.

March 31: Nuclear accident at Three Mile Island.

May 3: Margaret Thatcher elected British prime minister.

August 4 / 11: Led Zeppelin play Knebworth Festival, England.

August 15: *In Through the Out Door* released.

August 30: Earl Mountbatten killed by IRA bomb.

November 26: Iranian students seize hostages at US Embassy, Tehran.

December 21: USSR invades Afghanistan.

Movie: *Apocalypse Now.*

Music: Pink Floyd, *The Wall*; Michael Jackson, *Off the Wall*; Supertramp, *Breakfast in America*; the Police, *Outlandos d'Amour*; the Clash, *London Calling*; AC/DC, *Highway to Hell*; Blondie, "Heart of Glass"; Donna Summer, "Hot Stuff"; the Sugarhill Gang, "Rapper's Delight."

25

Presence

Led Zeppelin Then and Now

Laughing in the Rain: Led Zeppelin Parodies

The band's lofty status as inflated rock 'n' roll nobility has, fairly or not, made them inevitable targets for satire. The most conspicuous instances of comedians or musicians poking fun at Led Zeppelin are as follows.

Little Roger and the Goosebumps

In 1978 San Franciscans Roger Clark and Dick Bright recorded and released a well-executed cover of "Stairway to Heaven," only with the lyrics of the kitsch TV series *Gilligan's Island*—the lines actually fit into the original music pretty well. The effect of "Gilligan's Island (Stairway)" is to either elevate the banal sitcom into something profound, or to turn Led Zeppelin's solemn masterpiece into something goofy. The group's management soon threatened legal action and the single was withdrawn, but the music now circulates freely on the Internet.

Frank Zappa

The master rock satirist orchestrated a brass-heavy version of "Stairway to Heaven" in 1988, with vamped instrumental accompaniment that punctured the folk pretensions of the Zeppelin version. Though the song is not explicitly a send-up, there was a rather smug subversion in recreating the famous guitar parts for tuba.

Dana Carvey

While he didn't specifically reference Led Zeppelin, the American actor (*Saturday Night Live* and *Wayne's World*) performed a funny routine called

"Choppin' Broccoli," spoofing the pseudo-heavy, stream-of-consciousness lyrics of many rock anthems. "There's a lady I know, if I didn't know her, she'd be the lady I didn't know . . ." he begins, and climaxes with the heroine slicing the titular vegetable.

Dread Zeppelin

Probably the most successful purveyors of Led Zeppelin–based comedy, this Californian group has recorded a number of albums that remake Zeppelin music in a reggae style (with guitarist Jah Paul Jo, alias Joe Ramsey) and sung in the manner of Elvis Presley (Tortelvis, alias Greg Tortell). The results aren't so much parodies as just good cover versions that prove the appeal of the prototypes; the medleys of "Black Dog / Hound Dog" and "Heartbreaker (At the End of Lonely Street)" put Led Zeppelin in a new light. Dread Zeppelin's albums *Un-Led-Ed* (1990) and *5,000,000* (1991) enjoyed wide appeal at first release, and even earned commendations from Robert Plant himself, who was pleased to hear the Zeppelin legacy for once treated with friendly irreverence. "We were doing reggae versions of 'Stairway to Heaven' when Tortelvis was thin," he claimed to *Rolling Stone* in 1990. "Just doing sound checks and stuff like that. . . . It wasn't sending the thing up—it was just like, 'Here's another way of doing it.'" For those who can still appreciate the humor, Dread Zeppelin have also put out *No Quarter Pounder* (1995) and *The Song Remains Insane* (1996).

SCTV

Originally broadcast on the pioneering 1980s comedy series (and for copyright reasons blocked from its DVD releases), a mock K-tel-style advertisement promotes a ridiculous collection of "Stairway to Heaven" covers by Slim Whitman, Luciano Pavarotti, Barry White, Buffy Sainte-Marie, and others. The impersonations are spot-on and very funny—and note the fictionalized credit to Dolly Parton, who really did do her own "Stairway" version some years later.

Spinal Tap

Not a real band but a fictional outfit portrayed in the pioneering 1984 "mockumentary" *This Is Spinal Tap*, the hilarious representation of rock music's most embarrassing clichés has since entered the public mind as the obvious comparison to countless genuine acts—including Led Zeppelin. By showing heavy metal not as the majestic religion of its fans' fantasies but the juvenile schlock most outsiders considered it to be, *This Is Spinal Tap* brought a much-needed dose of irony to the genre. "I definitely recognized the band politics," even Jimmy Page said of the film. "People getting puffed up and self-important." Robert Plant saw himself in Spinal Tap too: "Getting lost on the way to the stage—that was us, playing in Baltimore. It took twenty-five minutes to do the hundred yards from our Holiday Inn through the kitchen to the arena."

Comprised of improvisational actors and accomplished musicians Christopher Guest (Nigel Tufnel, lead guitar), Michael McKean (David St. Hubbins, rhythm guitar and vocals), and Harry Shearer (Derek Smalls, bass), Spinal Tap hit all the right notes in depicting the decline of a British hard rock group whose prime was sometime in the 1970s: the moody virtuoso who solos with a violin scraped across the strings of his Les Paul, the outgoing blond singer trapped in a love-hate partnership with his foil, and the quiet bassist who sees himself as the middle ground between the vocalist's fire and the guitarist's ice. "I'm sort of lukewarm water," says Derek. There's also the late drummer who choked on vomit (though not his own) and the Stonehenge stage set that the real Led Zeppelin foreshadowed in Oakland in 1977. The bewigged Guest, McKean, and Shearer have occasionally "reunited" for more Tap projects over the years, and though Zeppelin never sank to their blundering depths, it's subsequently been hard to watch *The Song Remains the Same* with a straight face.

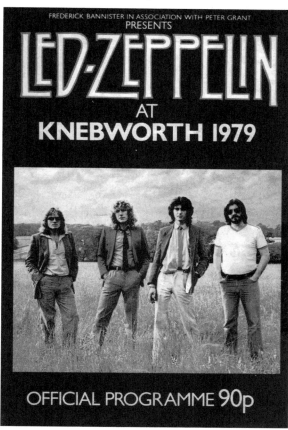

By the time of Zeppelin's last British shows in 1979, both pop music and world affairs had changed dramatically.

Courtesy of Robert Rodriguez

N-N-N-Nobody's Fault but Mine: Led Zeppelin Sampled

Since the appearance of analog and then digital audio sampling in the 1980s and '90s, many people have plundered the Zeppelin vault. In fact, given the nature of the techniques—overdubbing, repeating, or otherwise incorporating portions of previous songs into new music—there is no way to identify every single sampler who's ever taken a riff or drumbeat from a Zeppelin cut and made something else with it. Most of the Led Zeppelin sampling has likely been improvised in dance clubs where the piece was used by the house DJ only once, and never recorded or released as a new work, or known only by a small audience of clubbers. Because of the sonic clarity of Jimmy Page's productions, particularly his recording of John Bonham's drums, and because of the heavy impact of Bonham's drumming itself, Zeppelin music has been popular with turntable and digital players who isolate and reconfigure the sounds for their own purposes. Some listeners name Bonham as the single most sampled performer ever, although others give James Brown that credit.

Sampling, of course, has its opponents who complain that it is an inherently lesser art form than the playing of a "traditional" instrument, and the legality of recycling a few seconds of someone else's track into another's has been widely debated. Page himself once denounced the sample-reliant hip-hop medium thusly: "They steal your riffs and then shout at you," but many samples today are legitimately permitted and paid for. A roster of artists who've identifiably placed Led Zeppelin music into their own collages would include but is not limited to:

- Frankie Goes to Hollywood: "Relax" ("Moby Dick" sample)
- The Beastie Boys: "She's Crafty" ("The Ocean"); "Rhymin' and Stealin,'" "So What'cha Want" ("When the Levee Breaks"); "Beastie Groove" ("Black Dog"); "What Comes Around" ("Moby Dick")
- No Remorze: "Dark Malice '95" ("Whole Lotta Love")
- De La Soul: "The Magic Number" ("The Crunge")
- Sandra: "Hiroshima" ("Whole Lotta Love")
- Fort Minor: "Dolla" ("The Ocean")
- Ice-T: "Midnight" ("When the Levee Breaks")
- T.I.: "Make You Sweat" ("Black Dog")
- Son of Bazerk: "One Time for the Rebel" ("Whole Lotta Love")
- The Prodigy: "Rhythm of Life" ("Whole Lotta Love")
- Obie Trice: "You Burn" ("Black Dog")

- Chinese Man: "You Suck Me" ("You Shook Me")
- Sean Kingston: "Me Love" ("D'yer Mak'er")
- The Backyard Rangers: "What's It Gonna Be?" ("D'yer Mak'er")
- Sandy Vee: "Bleep" ("Immigrant Song")
- Fatboy Slim: "Going Out of My Head" ("The Crunge")
- Scatterbrain: "Down with the Ship (Slight Return)" ("Dazed and Confused," "Heartbreaker," "Rock and Roll")
- Double Dee & Steinski: "Lesson 3 (History of Hip Hop Mix)" ("The Crunge")
- Chapterhouse: "Pearl" ("When the Levee Breaks")
- Dr. Dre: "Lyrical Gangbang" ("When the Levee Breaks")
- Jake One: "Gangsta Boy" ("When the Levee Breaks")
- Enigma: "Gravity of Love," "Return to Innocence" ("When the Levee Breaks")
- Coldcut: "Beats and Pieces" ("When the Levee Breaks")
- Eminem: "Kim" ("When the Levee Breaks")
- Sophie Hawkins: "Damn I Wish I Was Your Lover" ("When the Levee Breaks")
- Robert Plant: "Tall Cool One" ("Black Dog," "Whole Lotta Love," "Dazed and Confused," "Custard Pie")
- Nikki Costa: "Hope It Felt Good" ("Whole Lotta Love")
- Schooly D: "Signifying Rapper" ("Kashmir")
- Puff Daddy / Jimmy Page: "Come with Me" ("Kashmir")
- Mike Oldfield: "Crystal Clear" ("When the Levee Breaks")
- Insane Clown Posse: "$50 Bucks" ("Ramble On")
- The Chemical Brothers: "Delik" ("The Crunge")
- MF Grimm: "Adam & Eve" ("Achilles Last Stand")

26

Thinking How It Used to Be

Zeppelin After Zeppelin

I've Got to Get You Together: Led Zeppelin Reunions

Technically, there haven't been any: Since the announcement of the band's dissolution on December 4, 1980, the original Led Zeppelin of Jimmy Page, Robert Plant, John Paul Jones, and John Bonham has ceased to exist. Since then, a handful of live or recorded pairings of two remaining members has attracted attention from fans, but can't really be counted as reunions. In a few public and private instances, the three Zeppelin survivors have gotten together to play Zeppelin music, notably:

Live Aid, Philadelphia, July 13, 1985

Page, Plant, and Jones, and drummers Phil Collins and Tony Thompson, played "Rock and Roll," "Whole Lotta Love" and (with Paul Martinez from Plant's band on bass) "Stairway to Heaven," but not very well, despite the rapturous reception of the crowd. Plant was hoarse and exhausted, Page's Les Paul was out of tune and he was plugged into a too-short cable for "Stairway," and the two drummers couldn't quite mesh together. The grand positive spirit of the Live Aid event overshadowed Led Zeppelin's troubled set. "Live Aid was like having the umbilical cord there for me to see again," Plant said in 1988. "But it also smacked of the shambles and shoddiness that Zeppelin could never get away with."

Bath, England, January 1986

At the suggestion of John Paul Jones, private rehearsals between Page, Plant, Jones, and Tony Thompson took place in a Corsham studio near this

English city after the Live Aid affair. Despite the best of intentions, it never quite came together. Thompson was soon injured in a car accident and was replaced by Plant's roadie Mike "Kiddo" Kidson, and Page and Plant no longer had the same master-protégé dynamic of 1968: Plant was riding high on an acclaimed solo career, while Page was still seeking a post-Zeppelin direction and coming off years of heavy indulgence. "It was the most bristlingly embarrassing moment, to have all that will and not knowing what to play," said Plant. The vocalist ended up contributing bass to some jams while Jones played piano and Page guitar. "It was pretty good. And there were two or three things that were very promising." "I don't know if Jimmy was quite into it, but it was good," Jones described the sessions politely. "What I recall is Robert and I getting drunk in the hotel and Robert questioning what we were doing. He was saying nobody wants to hear that old stuff, and I said, 'Everybody is waiting for it to happen.' It just fell apart from then." What might have come from these trials—or where the musicians wanted to take them—is anyone's guess, but it seems to have been the last time any new Led Zeppelin music was created.

Atlantic Records Fortieth Anniversary, New York, May 14, 1988

Intended as a highlight of a show that also featured sets by such legendary Atlantic acts as the Coasters, Wilson Pickett, and the Bee Gees, the surviving members joined with Jason Bonham on drums to perform uneven renditions of "Kashmir," "Heartbreaker," "Whole Lotta Love," and—grudgingly agreed to by Plant at the last moment—"Stairway to Heaven." The band waited backstage for too long: fraught with emotional tension, their spot was, in Peter Grant's word, "diabolical." "It's unfortunate to be measured by a one-off shot like that, when you haven't played in a while," Page said in *Musician* magazine later.

Carmen Plant's Twenty-First Birthday, Oldbury (near Birmingham), UK, November 21, 1989

The coming of age party for Plant's daughter saw an impromptu gathering of her father, Page, Jones, and members of Plant's band doing "Trampled Underfoot," "Misty Mountain Hop," and "Rock and Roll." Out of the public spotlight, the musicians were more relaxed and actually enjoyed themselves. "Pagey was playing so good—I had a big lump in my throat," recalled Plant.

Page-Plant tours were the closest many fans could come to witnessing a Zeppelin
reunion.   *Courtesy of Robert Rodriguez*

Jason Bonham's Wedding Reception, Bewdley, Worcestershire, UK, April 28, 1990

Another happy and private occasion for the Zeppelin family spurred a fun,
spontaneous jam where the groom, now married to Jan Charteris, took the
drum stool as his three "uncles" played "Bring It On Home," "Sick Again,"
"Custard Pie," "Rock and Roll," and Jerry Lee Lewis's "It'll Be Me."

Rock and Roll Hall of Fame Induction, New York, January 12, 1995

Part of an all-star get-together that included Jason Bonham on drums
(over Plant's objections), Aerosmith's Joe Perry and Steve Tyler, and fellow
inductee Neil Young, Page, Plant, and Jones got through "Bring It On
Home," "Train Kept A-Rollin'," "Baby Please Don't Go," and "When the
Levee Breaks." The ad hoc formation made for a ragged but passable show:
Referring to Jones's quip regarding the recent Page-Plant *No Quarter* project,
Neil Young nudged Plant and told him, "Don't forget his phone number
again!"

Ahmet Ertegun Tribute Concert, O2 Arena, London, December 10, 2007

A worldwide sensation that drew millions of applicants to an online lottery of just 18,000 available seats, this was the most successful Zeppelin reunion. Weeks of rehearsal between Page, Plant, Jones, and Jason Bonham, and careful recalibration of their best-known songs (some tuned down to accommodate Plant's lowered voice), resulted in a polished two-hour set that finally brought the band's legacy to an honorable close. Robert Plant told the *Telegraph* newspaper that the O2 performance was "the best Led Zeppelin gig since 1975."

Let Me Get Back: The Most Significant Posthumous Led Zeppelin Releases

Since the band's official breakup, the popularity and critical standing of Led Zeppelin has steadily risen. Both the solo efforts of the remaining musicians and the unearthing or repackaging of original Zeppelin material have added to the band's stature and revealed new dimensions to their oeuvre of 1969–79. The standout releases since 1980 have been the following.

Led Zeppelin Box Set, 1990

This celebrated four-disc collection updated the sound of the analog music to the CD era; the lavish presentation and comprehensive history of the band's nine official studio albums secured Led Zeppelin's position as one of rock's greatest, after years of being relegated to the heavy metal subcategory. Most impressive was Jimmy Page's thoughtful resequencing of the fifty-four tracks, which brought out his contrasting light-and-shade effects as never before. For once the cliché was accurate: Listening to this really was like hearing the songs for the first time.

Led Zeppelin DVD, 2003

The visual document of the quartet's finest performances that millions of fans were waiting for. Ranging from a 1970 Albert Hall gig on Page's birthday to Earl's Court in '75 and Knebworth in '79, these video gems once again validated Zeppelin as a brilliant live act. The revelatory coverage of John Bonham's insuperable drumming is alone worth the price of admission.

L e d   Z e p p e l i n

The lavish Led Zeppelin box set of 1990 won new respect for the group's musical legacy.   *Author's Collection*

How the West Was Won, 2003

Though bootlegs of these LA concerts from 1972 had circulated for many years, their cleaned-up release under official auspices offered more proof of Led Zeppelin's concert prowess. With the simultaneous issue of the DVD, the three CDs of this set effectively replaced *The Song Remains the Same*, hitherto doing lonely duty as the group's imperfect live collection.

BBC Sessions, 1998

Likewise heard in unofficial format for some time but finally given an authorized launch, these British live radio dates from 1969 and 1971 showed a hungry and ambitious Zeppelin before they became the regal superstars of later years. Highlights included the tentative first-ever broadcast version of "Stairway to Heaven," some funky excursions on "Communication Breakdown," a rollicking cover of Eddie Cochran's "Somethin' Else," and the killer riffing of "The Girl I Love She Got Long Black Wavy Hair," adapted into the Zeppelin idiom from an old Sleepy John Estes number.

Coda, 1982

This was the first posthumous Zeppelin record, fulfilling a contractual obligation Jimmy Page found "disgusting," but it did offer some provocative nuggets that had been left out of earlier albums. The driving folk stomp of "Poor Tom" from 1970 and the punk zeal of 1978's "Wearing and Tearing" proved the foursome's range, but it was the vast drum solo "Bonzo's Montreux" that best paid tribute to their late, great, and irreplaceable drummer.

Jimmy Page–Robert Plant, No Quarter, 1994

The reunion of the two Led Zeppelin showmen was a celebrated occasion that attracted much fanfare, and even some controversy due to the exclusion of John Paul Jones. But the album and video project, begun as an episode of MTV's *Unplugged* series, turned out to be a surprisingly inventive rethinking of the Zeppelin canon, with Celtic and Arabic takes on "Nobody's Fault but Mine," "The Battle of Evermore," "No Quarter," "Kashmir," and "Four Sticks." More striking still were the new songs, such as "City Don't Cry" and "Wonderful One," accompanied by indigenous Moroccan musicians. What could have been easy remakes turned into an intelligent exploration of Led Zeppelin's own distant influences.

Robert Plant, Now and Zen, 1988

Robert Plant's long-awaited reconciliation with his past included digital samples of "Black Dog," "Dazed and Confused," and "Whole Lotta Love," as well as actual collaborations with Jimmy Page on the album's moody hit singles "Tall Cool One" and "Heaven Knows." The singer's already strong solo career was boosted by this clever and sincere engagement with the Zeppelin legacy.

Jimmy Page–David Coverdale, *Coverdale-Page*, 1993

Derided by many as Page's settling for an inferior Plant substitute when he couldn't get the real thing, this earnest joint effort with former Whitesnake and Deep Purple front man David Coverdale revived the guitarist's fortunes somewhat and marked his return to heavy guitar heroics with "Feeling Hot," "Take Me for a Little While," and "Shake My Tree." "I enjoyed working with him, believe it or not," Page shrugged in retrospect.

John Paul Jones–Diamanda Galás, *The Sporting Life*, 1994

If his versatility was ever in doubt, John Paul Jones confirmed its existence with this out-of-nowhere pairing with Diamanda Galás, a dark and feisty

The Page-Plant *No Quarter* project was a surprising departure for the reunited hard rock heroes. *Author's Collection*

alternative screamer and pianist. Adding this credit to his already wide list of credentials put his work with Led Zeppelin into a fresh, even disturbing perspective. Asked if she thought the Gothic yowls and grinds of *The Sporting Life* were Zeppelin-influenced, the singer responded that instead it was Zeppelin who were Jones-influenced. Good point.

Robert Plant, *The Principle of Moments*, 1983

Plant's second official solo album gave him more momentum with the popular singles "Big Log," and "In the Mood," further distancing him from the rock-god persona he'd lived in Zeppelin. There was nothing heavy metal about the sophisticated post–New Wave sheen on display here, which was the way Plant wanted it.

The Honeydrippers, *The Honeydrippers, Volume One*, 1984

Still less evidence of Led Zeppelin was audible in this pseudonymous collaborative effort between Plant, Nile Rodgers, Jeff Beck, and Jimmy Page, as the Plant-instigated EP offered faithful versions of old rhythm 'n' blues favorites from the 1950s, including "I Get a Thrill," "Rockin' at Midnight," and the hit "Sea of Love." As on Plant's other work of the 1980s, he was obviously relishing the opportunity to sing how and what he wanted rather than any of the stadium-rocking anthems he was identified with.

The Firm, *The Firm*, 1985

Straining for artistic purpose and career relevance after Zeppelin's demise, Jimmy Page teamed up with Swan Song labelmate Paul Rodgers of Bad Company to form another four-piece rock act, with Chris Slade on drums and Tony Franklin of Roy Harper's band on bass. Some of the cuts, such as "Radioactive," "Closer," a cover of "You've Lost that Loving Feeling," and the grandiose "Midnight Moonlight" were appealing, but the largely generic '80s-era tones were not the powerhouse Led Company many fans had hoped for.

Jimmy Page–Robert Plant, *Walking into Clarksdale*, 1998

The second Page-Plant collection, this time of all-new songs without the support of English and Arabic backing players, was not the triumph the *No Quarter* comeback had been, but it did go off in some intriguing North

African and Middle Eastern directions. Memorable tracks included "Most High," "Heart in Your Hand," and "When I Was a Child."

Jimmy Page, *Outrider*, 1988

Page's first real solo album was a better outing than the Firm's two releases, boasting three intriguing instrumentals ("Emerald Eyes," "Writes of Winter," "Liquid Mercury"), a duet with Robert Plant ("The Only One") and piercing electric blues ("Prison Blues," "Blues Anthem"). The record had only modest sales, however, and Page has put out no solo music since.

Robert Plant–Alison Krauss, *Raising Sand*, 2007

Plant surprised his audience in this partnership with respected country soprano Alison Krauss. The unlikely vocal combinations of grizzled rocker and Dixie diva, produced by the much-admired roots scholar T Bone Burnett, became a major critical and commercial success. Among the songs performed were soulful versions of obscure bluegrass and R&B songs, as well as a remake of "Please Read the Letter," which was first heard on *Walking into Clarksdale.*

Them Crooked Vultures, *Them Crooked Vultures*, 2009

Never underestimate Jonesy. After years of eclectic and independent production and instrumental work for the likes of REM, the Butthole Surfers, Heart, Cinderella, the Sisters of Mercy, and Brian Eno, he turned around and formed a heavy rock band, with relative youngsters Dave Grohl, formerly of Nirvana and the Foo Fighters, and Josh Homme, of Queens of the Stone Age. Grungy nu-metal for frat boys and teenage skateboarders, from a man who'd played with Tom Jones, Petula Clark, and Herman's Hermits.

Do I Look the Same? Led Zeppelin Tribute Bands

There are many of them. From Elvis Presley to the Beatles, from Shania Twain to Frank Sinatra, and from Kiss to Metallica, there is a long showbiz tradition of providing eager punters with ersatz versions of distant or departed stars. Led Zeppelin, despite their unique sound and image, have been given the tribute treatment from far and wide. As long as guitarists have been figuring out Jimmy Page's idiosyncratic licks and tunings, as long as drummers have developed the muscle to hit like John Bonham, and as long as singers can grow hair and reach notes like Robert Plant, bar bands

Nineteen ninety-three's Coverdale-Page effort was an unlikely pairing of the Zeppelin guitarist and Whitesnake singer. *Author's Collection*

have made careers out of putting on replica Zeppelin shows. Some of these go for visual as well as musical spectacles—complete with appropriate costumes and instrumental lineups designed to mimic Madison Square Garden in '73 or Earl's Court in '75—but others aim to do the music alone with no theatrical gimmickry to distract, like Michael White's the White. Some acts stake out strictly local or regional turf, while others have built national followings. At least two all-female tributes, Lez Zeppelin and Zepparella, have put a very novel (maybe even a little discomfiting) slant on the original quartet. One American recreation, Led Zepagain, has been seen and endorsed by Jimmy Page himself, although Page has also said that he would be unlikely to drop in on any tribute show: "I'd probably get torn apart." In 2010 and 2011 John Bonham's son Jason toured with Jason

Jimmy Page's last solo record, *Outrider*, was released in 1988.   *Author's Collection*

Bonham's Led Zeppelin Experience, offering a singular link to the original no other tributes can.

With names that plainly spell out their premise, some of the current or past Led Zeppelin cover bands from the US, Canada, and Britain include: Swan Song, Kashmir, Custard Pie, Led Astray, Get the Led Out, Presence, Zeppelin Live, ZoSo, In the Light, Coda, Screamer, Heartbreaker, No Quarter, Led Hed, the Vibe Remains the Same, Valhalla, Led Zepland, Boot Led Zep, Physical Graffiti, Crunge, Ozone Baby, Led Zep Too, Led by Zeppelin, Black Dog, Fed Zeppelin, Let's Zeppelin, Stairway to Zeppelin, Letz Zep, and Whole Lotta Led. Perhaps the most musically accurate tributes have been performed by Classic Albums Live, a Canadian ensemble that performs note-for-note, song-by-song versions of legendary rock discs by the Beatles, Pink Floyd, the Rolling Stones, Fleetwood Mac, the Eagles, and Led Zeppelin.

Led Zeppelin Too: Led Zeppelin Tribute Albums

Another symptom of Zeppelin's enduring popularity has been the proliferation of collections that present covers of their songs. This too is an extensive subcategory of the music business, as completists and the curious provide a ready market for fresh takes on material by the Beatles, Elvis Presley, Bob Dylan, and other legends, all the way down to relative cult acts such as Leonard Cohen or Van Morrison. Some of these are random assemblies of work by well-known contemporary artists, while others are thematic remakes by studio teams. At last count there were at least twenty or thirty CDs devoted entirely to Led Zeppelin songs, including several all-orchestral packages. One album consists entirely of "Stairway to Heaven" remakes; it's called, oddly, *Stairways to Heaven.*

For those interested in hearing the band as you've never heard them before, check out:

- *Enconium: A Tribute to Led Zeppelin* featuring Sheryl Crow, Hootie and the Blowfish, Duran Duran, and Robert Plant and Tori Amos's duet on "Down by the Seaside."
- *Pickin' on Zeppelin: A Tribute.* Bluegrass guitar versions.
- *Rockabye Baby: Lullaby Renditions of Led Zeppelin.* She is only three years old and it's time to go nighty-night.
- *Long Ago and Far Away: The Celtic Tribute to Led Zeppelin.* Scottish-Irish folk stylings.
- *Going to California: A Classical Guitarist's Tribute to Led Zeppelin.* Acoustic virtuoso Richard DeVinck's covers.
- *Great Zeppelin: A Tribute to Led Zeppelin.* Popular 1980s hair band and Zeppelin sound-alikes Great White drop the pretense of "original" material to perform the real thing.
- *Chamber Maid: The Baroque Tribute to Led Zeppelin.* This is getting ridiculous.
- *Dead Zeppelin: A Metal Tribute to Led Zeppelin.* Ugly. Makes the prototypes, which were pretty metal in their day, sound like Nelson Riddle.

Valhalla I Am Coming: Awards and Honors Given to the Group or Its Members

Led Zeppelin often topped readers' polls of favorite groups in music papers such as *Melody Maker* and *New Musical Express* when they were a functioning band but seldom received any great kudos otherwise. However, since 1980 the group or its members have won laurels from all over. All of Led Zeppelin's music and video releases have been given special commemorative Gold and Platinum acknowledgements from countries around the world, signifying their high sales in many national markets; the Recording Industry Association of America (RIAA) has granted Diamond Awards to the five Zeppelin albums with certified sales of over 10 million units in the US, *Led Zeppelin*, *Led Zeppelin II*, *Led Zeppelin IV*, *Houses of the Holy*, and *Physical Graffiti.* As with many celebrations in the entertainment industry, some of these accolades are really promotional tie-ins meant to benefit the entire profession or advertise the outlets granting them (e.g., the group's premier rank in the *Classic Rock* Best 50 Live Acts of All Time or the *Mojo* Hall of Fame), while others are sincere accolades that indicate the genuine respect for Led Zeppelin and its individual members throughout the music business. Among the credits are:

Led Zeppelin

- *Q* magazine Merit Award, 1992
- Rock and Roll Hall of Fame induction, 1995
- International Artist Award, American Music Awards, 1995
- Ivor Novello Lifetime Achievement Award, 1997
- Lifetime Achievement Grammy Award, 2005
- Polar Music Prize, 2005
- United Kingdom Music Hall of Fame induction, 2006
- *Mojo* magazine Honors List for Best Live Act, 2008

Jimmy Page

- Rock and Roll Hall of Fame induction (the Yardbirds), 1992
- Hollywood Rock Walk star, 1993
- Lifetime Achievement Award, MTV Music Video Awards, Japan, 2002
- London Walk of Fame star, 2005
- Honorary Citizen of Rio de Janeiro, 2005
- Officer of the British Empire (OBE), 2005

Robert Plant

- Midlander of the Year Lifetime Achievement award, 2002
- Musical Event of the Year Country Music Association Award, 2008 ("Gone, Gone, Gone")
- Commander of the British Empire (CBE), 2009
- Album of the Year Grammy Award, 2009 (*Raising Sand*)
- Record of the Year Grammy Award, 2009 ("Please Read the Letter")
- Best Contemporary Folk/Americana Album Grammy Award, 2009 (*Raising Sand*)
- Best Pop Collaboration with Vocals Grammy Award, 2009 ("Rich Woman")
- Best Country Collaboration with Vocals Grammy Award, 2009 (*Raising Sand*)

◆   *Q* magazine Outstanding Contribution to Music prize, 2009

John Paul Jones

◆   Gold Badge from British Academy of Songwriters, Composers, and Authors (BASCA), 2010

Threads That Have No End: The Best Led Zeppelin Internet Sites

As with seemingly everything else that has ever existed, Led Zeppelin is now represented at numerous points on the Internet. Since 2007 the band's catalogue has been available for purchase online, and Robert Plant and John Paul Jones have official websites (Jimmy Page has an official domain registered in 2010, but there is no activity there). There is also an authorized Led Zeppelin site, ledzeppelin.com, that contains news, a discography, a timeline, and a busy and well-moderated fan forum. Licensed by the act's management, ledzeppelin.com began as an independent entity created by

Page composed the soundtrack for the 1982 film *Death Wish II*.   *Author's Collection*

webmaster Sam Rapallo, but such was his thoroughness and care with administering its information that it was remade as the formal Internet face of Led Zeppelin in 2007.

Other sites do not have the sanction of group but are nonetheless full of worthwhile material. Each has a particular appeal: On some forums, trading of bootleg recordings between members is tolerated; some promote fan fiction and other community interaction; some highlight Zeppelin-related musical or technical details; and some disseminate news tidbits and rare video clips. Newbies are more tolerated on some forums than others, and nasty cyber-scraps have broken out between posters as they debate (for example) Robert Plant's solo career, Jimmy Page's history of drug abuse, or the color of John Paul Jones's socks when he played Chicago in 1975 (the second show).

Numerous individuals have built their own blogs to discuss their Zeppelin fandom and solicit contact with like-minded surfers, and several pages about the group are now on Facebook. Original or homemade video clips of Led Zeppelin musical performances, bootlegs, and interviews are all over YouTube. Whether or not the sixty-something Jimmy Page, Robert Plant, and John Paul Jones are themselves pointing and clicking away out there is unknown—asked once if he used e-mail or the Web, Page said, "I wouldn't know how to turn on a computer." Like so much on the Internet, the online Led Zeppelin data should be scrutinized carefully and double-

Robert Plant's post-1980 career took him far away from his Golden God Zeppelin persona.   *Courtesy of Len Ward / The Rad Zone*

checked before confirming any details as factual. The most useful and visited Zeppelin sites available in English are:

- **jimmypageonline.com** Not affiliated with Page himself, this is a fan site with pictures, merchandise, and occasional news.

- **johnpauljones.com** Run by Sam Rapallo, the website offers the multi-instrumentalist's most recent news, itineraries, and pictures.

- **ledzeppelin.com** Great-looking graphics and a very active forum make this the first stop in cyberspace for many Zeppelin buffs. Its official status, however, means bootleggers are unwelcome.

- **led-zeppelin.org** Less flashy but still a commendable source of info, featuring tablature for guitarists, musical instrument analysis, song lyrics, interview transcriptions, and backstage secrets in an "Infrequently Murmured Trivia List."

- **ledzeppelin-database.com** An extremely thorough and navigable index to every single Led Zeppelin performance around the world between 1968 and 1980, offering fan photos, press coverage, set lists (with song timings and band members' onstage comments), and sound clips from audience recordings.

- **ledzeppelinnews.com** Steve Sauer posts the latest post-Zeppelin activities of the band members and their circle. Coverage is always timely and often exclusive.

- **planet-zeppelin.com** Geared toward more casual fans who're interested in meeting up and sharing stories online. Lots of interesting opinions, trivia, memories, and exchanges, and a friendlier tone among posters than in some other forums.

- **robertplant.com** The solo singer's official site features pictures, press clippings, a discography, videos, and interviews.

- **royal-orleans.com** Hard-core collectors and musos gather here to dissect the fine points of Led Zeppelin's official and bootlegged music; highly knowledgeable input concerning any and all technical aspects of the shows and the records can be found here.

- **tightbutloose.co.uk** From England's Dave Lewis, publisher of the long-running *Tight but Loose* fan magazine. This is the portal to the authoritative print journal, but the website also presents up-to-date news, diaries, and commentary (not all to do with Zeppelin) from Lewis; a very civilized place to go.

1980

May 19: Mt. St. Helens volcano erupts in US; 8 dead.

June 10: Comedian Richard Pryor badly burned in freebase cocaine accident.

June–July: Led Zeppelin tour Europe.

September 20: Iran-Iraq war begins.

September 25: John Bonham found dead.

November 4: Ronald Reagan defeats Jimmy Carter in US presidential election.

December 4: Press release announces the dissolution of Led Zeppelin.

December 8: Ex-Beatle John Lennon killed, New York.

Movies: *Raging Bull*; *The Elephant Man.*

Music: Bob Marley and the Wailers, *Uprising*; AC/DC, *Back in Black*; U2, *Boy*; the Pretenders, "Brass in Pocket"; Devo, "Whip It"; Kool & the Gang, "Celebration."

27

But in the Long Run

Led Zeppelin in Overview

If We Could Just Join Hands: Led Zeppelin as Supergroup

Rock music's unprecedented international success from the mid-1960s onward, in terms of economic impact, media notice, and critical respect, was marked by the growing numbers of acts comprised of members sprung from bands that had already enjoyed some measure of popularity. The term *supergroup* was first applied to Blind Faith in 1969, made up of Eric Clapton and Ginger Baker of Cream, Steve Winwood of Traffic, and Rick Grech of Family, all of them (especially Cream) with strong histories of record and ticket sales. Crosby, Stills, Nash & Young were another example of the phenomenon (they too debuted in '69), as David Crosby had emerged from the chart-topping Byrds, Graham Nash from the Hollies with their own string of hits ("Bus Stop," "Carrie-Anne"), and Stephen Stills and Neil Young from the Buffalo Springfield ("For What It's Worth"). Later the "supergroup" label was put to various highly successful bands, but it was most accurately employed as a description of ensembles made up of musicians boasting proven backgrounds in the business: Beck, Bogert & Appice; Emerson, Lake and Palmer; Asia; Damn Yankees; the Traveling Wilburys; and so on.

By some standards, Led Zeppelin was a supergroup, but by most they were not. Jimmy Page, Robert Plant, John Paul Jones, and John Bonham were all full-time working players when they joined forces in 1968; Page and Jones had established solid reputations as session men, and Page had been a member of the world-touring Yardbirds; Plant had recorded and released songs under the CBS label; and by '68 Bonham was drumming for the rising star Tim Rose as well as catching the ears of other comers such as Joe Cocker and Chris Farlowe. The 1968 Atlantic Records press release that announced the label's signing of Led Zeppelin boasted that the group "consists of four of the most exciting musicians performing in Britain today," portraying Plant as "one of England's outstanding young blues singers" and claiming that Bonham "caused a sensation with his drum solos." In contrast to previous generations of rock 'n' roll groups, Zeppelin were not a gang of teenage friends who'd worked their way up together playing dances, parties, and clubs in their home town—they were adult veterans signed on into serious performing and recording commitments from the start, and they were expected to deliver.

On the other hand, of all the men of Led Zeppelin only Page had been connected to a truly successful act, and it was his link to the Yardbirds that was put front and center in the group's earliest publicity handouts. Though Jones would certainly have continued to have an access to the higher levels of music production and management had Zeppelin not taken off, and though Plant and Bonham might have eventually found their own footings in the British music scene had Page taken on Terry Reid and B. J. Wilson as vocalist and drummer, respectively, none of them would have had the star factor of genuine supergroup recruits. If anything, it was generous of Page and Peter Grant *not* to extract a Jimmy Page Group or a Jimmy Page and the Mad Dogs out of the defunct Yardbirds, although in the long run the equal billing would give the foursome more credibility. Groomed to be a lucrative project of seasoned experts, Zeppelin nevertheless can't be properly put into the supergroup category. Surviving members have been involved in supergroups, though: Jones in Them Crooked Vultures, alongside Josh Homme of Queens of the Stone Age and Dave Grohl of Nirvana and the Foo Fighters, and Page in the Firm, with Paul Rodgers of Bad Company.

Have You Heard the News: Led Zeppelin as "Hype Band"

Just as Zeppelin's "supergroup" status may be confused by Page and Peter Grant's registering their music publishing company as "Superhype," so did the name virtually invite accusations that the band itself was no more than a product of corporate manipulation and capitalist greed. The charge is not without foundation, but neither is the way Led Zeppelin conclusively disproved it.

Following the watershed impact of *Sgt. Pepper* and the groundbreaking attractions of Cream and the Jimi Hendrix Experience, the record industry of 1968–69 had begun to codify some of the market trends observable during the era. Albums could be as lucrative as singles; artists didn't need Top 40 hits to draw a steady audience; blues-based, improvisatory electric guitar workouts were followed reverently by college-age fans; sexual, chemical, or other countercultural references in the music and on the record covers could be more and more overt; talking up the "mind-blowing" potential of new acts was a valid sales strategy. Atlantic Records took all these into account when signing Led Zeppelin in 1968 for a trade-headline-grabbing $220,000, a huge amount at the time and a sum few new acts have been granted since. With Cream disbanding and Jimi Hendrix, Iron Butterfly, Fleetwood Mac, the Who, and Vanilla Fudge more than demonstrating the continuing appeal of their heavy rock formula, Zeppelin looked and sounded like a good investment.

From the point of view of many punters, however, and certainly of many of the youthful reviewers writing for US rock magazines like *Rolling Stone*, *Creem*, and *Crawdaddy*, Led Zeppelin seemed to be a calculated ploy—a deliberately packaged band whose sound and style were designed to resemble those of a roster of famous acts, touted in the pseudo-groovy language that was even then creeping into the lexicon of Wall Street, Madison Avenue, and Hollywood. The aforementioned Atlantic press release, ascribed to Bob Rolontz of the label, told of the "hot new group" whose "pulsations" had caught the ears of "top English and American rock musicians," prompting comparisons "to the best of Cream and Hendrix." "Led Zeppelin is the eighth British group to be signed by Atlantic during the past 24 months," the statement closed. "The others are Cream, Bee Gees, Julie Driscoll-Brian Auger & The Trinity, The Crazy World of Arthur Brown, The Marbles, The Magic Lanterns, and Jimmy James & The Vagabonds." Oh yes, the incomparable Marbles and Magic Lanterns. Led Zeppelin's first promotional flyers and zeppelin-shaped giveaway balloons were replete with slogans like "The Only Way to Fly," "Isn't that a gas!" and "Led Zeppelin 2 . . . Now Flying!"

This was all hype—PR efforts to stimulate interest in a fresh act Atlantic Records had already wagered a lot of money on and which had to earn its keep. Around this time other big entertainment companies had tried to push the countercultural authenticity of their artists or movies and were met with suspicion by the hip youth market. There was MGM's "Bosstown Sound" attempts to sell Boston-based bands like Ultimate Spinach, Kangaroo, and Chameleon Church, all of whom flopped; ditto "now" Hollywood films like *Getting Straight* and *Zabriskie Point*, attempting to cash in on 1967's blockbusting *The Graduate* and 1969's *Easy Rider*. In this climate, given the kind of promo motifs used to introduce Led Zeppelin to North America, listeners had a right to be skeptical. An early *Creem* review called the band "only redone joplinshake heavybody drughendrix," while *Rolling Stone* dismissed the premier *Led Zeppelin* album as a template taken up in "the aftermath era of such successful British bluesmen as Cream and John Mayall."

Such criticism frustrated the four members of Led Zeppelin, and their intense run of touring and recording between 1969 and 1973 may be seen as an attempt to show how wrong the "hype" slander was. The untitled album usually designated *Led Zeppelin IV* was Jimmy Page's bid to refute any notion that it was the hype itself that drew fans: "We wanted to demonstrate that it was the music that made Zeppelin popular; it had nothing to do with our name or image." Ultimately they succeeded in winning over the rock intelligentsia through a respectably consistent career of albums and concerts, but their initial backing by a powerful media company, bragging of the potential they had yet to realize (let alone exceed), was not an uncommon problem for artists in the late 1960s. "All that stuff about us being a hyped band . . . ," John Paul Jones has reflected. "That didn't help us early on." The point is not that Zeppelin were not enthusiastically pitched by Atlantic Records and its field agents—they were—but that for once the act was worthy of the enthusiasm. Whenever salesmen have tried to plug a cool new product to a cohort resistant to the very notions of salesmen and products, red flags are raised (similar populist scorn greeted many of the post-Nirvana "grunge" acts signed out of Seattle in the early 1990s). Truly, *every* mass-marketed assembly of musicians, from the Texas Playboys and the Ink Spots to U2 and Public Enemy, has been a "hype band," even the ones that catered to the audience's conceits of integrity and independence. Insofar as Led Zeppelin was hyped, the gambit was one that backfired, and the group ended up having to make its case through music alone—which it more than did.

I Don't Know, But I've Been Told: Led Zeppelin as Heavy Metal

As late as the 1983 *Rolling Stone* review of *Coda*, Led Zeppelin was praised as "the greatest heavy metal band that ever strutted the boards." Around the same time they were included with other "Great Heavy Metal Bands" in *The Book of Rock Lists*, alongside Thin Lizzy, Uriah Heep, Blue Cheer, Grand Funk Railroad, and AC/DC, and a 1982 *Hit Parader* article titled "Heavy Metal: The Hall of Fame" decreed that "[q]uite simply, Led Zeppelin is, was, and will always be the ultimate heavy metal masters." The tag was stuck on the band early in their working life and they were saddled with it through the 1970s and beyond. Rock critics such as Dave Marsh and Lester Bangs included Zeppelin in their own definitions of the genre, and the average high school fan of 1974 would likely have classified the group's music as heavy metal. One Zeppelin tune, "Trampled Underfoot," actually uses the term in its lyrics, albeit as an automotive pun. Sociologist Donna Gaines's *Teenage Wasteland: Suburbia's Dead End Kids* (1991) reported on the alienation and aggression of the adolescent heavy metal cliques she interviewed in

New Jersey, calling them "The Children of Zoso," after Jimmy Page's runic signature from *Led Zeppelin IV*. Even today, few scholarly or popular studies of heavy metal as a social or musical subculture will fail to mention the centrality of Led Zeppelin.

This would not be such an issue if the members of Zeppelin themselves were not disappointed to be put into the company of Grand Funk Railroad and their ilk. "There was nothing heavy about that at all," Robert Plant said of the *Led Zeppelin* album in *Musician* magazine. "It was ethereal." To the *New York Post* in 1988 he also dismissed most of Zeppelin's imitators: "It's mindless, it's not a reflection of something sociological. I don't think Zeppelin was their inspiration—Tiny Tim was. . . . But this is some kind of demented dwarf giving strange hand signals as he walks out of a volcano onstage. It's tacky." Plant later told writer Chuck Klosterman that John Bonham had described acts like "Deep Sabbath" as "a conglomerate of English, sketchy, blues-based thud. . . . It was inane and no mystery to it at all." The other survivors, Jones and Page, have made equally distancing remarks about the band's relationship to the heavy metal format, Page pointing out the lack of "light and shade" dynamics in competitors like Black Sabbath, and Jones sneering at the "glowering, Satanic crap" of most metal acts. Page was quoted as saying, "I can't relate [the heavy metal term] to us because the thing that comes to mind when people say heavy metal is riff-bashing, and I don't think we ever just did riff-bashing at any point." "No one ever compared us to Black Sabbath after this record," was the bassist's blunt conclusion of *Led Zeppelin IV*'s impact. Yet even pundits who concede "Zep was always too arty and eclectic to be considered a real metal band" (*Guitar World*'s "Top 50 Heavy Metal Albums") allow that "[f]or sheer power chord mania and horny, guttural hoo-ha, it doesn't get any better than 'Whole Lotta Love' or 'Heartbreaker.'"

Jimmy Page and his bandmates were not alone in rejecting whatever pigeonhole they were consigned to. Most rock musicians at some point have complained about industry or critical simplifications of their work, a protest which usually tends to enforce their reputations all the more. "You cannot classify anything," Plant avowed to Chuck Klosterman. "Classification is a killer." Most artists in any medium, indeed, will resist being slotted into some or other stereotype, saying that their work is only their self-expression and that any generalization will miss the personal subtleties they try to impart to it; yet the defense of artistic freedom on the part of the creator is about as predictable as the inclination to format and sort on the part of the spectator or listener. As Led Zeppelin's players sought to demonstrate that they had more to offer than the one-dimensional boogie of Grand Funk—*Led Zeppelin III* was an early example of this—professional and amateur audiences strained to define their songs as *something*, and heavy metal was still the handiest option.

The Zeppelin-as-heavy-metal controversy says more about the rapid evolution of rock 'n' roll aesthetics over twenty or thirty years than any objective parameters of what the music itself sounds like. Critic Chuck Eddy's *Stairway to Hell* compendium goes so far as to include Miles Davis's *Live Evil* as one of "The 500 Best Heavy Metal Albums in the Universe," in with records by Metallica, Guns N' Roses, and, inescapably, Led Zeppelin. The origins of the genre are usually traced back to the Steppenwolf song "Born to Be Wild" (1968), with its celebration of "*heavy metal thunder,*" although other histories document the influences of Iron Butterfly, Vanilla Fudge, Cream, the Who, Jimi Hendrix, the Yardbirds, and the pioneering distorted guitar chords heard in the Kinks' "You Really Got Me" and "All Day and All of the Night" (both 1964). The very loud and sometimes deliberately primitive "acid rock" of the late 1960s, including the work of Blue Cheer, the Stooges, and the MC5 (Motor City 5), is also factored into some accounts. Of all the names linked to heavy metal's inception, it's notable that session man Jimmy Page played for two (the Kinks and the Who), was an official member of one (the Yardbirds), and that Led Zeppelin shared bills with two more (Iron Butterfly and Vanilla Fudge). Categorizing any music as heavy metal was perhaps no more than a convenient shorthand for fans and writers facing an expansive range of young people's pop music from 1965 onward—a way to distinguish it from the sophisticated harmonies of the Beatles and the Beach Boys, the acoustic introspections of Bob Dylan and Donovan, the soulful grooves of James Brown and Marvin Gaye, the ebullient melodicism of the Supremes and the Four Tops, the country-flavored craft of Creedence Clearwater Revival and the Band, or the bubblegum confections of the Archies, the Monkees, or the Ohio Express.

The common denominators of heavy metal are distorted electric guitars, keening vocals, and a powerful rhythmic base, which would certainly encompass the typical Led Zeppelin tune. But the popular Zeppelin numbers "Your Time Is Gonna Come," "Going to California," and "All My Love" can't qualify by these standards. Conversely, the Rolling Stones' "Gimme Shelter" meets the metal criteria, as do David Bowie's "Panic in Detroit"; Stevie Ray Vaughan's "Change It"; Funkadelic's "Mommy, What's a Funkadelic?"; Michael Jackson's "Beat It"; the Ramones' "Blitzkrieg Bop"; and Pantera's "Cemetery Gates." Heavy metal has changed over the decades, too: In 1971, it meant Alice Cooper and Mountain; in 1978 it meant Van Halen and UFO; by 1987 it was Exodus and Megadeth; in 1995 it was Nine Inch Nails and Marilyn Manson; by 2010 it was Converge, Mastodon, and

BBC Sessions was a successful 1998 release of the band's live radio appearances.

Author's Collection

Every Time I Die. Possibly the one constant in heavy metal is that most of its musicians are white males with very long hair.

Where Led Zeppelin fits in with any of these, let alone with Motörhead, Kiss, Godflesh, Venom, Judas Priest, or Iron Maiden, is the crucial question. Each successive generation of heavy metal artists seemed to take one element of a prior group's material and emphasize it, such that every few years someone emerged who looked and sounded like a cartoon version of someone else: louder, darker, faster, and more debased, but no less derivative. Who was Marilyn Manson if not Alice Cooper updated for the 1990s? Who did Guns N' Roses resemble more than a souped-up Aerosmith? In a mid-'70s *Rolling Stone* essay, Lester Bangs reduced Black Sabbath to a "sub-Zeppelin kozmic behemoth." The point is that, *pace* Page, Plant, and Jones, every heavy metal band from 1970 onward was consciously or unconsciously inspired by the Led Zeppelin of 1969–71. Rock author Charles

Shaar Murray has written that Jimmy Page and Zeppelin "professionalized" the hard electric blues timbres explored more haphazardly by Cream or Jimi Hendrix, and if by this he means that Page patented the sonic formula for the group's loudest and most propulsive riffs ("Communication Breakdown," "How Many More Times," "Whole Lotta Love," "Heartbreaker," "Immigrant Song," "Black Dog," et al), then there is no question that the patent was copied by a great many performers, among them the certifiably metallic.

In today's digitized, atomized music universe, the heavy metal appellation is largely obsolete, even after being broken up into subunits like death metal, speed metal, grindcore, and nu-metal. As with the "plagiarist" slur, calling Led Zeppelin a metal group is as indicative of the listener as the listened. To someone raised on the bright, catchy rock songs of the early British Invasion, Led Zeppelin was heavy metal; to a Deadhead, a New Waver, or a spandex-clad headbanger, they were hard rock; to rappers and hip-hoppers they might be an oldies act. Most remaining music retailers today find Led Zeppelin CDs between Lenny Kravitz and John Lennon in the mainstream "Rock / Pop" shelves, while their immediate followers and rivals Black Sabbath go in with Biohazard and Cannibal Corpse in the narrower "metal" aisle. In the family tree of rock genealogy, Led Zeppelin is at the root of several branches. Ultimately, Zeppelin began to transcend their characterization as a mere metal band only a few years into their active career and to an even greater degree thereafter, when critics and fans were forced to admit that their legacy had forever pervaded the whole field of rock 'n' roll.

Mama, Let Me Pump Your Gas: Led Zeppelin as Cock Rock

One of the more heated Led Zeppelin debates stems from their lyrical and visual representations of male and female identities. The term *cock rock* emerged out of the feminist movement in the 1970s, as progressive and newly politicized women (and men) began to question the traditional gender roles portrayed everywhere from classic novels and paintings to television and pop music. During the Rolling Stones' 1972 North American tour, handmade flyers decrying the Stones' swaggering masculinity were distributed among concertgoers, as covered by writer Terry Southern: "If you are male," the broadsheets read, "this concert is yours. . . . The Stones are tough men—hard and powerful. They're the kind of men we're supposed to imitate, never crying, always strong, keeping women in their place (under our thumbs). In Vietnam, to save honor (which means preserving our manhood), our brothers have killed and raped millions of people in the name of this ideal. . . . We resent the image the Stones present to males as examples we should imitate. . . ." In 1978, British critics Simon Frith and Angela McRobbie's article "Rock and Sexuality" was published in the book *On Record: Rock, Pop and the Written Word*, where they named Mick Jagger, the Who's Roger Daltrey, and Zeppelin's Robert Plant as prime exponents of the style: "Cock rock performers are aggressive, dominating, and boastful, and they constantly seek to remind the audience of their prowess, their control. . . . In these performances mikes and guitars are phallic symbols; the music is loud, rhythmically insistent, built around techniques of arousal and climax; the lyrics are assertive and arrogant, though the exact words are less significant than the vocal styles involved, the shouting and the screaming."

As much as they embodied personas as long-haired, dope-smoking outlaws, male rock stars of the 1960s and 1970s were no advocates of Women's Liberation, and the cock rock charge was an important corrective to their supposedly "revolutionary" values. Many Led Zeppelin songs—"Dazed and Confused," "Your Time Is Gonna Come," "How Many More Times," "Heartbreaker," "Living Loving Maid (She's Just a Woman)," "The Lemon Song," "Since I've Been Loving You," "Black Dog," "Custard Pie," "Trampled Underfoot," and others—depict women as crudely and as chauvinistically as any leering hard-hat or patronizing business executive of the same time. Likewise, the sexual or martial boasting of "Good Times Bad Times," "Whole Lotta Love," "Ramble On," "Immigrant Song," and "No Quarter" cast the singer and his ensemble as conquering, untamable bad boys never to be tied down by any domestic conventions. Add to these the live performances of the band, their amplifiers cranked, their shirts open, and their pants bulging, and Led Zeppelin does seem like a prime example of cock rock at its hardest, loudest, and most offensive.

There are several reasons, if not excuses, for Zeppelin's macho exaggerations. Given that the band was an all-male act of individuals in their early to mid-twenties, of course there was bound to be a surfeit of testosterone flowing around onstage and in the studio. Many of their songs were taken directly or indirectly from blues or blues-rock antecedents, and the blues was rife with blaring declamations of male dominance and sexual power, Bo Diddley's "I'm a Man," Howlin' Wolf's "Back Door Man," B. B. King's "Ain't Nobody Home," Jimi Hendrix's "Stone Free," and Robert Johnson's "Traveling Riverside Blues" being only the most memorable examples. This posture itself was something of a façade, a way for otherwise poor and disenfranchised men to assert their authority over anyone at all, their wives and lovers often being the closest people they could turn to for validation. Blues-based music could reverse the received structures of male-female relationships, as it became the *men* who could sing of being done wrong by a cheating partner (e.g., "Your Time Is Gonna Come," "Black Dog"), or of being hopelessly, romantically in love with a woman who rejects their affection ("Dazed and Confused," "The Lemon Song"), an appealing pretense for rock stars who were themselves usually doing the cheating and rejecting. In time the bluesy brag would degenerate into the bathroom-wall dreck of Bon Jovi's "You Give Love a Bad Name," Mötley Crüe's "Looks That Kill," and AC/DC's "Let Me Put My Love into You."

The stark truth is that Led Zeppelin's cock rock—and that of most other rock 'n' roll bands of the period—was borne of the musicians' experiences in the real world of touring and giving shows. Male entertainers have always held special attractiveness to female followers, and the uninhibited years of the sexual revolution allowed them to take Dionysian advantage of this. Nubile young women came to their concerts, worked their way backstage, and convened at their hotels and barrooms; by Jimmy Page and Robert Plant especially, their attentions were taken for granted. Lyrics like those of "Living Loving Maid (She's Just a Woman)," though not deeply thought out, were accurate reflections of the players' feelings toward their most devoted admirers—the girls were at best disposable and at worst nuisances. Page's much-repeated remarks to journalist Ellen Sander in 1969 ("Girls come around and pose like starlets, teasing and acting haughty. . . . I haven't got time to deal with it") were, for better or worse, his summary of casual sex as an occupational hazard rather than an emotional commitment or personal responsibility. His approving reference to Aleister Crowley ("Crowley didn't have a very high opinion of women and I don't think he was wrong") is scarcely more sensitive. Writer and Zeppelin supporter Cameron Crowe, describing the real-life milieu that inspired his 2000 film *Almost Famous*, remembered how the 1970s rock 'n' rollers he covered regarded their female followers as "trinkets," and Bebe Buell, who had a fling with Page in 1974, overheard the guitarist say of her to Plant and Peter Grant, "She's not a coke whore," which other women around them presumably were. With such disdainful if not misogynistic impressions, it was inevitable that a jaded, imperial arrogance would seep into Led Zeppelin's music.

What the cock rock indictment significantly overlooks is that many women were Zeppelin fans, found the male musicians attractive, and responded to the sexual overtones of the songs as much as any boy or man buying the records or attending the concerts. Though Led Zeppelin had never been a teenybopper act of winsome youngsters like their contemporaries the Osmonds or the Bay City Rollers, teenyboppers had older sisters and in time grew up themselves, and chaste fantasies of doe-eyed Donny or Woody evolved into more explicit ones of sweaty Robert or mysterious

Jimmy. Cock rock worked both ways: the performers expressed it (Mick Jagger rode an inflatable oversize phallus during the Rolling Stones' 1975 US tour), and both sexes in the audience encouraged it. Though there were probably many women put off by Led Zeppelin's overt machismo and crushing rhythms, preferring the sensitive tones of a James Taylor or a Van Morrison, or instead identifying with the lyrics of a Joni Mitchell or a Carole King, there were still plenty happy to find in Zeppelin a larger-than-life eroticism the musicians could not help but convey. For a term intended as a rebuke, Zeppelin's "cock rock" was sometimes exactly what listeners wanted to see and hear.

Airwaves to Heaven: Led Zeppelin as AOR Band

The band was one, but not intentionally. The group's debut in 1968 was in part planned around the rise of "free-form" FM radio in North America, stations that broadcast music far removed from the sanctioned two-minute ditties of their AM rivals. In the 1960s the coolest FM outlets might play extended sides of jazzer Sun Ra, avant-gardist Captain Beefheart, or sitar virtuoso Ravi Shankar; or choose from among the best new tracks by Iron Butterfly, the Band, or Jimi Hendrix; it was these stations that the young baby boomers turned to when seeking out the most progressive sounds. FM came through in stereo, as well, adding a new dimension to the already expanding home sound systems proliferating in the basements, dorm rooms, and campus pubs of the era. At the time of Led Zeppelin's appearance such stations were considered "underground," but into the next decade the format was popular enough to be reconfigured into "Album-Oriented Radio" or "Album-Oriented Rock." "FM radio was just beginning to have a huge influence," John Paul Jones acknowledged of Zeppelin's initial marketing mediums. "They weren't afraid to play longer tracks or even whole albums. We went around to a lot of radio stations to plug the record." Publicist Danny Goldberg added that "rock stations like WCBN in Boston, KMET in LA, and KSAN in San Francisco really made Zeppelin very big, very fast."

AOR was both the expression and the basis of a music industry whose prime product had become the long-playing 33 -rpm record. Audiences were now affluent enough to afford the discs in large numbers, competing with (though not completely eliminating) the market for 45-rpm singles. Both rock artists and rock audiences came to revere the album format as a more personal or serious art, less constricted by the time and content regulations of AM, and the most important rock albums were compared to the most important novels, plays, or films of older generations. To Peter Grant and Led Zeppelin, AOR was the perfect complement to their strategy of album-only releases, where the quartet's AM-friendliest singles ("Communication Breakdown" or "Immigrant Song") were no more helpful to the bottom line than the longer album cuts featured on FM ("Dazed and Confused," "Stairway to Heaven," or "Kashmir").

But from the middle of the 1970s onward, AOR became synonymous with a smug and cynical business culture that was a natural product of rock's billion-dollar revenues. Staple AOR acts such as Fleetwood Mac and the Eagles were derided as spoiled prima donnas disconnected from the day-to-day lives of their middle-class fans, and fresh AOR additions like Boston, Styx, Journey, Kansas, and Supertramp seemed to have been specifically crafted for the highbrow pretensions of listeners raised on *Abbey Road, Dark Side of the Moon,* or *Tommy.* Drug-based corruption was endemic between record labels and disc jockeys, with cocaine replacing payola as the standard currency of greased palms; AOR playlists shrank to almost exclusively white rosters, the occasional exception being a song from Jimi Hendrix or Stevie Wonder (some called it Apartheid-Oriented Radio). "Through AOR," noted 1995's *Rolling Stone Encyclopedia of Rock & Roll,* "FM radio became almost as, and some would argue substantially more, conservative than the AM radio of the Sixties to which FM had been an alternative. . . . AOR music, which is now termed 'classic rock,' is played all the time because it's popular; it remains popular because it's played all the time."

As anyone who has listened to a local classic rock radio station for an hour or so will confirm, Led Zeppelin was an early pillar of AOR airplay and has been ever since. This was a good thing for the band while they were making records, but since their demise the prevalence of the fistful of Zeppelin cuts in heavy rotation on FM radio—"Whole Lotta Love," "Ramble On," "Black Dog," "Over the Hills and Far Away," and, notoriously, "Stairway to Heaven"—has misrepresented their overall canon and gotten them lumped them in with a range of other acts and tracks whose familiarity has muted their original appeal. Today the inescapable AOR classic "Stairway to Heaven" is reviled as much as it's revered, in company with the Who's "Won't Get Fooled Again," the Rolling Stones' "Jumpin' Jack Flash," AC/DC's "Back in Black," plus Boston, Styx, Kansas, Journey, Supertramp, Fleetwood Mac, and the Eagles. On their own, all of these are fine works and fine musicians whose continued fame is justified, but repeated ad infinitum on AOR they have suffered grievous overexposure. What began as a trade term subsequently became a derogatory epithet, and Led Zeppelin and other artists have been tarred by association.

A Minute Seems like a Lifetime: How "Classic Rock" Radio Represents Led Zeppelin

Since the early 1980s Album-Oriented Radio has been transformed into classic rock, a programming format devoted to the rock music of roughly 1966 to 1980—AOR frozen in time. Just as it was in the 1970s, Led Zeppelin has been prominent on classic rock stations, and the broadcasters have played a large part in the band's continued popularity with generations too young to remember them from their heyday. Whereas many of Zeppelin's onetime peers on the charts and tour circuits have been relegated to the oldies, "soft favorites," or "where are they now" categories (say, Three Dog Night, Paul Simon, Stealers Wheel, or Van Morrison), Zeppelin are thriving on classic rock stations, where the children and perhaps even grandchildren of their original fans can still catch their hits at all hours of the day. Because of classic rock radio, Led Zeppelin's posthumous releases, such as the box sets of 1990 and 1993, the *BBC Sessions* of 1997, and the *Mothership* collection of 2007, have all found ready markets. By maintaining Zeppelin's favored status on its airwaves (and offering syndicated shows like *Get the Led Out* and other Zep-focused program blocks), classic rock has been the group's best marketing vehicle for some thirty years.

Like the earlier AOR, however, classic rock broadcasting has tended to adhere to rigidly controlled selections of songs and an entrenched mythology that has had the unfortunate effect of making the music less and less interesting. Even Led Zeppelin's boosters admit that the band's place in the classic rock system has harmed the group as much as it has helped them: in his liner notes to the 1990 Zeppelin four-CD box set, critic Robert Palmer wrote, "The preponderance of 'Led Clones' on American FM radio, and continuing frequent airplay for the original recordings, have kept the band's legacy alive. They have also done our memories of the band a great disservice by carrying on as if 'Stairway to Heaven' and a few crunching, blues-based riff tunes . . . represented the entire scope of the Led Zeppelin heritage." As the years go on, defenders of Zeppelin have had to distinguish the true richness of classic rock, the genre, from its caricature in classic rock, the sales pitch.

Ironically, the initial attraction of classic rock was that most of its tunes had rarely been heard on the conventional AM stations and might thus be thought of as heavier or cooler than the happy pop hits of the 1970s or 1980s. Likewise, the advent of music video in the 1980s came as a garish contrast to the substance of rock 'n' roll's greatest decades of creativity and artistic freedom, as noted by Brad Tolinski in *Guitar World* in 1993: "Thanks to constant exposure on MTV, today's pop heroes somehow seem smaller, more disposable than their predecessors. But pre-MTV bands like Queen, the original Kiss, and Led Zep have retained a powerful mystique. Unlike today's overexposed supergroups, those Classic bands were rarely captured on film, and when they were, they left distant, grainy images which have themselves taken on an almost mythic power." But by 2010 even the best-loved tracks by Queen, the original Kiss, and Led Zep had been almost exhausted by continuous airplay on classic rock radio, especially under an enforced regimen that has shrunk their catalogues (and those of other classic rock stalwarts like Pink Floyd, Lynryd Skynyrd, and Steve Miller) to but a fraction of their depth.

Disc jockey Jon Shap of WKOT in Illinois, a Zeppelin lover who asserts that "Led Zeppelin will always have a place on classic rock radio," nonetheless harbors reservations over they way the band are covered on his own and other stations. "Without a doubt, 'Stairway' and 'Whole Lotta Love' are on their own overplay level. . . . Air Talent (DJs) really have *no* freedom [as to] what goes on the air. Everything is picked ahead of time by the programming department and then scheduled by a computer. Some programmers base their playlists on research done with target listeners, or test songs on how quickly listeners recognize them. Other programmers are told what to play by consultants, and check with their consultants for everything! It's nuts!" One on-air personality confesses anonymously that he breaks ranks by playing the Led Zeppelin drum solo "Moby Dick" every year on the anniversary of John Bonham's death. Many classic rock outlets now cater to a middle-aged male audience, with DJs telling dirty jokes and cueing up advertisements for power tools and military recruiters between spinning forty-year-old anthems of personal and social liberation. If you want to hear a Led Zeppelin song on the radio, tune to classic rock—if you want to really hear Led Zeppelin, turn to your own collection.

Takin' Home My Hard-Earned Pay: Led Zeppelin as Corporate Rock

Like pornography, corporate rock is something hard to define—but you know it when you hear it. The phrase cropped up orally and in print around the time of the punk rebellion of 1976–79, although by the late '60s some acts, including Led Zeppelin, had their countercultural bona fides questioned by the most politically vociferous segments of the youth movement. The disco craze of the late 1970s, driven by anonymous dancers, DJs, and club hits like Sister Sledge's "We Are Family" and the Commodores' "Brick House," likewise made four- or five-man collections of millionaire hippies look much less populist than they thought themselves to be.

Corporate rock refers to the music made by artists so commercial, so conspicuously rich, or with such confident label promotion, that its spontaneity, humanity, and air of social menace have been all but suppressed. Some critics have written off nearly every pre-punk pop record of the decade as corporate rock, as the *New York Times*'s Howard Hampton did in 2001:

> Something happened to rock music in the 1970s that it has never quite recovered from: the sound congealed into a dense, ponderous and soporific mass. . . . Where playfulness, humor, chaotic weirdness and wayward passion had reigned supreme, now even excess and outrage came to seem stage-managed by an invisible bureaucracy of FM station consultants, management firms, technocrat producers, and record company apparatchiks. . . . FM rock's infamous disco-bashing campaign was an understandably panicked, phobic reaction, given how insular rock culture had become by that point.

The first of corporate rock's prime suspects might include the flamboyant Elton John, the gaudy Queen, the faceless Doobie Brothers, the imitative Blue Öyster Cult, or the arena demagogue Ted Nugent. Others might cite the proliferation of extravagant artist-owned record companies (the Beatles' Apple, the Rolling Stones' Rolling Stones, and Zeppelin's Swan Song) or the prominence of oversold live albums like Peter Frampton's *Frampton Comes Alive*, Kiss's *Alive!* and Cheap Trick's *At Budokan* as crucial indicators of corporate rock's arrival.

Along with their manager Peter Grant, the men of Led Zeppelin earned a lot of money for themselves (so much that they could only keep it by going into tax exile); they were treated like royalty by industry personnel; and their records and promo paraphernalia turned a neat profit for their financial backers, so by that definition the band was certainly corporate rock. Of course, no performers would ever identify themselves as such, and the term *corporate rock* is purely a derogatory one that can be thrown at anybody deemed too popular or successful for the thrower's liking. Such an epithet also disregards the very real struggle and hard work that a group like Led Zeppelin underwent before getting to their vast stadium shows and decadent private jets of later in their career. A more judicious application of the label would be to the ready-made superstars whose airplay and revenue piled up a little too fast and more easily than their music warranted: Toto, REO Speedwagon, Night Ranger, Foreigner, Meat Loaf. The whiff of corporate rock was also strong off of works heavily produced, cowritten, or otherwise doctored by employees or supervisors of the named artist: Bryan Adams, Bon Jovi, Carly Simon, latter-day Aerosmith, and the antiseptic Starship, whose '80s hit "We Built This City" must surely be liable in some kind of corporate rock class-action suit. Next to these, Led Zeppelin were no more than a mom 'n' pop operation dispensing handcrafted merchandise at honest prices.

Payin' Your Bills: Led Zeppelin Music Licensed for Use in Advertisements or Films

Because the surviving members, together with the heirs of John Bonham and Peter Grant, continue to own the rights to Led Zeppelin's back catalogue and its associated trademarks (as stamped on merchandise like clothing or posters), the band has not suffered the indignities of having their name, songs, or likenesses used to promote an incongruous or tacky line of other products without their consent. (In the early 1980s Robert Plant sold his financial stake in prospective sales of the original Zeppelin albums, but as co-songwriter he continues to have a share in publishing and other revenues.) The retention of Led Zeppelin's mystical or occult aura over almost four decades has been due at least in part to Grant's earliest decisions not to plaster the quartet's images in every conceivable medium, as he told *Billboard* magazine in 1979: "One of the keys to Zeppelin's longevity is that its appearances have been well-spaced, preventing overexposure." As the policy was kept up following Bonham's death and the group's breakup in 1980, Led Zeppelin have enjoyed an untouchable remoteness shared by few artists from their time.

Some Zeppelin songs have been heard in movies, but only after determined (and costly) negotiation by the producers. "Kashmir" was used in 1979's *Fast Times at Ridgemont High*, written for the screen by Zeppelin admirer Cameron Crowe, and Crowe's *Almost Famous* of 2000 used "That's the Way," "Misty Mountain Hop," "The Rain Song," "Bron-yr-Aur," and "Tangerine." *School of Rock* from 2003 featured "Immigrant Song," as did 2007's *Shrek the Third*, and the 2003 documentary *The Mayor of the Sunset Strip* sounded "Sick Again." *School of Rock* got to use Zeppelin music only after its star, Jack Black, filmed his own humble request to "the Gods of Rock" and had it shown to Page, Plant, and Jones. "Come with Me," Jimmy Page and Puff Daddy's rewrite of "Kashmir," made it to the soundtrack of the 1998 blockbuster *Godzilla*, although in 1994 Page and Robert Plant had sued the producers of the film *Bad Lieutenant* to remove "Signifying Rapper," an unauthorized track also based on "Kashmir," from the movie. More Zeppelin songs have been used in films and TV shows from outside the English-speaking market (the same way American or British movie stars will act in advertisements shown only in Japan), and in 2001 Warner Brothers released a limited-edition three-CD set of songs aimed at soundtrack programmers and licensing consultants. Among the tracks were "Stairway to Heaven" and "Whole Lotta Love." Although in the case of Led Zeppelin the artists themselves have the final say in whether or not the numbers can be sold, they are advised by managers and agents who take into consideration the intended use of the material (timed as a "needle drop" that usually does not capture the entire song), the potential audience, and the prospective fee.

As a session man in the mid-1960s Page almost certainly played on some commercial jingles and industrial film soundtracks, and his recollections of accompanying saxophonist Tubby Hayes link him to Hayes's confirmed work for Cadbury and Hush Puppies in this vein. In the Yardbirds he contributed to the band's version of "Over Under Sideways Down" adapted to a jingle for the Great Shakes soft drink (*"Any place can be a soda fountain now, with Great Shakes, new Great Shakes. . . ."*). A generic version of "Whole Lotta Love," performed by the Collective Consciousness Society, was for many years the theme song of the popular British music show *Top of the Pops*. During the Zeppelin years and after, members of the group were seen in print advertisements endorsing musical instruments and accessories, and Page has allowed the Gibson guitar company to issue "signature" models designed to resemble his personal Les Pauls and double-neck. The guitars signed and inspected by Page himself have retailed for as much as $30,000. Jimmy Page has also been immortalized in three mass-produced plastic figurines that

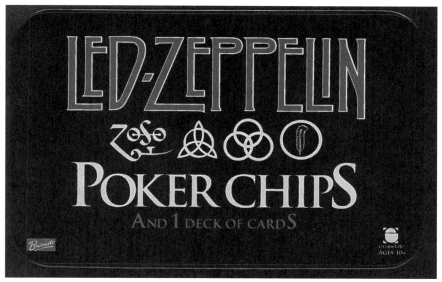

Over the years, the Zeppelin trademarks have been licensed for use on a variety of products.   *Courtesy of Len Ward / The Rad Zone*

depict him in his dragon, poppy, and SS suits of 1975 and '77 (keep him away from Barbie and Strawberry Shortcake). In the 1980s Robert Plant's solo hit "Tall Cool One" was used in a Coke TV ad that concluded with the singer guzzling a bottle of the Real Thing, probably not the coke he was used to, and in 2002 excerpts from "Rock and Roll" were heard in a North American TV spot for Cadillac cars, a move that drew much publicity and some criticism. A short-lived Hard Rock theme park in Myrtle Beach, South Carolina, took thrill-seekers on "Led Zeppelin—the Ride," a roller-coaster attraction set to the screams and stutters of "Whole Lotta Love." Since 2007 Led Zeppelin music has been sold and available for download over the Internet, although Page, Plant, and John Paul Jones have resisted the offers to incorporate the catalogue into such popular video games as *Guitar Hero* and *Rock Band*.

Judged against the legacy of some of their contemporaries, like the Beatles, the Rolling Stones, Jimi Hendrix, and the Who, Led Zeppelin's artistic integrity has been less sullied by commercialism or embarrassing appropriation into cheesy mediums. Absolut vodka has used classic portraits of John Lennon, Miles Davis, and David Bowie in its ads; the Stones' "Start Me Up" was used to announce the debut of the Windows 95 computer program; Deep Purple had their biggest hit bastardized into Burger King's "Smoke on the Whopper"; and Kiss have become more brand than band, putting their logo on everything from condoms to credit cards to caskets. As the years go on, however, some of the opposition to overexposure that has always set Zeppelin apart may be mooted by forty years of public demand and acceptance of their worldwide familiarity, and we may see more officially licensed clothes, art, and collectibles put out to satisfy the consumer appetites of the group's millions of fans.

Coda: How Led Zeppelin Stayed So Popular So Long After They Broke Up

The frank answer may be that they are still popular *because* they broke up. During the last half of the 1970s Zeppelin had become among the most famous and successful rock 'n' roll acts in the world, racking up number one albums and sold-out concerts around the globe, but they were nonetheless overshadowed by older bands like the Rolling Stones, the Who, and the Grateful Dead; individual superstars like Elton John and David Bowie; and fresh megasellers like Peter Frampton, the Bee Gees, and Queen. In April 1981, only a few months after John Bonham's death and the band's official split, Robert Plant played a series of Honeydrippers shows in small British venues, and was asked by a local interviewer if Led Zeppelin would forever be an "albatross" for him and the remaining members of the group. "It wasn't like the Beatles," he answered. "They encompassed everything, really . . . whereas [Led Zeppelin] had a sort of niche. So whatever happens . . . I don't think it can happen really because there are loads of bands coming along and taking the majority of our audience away already." Little did he know.

Over the next decade it gradually emerged that Led Zeppelin, despite one-off reunions in 1985 and 1988, was indeed gone for good. Meanwhile, the proliferation of heavy metal and hard rock bands claiming Zeppelin as a prime influence, Zeppelin's ongoing deification by classic rock radio, the transformation of the music industry by the compact disc, and the release of Stephen Davis's best-selling tell-all *Hammer of the Gods* breathed surprising new life into what a few years before had been reviled as a dinosaur act. Contrary to Robert Plant's expectations, Led Zeppelin actually rose in stature to become like the Beatles—both to the record-buying public as an undisputed giant of rock's glorious past, and to Plant, Jimmy Page, and John Paul Jones, as a peak achievement they would always have to account for. Between 1990 and 1999 some five million copies of *Houses of the Holy* were sold in the United States, along with six million copies of *Led Zeppelin II*, numbers to delight any contemporary group, let alone one whose records were twenty years old. Though the foursome's own visual and musical history was of course a major factor in this, the relative diminution of their erstwhile competitors had also played a part.

Led Zeppelin are one of the very few big-name music acts whose retirement has been a real one. The Rolling Stones, whose first records came out in 1964, have kept going beyond the death of their founder Brian Jones in 1969, the departure of Jones's replacement Mick Taylor in 1974, and the resignation of original bassist Bill Wyman in 1993, and the legendary quintet now exists as a four-piece band, with bass player Daryl Jones demoted to auxiliary status. Pink Floyd kept going despite bassist and lyricist Roger Waters's acrimonious break in the early 1980s, the group centered around guitarist David Gilmour and drummer Nick Mason, with an extensive cast of supporting players. Like Led Zeppelin, the Who also lost their drummer (in 1978), but replaced Keith Moon with Kenney Jones, later Jones with Zak Starkey, and singer and guitarist Roger Daltrey and Pete Townshend continue to perform under the name even after the death of bassist John Entwistle in 2002. The Doors should have been absolutely defunct after the death of singer Jim Morrison in 1971—and were for a long time—but in the early 2000s keyboardist Ray Manzarek and guitarist Robbie Krieger began an ill-advised revival with Ian Astbury of the Cult taking Morrison's place and original drummer John Densmore denouncing the affair from the sidelines.

The pioneering glam-shock rockers Kiss reunited with costumes and makeup to spectacular effect in 1997, but the novelty wore off as guitarist Ace Frehley and drummer Peter Criss were once again given walking papers, and their parts and trademark images have been taken up by younger musicians; they are currently back on the casino circuit. The Eagles, who had gone through several personnel changes while they were a productive band in the 1970s, put on a lucrative reunion in 1994 (the *Hell Freezes Over* album and tour), but, like the Rolling Stones, are now down to four members following guitarist Don Felder's rejection of a deal that put him in a subordinate position to lead vocalists Don Henley and Glenn Frey. AC/DC, like Led Zeppelin, lost a key member to overindulgence in 1980 (singer and lyricist Bon Scott), but they soon found Brian Johnson to take his place at the microphone, and core members Malcolm and Angus Young have also toured and recorded with a variety of drummers and bassists. Lynyrd Skynyrd suffered a devastating plane crash that claimed the life of vocalist-wordsmith Ronnie Van Zant, guitarist Steve Gaines, and backing vocalist Cassie Gaines in 1977, but the band reformed in 1990 (with Van Zant's younger brother Johnny filling his spot) and have been a viable touring draw ever since, particularly in the US heartland. Heavy metalers Judas Priest, Metallica, and Mötley Crüe have all carried on with voluntary and involuntary lineup changes.

Without any premature deaths on their records, Zeppelin's closest English rivals, Black Sabbath and Deep Purple, have each gone through a bewildering roster of new, old, and new-old players, staging occasional reunions before dissolving once again, making them rich subjects for rock genealogists and satirists. Van Halen booted the flamboyant vocalist David Lee Roth in the 1980s, carried on successfully with Sammy Hagar for several years, tried Extreme front man Gary Cherone for one album, and have lately regrouped with Roth but inexplicably substituted guitar hero Eddie Van Halen's young son Wolfgang for original bassist Mike Anthony. The Beach Boys, Creedence Clearwater Revival, the Band, the Animals, and Sly and the Family Stone have disintegrated into various competing sects of one or two founding members and whatever backup players can approximate the remainder, often with dire and legally contentious results. Famously iconoclastic punk rockers the Sex Pistols, whose brief career of 1975–78 was one of rock 'n' roll's most influential, launched their own "Filthy Lucre" comeback in 1996 and have put on subsequent gigs under the Sex Pistols name, Glen Matlock taking over from the deceased Sid Vicious who had himself been dropped into Matlock's bass role. Modern recording technology enabled even the Beatles to make a long-awaited reunion in 1995, augmenting two rough demo tapes by the late John Lennon, "Real Love" and "Free as a Bird," with the voices and instrumentation of Paul McCartney, George Harrison, and Ringo Starr.

Led Zeppelin stand out from all these. The closest to a continued revival staged by the band have been the Page and Plant concert tours of 1995-96 and 1998, along with the duo's *No Quarter* and *Walking into Clarksdale* albums of 1994 and 1998; with John Paul Jones and John Bonham's son Jason, a band billed as Led Zeppelin have played at the Atlantic Records fortieth-anniversary show in 1988, the Rock and Roll Hall of Fame induction in 1995, and at London's O2 arena in 2007. In 1986 some fumbled private jams between Jimmy Page, Robert Plant, John Paul Jones, and drummer Tony Thompson took place in England (after an unimpressive performance together at 1985's Live Aid in Philadelphia), but personal and health issues, and Thompson's injury in a car accident, brought this to a quick close. While Page has over the years made known a desire to participate in a permanent or semi-permanent Zeppelin reunion, and Jones has also expressed a willingness to join, the reluctance of Plant to be involved would seem to have squashed any possibility of such a project.

However disappointing the lack of a full-fledged resuscitation might be to some of Led Zeppelin's musicians and millions of the group's fans, much of the Zeppelin legend rests on their tragically shortened biography. Had John Bonham not died in 1980, or had he been soon replaced with another drummer, the quartet's most powerful music would already have been ten years old or more and they might have declined into self-parody—as it was, their last two years of playing and recording are already regarded as their weakest—or have become merely irrelevant. While titans like the Rolling Stones, Metallica, or the Eagles might continue to top charts and fill stadiums, even their most loyal fans quietly concede that their contemporary incarnations "aren't the same" and speculate wistfully about seeing them in better (thinner, younger, cheaper, more dangerous) days. Something similar would have happened to Led Zeppelin post-1980. Premature show business deaths have often been called good career moves by the cynical (think of James Dean, Marilyn Monroe, Hank Williams, Buddy Holly, or Zeppelin's primordial inspiration Robert Johnson), but beyond the human loss of Bonham as friend, son, brother, husband, and father is the stark fact that his irreplaceable passing probably helped rather than hurt Led Zeppelin's long-term popularity.

Everything Still Turns to Gold: Led Zeppelin's Lasting Legacy to Popular Culture

Many rock historians have argued that, after the ascendancy of Bob Dylan and the Beatles-led British Invasion in the mid-1960s, the most important development in the genre was the punk explosion of the later '70s, which finally shattered the complacency of the previous ten years' run of super-groups, heavy metal, cock rock, and AOR bands. Robert Palmer wrote in 1983 that "the most popular of the younger groups and soloists were simply *recycling* the Sixties with an added layer of studio sheen that fooled a surprisingly large number of fans, kids and otherwise, into thinking they were hearing something new. There wasn't much rock & roll around that was really worthy of the name—not until 1976 or so." In that light, Led Zeppelin, in spite of their mammoth stadium concerts and string of multimillion-selling albums, were only a footnote to a broader story.

The most significant innovations in pop music during the later twentieth century predated Led Zeppelin: self-contained acts whose personnel both wrote and performed their own music; the shift to LPs from 45s as the medium's favored format; introspective or "poetic" lyrics that transcended the conventions of boy-meets-girl; and artists incorporating into their own work a range of technical advances in sound recording. Zeppelin *capitalized* on these changes to powerful effect, to be sure, and accelerated their influence throughout the industry, but the band were not the ones who instigated them. Led Zeppelin's true impact across the field of commercial entertainment came in three fundamental breakthroughs.

With the trademark heavy guitar riffs of their first four albums—"Dazed and Confused," "Communication Breakdown," "Whole Lotta Love," "Heartbreaker," "Immigrant Song," "Black Dog," and "Rock and Roll"—Led Zeppelin completed the music's transition from pop to rock, where the sonic weight of the records became as much a part of the listening experience as any appreciation of the words or the tunes. Jimmy Page's guitars on these tracks are as percussive as they are melodic, and at times with John Paul Jones's and John Bonham's rhythm section the three sound like a single relentless timekeeping device: music as machine. Zeppelin's attack was not the raw abandon "super hooligan music" Page had envisioned, but a precisely controlled sound whose very meticulousness gave it all the more impact.

Although other rock 'n' rollers had used the studio or outboard effects as instruments unto themselves (e.g., the Beatles with *Sgt. Pepper*, the Rolling Stones with the fuzz-boxed intro to "Satisfaction," plus Jimi Hendrix, the Who, and Cream), it was Led Zeppelin who made the effects do more of the

Mothership, released in 2007, coincided with the historic Zeppelin reunion show in London.
Author's Collection

work, taking a minimum of harmonic variation and amplifying it into something as portentous as *Led Zeppelin II*. "[I]t seems as if it's just one especially heavy song extended over the space of two whole sides," ran *Rolling Stone*'s review of the 1969 sophomore disc, a more insightful observation than the writer likely knew. The band have many memorable songs, but they tend to be classics of performance and audio presentation more than of composition; transcribed as sheet music, "How Many More Times" or "Bring It On Home" don't feature particularly brilliant arrangements or clever rhyme schemes. The unique acoustics of "Black Dog," "When the Levee Breaks," or "Hats Off to (Roy) Harper" are what define the cuts, not their underlying blues bases. Today the sheer sensory punch of popular music in all genres, with its intensities of loudness, terraced shifts in sound texture, and woofer-shredding bass frequencies, owes much to the formal experiments audible in Led Zeppelin. The difference is that modern pop is dependent on digitized recording equipment that boosts levels, edits takes, samples notes, and repeats rhythms at the push of a button, whereas the inhuman drive and force of Led Zeppelin's best material was created by four human beings playing to and off each other in real time. Even the deafening sound projection in contemporary movie theaters and the clarity and richness of television soundtracks can be indirectly attributed to the way Zeppelin changed the audience's expectations of volume, stereo dimensionality, and equalization. Love it or hate it, Led Zeppelin is one of the key shapers of the twenty-first century's postindustrial sonic environment.

The second landmark creditable to the quartet is in the earning potential of popular musicians. Of course, singers and instrumentalists could become rich before Led Zeppelin; Elvis Presley had moved into his palatial Graceland before the band had even formed. But until Zeppelin it was more common for young pop sensations to lose as much wealth as they made. Peter Grant's unyielding business savvy and Jimmy Page's oversight of all aspects of the Zeppelin empire established an artistic and financial control over the group's work that other acts—even those, like the Beatles and the Rolling Stones, who sold as many records and concert tickets—could only envy. Thus Page and his fabulous homes, John Bonham with his fleet of hot rods, and Robert Plant and John Paul Jones with their country estates became the benchmarks for how many entertainment dollars or pounds could be retained by the performers themselves, not just their agents, handlers, promoters, and label executives. "All the deals I did with [lighting company] Showco and the traveling and things like the deal I got to use the *Starship* . . . It all protected the profits," Grant summed up to Dave Lewis. "I'm not saying we didn't spend a lot individually because we all did, but as for the overall earnings we played it clever for a very long time." In an decade when other rock and soul stars might still be forced into bankruptcy (Marvin Gaye in 1978, Tom Petty in 1979, to name two), the four players of Led Zeppelin and their manager enjoyed the security of knowing that every Zeppelin album, poster, or arena seat purchased anywhere in the world meant more money in their bank accounts. Today Metallica, U2, Celine Dion, Madonna and others in the same stratospheric bracket are worth millions in part because of the business blueprint laid out by Led Zeppelin, whereby the talent rather than the backstage support take in the biggest slice of any transaction conducted in their name.

Finally, Led Zeppelin's most distinctive cultural legacy is in the way they exemplified the mythology of rock music itself. The dry ice and lasers of their concerts, the arcane imagery of their album covers, the instrumental virtuosity and unknowable lyrics of their greatest songs, the whispered stories of the musicians' private lives: all of these have defined the ideals of rock stardom for at least two generations. Though others have had a comparable mythology thrust upon them—Elvis the King, the Beatles the Fab Four, Dylan the Protest Bard, the Rolling Stones as the World's Greatest Rock 'n' Roll Band—they were usually too modest, or their work was too erratic, to fully go along with it. Zeppelin was the exception. They willingly played *up* to their public image, or at least made little effort to disown it, and thus their music and performances took on the majesty and drama that is easily parodied in lesser bands but which was hugely impressive to the rock audience of the 1970s and is still striking today. As pretentious or as overblown as Zeppelin's material or stage moves might appear in our contemporary media-glutted, irony-saturated climate, only the most self-conscious, tone-deaf, or perversely hip listener can fail to be moved by them.

Led Zeppelin's working life coincided with the climactic wave of rock 'n' roll as a social phenomenon, spanning the middle of the 1960s to the late 1970s. As were many of their peers, rivals, and inspirations, the four players in the group were taken aback to encounter the reception they did. They had not imagined that their music would become a giant business taking them around the world while they became idolized as a mass-marketed secular religion for millions of people. They never guessed that ballads or boogies dashed off in an hour or two would become hymnal observances four decades later, or that concerts they barely remember giving would be renowned as generational landmarks of community and ritual, or that their youthful indiscretions and misadventures would be upheld as timeless symbols of glamour, power, and decadence. For this reason some of the improvised or offhand gestures they made while members of Zeppelin have only been revealed as such long afterward; to different degrees the middle-aged Jimmy Page, Robert Plant, and John Paul Jones have been candid in explaining musical techniques, backstage issues, and creative muses that fans had assumed to be divinely (or diabolically) ordained. Other participants in their story, and outside researchers, have also been diligent in disabusing the public of its illusions as to what the quartet were really up to in the studio, on the stage, or on the *Starship*. Led Zeppelin's mythology, like that of the Beatles, Dylan, the Stones, et al, was really something projected onto them by an economically and demographically dominant audience that *wanted* its entertainment to be more heroic or more meaningful than its makers at first intended. Yet long after the artists and their constituencies have admitted to acting out a collective fantasy mere mortals could never fulfill, the fact remains that Led Zeppelin, in the grandeur of their songs, in the scale of their shows, and in the richness of their mystique, did more than anyone to bring the fantasy to life.

Selected Bibliography

In order to make *Led Zeppelin FAQ* the comprehensive work I had intended it to be, a very wide range of source material was consulted in researching the names, numbers, dates, addresses, titles, and quotations featured in its pages. Core texts in my research include the Dave Lewis compendia *A Celebration*, *Celebration II*, and *The Concert File*, as well as Mick Wall's *When Giants Walked the Earth*, Susan Fast's *In the Houses of the Holy*, and Jon Bream's *Whole Lotta Led Zeppelin*. Each of these is recommended for further reading.

However, to do Led Zeppelin justice I also took care to look further afield than the standard partisan studies of the group itself to consider general overviews of rock history, folk and blues music, guitar craft, the occult, the sex-and-drug cultural revolution, and other areas where the Zeppelin story is fit into a much wider perspective. Examples here would be Pamela Des Barres' *Let's Spend the Night Together* and *I'm with the Band*, Gary Herman's *Rock 'n' Roll Babylon*, Dave Marsh and Kevin Stein's *The Book of Rock Lists*, Francis X. King's *Witchcraft and Demonology*, Colin Larkin's *Virgin Encyclopedia of the Blues*, Robert Walser's *Running with the Devil*, and Michael Walker's *Laurel Canyon*.

As well, many journal interviews provided contemporary and historic anecdotes and quips from individuals from within and outside Led Zeppelin. Key magazines (printed and electronic) were *Rolling Stone*, *Guitar World*, *Goldmine*, and *Mojo*.

Finally, Internet sites ledzeppelin.com, royal-orleans.com, led-zeppelin. org, and ledzeppelin-database.com were frequently checked for the latest confirmed details of (and ongoing debates over) Zeppelin's discography, chronology, instrumentation, and itinerary.

Detailed information on various sources is indicated in this bibliography.

General Reference Works

Barry, Dave. *Dave Barry's Book of Bad Songs*. Kansas City, MO: Andrews and McMeel, 1997.

Bream, Jon. *Whole Lotta Led Zeppelin: The Illustrated History of the Heaviest Band of All Time*. Minneapolis: Voyageur Press, 2008.

Case, George. *Out of Our Heads: Rock 'n' Roll Before the Drugs Wore Off.* New York: Backbeat, 2010.

Coleman, Satis Naronna. *Songs of American Folks.* Freeport, NY: Books for Libraries Press, 1968.

Crowe, Cameron. *Led Zeppelin / Light and Shade* (Led Zeppelin Box Set Notes). New York: Atlantic Records, 1990.

Crowley, Aleister. *The Book of the Law.* York Beach, ME: Samuel Wiser, Inc., 1976.

Crowley, Aleister. *Magick in Theory and Practice.* Book Sales, 1992.

Dalton, David, ed. *The Rolling Stones: The First Twenty Years.* New York: Alfred A. Knopf, 1981.

Davis, Stephen. *Hammer of the Gods: The Led Zeppelin Saga.* New York: Ballantine, 1986.

Des Barres, Pamela. *Let's Spend the Night Together: Backstage Secrets of Rock Muses and Supergroupies.* Chicago: Chicago Review Press, 2008.

Fast, Susan. *In the Houses of the Holy: Led Zeppelin and the Power of Rock Music.* New York: Oxford University Press, 2001.

Godwin, Robert. *Led Zeppelin: The Press Reports.* Burlington, Ontario: Collector's Guide, 2003.

Herman, Gary. *Rock 'n' Roll Babylon.* London: Plexus, 1994.

King, Francis X. *Witchcraft and Demonology.* London: Hamlyn, 1987.

Klosterman, Chuck. *Chuck Klosterman IV: A Decade of Curious People and Dangerous Ideas.* New York: Scribner, 2006.

Kureishi, Hanif, and Jon Savage, eds. *The Faber Book of Pop.* London: Faber and Faber, 1995.

Larkin, Colin. *The Virgin Encyclopedia of the Blues.* London: Virgin in Association with Muze UK Ltd., 1998.

Larkin, Colin. *The Virgin Encyclopedia of Dance Music.* London: Virgin Books, 1998.

Lewis, Dave. *Led Zeppelin: A Celebration.* London: Omnibus, 2003.

Lewis, Dave. *Led Zeppelin: The Tight but Loose Files—Celebration II.* London: Omnibus, 2003.

Lewis, Dave, and Simon Pallett. *Led Zeppelin: The Concert File.* London: Omnibus, 2005.

Loder, Kurt. *The Rolling Stone Interviews: The 1980s.* New York: St. Martin's Press, 1989.

Lomax, Alan. *The Folk Songs of North America in the English Language.* Garden City, NJ: Doubleday, 1960.

Marcus, Greil. *Like a Rolling Stone: Bob Dylan at the Crossroads.* New York: Public Affairs, 2005.

Marsh, Dave, and Kevin Stein. *The Book of Rock Lists.* New York: Dell, 1984.

Menn, Don. *Secrets of the Masters: Conversations with 40 Great Guitar Players.* San Francisco: GPI Books, 1992.

Miller, Jim, ed. *The Rolling Stone Illustrated History of Rock & Roll.* New York: Random House, 1976.

Palmer, Robert. *Led Zeppelin: The Music* (Led Zeppelin Box Set Notes). New York: Atlantic Records, 1990.

Palmer, Robert. *The Rolling Stones.* Garden City, NJ: Doubleday, 1983.

Perry, Tim, and Ed Glinert. *Fodor's Rock & Roll Traveler USA.* New York: Fodor's Travel Publications, 1996.

Robson, Peter. *The Devil's Own.* New York: Ace, 1969.

Romanowski, Patricia, and Holly George-Warren, eds. *The New Rolling Stone Encyclopedia of Rock & Roll.* New York: Fireside, 1995.

Rosen, Steven. *Black Sabbath.* London: Sanctuary, 2002.

Shadwick, Keith. *Led Zeppelin: The Story of a Band and Their Music, 1968–1980.* San Francisco: Backbeat, 2005.

Sherman, Dale. *Urban Legends of Rock & Roll (You Never Can Tell).* Burlington, Ontario: Collector's Guide, 2003.

Silber, Irwin. *Folksinger's Workbook.* New York: Oak Publications, 1973.

Simpson, Claude M. *The British Broadside Ballad and Its Music.* New Brunswick, NJ: Rutgers University Press, 1966.

Spence, Lewis. *An Encyclopedia of Occultism.* New Hyde Park, NY: University Books, 1960.

Spence, Lewis. *The Magic Arts in Celtic Britain.* Mineola, NY: Dover Publications, 1999.

Walker, Michael. *Laurel Canyon: The Inside Story of Rock and Roll's Legendary Neighborhood.* New York: Faber and Faber, 2006.

Wall, Mick. *When Giants Walked the Earth: A Biography of Led Zeppelin.* London: Orion Press, 2008.

Walser, Robert. *Running with the Devil: Power, Gender, and Madness in Heavy Metal Music.* Hanover: Wesleyan University Press, 1993.

Wyman, Bill. *Rolling with the Stones.* New York: Dorling Kindersley, 2002.

Yorke, Ritchie. *Led Zeppelin: The Definitive Biography.* Novato, CA: Underwood-Miller, 1993.

Memoirs and Biographies

Bockris, Victor. *Keith Richards: The Biography.* New York: Poseidon Press, 1992.

Booth, Martin. *A Magic Life: The Biography of Aleister Crowley.* London: Hodder & Stoughton, 2000.

Buell, Bebe, with Victor Bockris. *Rebel Heart: An American Rock 'n' Roll Journey.* New York: St. Martin's Press, 2001.

Case, George. *Jimmy Page: Magus, Musician, Man: An Unauthorized Biography.* New York: Backbeat, 2009.

Clapton, Eric. *Clapton: The Autobiography.* New York: Broadway Books, 2007.

Cole, Richard, with Richard Trubo. *Stairway to Heaven: Led Zeppelin Uncensored.* New York: Harper Collins, 1992.

Crowe, Cameron. *Almost Famous* (Screenplay). London: Faber and Faber, 2000.

Des Barres, Pamela. *I'm with the Band: Confessions of a Groupie* (Updated Edition). Chicago: Chicago Review Press, 2005.

Des Barres, Pamela. *Take Another Little Piece of My Heart: A Groupie Grows Up.* New York: William Morrow, 1992.

Giuliano, Geoffrey. *Behind Blue Eyes: The Life of Pete Townshend.* New York: Dutton, 1996.

Goldberg, Danny. *Bumping into Geniuses: My Life in the Rock and Roll Business.* New York: Gotham Books, 2008.

James, Catherine. *Dandelion: Memoir of a Free Spirit.* New York: St. Martin's Press, 2007.

Leitch, Donovan. *The Autobiography of Donovan: The Hurdy-Gurdy Man.* New York: St. Martin's Press, 2005.

Mason, Nick. *Inside Out: A Personal History of Pink Floyd.* San Francisco: Chronicle Books, 2005.

Murray, Charles Shaar. *Crosstown Traffic: Jimi Hendrix and Post-war Pop.* London: Faber and Faber, 1989.

Oldham, Andrew Loog. *Stoned.* London: Secker & Warburg, 2000.

Walker, Clinton. *Highway to Hell: The Life & Times of AC/DC Legend Bon Scott.* Portland, OR: Verse Chorus Press, 2001.

Welch, Chris, and Geoff Nichols. *John Bonham: A Thunder of Drums: The Powerhouse Behind Led Zeppelin and the Godfather of Heavy Rock Drumming.* San Francisco: Backbeat, 2001.

Welch, Chris. *Peter Grant: The Man Who Led Zeppelin.* London: Omnibus, 2001.

Welch, Morgana. *Hollywood Diaries.* Xlibris, 2007.

Wenner, Jann. *Lennon Remembers.* New York: Fawcett, 1972.

Williams, David. *First Time We Met the Blues: A Journey of Discovery with Jimmy Page, Brian Jones, Keith Richards and Mick Jagger.* London: Music Mentor Books, 2009.

Wood, Ronnie. *Ronnie.* London: MacMillan, 2007.

Newspaper and Magazine Articles

"The 100 Sleaziest Moments in Rock." *Spin,* September 2000.

"Go Behind the Boards with Led Zeppelin." *Goldmine,* October 10, 2008.

"Still Ramblin' On?" *Mojo,* August 2008: 18.

Billiter, Bill. "Satanic Messages Played Back for Assembly Panel." *Los Angeles Times*, April 28, 1982: A3–21.

Clines, Francis X., and Warren Weaver, Jr. "Ban on Devil's Advocacy." *New York Times*, June 30, 1982: A 20.

Considine, J. D. "Led Zeppelin." *Rolling Stone*, September 20, 1990: 56 +

Crowe, Cameron. "Secrets of the Object Revealed." *Rolling Stone*, June 3, 1976.

Datskovsky, Miriam. "Stairway Surprise." *Condé Nast Portfolio*, July 2008: 42.

DeCurtis, Anthony. "Refueled and Reborn." *Rolling Stone*, February 23, 1995.

Epstein, Andrew. "Did the Devil Make 'Em Do It?" *Los Angeles Times*, May 9, 1982: J 60

Fox, Brian. "Returning Fire: John Paul Jones, Rock's Ultimate Wingman, Reunites with Led Zeppelin." *Bass Player*, February 2008: 54 +

Fricke, David. "The Return of Led Zeppelin." *Rolling Stone*, December 13, 2007: 58–68.

Geist, Brandon, and Chris Krovatin. "Led Zeppelin's Houses of the Holy: The Stories Behind Metal's Greatest Album Covers." *Revolver*, February 2009: 82.

Gold, Jude. "Songs That Didn't Remain the Same." *Guitar Player*, September 2003: 85–87.

Goodman, Fred. "Vanity Labels: Good Business or an Ego Boost?" *New York Times*, May 10, 1992: 24.

Greenblatt, Mike, ed. "Led Zeppelin & Current Metal Kings." *Superstar Facts & Pics #25*, 1991.

Hampton, Howard. "70s Rock: The Bad Vibes Continue." *New York Times*, January 14, 2001: 2-1.

"Illustration's Expanding Universe." *Creativity*, December 2006: 10.

Kurtz, Steve. "Flying High." *New York Times Magazine*, Fall 2003: 56–58.

Powers, Ann. "The Male Rock Anthem: Going All to Pieces." *New York Times*, February 1, 1998: Section 2-46.

Ross, Dalton. "Plant Life." *Entertainment Weekly*, May 13, 2005: 49.

Scaggs, Austin: "Q & A: Robert Plant." *Rolling Stone*, May 19, 2005.

Thorne, Stephen B., and Philip Himelstein. "The Role of Suggestion in the Perception of Satanic Messages in Rock-and-Roll Recordings." *The Journal of Psychology*, 1984: 245–48.

Tolinski, Brad. "Black Beauty Rides Again." *Guitar World*, January 2008: 76

Tolinski, Brad. "The Fab IV." *Guitar World*, January 2002: 62–100.

Tolinski, Brad. "Flying High Again." *Guitar World*, January 2008: 70–106.

Tolinski, Brad. "The Greatest Show on Earth." *Guitar World*, July 2003: 80–165.

Tolinski, Brad, with Greg Di Benedetto. "Light and Shade." *Guitar World Presents Guitar Legends*, Winter 2004.

Internet

www.johnpauljones.com
www.ledzeppelin.com
www.led-zeppelin.org
www.ledzeppelin-database.com
www.ledzeppelinnews.com
www.planet-zeppelin.com
www.royal-orleans.com
www.stormthorgerson.com
www.tightbutloose.co.uk
www.uncut.co.uk

Index